SITTING IN AND SPEAKING OUT

SITTING IN
AND
SPEAKING
OUT

Student
Movements
in the
American
South
1960–1970

JEFFREY A. TURNER

THE UNIVERSITY OF GEORGIA PRESS

Athens & London

© 2010 by the University of Georgia Press
Athens, Georgia 30602
www.ugapress.org
All rights reserved
Designed by Walton Harris
Set in 10/13 Minion Pro

Printed digitally in the United States of America

Library of Congress Cataloging-in-Publication Data

Turner, Jeffrey A.
Sitting in and speaking out : student movements in the
American South, 1960–1970 / Jeffrey A. Turner.
    p.   cm.
Includes bibliographical references and index.
ISBN-13: 978-0-8203-3593-3 (hardcover : alk. paper)
ISBN-10: 0-8203-3593-2 (hardcover : alk. paper)
ISBN-13: 978-0-8203-3599-5 (pbk. : alk. paper)
ISBN-10: 0-8203-3599-1 (pbk. : alk. paper)
1. Student movements — Southern States — History —
20th century. 2. College students — Political activity —
Southern States — History — 20th century. 3. Civil
rights movements — Southern States — History — 20th
century. 4. Whites — Southern States — History — 20th
century. 5. African Americans — Civil rights —
History — 20th century. 6. Southern States — Race
relations. I. Title.
LA229.T87 2010
378.1'981097509045 — dc22   2010006351

British Library Cataloging-in-Publication Data available

To Fran

CONTENTS

ACKNOWLEDGMENTS

IT IS NOT UNCOMMON for scholars of the 1960s to begin their treatments of the decade with a bit of autobiography. The decade at times seems to demand a taking of sides, a declaration of identity. I see nothing inherently wrong with this tendency, the existence of which points to the passions that events continue to inspire. In the years I spent on this project, I witnessed this passion time after time in formal interviews and informal conversations with those who lived through those years. The process can be a little daunting for someone who is not old enough to have specific memories of the decade, and at times I have felt like an interloper. I am not the first — nor will I be the last — member of a post-1960s generation to write about the decade. I am, however, conscious of the ways in which the events described in this book have shaped my life. In important respects, the questions that gave rise to this study began in the mind of a boy growing up in suburban Atlanta in the 1970s and 1980s, hearing stories from his parents about coming of age in Birmingham during the 1950s and 1960s, and trying to make sense of both the apparent change and the continuity. I only hope that what follows does justice to the people who lived and created these stories.

This book took a long time to write, and I accumulated many debts along the way to its completion. The project began as a suggestion from Clarence Mohr and took root during the 1990s in the Tulane University history department. Clarence provided a passion for the topic and the model of his own outstanding work in the history of the U.S. South. His advice and criticism were crucial, but he also demonstrated great patience as I found my own way back to the 1960s. The project began to take shape in seminars led by Patrick Maney and Ralph Lee Woodward Jr. and made its way through the dissertation stage thanks in part to the assistance of Lawrence Powell and Donald Devore. Along the way, I benefited from the friendship and commentary of fellow graduate students Charles Chamberlain, Emily Clark, Kent Germany, Michelle Haberland, Kahne Parsons, and Carolyn Thompson. I am grateful to Tulane for providing a Dissertation Year Fellowship in 1998–99.

I completed the project while living and working in Richmond, Virginia. St. Catherine's School has provided a nurturing environment, the freedom to work out my own salvation in the classroom, and the encouragement to continue doing the work that historians do. I could not have completed this project without the generous benefit of a half-year sabbatical in 2008–9. I thank my colleagues for their support and camaraderie and my students for their curiosity.

Portions of this book appeared in "Power, Black Power, Class Power: Race, Class, and Student Activism on Two Southern Commuter Campuses," *Gulf South Historical Review* 16 (Fall 2000): 48–70, and "From the Sit-Ins to Vietnam: The Evolution of Student Activism on Southern College Campuses, 1960–1970, *History of Higher Education Annual* 21 (2001): 103–35 (Copyright 2001 by Aldine Publishers. Reprinted by permission of Aldine Transaction, a division of Transaction Publishers). I thank the publishers of both journals for permission to use the material.

I have nothing but praise for the good people at the University of Georgia Press, especially Derek Krissoff, Andrew Berzanskis, and John Joerschke and I thank them for their support and patience. Robert Cohen and Gregg Michel, the reviewers for the press, offered thoughtful critiques that made this manuscript better and saved me from a number of errors. I have not chosen to follow all of their suggestions but appreciate their careful reading. Ellen D. Goldlust-Gingrich, as copy editor, provided a remarkably careful reading that saved me from many more mistakes. Of course, any errors that remain are my responsibility.

I thank friends and family for providing support and a respite from the work over the years. The good folks on the block obligingly participated in minicelebrations at each step along the home stretch. My parents, Roger and Sherry Turner, made this book possible in many ways. Katie was born as I began this project, and Lilly came along about halfway through. They are both budding writers, and they inspire me. Finally, Fran Turner has lived this topic with me for most of our two decades together. She has made many concessions to the demands of the book yet always reminds me of what is truly important. Fran is a good editor, and on more occasions than I can count, she has offered encouragement that kept me going. For all of that and for so much more, I thank her.

SITTING IN AND SPEAKING OUT

INTRODUCTION

IN MAY 1970, Jerry Rubin, the infamous Yippie activist, delivered a speech at the University of Alabama. By then, Rubin was a national figure, admired by some, reviled by others. The University of Alabama also had claims on the national consciousness — as the scene of the segregationist Governor George C. Wallace's audacious 1963 attempt to block the school's integration and as the home of the Crimson Tide, Bear Bryant's football powerhouse. Neither, however, meant much to campus progressives who rejected hidebound traditions and sought to move the university and the state toward their vision of racial progress — those, in short, who envisioned the emergence of a new 'Bama. To activist students, the fact that someone of Rubin's renown had come to Tuscaloosa symbolized the dawning of a new era. "Just his presence meant something," recalled Mike O'Bannon, at the time an undergraduate psychology major and campus activist. "To a lot of people it meant that we had, in a lot of ways, arrived." Alabama activists, according to O'Bannon, believed Rubin's Tuscaloosa appearance said to the rest of the country, "Look, the University of Alabama is part of this whole thing." In May 1970, a reporter for *Time* magazine wrote, "Consider the University of Alabama, which has long been a bastion of idolized athletes and lionized coaches, pretty coeds, fervent fraternity men and racism. Today, Alabama is aroused — and politicized."[1]

The *Time* reporter's assessment of 'Bama's student culture was true as far as it went. Football, frats, and belles had long dominated student life. And, in fact, the campus political culture had undergone a significant transformation, making space for new forms of dissent. But the university's politicization — its status as a battleground for conflict over serious political ideas — was nothing new. Since at least 1956, when rioting by segregationist students and community members blocked the attempted entrance of an African American student, the campus had been politicized, though in ways that varied from the examples set by "Berkeley, say, or Cornell, or Columbia"[2] — schools that seemed to provide the model the *Time* reporter used to understand the emergence of "aggressive moderates" at the University of Alabama and similar places.

To the extent that white students on southern campuses now vigorously debated the full range of issues — from American policy in Southeast Asia to racism at home — that development could be attributed to the activism of black students on other southern campuses a decade earlier. In 1960, students on the region's historically black campuses organized nonviolent direct-action campaigns against segregated public establishments. The resulting crusade, as much as any other phenomenon, generated a student movement that was more commonly represented by images from the University of California's Berkeley campus in 1964 and Columbia University in 1968. By the late 1960s, American students had become a force in politics and American society, engaged in national and international issues as well as in an effort to remake their campuses. Southern students were a part of this phenomenon — part of the "sixties generation" — but were no longer helping to set the tone for student political mobilization. *Time*'s treatment of student activism at 'Bama in 1970 indicated a prevailing sense of what student activism meant and where it was expected. And as O'Bannon's comments suggested, even southern student activists sometimes had difficulty seeing themselves as "part of this whole thing."

Where do the South and its students fit in the story of the 1960s student movement? *Sitting In and Speaking Out* studies a dramatic decade that began with a student-led assault on segregation and ended with demonstrations over the war in Southeast Asia. It tells the story of southern black and white kids confronting social, political, and cultural issues and participating in a movement that redefined southern and American society. It is also the story of limits, of a region whose hostility to dissent presented fundamental obstacles to student political mobilization and of students' efforts not only to mobilize despite those obstacles but also to destroy the obstacles themselves.

Student activism during the 1960s has continued to generate controversy. Politicians and commentators have labeled 1960s student protest a source of everything from "political correctness" and "illiberal education" to the destruction of an American Left that formerly united labor and the academy. The images that inform these interpretations, however, are often drawn from a few highly publicized campuses and national organizations. Though television relayed events at Berkeley and Columbia to living rooms throughout the country, this immediacy does not mean that explaining the events on those campuses — or a handful of others on the coasts or in the Midwest — necessarily explains the student movement. Nor do the inner workings of the national office of Students for a Democratic Society (SDS) necessarily reveal the student movement as most students experienced it.

Sitting In and Speaking Out differs in two important ways from most previous studies of the 1960s student movement. The fundamental difference is in its geographic focus. The most influential studies have been national in scope and usually have focused on SDS, the organization that for most people came to embody the New Left, or on the Student Nonviolent Coordinating Committee (SNCC), which channeled much of black students' activism.[3] More recently, a number of historians have produced local studies of the New Left.[4] Although both the national and local tendencies offer much that is useful, this study concentrates on a region. Implicit in this geographical focus is an assumption that certain elements of the South's history have set it apart in important ways from the rest of the nation. At the same time, one of the central questions of the post–World War II South has been the degree to which the end of legalized segregation and disfranchisement as well as broad economic trends have dissolved the most important differences between the South and the nation at large. Thus, by analyzing student activism in the South at a time when the definition of *southernness* was itself in transition, this study contributes to the ongoing discussion over regional consciousness in the modern South.[5]

This study also differs from other examinations of the student movement by adopting a biracial focus. Studies of the New Left that pay attention to student activism have tended to concentrate on white students. If they deal with the political mobilization of black students, the coverage is limited to the sit-in movement of the early 1960s. Fuller discussions of black student activism usually appear in studies of the civil rights movement, but these works generally avoid sustained attention to black students acting as students.[6] Much bound together the activism of black and white students during the 1960s. Historians have documented some of the ways in which the white New Left took cues from the black freedom struggle, but the connections went deeper. Black and white students were part of the larger youth culture that fed the student movement of the 1960s.[7] They were also part of the movement for university reform and student power that helped generate a wave of educational experimentation during the decade. Race modified the form and content of student activism, but only from a biracial perspective can one evaluate the roles of racial identity, youth identity, and student identity in creating a movement culture.

More important, this study's biracial focus brings to light the centrality of the ongoing process of desegregation in the development of southern student activism. The story of the student movement in the South becomes in important respects the story of students grappling with the implications of desegregation in a region that for many years maintained dual systems of higher education. A decade that began with interracial demonstrations and the initial desegregation of previously all-white universities ended with ambiguity, as white resistance and reluctance converged with a heightened black consciousness to limit the integration of the region's dual educational systems.

The Emerging Sixties

Despite the prominent role of African American students in the sit-in movement of the early 1960s, a sense that southern conservatism militated against the development of the (presumably white) student movement in the South was common in the 1960s and held sway for decades. Recent studies of student activism in places such as Austin, Texas, and Chapel Hill, North Carolina, along with a study of the Southern Student Organizing Committee, have largely dismantled the idea that the South's rocky soil prevented the growth of student political mobilization. They join efforts by scholars to develop other glimpses of the 1960s that either flesh out or complicate earlier interpretations. What did struggles for social change look like outside of the ranks of the New Left or civil rights leadership or outside of select locations on the coasts? *Sitting In and Speaking Out* joins this new wave of scholarship in both fleshing out and complicating earlier views of a tumultuous decade.[8]

"There is a 'movement' on Southern campuses," the *Southern Patriot*, a monthly newspaper published by the Southern Conference Educational Fund, assured its readers in January 1966. The *Patriot*, always eager to document any evidence of liberal or radical activity in the South, acknowledged that the movement was not as large there as in other parts of the country, though the publication contended that the southern movement was "still like an iceberg with its most significant parts hidden from general view." But the *Patriot*'s editors believed that the southern variant had the potential to make a significant impact.[9] A year later, journalist Haynes Johnson reported that students on the campuses he visited throughout the country exhibited "a striking unanimity" on social and political issues. "The difference between the coed at Berkeley and her more cloistered collegiate sister at Agnes Scott [in Atlanta] is only one of degree," Johnson suggested. "Everywhere, regional patterns which once separated Eastern from Western and Midwestern from Southern are disappearing."[10]

Those who long assumed that little of substance could happen in the South based their assumptions not only on preconceived notions of the region's political tendencies but also on preconceived ideas about student activism itself. When tracking the path of student activism through the decade, textbooks commonly begin with the Berkeley Free Speech Movement, move quickly to Columbia in 1968, and then conclude with Kent State in 1970. When southern universities appear, they usually are represented by the riots surrounding the entrance of James Meredith into the University of Mississippi in 1962 or Wallace's "stand in the schoolhouse door" at the University of Alabama a year later.[11] Given these guideposts, it is perhaps not surprising that some observers have found student activism in the South difficult to imagine. "This campus has no Telegraph Avenue, no Harvard Square, no Marcuse, no Savio, no Rudd, no Rubin," journalist Peter Schrag noted in a *Saturday Review* article on the University of Alabama in the early 1970s. "Its traditions are more visibly enshrined in the photo-murals of bowl games outside coach Paul 'Bear' Bryant's office than they are in intellectual distinction or social reform."[12]

There is merit to the idea that the South's historical antipathy to dissent made left-liberal student activism difficult to develop. In fact, empirical studies conducted in the late 1960s and early 1970s found a measurable level of activism on southern campuses, though the region as a whole tended to be less active than did other parts of the country. In a May 1968 survey of more than twelve hundred universities, two researchers found that 36 percent of the responding institutions in the South reported some sort of demonstrations during the preceding academic year. By comparison, 49 percent of responding northeastern institutions reported protest, while 44 percent of midwestern universities and 40 percent of western universities noted demonstrations. However, 57 percent of predominantly black institutions, almost all of them in the South, reported demonstrations during the year.[13] At the very least, the numbers suggest that even if the South's universities had somewhat less activism than the rest of the nation, the numbers were not staggeringly small. More important, they suggest that, if anything, the South was something of a hotbed for black student activism.

If student activism in fact occurred in the South, then what did it accomplish? What did it mean? Was it an export from Berkeley and Columbia and the result, as conservatives often charged, of "outside agitators?" If so, then stories of activism on individual campuses should more or less fit comfortably into the existing accounts of the New Left and constitute a chapter in the history of the American Left. Conversely, could southern student activism have been an indigenous phenomenon that grew from local and regional factors? If so, then the story is a chapter in the history of political dissent in the South.

These questions suggest the existence of a historiographical gap between the study of the South and the study of the 1960s. To the extent that historians of the 1960s in general and the New Left in particular have ignored the South or relegated it to a marginal role, they have unnecessarily narrowed their approach. The South must lie at the center of any true understanding of America in the 1960s. Viewing the region not as a backwater that received its activism secondhand from Berkeley and Columbia but as the epicenter of a national debate over fundamental moral and political issues refocuses the story of social change in the decade.

In light of the political mobilization of black southern students, the image of relatively inactive southern campuses becomes even more troublesome. In 1960 and 1961, black southern campuses served as the staging grounds for the sit-in movement. In the late 1960s, the institutions themselves became targets of discontent, as black students rebelled against hoary regulations and curricula and called for the creation of "black universities" that would serve as instruments of liberation for the African American community. In a significant number of instances, the mobilization of black students on black campuses prompted a quick and drastic response from law enforcement officials. Students died in violent clashes with police at South Carolina State College, North Carolina Agricultural and Technical College, Jackson State College in Mississippi, and Southern University in Louisiana. On several other occasions, violent showdowns were only narrowly avoided. Black students on recently desegregated and predominantly white campuses also mobilized behind an agenda inspired by Black Power during the closing years of the 1960s.[14]

Although they give due attention to the sit-ins and the freedom rides, in which southern black students played key roles, studies of movement organizations such as SNCC and the Congress of Racial Equality offer little insight into the political consciousness of black students. After attempting to coordinate the sit-in movement of 1960–61, SNCC shifted its attention from the campus to voter registration and community organizing. And by the mid-1960s, both organizations shifted their focus from the South to the urban North. Local and state studies have made some headway in describing post-1965 events in the South, but by their nature, these local studies give little attention to the broader patterns apparent throughout the South. As these studies have suggested, local conditions played a crucial role in determining the form and content of activism in particular locales. However, broader regional factors, including changes in southern politics and southern higher education, also affected and were effected by student activism.

Sitting In and Speaking Out fills not only the gap between histories of the South and of the 1960s but also the gap between studies with local and national focuses. It joins other recent studies questioning the decline from liberal reformism to destructive radicalism as the dominant story of the 1960s student movement. While elements of that narrative arc appear here, other themes assume greater importance. First, the civil rights struggle and the politics of desegregation emerge as central elements in the story. Long before the SDS old guard began exploring the possibilities for student engagement in social and political issues, southern students faced very real issues in their own backyards — the future of the South's dual systems of higher education and the fallout from a civil rights movement that was developing in localities throughout the region.

During the early 1960s, the sit-in movement and the high-profile desegregation of institutions such as the Universities of Mississippi, Alabama, and Georgia provided much of the context for the engagement of southern students. But the drama of desegregation did not end with the fading of the sit-in movement and the admission of the first African American students to formerly white Deep South universities. Instead, a larger story continued throughout the decade. What would desegregation mean on campuses — both those that had previously been all white and those that had previously been all black — where segregation had been deeply embedded in the culture? Southern students wrestled with these and other related questions throughout the decade, with race remaining the taproot for southern student activism.

Southern students engaged race and other issues with the knowledge that their actions could have severe consequences. Southern students who chose to become involved risked much. Activists struggled with what they could and could not say and do. These limitations on activism and students' responses to them constitute a second theme of this book. On the eve of World War II, W. J. Cash's *The Mind of the South* painted a portrait of a regional mind-set that conformed to the "savage ideal," an "ideal whereunder dissent and variety are completely suppressed and men become, in all their attitudes, professions, and actions, virtual replicas of one another."[15] Historians debate whether the savage ideal resulted in greater restrictions on academic freedom in southern universities than outside the region. Regardless, southern colleges and universities experienced their share of conflicts over academic freedom in the first half of the twentieth century. Dissenters from regional orthodoxy, especially those who questioned the racial status quo, on many occasions prompted conflicts over the freedom of students and faculty members to teach, inquire, and dissent.[16]

These forces did not eliminate activism from the South's college campuses but played a significant role in shaping the form and content of that activism. One result of this dynamic was a tendency for student activism to flow into established channels such as student government or officially sanctioned programs. This process moderated the tone of southern campus activism, even as national movement leaders won media coverage with heated, often violent rhetoric. While some elements of "declension" — the destructive militance of the late 1960s — appeared on southern campuses, this militance usually was more rhetorical than actual. Some black and white southern student activists used violent rhetoric at the decade's end, but the thrust of southern student activism remained liberal in the sense that the activists pushed primarily for the reform rather than destruction of existing institutions. Southern student activism also demonstrated a tendency to concentrate on "safer" issues with broad appeal, such as curfews or student participation in campus governance. At the same time, the limits on dissent often became mobilizing issues in their own right. Speaker bans and censorship of student publications were potent issues that could and at times did mobilize large numbers of students across the political spectrum. But the centrality of civil libertarian issues was a two-edged sword. While students mobilized in opposition to limits on speech, they sometimes had trouble transcending the question of what they could and could not say to get to more substantive issues.

Students, the South, and Higher Education

An analysis of student activism in the South reveals distinctive regional patterns, yet none of these patterns points to a monolithic South. Campus travelers for activist organizations frequently noted the particularism that existed throughout the region; at a more general level, many activists recognized that despite the regional tendency toward Cash's savage ideal, some places welcomed dissent more readily than did others. One pattern that emerges in this study is a difference between the more insular and atavistic Deep South (roughly, the states running west to east from Louisiana to South Carolina) and the more cosmopolitan areas of the Upper or peripheral South (Tennessee, North Carolina, and Virginia in the east; Texas in the west). Variations existed within these two general areas. Most important, in the Deep South, larger cities, especially Atlanta and New Orleans, served as pockets of relative openness.

A second pattern relates to institutional type. In important respects, the issues addressed by activists on both historically black and predominantly white campuses differed according to whether a campus was publicly or privately funded and run. Private institutions at times were more insulated from political currents and especially the pressures of politicians who sometimes benefited from using the campus Left as a foil for political gain. But the dynamic could be reversed; activists on public campuses at times used politicians' repressive policies to mobilize large numbers of students.

The story of higher education in the postwar South to a great extent revolves around the tensions created by two somewhat contradictory impulses. During the 1950s and 1960s, resistance to integration and anticommunism combined to produce heightened levels of intolerance for dissent. At the same time, however, an increasing number of southern universities sought admission into the upper echelons of American higher education. Institutions making this transition had to adopt the values that dominated American higher education during the 1960s, including an emphasis on academic rigor and intellectual freedom and an acceptance of individual merit as a core principle. Segregation was incompatible with this milieu.[17]

The sit-in movement and subsequent student mobilizations played a significant role in exposing these tensions, as did the simultaneous process of institutional desegregation. Thus, black and white southern college campuses served as a sort of political testing ground where emerging social issues collided with broad forces. Students stood at the center of these events, participating in local struggles that marked them indelibly as members of the 1960s generation.

Beginning in the 1950s, black students challenged segregation by attempting to enroll in all-white schools and by participating in local direct-action campaigns. Then came February 1960, when black students transformed the civil rights movement and the southern political terrain by taking the lead in a sit-in movement against segregated public establishments. Both developments opened up new possibilities for the political mobilization of white students. Indeed, for southern students, the story of the first half of the 1960s became the effort to sort out the impact of the politics of desegregation. By the time of the Berkeley Free Speech Movement in the fall of 1964, southern college campuses had for many years been at the center of the region's most intense political battles.

Berkeley occurred during a transitional period in the history of the southern student movement, as organizations such as the U.S. National Student Association, SDS, and the Southern Student Organizing Committee attempted to pull together the separate strands of activism that were present in pockets throughout the region and nudge southern students toward activism. Such halting efforts revealed the challenges inherent in organizing a regionwide student movement; nevertheless, despite the challenges posed by conservatism and apathy, racial divisions, and strategic and philosophical difficulties, a movement that included black and white students was developing in the South by 1965. This movement addressed a wide array of national — and, with the deepening U.S. involvement in Vietnam, international — issues, but students always filtered those issues through a local lens. And on college campuses, "local" usually meant that the student movement was grounded in concerns about students and education. What emerged was a reciprocal process through which identities as students shaped the development of political consciousness at the same time that rising awareness altered the shape and content of student life. The academic environment in which student activism emerged provided the common thread that tied together a diverse array of movement issues, from racism and imperialism to the academic rights of students.

At mid-decade, as students wrestled with university reform and student power, three developments — the end of legalized segregation, the emergence of Black Power, and America's deepening involvement in Vietnam — signaled a shift in the trajectory of the southern student movement. On formerly all-white campuses, the admission of the first one or two black students was only the beginning of another story in which black and white students began wrestling with the question of what desegregation should mean and how it should look. An initial period of tentativeness preceded a post-1966 phase in which black students began to assert their rights as academic citizens. This era of greater assertiveness corresponded with the rise of Black Power, a broad movement encompassing many ideological orientations but united in the pursuit of the psychological liberation of African Americans. While Black Power helped fuel the political engagement of African American students on predominantly white campuses, it called into question the interracialism that provided the initial impetus for activism among white students. For some white liberals on southern campuses, the separatist element of Black Power was an obstacle too great to transcend. Other white activists, however, accepted the principles of Black Power; supporting black activism provided an important avenue for these students' radicalization.

On black campuses, the emergence of Black Power intensified the scrutiny that had been unleashed during the sit-in movement. Drawing not only on Black Power rhetoric but also on the currents of generational revolt and the idea of student power, black students addressed most of the moral and political issues that animated campus protests within and outside the South. Their central concern, however, remained loosening the grip of in loco parentis regulations and changing curricula to focus more on African American history and life. Violent rhetoric on black campuses went hand in hand with modest goals. But the white politicians' and law enforcement officials' hair-trigger tendency to clamp down on activism at black institutions, especially public ones, resulted in some violent clashes.

By the late 1960s, Vietnam had emerged to rival race as a motivating factor in the southern student movement. For many students, especially whites, Vietnam's role in the late 1960s resembled that of integration earlier in the decade, providing a foundation on which activists could erect a larger edifice of dissent. To the extent that this dynamic occurred, the emergence of Vietnam — an issue that, unlike integration, was not particularly tied to one region of the country — served as a factor in the "de-southernizing" of southern student dissent. Frustration over the continued escalation of the war also contributed to the heightened militance of southern student radicals. At the same time, however, the South's pro-military tendencies and unwillingness to express "anti-American" views complicated the process of mobilizing against the war. The power of anticommunist orthodoxy along with the predominance of civil rights resulted in a southern, campus-based peace movement that proceeded in fits and starts. While more and more students opposed the war, activists had trouble channeling that dissent into a real movement. The demonstrations that occurred in the aftermath of the Cambodia invasion and the deaths at Kent State in May 1970 brought student disaffection to a momentary peak. Student activists lashed out not only against the war but also against all of the grievances that had been brewing on their campuses. But when students returned to campus in the fall of 1970, activism generally sank back to its pre-1970 level. With national and regional organizing groups such as SDS, the Southern Student Organizing Committee, and SNCC now defunct and with the Nixon administration implementing a policy of "Vietnamization," activism tapered off during the early 1970s.

The rise and fall of activism on southern college campuses had an impact that went beyond its uncertain effects in shortening the war. At the top of the list are changes in curricula, campus regulations, and students' roles in the campus decision-making process. But such results only scratch the surface of the student movement's impact and meaning. One of the movement's greatest but least-appreciated legacies was in the way that it changed the dominant culture of southern campuses, particularly in the areas of race and gender relations.

This study represents an effort to combine depth with breadth. I have read widely in the literature of the New Left, the civil rights movement, and southern higher education and have conducted research on a variety of college and university campuses. Cognizant of the dangers of missing the nuances associated with the development of student activism at the local level, I might have picked one or two campuses in the South and projected these stories onto the region at large. I have chosen a different route in the belief that no single case study or series of case studies could adequately convey the full dimensions of the story. In all, my research took me to some twenty colleges and universities — public and private, Upper and Deep South, in cities and in more provincial locations, and historically black and predominantly white. My research in these locations has centered on student newspapers, presidential records, and the records of student organizations and faculty governing bodies. On- and off-campus underground newspapers have also been useful in placing student activism within a community context. I interviewed some participants to supplement areas where the documentary evidence is thin, and I have drawn on recordings and transcripts of interviews conducted by other scholars.

Visiting these and other institutions has offered me the opportunity to observe variations in campus cultural composition. To some extent, these variations are a product of the institutional type. For example, the University of Alabama and the University of Richmond differ in several important respects. One is a large, public institution in the Deep South that draws most of its student body from within the state. The other is a smaller, private institution with a healthy representation of students from the Northeast. Similarly, two historically black institutions, Morehouse College in Atlanta and Southern University's New Orleans campus, differ in many respects. One is a small, private institution that historically has catered to the black middle class and continues to draw its students from throughout the country. The other is a relatively recent creation that seeks to meet the educational needs of African Americans from more modest socioeconomic backgrounds.

These comparisons only hint at the range of variation in the South's institutions of higher education. Many factors — including the college's proximity to an urban center, the composition of the student body and the faculty, its institutional mission, and the political culture of the surrounding community and state — can modify the student experience. Nevertheless, there is also value in an approach that at times flattens out local variations to uncover broader regional patterns. To get at this larger perspective, I have consulted collections of documents from movement organizations and activists, which offer a broader view of southern student activism.

Over the course of the 1960s, the South changed in many respects, and southern universities and their students were at the heart of that change. As the *Southern Patriot* suggested in early 1966, southern campuses indeed had a student movement. In some respects, it contradicted people's preconceived notions about what a student movement should look like. And ultimately, it did not live up to the hopes and expectations that the *Southern Patriot* and other progressives envisioned. But its story nevertheless looms large for anyone seeking a better understanding of cultural, racial, and academic politics in the modern South and the modern United States.

CHAPTER ONE

Southern Campuses in 1960

TRENT LOTT LATER RECALLED being overwhelmed — "in the thrall of the colorful pageant that is Ole Miss" — by the campus of the University of Mississippi. It was the fall of 1959. He was a freshman from Pascagoula, in southern Mississippi, and had considered attending Tulane University in New Orleans before choosing the University of Mississippi because he preferred its law school curriculum. The decision had been a practical one, but the emotional connection developed almost immediately after his September arrival. Rush week, when fraternities and sororities sorted through and selected or rejected prospective members, had already begun, and Lott decided to submit himself to the process, to being "figuratively poked and prodded." Though he received other offers, he eventually pledged Sigma Nu, a fraternity founded in 1861 at Virginia Military Institute and "grounded in old Southern tradition" and "attuned to the principles of honor, brotherhood, and religion." In the following weeks, he helped to form a singing group called the Chancellors and won himself a place on the cheerleading squad after trying out at the insistence of an older fraternity member. He became involved in student politics and, later, as a senior, in politics of a different sort.

In 1962, when James Meredith's matriculation at the University of Mississippi prompted violent resistance by segregationists, Lott, now president of the Inter-Fraternity Council, made it his mission to keep his fellow Sigma Nus out of the violence. "Integration was steamrolling through the South," he later wrote of the tumultuous episode. "Its time had come." By the time the violence ended, Lott, by his own recollection, had kept his fraternity out of the chaos, but though he accepted the inevitability of desegregation, he could not have been classified as an active proponent of the process, at least as it unfolded at Ole Miss. He "felt anger in my heart over the way the federal government had invaded Ole Miss to accomplish something that could have been handled peacefully and administratively," the future U.S. senator (and, for a time, Senate majority leader) later declared. The episode, he seemed to suggest, had harmed the seemingly idyllic campus: "Ole Miss was a different school from then on. And our innocence was gone."[1]

Some 250 miles to the northeast, in Nashville, another southern collegiate career that eventually led to Congress was also playing out. In some respects, it could not have contrasted more sharply with Lott's undergraduate experience. In September 1957, John Lewis was an African American from rural Alabama entering a tiny, religiously affiliated college in a southern city with a reputation for racial moderation. The campus of American Baptist Theological Seminary (ABT) could scarcely have competed with the magnolias and Doric columns of Ole Miss. But to Lewis — "just a boy from the woods, nervous and unsure" — the experience was perhaps as overwhelming as Lott found entering the Oxford campus. "Spartan, cramped, yes," Lewis later recalled of his dormitory. "But back on that September afternoon in 1957, through my seventeen-year-old eyes, these dorm rooms looked palatial."[2]

The cultural currents that shaped Lott's undergraduate life — Greek societies, football games, student politics as a springboard to a state political career — did not exist at ABT. Those outlets were available, in their own way, for the black students at nearby Fisk University, but for Lewis and his cohort at American Baptist, a seminary for African Americans that operated under the auspices of the Southern Baptist Convention, college was about one thing — training for the ministry. According to Lewis, the most important question at ABT was, "Can you *preach*, boy?"[3]

Despite these profound differences — in campus architecture, in institutional role, in student life — the undergraduate careers of Lewis and Lott were connected in at least one important respect. Both men, though in dramatically different ways and with profoundly divergent outcomes, were drawn into the battles of the desegregation era. Lewis eventually participated in seminars on nonviolent direct action led by another Nashville student, James M. Lawson Jr., who was in Vanderbilt University's graduate divinity program. In the spring of 1960, that group launched an attack on segregation that provided one of the foundations of the 1960s southern student movement.

These two men's experiences provide glimpses into the range of ways that youth experienced southern college life on the eve of the 1960s as well as some of the ties that could connect seemingly disparate experiences. There was no one "typical" collegiate experience in the South. An array of forces — including race, gender, institutional purpose, class background, and religious beliefs — modified collegiate life. Yet this diversity developed in a historical context that connected college students throughout the region and prepared the ground on which a uniquely southern student movement grew in the 1960s.

On the surface, college campuses in the American South seemed quiescent, unlikely incubators for a student movement that ultimately left a deep imprint on southern and American politics and society. Compared with their counterparts in the rest of the country, southern students were less academically accomplished and more provincial. The student cultures on both black and white southern campuses — at the larger institutions, usually dominated by members of Greek societies — contained heavy doses of political and social conservatism and apathy. Campus newspapers published articles about blood drives, beauty pageants, dances, and other organizational activities, all evidence of that particular school's spirit. When they addressed international events, writers in these campus publications frequently used the language of the Cold War and either implied or explicitly stated the superiority of the American system and way of life over those of the communist world; such declarations usually went unchallenged — at least in the pages of the campus papers. Student government organizations often thrived as arenas in which aspiring leaders could develop their skills and resumes. Relatively rare were the instances in which student government offered a forum for the serious engagement of social, political, or educational issues.

Amid these conditions, however, existed related but contradictory others that fed student activism in the early 1960s. A conservative collegiate subculture dominated most campuses, but the southern student body was not monolithic. On the periphery of many campuses, handfuls of rebels — outliers as a result of their religious and political beliefs, their cultural values, their class background, or other factors — developed critiques of their schools and occasionally of southern society. Among the seemingly toothless campus groups were religious organizations that at times engaged social issues. And though campus politics usually seemed vapid and lacking in substance, southern students could not entirely avoid serious political issues, for southern higher education, which was distinguished from the rest of the nation by its rigidly segregated nature, found itself at the center of a gathering political storm. The politics of the desegregation era — the outcome of years of battles in the court system as well as a growing movement against de jure segregation of all types — disrupted the seemingly placid surfaces of many southern campuses.

The Evolution of Higher Education after World War II

Southern higher education was provincial and racially segregated throughout the first half of the twentieth century. After World War II, however, important developments challenged both of those characteristics. In some respects, the war itself served as the watershed event for both the expansion of southern higher education and the challenge to segregation, which defined not only southern higher education but all aspects of public life in the region. By incorporating higher education into the fight against fascism, the federal government jump-started a process by which American colleges and universities became, as Clark Kerr later termed them, "instrument[s] of national purpose."[4] Wartime training programs on southern campuses provided seeds for the postwar expansion and democratization of education. Inequities existed in the implementation of these programs; the region's Negro colleges were limited in their ability to secure federal funding, and college women benefited little from wartime programs. Nevertheless, southern colleges and universities expanded in terms of enrollment and institutional scope. Spurred initially by the Servicemen's Readjustment Act, known popularly as the G.I. Bill, enrollments skyrocketed in the South, as they did nationally. By the early 1970s, the number of students attending college had increased by 700 percent from 1940.[5]

Improvements were not simply quantitative but also qualitative. During the first half of the twentieth century, little research and by extension little graduate education occurred on southern campuses. Wartime defense needs, followed quickly by Cold War defense programs, brought southern institutions a growing share of the federal research budget. This money helped to spur the growth of graduate programs, helping to raise the stature of southern research institutions. By the mid-1960s, the Universities of Texas, North Carolina, Florida, and Virginia, as well as Duke, Vanderbilt, Tulane, Emory, and Florida State, ranked in the middle third of the nation's research institutions. Nevertheless, they lagged the rest of the nation by most qualitative measures.[6]

Advances by select research universities were not uniformly reflected by other institutional types, however. Well into the 1950s, higher education for women in the South remained focused primarily on private institutions and normal colleges, with curricula that tended to offer, as historian Roger Geiger phrases it, "a practical education for future work rather than a liberal education for intellectual development."[7] More conspicuously, the South's Negro colleges continued to operate under conditions that were inferior to those of their white counterparts. Whether public or private, most black institutions were poorly funded; few offered the opportunity for serious graduate study. In 1947, when President Harry Truman's Commission on Higher Education proposed eliminating the South's segregated educational system, the southern members of the commission dissented, but only after acknowledging the significant inequities in educational opportunity for black southerners: "We recognize that many conditions affect adversely the lives of our negro citizens and that gross inequality of opportunity, economic and educational, is a fact. We are concerned that as rapidly as possible conditions should be improved, inequalities removed and greater opportunity provided for all our people." The dissenters — three university administrators and Virginia journalist Douglas Southall Freeman, who served as rector of the University of Richmond — argued that improvements in education for African Americans should occur within the context of the South's "established patterns of social relationships."[8]

The South's more than one hundred historically black colleges and universities had their roots in the years after the Civil War, when schools were created to serve former slaves. The American Missionary Association and other northern groups had played an important role in establishing such black colleges as Fisk, Howard, Hampton, Talladega, Atlanta University, and others. The association's schools originally emphasized a classical liberal arts education, but after the 1880s, philanthropic agencies increasingly emphasized industrial training, following the Hampton-Tuskegee model propounded by Booker T. Washington. During these years, segregation was codified, disfranchisement was implemented, and violence against black people increased. Washington emerged as the country's most powerful African American leader by delivering a message that was palatable to white paternalists already suspicious of black education. He stressed the need for cooperation with white southerners and deemphasized political participation. In the realm of education, Washington favored a vocational curriculum over a classical course of study, which he saw as "mere book learning." Washington's approach was applied not only to private institutions but also to state institutions, especially after the 1890 passage of the second Morrill Act, which required segregated state systems to distribute federal money to black schools. The curricula at those state-supported institutions often offered little in the way of collegiate programs. To white southerners — and to most white Americans in an age that historian Rayford Logan has called the "nadir" of African American history — industrial training seemed more appropriate for a laboring class and less likely than a liberal education to plant "dangerous" ideas in black southerners' heads. A monumental 1916 study of Negro education funded by the U.S. Bureau of Education and the Phelps-Stokes Fund buttressed the view that black collegiate education should emphasize vocational training.[9]

Despite his considerable power, Washington always had opponents within the black community. After the turn of the century, W. E. B. Du Bois, a graduate of Fisk and Harvard, offered the most articulate opposition to the Hampton-Tuskegee program. In "Of Mr. Booker T. Washington and Others," from *The Souls of Black Folk*, as well as in other forums, Du Bois argued that a broad liberal training was necessary for the development of a coterie of exceptional black men who would lead their race — the "Talented Tenth." The brightest black minds, like the brightest white ones, should have access to the best of human thought to prepare them for leadership, Du Bois argued. At the same time, however, he believed that black colleges should be centers for sociological research on African Americans, highlighting the race's contributions to American life as well as attempting to come to grips with the peculiar problems of black people. For more than a decade in the early 1900s, Du Bois directed a series of research conferences on black life at Atlanta University, thus becoming one of the earliest proponents of what would be known as black studies.[10]

The differences in educational philosophy represented by Washington and Du Bois and the apparent triumph of industrial training over liberal education in southern black colleges provided the backdrop for a series of revolts on black campuses in the 1920s. These revolts constituted one manifestation of a larger post–World War I rise in militancy among African Americans that also took the form of resistance to white mob violence in 1919 and the "New Negro" movement of intellectuals and artists in the 1920s. Du Bois, who chronicled the revolts in the pages of *The Crisis*, a magazine published by the National Association for the Advancement of Colored People (NAACP), and in lectures, provided much of the intellectual rationale for the wave of protests. In fact, Du Bois played a direct role in a showdown at Fisk University, leading a 1924–25 movement of alumni and students against the restrictive policies of President Fayette McKenzie.[11] The demonstrations at Fisk represented the fullest development of trends manifested on many of the region's other campuses.[12] Some were short-lived and less substantive than the Fisk movement in terms of the issues addressed. In a few instances, as at Fisk, these demonstrations produced curricular changes and loosened the colleges' tight grip on students' lives. In other cases, the protests resulted in the appointment of African Americans as college presidents. But the realities of race relations in the South and the continuing financial exigencies at black colleges and universities severely limited the amount of change that could occur.[13]

By the 1950s, the South's black colleges and universities ranged widely in size and quality. The top black colleges — Fisk in Nashville, the congeries of schools in Atlanta, and Howard University in Washington, D.C. — were quite cosmopolitan. They attracted important speakers from all over the world and trained many of the most significant African American leaders. Large state-supported institutions such as Southern University in Baton Rouge, Florida Agricultural and Mechanical College in Tallahassee, and North Carolina Agricultural and Technical University in Greensboro, with enrollments in the thousands, had much more limited curricula than flagship white institutions but often offered vibrant campus lives. A handful of church-funded colleges, among them Tougaloo College in Mississippi and Talladega College in Alabama, claimed academic reputations and a degree of cosmopolitanism that rivaled those of Fisk and the more elite Atlanta schools. Most black, church-funded institutions, however, struggled with poor facilities and a low instructional quality. Anne Moody, who attended Baptist-affiliated Natchez Junior College beginning in 1961 before transferring to Tougaloo in 1963, drew out the differences between the two schools in her autobiographical *Coming of Age in Mississippi*. "Is *this*

Natchez College?" she asked disbelievingly when she first arrived to find "only three little old brick buildings." Tougaloo was a different world, however: "It was large and spacious. There was evenly cut grass everywhere and huge old oak trees with lots of hanging moss." More notable to Moody was the preponderance of "high yellow" students and the presence of white faculty members. An African American student who had never studied under a white teacher, Moody found the white instructors especially intimidating, though she adjusted to the new academic environment.[14]

Though black and white institutions were often located merely a stone's throw apart, the wall of segregation created profound divisions, at least from the students' perspective. And those divisions seemed to widen after the 1954 *Brown v. Board of Education* decision. For students, contact with contemporaries across the color line was rare and freighted with significance, especially in the context of the rise of massive resistance in the late 1950s. Nevertheless, the *Brown* decision irrevocably connected race and education in the South for the rest of the decade. It heightened a sense of expectation of change among black southerners and a sense of dread among many white southerners. It raised the possibility of a diminution in the divide between white and black institutions without providing a road map for how that divide would be diminished.

By the 1960s, the "multiversity" — the large, impersonal institution so closely connected with government and corporate interests — became a target for disenchanted students. This critique emerged not only at institutions such as the University of California at Berkeley but also on southern campuses. In the South, however, the expansion and democratization of higher education coincided with and even exacerbated the challenge to segregation. As civil rights moved to the top of the liberal reform agenda, southern segregation became increasingly isolated as the nation's Achilles heel. At the same time, the race-neutral standard of individual merit now stood at the core of the values that dominated American higher education. As segregated southern colleges and universities moved to enter the national mainstream, tensions between national and southern mores were exposed.

Student Cultures

Southern higher education evolved in the context of more dramatic social and economic trends that were remaking the region. An increasingly urban and suburban South struggled to reconcile its traditional value system, rooted in communities and based on family, place, and stability, with newer individualistic ideological currents. In some respects, the new competitive individualism was liberating; in elevating individual merit, it fundamentally challenged the logic of both Jim Crow and gender discrimination. But the accompanying emphasis on the marketplace as the ultimate arbiter of value led some observers to bemoan the materialism and shallowness of middle-class life.[15] While some southerners voiced this criticism, the line of attack was not peculiarly or even primarily a southern phenomenon. From David Riesman to the Beats, scholars, writers, and artists mourned the rise of soulless, other-directed middle-class Americans. One vein of this line of criticism was directed at young people.

As early as 1951, commentators noted the quietude of American youth. In November of that year, *Time* magazine made one of the earliest references to the "silent generation": "Youth today is waiting for the hand of fate to fall on its shoulders, meanwhile working fairly hard and saying almost nothing. The most startling fact about the younger generation is its silence." The *Time* essay went on to catalog what would become the familiar criticisms of 1950s American youth — in particular, apathy toward politics and social issues and crass materialism — though the article seemed to exhibit a grudging admiration for their mature realism.[16]

Scholars who have examined the culture of American college students have suggested that despite the transitory nature of student life, several well-defined subcultures developed beginning early in the twentieth century that provided students with ready-made categories with which to define themselves and their relationship with their fellow students and the institution. Helen Lefkowitz Horowitz delineates three undergraduate subcultures: "college men and women," "outsiders," and "rebels."[17] On white campuses in the South, like those throughout the nation, a "collegiate" subculture built around fraternities and sororities and emphasizing interpersonal skills and cultural conformity, often to the exclusion of intellectual life, dominated. Despite its anti-intellectual elements, this cultural category gained acceptance from many campus administrations between 1920 and 1960. Fraternities and sororities, the institutional expression of this category, grew in numbers and wealth, and their customs often became the unofficial practices of the campus.

For countless students, these customs lay at the core of what became happy memories of innocence on the cusp of the tumultuous 1960s. A 1955 article in the Vanderbilt *Hustler* offering an overview of the campus from the perspective of a new student provides a glimpse of this seemingly benign world. "With sincerity, no student can ever complain of not having anything to do in the way of social activities," declared student Larry McGinty. "Apart from sorority and fraternity functions, the activities provided for all are numerous and widespread. For example, last quarter there were nearly a dozen dances open to all." To those events, McGinty added attendance at on-campus football games as constituting the foundation for a healthy campus social life. "There is seldom a week-end that something for the entire campus is not offered," McGinty concluded. "No sir! social activities are not slighted on this campus. . . . In summary the atmosphere at Vanderbilt is wholesome, healthy and clean. It is friendly, intellectual, and religious."[18]

Despite McGinty's characterization, some students found the environment less welcoming. The dominant fraternities and sororities were, by definition, exclusive. Greek societies at Vanderbilt and throughout the South picked their members during a series of social functions known as rush week. At the same time that McGinty was making his claims in the campus newspaper, a Vanderbilt faculty committee was wrapping up a report critical of the organizations' exclusiveness and proposing that they move toward a policy of openness. "We hope the fraternities can eventually adopt the attitude that: If you are good enough for Vanderbilt, you are good enough for me, but we can make you a better person," the committee declared. Specifically, the committee called for a strong faculty endorsement of the concept of openness, though it opted for a voluntary approach over requiring the organizations to end restrictive policies. The proposal met with strident opposition from a *Hustler* editor who argued that it would end the Greek system at Vanderbilt, in which some three-quarters of the student body participated. The editorial also called into question the concepts of social reform and egalitarianism, associating the faculty proposal with "liberalism," "ultra-liberalism," "social reform," and "radical change." Moreover, he argued, "Not all Vandy students are equal in ability, intelligence, personality, desirability, or background. . . . This is not a snobbish attitude. It is a fact. It is a realistic, not idealistic, approach." He concluded by taking aim not only at the specific faculty proposal but at government economic planning more generally: "The liberal attitude that every student must be socially protected from 'cradle to grave' or in our language, 'registration to graduation,' is an idealistic theory which seems totally foreign and a radical departure from the purposes of the university."[19]

In fact, the number of students who tried but failed to get into Vanderbilt's fraternities in the mid-1950s was relatively small. According to the dean of students, usually fewer than ten men were left without bids each year, though the number was somewhat higher for women. Nevertheless, the faculty committee insisted that restrictiveness had broader effects: students chose not to rush for fear of embarrassment at not being selected, and students who did not make the cut could suffer considerable psychological consequences. "Many members of this faculty have known students who have experienced the feeling of utter dejection and defeat as the spotlight of fraternity rejection set them apart from their peers," the faculty report declared, adding that the bases for such "blackballing" included "religion, race, family income, 'social acceptability,' and other such variables which this University does not consider either important or relevant for satisfactory status as a student in an institution of higher learning." Patricia Foster, a student at Vanderbilt during the 1960s, later described her reaction at receiving the news that she had not received a sorority bid: "Later I'll be bitter, but now I'm only ashamed. How can I tell my parents?" Foster noted the connections between the southern class system and the campus fraternity and sorority system. ("Everyone will tell me it's not my fault, but secretly they'll believe it is, for I haven't learned how to be a successful middle class girl.") But Foster eventually "learned to take pride in my outsider status."[20]

Like Foster, other students who were not part of the dominant collegiate subculture had other categories with which to define themselves. Though difficult to find in the pages of campus newspapers that chronicled the comings and goings of Greek societies in often excruciating detail, students who came to college with clearly defined professional ambitions sometimes made little time for the distractions of campus social life. Immediately following World War II, the military veterans who flooded southern campuses on the G.I. Bill provided a model for this sort of means-to-an-end approach to education. But even after the wave of veterans subsided, as Horowitz notes, "their insistence that they were in college to study and do well" lingered.[21]

A handful of other students rejected both the social emphasis of college life and a determined concentration on the classroom. These "rebels" were inclined toward political activism or artistic interests. Occasional bursts of student rebellion had occurred in the South during the 1930s and early 1940s, but a variety of forces combined to mute campus dissent in the 1950s. To some extent, the dynamic was national, a function of the Cold War's chilling effect. During the 1930s and 1940s, social scientists found that students became more tolerant and liberal in college. In the 1950s, in contrast, going to college made students not simply politically conservative but perhaps even more politically apathetic. Surveys conducted during the 1950s found that Republicans narrowly outnumbered Democrats 29 to 26 percent nationwide, but 42 percent of college students declared themselves "aloof from either political party."[22] In the South, the connections between the Cold War and resistance to integration combined substantially to mute cultural rebellion and political dissent, probably to a greater degree than in the rest of the nation.

The result of this cultural mixture could be a campus that casual observers would perceive as lacking in signs of intellectual life. When journalist Calvin Trillin visited the University of Georgia during the desegregation crisis of the early 1960s, he noted a dearth of posters advertising lectures, concerts, or plays. "Actually, a large number of things go on," Frank Gibson, a political science professor, told Trillin, "but you'd never know it from walking around the campus. We have a good concert series; the philosophy department has brought in some outstanding speakers. Perhaps because all these events are attended almost exclusively by faculty members, they don't bother to advertise. The faculty already knows about them." For students, social institutions provided order and structure on the campus. In fact, Gibson noted, the university was not very well prepared to handle independent students, as the student center was poorly equipped and offered limited facilities.[23]

Willie Morris captured well the mood of student life on white southern campuses when he described the University of Texas campus of the 1950s in the autobiographical *North toward Home*. "The 1950s were a quiescent time at the University, just as they were not a very poetic time in America," Morris noted.

> Led by the organized structure of the fraternities and sororities, the great hotbed of philistinism in the 1950s, this campus, as others surely did, reached unprecedented heights of carefully planned frivolity — parades with homemade floats, sing-songs, carnivals — anything, in fact, to do something meaningless with all that energy. It was the era of the beauty queens, bless their souls and bodies, and they decorated the front pages of *The Daily Texan* and inspired their own mystique, like Hollywood starlets tied down unfairly by classes and lectures.[24]

Black Campuses: Apathy and Activism

The prominent criticisms of complacent 1950s college students were not restricted to white students. And, indeed, black colleges were capable of producing their own versions of Morris's "carefully planned frivolity." A regular feature of the Fisk University alumni publication in the 1950s and early 1960s was "From Jubilee Bell Tower," an article by a Fisk student summarizing the significant events of the preceding season. These reports generally noted such events as beauty pageants, homecoming parades, and athletic events. Readers of the winter 1960 edition learned that Phyllis Crowder Lett, the newly crowned Miss Fisk, "wore a striking white floor length gown and her attendants . . . wore lovely white ballerina length dresses." They read that Fisk had defeated Knoxville 16–0 in the annual homecoming game. And they were told of a homecoming parade, the results of the annual marching band contest, and the winner of prizes for float and yard displays.[25] Indeed, some critics of the campus culture at Fisk and of black colleges in general during the era found much frivolity and complacency.

As early as the 1930s, Du Bois, Carter G. Woodson, and others complained that insular black colleges encouraged self-absorption among students. "Our college man today is, on the average, a man untouched by real culture," Du Bois declared in a 1930 commencement address at Howard University. "He deliberately surrenders to selfish and even silly ideals, swarming into semiprofessional athletics and Greek letter societies, and affecting to despise scholarship and the hard grind of study and research." Du Bois and other intellectuals complained that black students were abandoning their responsibility to serve as race leaders. This argument received its fullest exposition a quarter of a century later in E. Franklin Frazier's scathing analysis of the black middle class, *Black Bourgeoisie*. Frazier argued that black colleges made "money-makers," members of a black bourgeoisie "without cultural roots in either the Negro world with which it refuses to identify, or the white world which refuses to permit the black bourgeoisie to share its life." Black students were listless, interested less in learning than in the social activities of the Greek societies. Black teachers held their positions merely to ensure their social status; they had little interest in literature or ideas, were conservative politically, and paid little attention to social questions.[26]

Some observers argued that Frazier overstated his case. As historian August Meier pointed out in a review of *Black Bourgeoisie* published in *The Crisis*, Frazier at times "substituted highly critical and often sweeping, and therefore misleading, generalizations" for a judicious and scholarly approach. Nevertheless, Meier, a white historian who taught at various black colleges from the 1940s into the 1960s, seemed to agree with some of Frazier's criticisms, particularly his assessment of black professors: "As Frazier suggests, the average Negro professor has more in common with prejudiced middle-class whites than with the liberal white professors on the campus."[27] African American administrators similarly received criticism for limiting the possibilities for a more effective challenge to racial inequality in the South. Ralph Ellison's portrayal of Dr. Bledsoe, the president of a black college in the Deep South in *The Invisible Man*, became an archetype for the Uncle Tom administrator who kowtowed to white philanthropists while ruthlessly maintaining his power over the institution. Ellison had been a student at Tuskegee Institute in the 1930s, and his portrayal of Bledsoe and his college was a none-too-discreet indictment of Washington and Tuskegee.[28] But the critique lent itself to applications at other black colleges and universities, public as well as private. Articles in the Fisk campus newspaper in the late 1950s examined the university and found it wanting in a number of areas. A 1957 editorial in the *Forum* listed "The Five Liabilities of Fisk": a large annual faculty turnover, a one-man history department, a poorly administered library, an inefficient and weak student council, and "an overdose of student apathy." "As long as the irresponsible, indolent, anti-intellectual attitude of this student body exists, the name of our college is going to become increasingly less meaningful," the editorial declared.[29]

Despite the criticisms, the South's Negro colleges inherited a legacy of protest that made them logical sources for the civil rights movement and the student movement. In their protests of the 1920s, southern black students had addressed racial discrimination, educational policy, and the connections between the two. These protests demonstrated that even policies as seemingly arcane as curfews and dress codes could have important political implications if students recognized the social and political context in which those regulations developed. From the 1930s through the 1950s, black colleges continued to serve as home bases for leaders working toward the eventual end of segregation — among them Benjamin E. Mays of Morehouse College, Rufus Clement of Atlanta University, Mary McLeod Bethune of Bethune-Cookman, Albert W. Dent of Dillard University, Gordon B. Hancock of Virginia Union University, and Charles S. Johnson of Fisk University.[30] These leaders participated in regionwide organizations, such as the Southern Conference for Human Welfare and the more moderate Southern Regional Council, and played important roles in local movements. In Tuskegee, for example, sociology professor Charles Gomillion spearheaded a local civil rights movement beginning in the 1930s.[31] Progressive academicians counterbalanced the more conservative faculty administrators and faculty members who had disturbed observers such as Du Bois and Frazier and ensured that the black college, along with the black church, would be a central element in the rekindled civil rights movement of the 1950s and 1960s.

In fact, readers of the winter 1960 "Jubilee Bell Tower" also learned of "stand-outs," demonstrations against segregated restaurants in the Nashville area. And the same issue of the Fisk *Forum* that listed the university's liabilities also featured a front-page article on student involvement in an anti–Jim Crow boycott. At Fisk and on many other black campuses, apathy and activism existed in tension with each other.

Women on Campus

As Morris's reference to the "souls and bodies" of beauty queens suggests, the 1950s was a decade of retrenchment, of limited opportunities, of what by later standards could only be termed sexism for the South's coeds. The dominant assumptions about the role of and purposes for women in higher education held, among other things, that women were to be educated for domesticity and protected while they were students. Nationally, the years immediately following World War II had seen a backlash against women who pursued higher education as anything more than preparation for domesticity, with scholarly and popular literature frequently arguing against careers for women. In the South, men dominated public and private coeducational campuses, both numerically and institutionally. Several land-grant campuses either excluded women entirely or severely limited their numbers. At the same time, a system of public and private women's colleges remained viable. On campus, a collection of sometimes draconian rules and regulations, including separate curfews for women that were always earlier than those for men, circumscribed coed behavior. Rules also defined women's attire both on and off campus and, perhaps most important, restricted "visitation" with male students. "Regardless of their race or college," notes historian Amy Thompson McCandless, "Southern women were expected to behave as 'ladies' on and off the campus."[32]

The *Georgia Belle* handbook listed the rules of conduct for women enrolled on the Athens campus. Women could attend only those social functions listed on a weekly social calendar, and they were required to return to their dormitories within thirty minutes of the function's conclusion. They could visit men's apartments only with parental permission; at least three people had to be present, and women had to sign out of their dorms. Women had to dress in "authorized attire," which included dresses, skirts, blouses, sweaters, and neat "hair-dos." And if a physical education class required women to wear sports attire, they had to cover up with skirts or nontransparent coats while on their way to class. Unlike men, women could not drink alcoholic beverages on campus, even if they were of legal drinking age.[33]

Years earlier, Alabama writer Carl Carmer had captured something of the essence of the symbolic meaning that women held for men at southern universities. During one 1930s dance at the University of Alabama, someone offered a toast: "To Woman, lovely woman of the Southland, as pure and chaste as this sparkling water, as cold as this gleaming ice, we lift this cup, and we pledge our hearts and our lives to the protection of her virtue and chastity." To W. J. Cash, this toast demonstrated the continuing power of the "cult of Southern Womanhood."[34]

Objectification of the "souls and bodies" of college women took many forms. At Vanderbilt, the Social Standards Committee sponsored Charm Week "to encourage campus coeds to 'look their charming best.'" At the University of Alabama, a regular feature of the campus newspaper as late as 1969 was the "Bama Belle," a photograph of a coed, often accompanied by references to her appearance.[35] Similarly, at Birmingham-Southern College, an observer wrote in 1960 that "one of the striking features of life" was the "deep bow to feminine beauty. Every issue of the school newspaper has some cautious but worshipful cheesecake. Every fraternity has a sweetheart elected with great fanfare. The grand climax of the school year is the selection of Miss Southern Accent." As McCandless notes, the rituals and institutions of southern colleges — newspapers, yearbooks, literary magazines, May Day festivities, cotillions, and fraternity and sorority functions — "portrayed the woman student as a white, upper-class lady who was worshiped and protected by an attractive and rich Southern gentleman who sought her for his wife. The ideal woman possessed a child-like innocence and dependence; she was not likely to challenge the status quo. Female students who were not rich or white were encouraged to attain the ideal by acting like ladies."[36] For many college women, the overwhelming message and purpose of college was marriage, quickly followed by motherhood.

Those students whose intellectual interests challenged the dominant assumptions about the purpose of college for women found themselves having to justify their behavior. In 1957, Lovey Jane Long of Onancock, Virginia, won the distinction of being named the "most beautiful senior" at Westhampton College, the women's branch of the University of Richmond. An article in the campus newspaper, the *Collegian*, focused on the oddity of Long's academic interests: "Thoughts of elections and politics — not love and marriage — are uppermost" in her mind. Long, an ardent Republican whose senior thesis compared elections in two Virginia congressional districts, aspired to a career as a "behind the scenes politician" but had "no immediate desire or plans for marriage." Long's challenge to gender expectations had limits, however. For one, she did not look to a future with a woman president. In fact, she expressed discomfort with the idea of women on the front lines of politics at any level. "I guess I'm just old-fashioned," she said, "but I think women are better managers than candidates or officers. I still feel that a woman's place is in the home."[37]

Similar ideas existed at black colleges and universities. At Atlanta's Spelman College, an old saying held, "You can always tell a Spelman girl." According to Howard Zinn, a historian who served on the Spelman faculty in the 1950s and early 1960s, "The 'Spelman girl' walked gracefully, spoke properly, went to church every Sunday, poured tea elegantly, and in general had all the attributes one associates with the finishing school." Zinn likened the walls that separated Spelman students from the outside world to "a kind of chastity belt" that "confined young women to a semi-cloistered life in order to uphold the prevailing conception of Christian morality."[38] Novelist Alice Walker, a Spelman student in the early 1960s whose *Meridian* offers a fictionalized version of Spelman, "Saxon College," wrote, "A saying about Saxon was that you could do anything there, as long as you wore spotless white gloves. But because the gloves must remain clean and white, there was very little you could do."[39]

During the late 1960s, the dominant assumptions about college women came under attack on southern campuses. But two earlier events — the launching of Sputnik and the subsequent passage of the National Defense Act of 1958 — initiated a long-term process that helped to offer other opportunities for college women inside and outside the South. The 1958 legislation was designed to enlist America's top talent, including women, in the battle against communism. It provided aid to enable students to pursue studies in the humanities and the sciences and in the process opened avenues to women.[40]

But despite the changing material conditions, the cultural attitudes about women on southern campuses were slow to change, and most college women continued to play the roles assigned to them by this culture. As Walker's "white gloves" and Long's comments suggest, concepts of "ladyhood" — black or white — militated against most forms of political action. "The upbringing of southern white women with my class background was more repressive than most of us can comprehend these many years later," observed Dorothy Dawson Burlage, an activist student at the University of Texas in the 1950s who continued into full-time movement work in the 1960s.[41] Yet some southern women rebelled against the limitations placed on them by southern society through gender.

Dawson, raised in an upper-middle-class household in Mississippi and Texas, left home in 1955 for Mary Baldwin College, a private women's school in Virginia, "partly for the educational opportunities and partly to be 'finished.'" But despite a childhood that was in many ways conventional, she had been "inwardly preoccupied with issues of social justice and the moral teachings of the church." At Mary Baldwin, she ran afoul of her fellow students when she wrote a paper challenging school segregation and attended an interracial meeting of the U.S. National Student Association. Their reaction made her feel "like a traitor." The following year, she transferred to the University of Texas. Again, she followed convention by pledging a sorority; again, her concern with issues of social justice, especially race relations, caused her to step outside those conventions. She quit her sorority because of its "whites only" membership clause, "a decision that shocked my sorority sisters and violated the stereotype of the southern lady." She became involved with the YWCA, an interracial organization that became an important organizer for the civil rights movement in Austin, and attended lectures at the Christian Faith and Life Community, an interracial off-campus residence. By the late 1950s, she was involved in desegregation demonstrations. However, Dawson also maintained connections to conventional university activities for women, receiving honors such as Outstanding Student, Goodfellow, and a nomination for University Sweetheart. Her memoir of the period reflects on the ongoing struggle to reconcile the tension between her upbringing and her evolving concern with social issues. Though Austin was in a politically conservative state, it was, in Burlage's words, a "liberal oasis" and therefore exposed her to both religious and secular ideas that countered southern cultural and political orthodoxy.[42] For Burlage, a religiously inspired concern with social justice blossomed in the context of a vibrant community of religious liberals and radicals in a relatively open, cosmopolitan environment. But such circumstances did not hold for most college women in the South during the 1950s.

Joan C. Browning's rebellion grew out of similar religious beliefs. Raised on a farm in rural South Georgia, Browning was influenced by "an exuberant, joyful, life-affirming" Methodism that eventually led to her involvement in the civil rights movement. She entered the Georgia State College for Women in Milledgeville in the fall of 1959 and threw herself into her studies, ran for class president, served on the student newspaper, and took a job in the dining hall.

Browning collected signatures in opposition to proposals to close schools to avoid desegregation, but this activity did not place her "outside the magic circle." Rather, her attendance at a local black church, followed by her involvement in desegregation demonstrations in Augusta, caused not only other students to exclude her from mainstream college life but also the college administration to force her out altogether. By that time, the student-led sit-in movement was in full swing, and Browning moved toward deeper involvement in Atlanta. But her initial participation came from a belief that she was "exploring new dimensions of my own Christianity." Those actions caused her and a friend and activist partner at the college to be "perceived as actively rejecting segregation's protection from miscegenation."[43]

Religiosity

Southern campuses in the 1950s were steeped in what historian Paul Conkin has called a "conventional religiosity" that in many respects merely reflected national trends. The South had been dominated since the nineteenth century by a Protestant evangelicalism that emphasized a need for personal salvation while generally avoiding any tendencies to address broader social problems. In many respects, this form of religion adapted easily to the bland, Cold War–tinged religiosity that swept the United States in the 1950s. Throughout the South, the institutional church was in the midst of a metamorphosis, as white, metropolitan, middle-class churches of a variety of denominations grew in prominence. At the same time, black churches became increasingly secular, dominated by members of the black middle class who, as Frazier argued, sought to sever their ties to the black masses. Yet despite the transformations that were under way, southern religion on both sides of the color line continued to emphasize born-again salvation above all else. Despite their changing material conditions, urban and suburban southerners with fundamentalist backgrounds continued to espouse those beliefs.[44]

On southern college campuses, declarations commonly proclaimed the superiority of an American society that retained faith in a more or less generic God while locked in battle with godless communism. As was true throughout the region, fundamentalist beliefs were clearly evident, perhaps even dominant, among southern students, at least in terms of a general assent if not in terms of consistent action. But fissures, often but not always prompted by race, lay not far beneath the surface of conventional 1950s southern religiosity. The stories of Burlage and Browning, along with those of many other students who became involved in the civil rights movement, testify to the potential for Christian beliefs to inspire a desire for social justice in this world rather than an emphasis on individual salvation with a corresponding wait for justice in the next world. For many white and black southern students, religious discourse was an exercise in affirming and strengthening beliefs that were consistent with southern orthodoxy. But for some students, religiosity opened up avenues for social criticism and political action.

Many southern colleges had Religious Emphasis Week (REW), during which speakers engaged broad religious topics. REW was often an exercise in instruction in the rudiments of Christianity and its application in daily living. At the Baptist-affiliated University of Richmond, the campus newspaper noted that 1955's REW was designed "to present the Christian faith in terms understandable to college men and women and to point out the relevance of that faith to daily living and to the great issues of our time." A year later, organizers tweaked the program so that it also constituted "a period devoted to an understanding of the Bible's importance and a systematic study of it." Coverage of the program in the Richmond campus newspaper did not hint at the engagement of controversial issues. The 1955 program, "On to Maturity," featured representatives from a number of professional fields, apparently with the goal of presenting career opportunities with a religious perspective.[45]

Only slightly more intellectually adventurous was Vanderbilt University's inaugural 1955 REW program, "Religion — Believe It or Not," which examined tensions between faith and reason. The program's sponsor, the Student Christian Association, suggested that REW was part of an evolving understanding of the concept of truth at the university. "Once every college was founded on a religious basis, to spread truths, rather than find truth, a task it has adopted today," a description in the campus newspaper suggested. "Soon, however, there was a de-emphasis of religion because of the tendency it had to cause the university to become sectarian and static." But "20 or 30 years ago," the article continued, educators became concerned that the modern college had lost its way, and "in seeking freedom the college had become nebulous and vague in its very being." REW had thus been designed "to show the inadequacy of knowledge purely for the sake of knowledge; to show as the prophets of our day have been saying, that each person and each institution lives in some way by a faith to fulfill a purpose." Sessions included a sampling of offerings related to religion in daily life, including a seminar at the Delta Delta Delta sorority house whose organizers asked, "In order for there to be a difference between religion and none at all, religion must make a difference. Does it for you?" Meatier topics included physics professor Arthur Compton's presentation on "Enrico Fermi and Atomic Power." Most notably, Charles M. Jones, a minister from Chapel Hill, North Carolina, who two years earlier had been dismissed from a Presbyterian church for his support for civil rights activities, led a session in the Alumni Hall snack bar, "The Christian and Race Relations." "Do you know the facts about employment, educational, civic, and social discrimination faced by negroes and other minority groups?" a description of the session asked. "What are our Christian obligations in the face of these facts?"[46]

Jones's program hints at religious discussion's potential to provide a forum for just such an engagement, even in a region dominated by a form of Protestant evangelicalism that attempted to steer clear of social issues. Though not shared by a majority of white southern students, religious belief could and sometimes did lead students toward a heightened social consciousness, as was the case with Browning and Burlage. The *Brown* decision prompted southern denominations to take a position on desegregation. The major denominations initially cautiously endorsed white Christians' general need to welcome their black brothers and sisters. By the late 1950s, some segregationists attempted to connect fundamentalist beliefs and segregation, even as liberal church people sought to prod their congregations toward an acceptance of integration and the amelioration of the conditions in which black southerners lived.[47]

Those tensions exploded in Mississippi in 1956, when Will Campbell, a Baptist campus minister at the University of Mississippi, created controversy during that school's REW program. Campbell invited Alvin Kershaw, an Episcopal priest from Ohio who recently had won $32,000 on television's *The $64,000 Question*, to speak. Kershaw, whose chosen subject on the game show was jazz, had become a minor celebrity — a white preacher who was an expert on jazz. But Kershaw became more than merely an oddity when he announced that he intended to give some of his winnings to the NAACP. Campbell had no problem with Kershaw's decision: Campbell had intended to make REW a forum for race relations, a topic that was taboo in the classroom, and to that end had engineered a slate of speakers, including Jesuit sociologist Joseph Fichter of Loyola University in New Orleans, who was sympathetic to racial equality. University officials, however, refused to allow Kershaw to speak. The cancellation received national attention, and all of the other scheduled speakers withdrew in protest. For his part, Campbell announced that he would sit silently in Fulton Chapel each day at the time when the events had been scheduled to take place, arranging two vacant chairs spotlighted on the stage. Hundreds joined Campbell in the silent protest. Subsequent controversies eventually prompted Campbell to depart for Nashville, where he became a representative of the National Council of Churches on the issue of race relations.[48] Shortly thereafter, a similar controversy occurred at Mississippi State College, where the Reverend Duncan Gray from Cleveland, Mississippi, declared his belief that segregation and the Christian faith were incompatible. In response, the school's president requested that participants in the program avoid discussion of segregation because it was an inflammatory issue, thereby prompting several invitees to withdraw.[49]

At one level, these controversies reveal the possibilities for dissent despite southern religion's largely conservative nature. But the results — the shutting down of the programs in Mississippi and Campbell's exile — also suggest the limits on discussion, let alone dissent. The confluence of Cold War tensions and the rise of militant resistance to integration constituted a potent force in opposition to any form of dissent, especially on the issue of race.

Anticommunism and Dissent

Southern politicians' tactic of merging the threats of communism and integration was not new. Even before the emergence of the domestic Cold War consensus, Georgia governor Eugene Talmadge conducted a campaign in the early 1940s to purge the University of Georgia system of "dangerous" people. He focused much of his attention on Walter Dewey Cocking, dean of the University of Georgia's College of Education. At the request of the board of regents, Cocking had conducted a study of state-supported higher education that pointed out some of the inequities produced by the doctrine of "separate but equal." Some Georgians viewed the report as an endorsement of social equality for African Americans, and one disaffected former instructor in the university's laboratory school embarked on a campaign against Cocking. Talmadge eventually reconstituted the board to remove Cocking and others who stood for "communism or racial equality." The purge prompted the General Education Board, a philanthropic organization that supported higher education, to discontinue funding and the Southern Association of Colleges and Schools to withdraw accreditation. The governor's actions also incited students at the University of Georgia. In the fall of 1941, they burned Talmadge in effigy on three occasions, while many actively worked for the campaign of Ellis Arnall, Talmadge's 1942 gubernatorial opponent. The backlash propelled Arnall to victory, and he set about introducing reform bills that would insulate the state's higher education system from political attack. The Southern Association eventually restored the university's accreditation. The events showed that southern students, though not firebrands in any sense, might mobilize politically when the circumstances were right. Moreover, when students perceived their interests to be at stake, they could even organize against segregationists. In this case, Talmadge's power play endangered the legitimacy of degrees awarded by the university, a matter serious enough to cause students to support his opponent.[50]

Nevertheless, this brief political awakening of students was a blip on the radar screen, not a sign of a burgeoning southern student movement.[51] With the close of World War II, veterans flooded southern campuses. Older and often with families, these students brought to campus not only a new seriousness but also a reluctance to set aside their studies in favor of extracurricular political activism.[52] Combined with the growth of what would become known as McCarthyism, which stifled campus dissent, this influx of veterans created a campus political environment that by the 1950s was practically devoid of activism, in the South as well as the nation at large.

The chilling effect of anticommunism became the more powerful and longer lasting of the two forces limiting campus activism. The anticommunist assault on higher education was often driven by opportunistic politicians who recognized the possibility of capitalizing on American fears of communist infiltration and a strain of anti-intellectualism with deep roots. University presidents typically responded defensively, in most cases conceding that although they believed the concept of academic freedom should be preserved, certain limitations were necessary. A consensus emerged among academic leaders: professors who joined the Communist Party had surrendered their intellectual independence and thus were unqualified to teach. As a result of McCarthyism's assault on suspected communists or fellow travelers, almost one hundred academics nationwide lost their jobs for refusing to cooperate with investigations.[53] But the impact was felt by more than the people who were fired. McCarthyism generated a need for self-censorship, limiting both scholarly critical inquiry and faculty and students' tendency to connect their academic work with social and political issues.

McCarthyism was a national phenomenon, and both southern and non-southern universities struggled to maintain their autonomy in the face of loyalty oaths and political attacks on radical faculty members. The threat in the South does not appear to have been greater than that outside the region. In the South, however, race became intermingled with anticommunism, which then provided a pretext for political attacks on civil rights movement activists.[54] The fullest manifestation of this tendency developed in the 1960s, when state legislators in North Carolina banned communist speakers at state institutions in response to civil rights activities in Chapel Hill.[55] Throughout the region, opponents of the civil rights movement found that raising the specter of communism could be a potent tool to stifle dissent from the South's racial orthodoxy.

Campus Politics

The southern campus political culture, especially in the Deep South and on campuses in less cosmopolitan locales, was decidedly unfriendly to any sort of progressive activism. To some extent, black campuses experienced a similar dynamic, though the limits on black activism, often generated by repressive white governing boards at public institutions or by cautious administrators at private institutions, were if anything even more severe. On black as well as white campuses, the possibility of loss of employment or expulsion always loomed. For black southerners, however, the threat of violence also remained ever present. Black campuses shared some characteristics of white campuses, chiefly the apolitical if not conservative tendency to see college life either as an opportunity for "planned frivolity" or as a pathway to middle-class success. Running counter to these forces, however, was a history of resistance to racial exploitation that resulted in a greater proclivity for activism on black southern campuses.

These factors informed the environment that Harry H. Lunn Jr. experienced in February 1955 when he visited college and university campuses throughout the South. The president of the U.S. National Student Association (NSA), Lunn wanted a close-up view of the campuses that made up the NSA's Great Southern Region. The NSA was founded in 1947 at a convention of students representing some 350 colleges and universities. The organization had no official connection to any national political group; student governments at member institutions simply voted to affiliate. But the organization did not avoid political issues. At the founding convention, held on the campus of the University of Wisconsin in Madison, attendees passed a Student Bill of Rights that laid out concepts of student academic rights and civil liberties and, significantly for the South, declared that those rights should not be limited on the basis of race, religion, or political views. This stand against racial discrimination caused many conservative white students in the South to view the NSA as a liberal organization. Indeed, the organization's white southern critics, who occasionally demonstrated a proclivity toward imprecision in their political rhetoric, sometimes labeled the NSA "communistic." Ironically, in 1967, *Ramparts* magazine uncovered a relationship between the NSA and the Central Intelligence Agency, which had been funding the organization as a competitor against Soviet student groups. Nevertheless, the NSA's position on race drew attention in the South, and in the 1950s, the organization sought to attract black as well as white member institutions. A number of black colleges and universities joined, but the NSA struggled to attract and maintain white institutional members.[56]

Well versed in the dynamics of student politics, Lunn was in a unique position to observe the state of southern student politics. Since Lunn was primarily interested in shoring up the ranks of NSA's membership and since the NSA welcomed both white and black institutions, his observations present a biracial view of southern student politics that is unusual in its breadth. Lunn spent eighteen days visiting nineteen institutions — white and black, public and private, coeducational and women-only.

It was Lunn's first visit to the South, and he apparently was somewhat unnerved by the role that race played. "As I told many of the audiences I spoke to, it is rather hard for a white man from the North to visit the Deep South for the first time, particularly to see the segregation in higher education," he noted. "As one who had been educated in mixed schools all my life (although coming from a predominantly white neighborhood in elementary–high school) I cannot share the apprehensions and statements offered to support segregated systems of higher education." Lunn described an encounter over coffee with James E. Foy, dean of students at Auburn University in Alabama, during which Foy commented, "If you were a nigger, I don't suppose we could be sitting here talking."[57]

Lunn related the Foy episode in the context of a larger discussion about the role of race — what he termed "the racial problem" — in complicating NSA membership in the South. As Lunn noted, the NSA performed a sometimes difficult balancing act in encouraging black schools to participate while avoiding the alienation of white member institutions. This balancing act prompted the NSA to "keep down the number of Negro schools" and to follow an informal prohibition against appointing a black regional chair. Nevertheless, Lunn's observations suggest that southern campus politics was not dominated by racial issues — or, for that matter, by any issue ("Issues in elections are virtually unknown," he noted at one point). Lunn painted a portrait of often-vibrant southern campus political participation and influence with significant weaknesses that reflected weaknesses in "adult" southern politics. "One often hears someone comment that attendance at the state university is the only stepping-stone to state politics," Lunn noted, adding an anecdote about the involvement of state politicians in student elections at the University of Florida. "What does all this lead to? On the surface it seems to be good — here are all these people engaging in on the spot leadership training which is directly related to future life in the community: the essence of our argument for student government." But Lunn stopped before offering a full endorsement of this version of what the Port Huron Statement later called the "let's pretend" approach to student politics, suggesting instead that a closer look sent a more "disquieting" message. Too often, according to Lunn, "the students are receiving training in *undemocratic* methods or, at least, are being taught very questionable value standards. The motivation is bad and the training points them into the same thought patterns as their elders — certainly not a very hopeful sign for Southern leadership."[58]

Lunn described one distinguishing characteristic of southern campus politics as most schools' tendency to have a strong political party system, which inevitably led to tensions between "independents" and "fraternity men," cultural categories that nevertheless lacked any connection to real campus issues that good student governments should address. "Since the living arrangements on campus provide some of the easiest channels for political activity, it is natural for the greek-independent split to occur, even though there may be no underlying issues affecting the campus which would cause a rift normally," Lunn stated. The party system thus played into the worst aspect of southern student politics: the tendency to serve merely as career-building vehicles for student politicians.

The dynamic was decidedly unfavorable to the NSA. "Since there are few issues, if any, affiliation or disaffiliation is a perfect political football, particularly with the racial issue thrown in," Lunn declared. "If someone endorses the Association and you are his political enemy, all you have to do is get some really good smear charges and scare slogans together and you probably can defeat him."[59]

The split between fraternities and independents, the absence of substantive issues, and the tendency for race to emerge occasionally as a divisive issue operated to varying degrees on large white public and private campuses throughout the 1950s. Fraternities generally dominated these campus political systems, and when race emerged, the racial progressives did not win the day. One exception to this pattern might have been the Chapel Hill campus of the University of North Carolina, possibly the brightest star in the NSA's southern constellation. UNC was one of the few places in the South where liberal sentiment survived. Liberal activist Allard Lowenstein studied there in the 1940s and subsequently remained a campus and NSA force. And as Eli Evans, a UNC student in the late 1950s, recalled, the student government provided the primary channel for liberal students' actions: "We projected our concern onto student government, because that was the only outlet for action our generation of students perceived." He continued, "Demonstrations and overt defiance were out of the question, for an arrest or expulsion would be reported on our college records and surely be judged by future employers, graduate schools, and bar examiners. Such were the restraints at the end of the McCarthy era. We treated the smallest risk-taking as a sign of our courage, especially any signal of sympathy for the cause of Negro advance."[60]

The UNC political scene during these years was dominated by two parties, the University Party and the Student Party. The University Party generally was the stronghold of the fraternities, while the Student Party was dominated by groups of nonfraternity interests. According to Evans, some ideological differences distinguished the two groups. The Student Party was more liberal, though it had to couch its terms on race carefully to avoid scaring off student voters. While the University Party was concerned primarily with doling out honors to Greeks, the Student Party "attracted to party meetings all the boys who took themselves terribly seriously — earnest do-gooders, the verbose intellectuals, the consumed activists, the small-town high school class officers hungry for recognition and struggling to articulate issues they had never thought about before." Nevertheless, Evans points out, the ideological differences between the two parties meant more to the leadership than to outsiders. Party leaders "exaggerated the differences out of self-importance, a need to believe, no matter how fanciful, that the state and nation were listening, thereby adding importance of our great debates and rationalizing the time student politics soaked up."[61]

The issue of the segregation of UNC's black students onto one floor of a dormitory emerged during Evans's campaign for student government president in 1957. During a debate, Evans's opponent stated that he would not "agitate" to change the situation "because the student body is not yet ready to cope with it," while Evans criticized the policy of "segregated integration" and said that the purpose of student government was "to see that each student is treated equally." He later recalled that "the audience applauded vigorously, but these were the goody-goody religious liberals." In the aftermath, though Evans received the praise of northerners in his fraternity, the Student Party precinct captains believed he had blown the election. As a reflection of campus cultural divisions, however, the election was something of an anomaly. Evans, a member of one of the university's Jewish fraternities, was the nominee of the normally "independent" Student Party; the University Party, typically the domain of the fraternities, nominated a popular "independent." Evans benefited from an irrepressible campaign manager whom University Party leaders despised because "he outworked them and out-thought them and they viewed him as some sort of eccentric politico who took the game much more seriously than it deserved to be taken." In the end, despite Evans's forthright declaration, he became UNC's first Jewish student government president.[62]

As significant as Evans's victory might have been for the University of North Carolina, it did not indicate an incipient regionwide southern glasnost. Chapel Hill's campus political environment differed greatly from that in much of the rest of the South. UNC was a rarity, a southern university with a historical memory that included a vibrant liberalism. Chief among the progenitors of UNC liberals in the 1950s was Frank Porter Graham, the school's president from 1930 to 1949. Graham had left UNC to fill an unexpired term in the U.S. Senate, and when he ran for election to the seat in 1950, he lost after a campaign in which his opponent, Willis Smith, attacked Graham's liberalism in general and his positions on race in particular. The campaign revealed the limits of North Carolina's liberalism, and that reputation came under further assault during the 1960s from radical student activists who viewed it as a facade. Nevertheless, the political climate at UNC was remarkably open compared to that in the rest of the South.[63]

Chapel Hill and nearby Durham thus became an important center for 1960s southern student activism, even as UNC fought off Jesse Helms and the state legislature during the Speaker Ban controversy. Evans's portrait of student politics emphasizes the limitations and complications of Chapel Hill's student liberalism in the context of the 1950s. The "new southerners" with whom Evans associated, operating in the post-*Brown* South, were cautious liberals who struggled to find their moorings while the sands shifted beneath them. "Suddenly we were aware of just how little we really knew about him, the black stranger, who was neither meek nor aggressive, suffering nor lustful, pitiable nor irresponsible, as we had been taught," Evans recalled. How to proceed in this new world, in which old assumptions were revealed to be mistaken? Evans suggests a contrast between members of his generation and those who followed in the 1960s: "But we were not an outraged generation; we were the first generation of Southerners in the new age, and the style of the decade dictated a cool, detached, play-it-safe response with quiet resolves supplanting personal action."[64] In the increasingly heated political environment of the late-1950s South, campus liberals, like their "adult" counterparts throughout the region, struggled to find firm footing on the contested ground between the strident segregationist forces on the right and increasingly aggressive black activists on the left.

The Challenge to Segregated Education

Racially segregated colleges and universities were part of a larger system of political and social subordination. Beginning in the 1930s, however, the NAACP embarked on a legal challenge to segregated education that profoundly affected the South's political terrain. Segregated higher education began to crumble in 1938, when the Supreme Court ruled in *Gaines v. Canada* that southern states must offer equal opportunities for blacks in all areas of higher education, including law and medicine. In June 1950, the Supreme Court ruled in the *McLaurin* and *Sweatt* cases that the segregated arrangements for black graduate students in Oklahoma and Texas were unacceptable. The University of Oklahoma had required George W. McLaurin, a graduate student in the School of Education, to attend classes in a separate room and use a variety of separate facilities on the campus; officials had responded to Heman Sweatt's application to study law at the University of Texas by creating a segregated facility. These efforts to circumvent integration were now illegal. With "separate but equal" hanging by a thread, some states responded by instituting token desegregation. The University of North Carolina admitted four black graduate students in 1951 as a result of a court order, without incident and with little public attention. By 1952, forty-nine previously all-white institutions of higher education (twenty-two of them public and twenty-seven private) had desegregated.[65]

Five states — Mississippi, Alabama, Georgia, Florida, and South Carolina — had not yet admitted any African Americans into public historically all-white institutions. And those institutions that had desegregated had generally committed only to token levels of desegregation, usually in graduate and professional schools. By 1954, recently desegregated public institutions enrolled no more than one thousand black students, one-fifth of them at the

University of Arkansas. White southerners generally had reacted largely with indifference.[66]

The climax to the legal challenge to segregated education came in 1954, when the U.S. Supreme Court ruled in four cases collectively known as *Brown v. Board of Education of Topeka, Kansas* that "the doctrine of 'separate but equal' has no place" in the nation's public education systems. The ruling, along with its implementation ruling a year later, left unanswered many questions regarding how and when desegregation would occur. Southern African Americans hoped for a hasty end to Jim Crow, while southern whites soon stiffened their resolve to resist integration. The 1957 clash over the entrance of the first black students at Central High School in Little Rock, Arkansas, demonstrated that integration would not occur quickly or easily and dashed the early optimism of many African Americans. Nevertheless, the *Brown* ruling continued to serve as "a yardstick of color-blind justice" against which Americans could measure racial progress.[67]

The *Brown* ruling fundamentally altered the southern political scene and set in motion a chain of events that placed southern college campuses at the center of the political turmoil. *Brown* sounded the death knell for liberal gradualism, which had been under assault since the end of World War II. Outside the South, liberals had been concentrating their fire on segregation, which they viewed as a national embarrassment that crippled the United States in its rhetorical battle against communism. While a few southern liberals — notably, members of the Southern Conference for Human Welfare — agreed that segregation should be ended, most southern liberals continued to support the gradual amelioration of the conditions of African Americans under a separate-but-equal framework. By placing the U.S. Constitution firmly behind integration, the *Brown* ruling set a new standard for the improvement of the lives of African Americans in the South. Proponents of massive resistance insisted that the ruling was wrong-headed and should be overturned, but a gradualist program was no longer tenable. As southern college campuses became the scenes for showdowns over integration, liberal white students, caught in the middle of the battle, embraced integration in a variety of ways and helped move southern liberalism closer to its northern counterpart.[68]

At the same time, however, massive resistance in the second half of the 1950s began slamming the door on some tentative moves toward limited desegregation. Just two months after the *Brown* ruling, Southwestern Louisiana Institute (later the University of Southwestern Louisiana) became the South's first previously all-white, state-supported college or university to admit African Americans to undergraduate programs. The admission of John Harold Taylor of Arnaudville, Louisiana, came as the result of a lawsuit. Other black students followed, and by September 1954, eighty black students attended Southwestern Louisiana without disturbance. Within two years, however, as massive resistance to desegregation picked up momentum, the Louisiana legislature moved to slow down desegregation. One law barred school officials from supporting integration, including signing certificates of good moral character for black students seeking to enter previously all-white schools, while another law required such certificates to enter college. The laws had the desired effect of decreasing black enrollment at Southwestern Louisiana Institute until they were declared unconstitutional a year later.[69]

Resistance to desegregation also increased at private universities, which arguably were not affected by the *Brown* ruling. Tulane University in Louisiana began moving toward desegregation in the early 1950s. The primary stumbling block was a stipulation in Paul Tulane's endowment that the money be used for the education of "young white persons in the city of New Orleans." The university had long admitted people from outside the city as well as outside the United States, but admitting black students was another matter. In 1952, President Rufus Harris suggested to Vanderbilt chancellor Harvie Branscomb that the two private universities desegregate together. Vanderbilt's board rejected the offer, and though the university soon desegregated its graduate program in religion, Vanderbilt waited until 1963 to admit undergraduate black students. Although some members of Tulane's board of administrators had seemed amenable to the idea of desegregation, the window of opportunity closed abruptly in 1954, and Tulane, too, did not admit its first black students until 1963.[70]

A similar dynamic occurred at the University of Alabama, where an apparent opening to desegregation appeared in the mid-1950s only to close shortly thereafter. In 1954, President Oliver C. Carmichael ventured a tentative opinion that "nonsegregation" could occur under the right circumstances, but he quickly disavowed that opinion when it met with opposition from Birmingham journalist John Temple Graves as well as the university's conservative, self-perpetuating board of trustees. Without strong leadership from the president, the forces of massive resistance gained precious time to build their strength. When Autherine Lucy attempted to become the first African American student at the university in 1956, opponents of desegregation, led by blue-collar workers and Klansmen from Tuscaloosa, along with several dozen segregationist students, rioted on the campus. The university responded by expelling Lucy, giving segregationists a victory in the first round in the battle to "keep 'Bama white."[71]

The 1956 riots at the University of Alabama, like later ones at the Universities of Georgia and Mississippi, were not typical developments in the process of desegregating the South's higher education system. Despite the strength of anti-integration sentiment, court rulings indicated that segregated education—

indeed, the entirety of the South's superstructure of segregation — was on its way out.[72]

Nevertheless, the Alabama riots were revealing. The intrusion of serious racial politics forced students to consider the future of segregation. In the aftermath of the riots, notes E. Culpepper Clark, some students "learned valuable lessons about speaking in a crisis, and still more learned about values and morality in a racially divided society. Student religious groups and classrooms became forums for talking about 'the' issue." The vast majority of 'Bama students likely opposed both the Supreme Court's ruling and demonstrations against Lucy's matriculation. Though many students subsequently went to great lengths to argue that outsiders — local toughs and Klan members — were responsible for the rioting, students had played an important role in the riots, and the riots had been key in the decision to expel Lucy.[73]

The riots demonstrated some of the possibilities for student mobilization at a time when many observers assumed that students were too apathetic and self-absorbed to engage the major political and social issues of the day. Progressive activists in general and supporters of a move toward racial justice in particular faced the challenge of capitalizing on students' potential to influence developments not only at their institutions but also throughout the region. Even if the Alabama rioting did not indicate that all or even most students violently opposed integration, the incident could not have been particularly encouraging to progressive activists looking for evidence that white students wanted racial change. Only a small number of students and faculty had voiced their support for Lucy and a desegregated University of Alabama. In the late 1950s, most white students still accepted the tenets of segregation.

But students also cared about their institution's prestige and the value of their degree. And in the aftermath of the Lucy episode, Alabama students watched as their university took a beating in the national press, as Dennis Holt, president of the Arts and Sciences College Council, must have realized as he addressed the University of Alabama Student Government Association. Holt had worked with university officials during the riots, at one point personally turning back would-be demonstrators. "Our University and its trustees may well be famous for all time for running away from a fight. They have acquiesced to the mob. Let us face it: The mob is king on the campus today. We must all think a little bit about the fact that the mob won." Holt introduced a resolution condemning mob violence and favoring "law and order." It did not support integration. Holt thus embodied the limitations of the South's liberal gradualists.[74] Nevertheless, Holt's actions, echoing as they did those of University of Georgia students who had mobilized in opposition to Eugene Talmadge in the 1940s, demonstrated that potential for progressive white student mobilization existed when conceptualized in the right way — if not for integration, then for law and order or for the preservation of the autonomy of one's alma mater.

But in the late 1950s, the solution to the problem of finding ways to mobilize students around student issues remained a few years away. The first item on the agenda for white students in the South was to sort out a response to an emerging assault on an approach to race relations that lay at the heart of southern culture. Developments throughout the region — the Montgomery Bus Boycott, the Lucy episode, the Little Rock crisis — raised the stakes for all southerners. Then, in February 1960, black college students surprised many observers by organizing a movement that raised the stakes even more.

CHAPTER TWO

Nonviolent Direct Action and the Rise of a Southern Student Movement

THE TENSION BEFORE a demonstration was palpable, enough to make it difficult for a student to concentrate on her professor, on the day's material. Looming in the near future was another sit-in and the possibility of jail, violence, or both. These were heavy burdens for someone in late adolescence, especially when she tried to juggle the demands of a movement with the more mundane but no less important responsibilities of a college student. Some observers suggested that students had less to lose than "adults" did by participating in demonstrations, but the costs could still be great: parental disappointment, the shame of jail, the possibility of expulsion and with it the loss of an important avenue to upward mobility and a better life. "People used to tickle me, talking about how brave I was, sitting in, and marching, and what have you, because I was so scared," Nashville activist and Fisk student Diane Nash later recalled. "All the time. It was like wall-to-wall terrified. I can remember sitting in class, many times, before demonstrations, and I knew, like, we were going to have a demonstration that afternoon. And the palms of [my] hands would be so sweaty, and I would be so tense and tight inside. I was really afraid."[1]

Carolyn Long, a student at Clark College in Atlanta, later recalled dealing with the challenge of balancing activism with academics: "While we were in jail, we had books and things brought to us, and we studied while we were there. We never missed classes. . . . It was like the whole purpose of going to school was to get an education, and nothing was more important than that." Thus, Banks was "devastated" when, in the midst of the Atlanta student campaign against segregation, she received a D in conversational French. The professor, who was white, combined the low grade with "a very, very long dissertation on why blacks should stay in their place." She later took the same class at nearby

Morris Brown College and received an A. And she continued her activism and her collegiate career, eventually earning a degree and getting a job at the same Rich's department store she had helped desegregate in the early 1960s.[2]

Nash, Long, and other undergraduates in their late teens or early twenties fueled the sit-in movement, a dramatic, nonviolent challenge to segregation that swept much of the South in the early 1960s, changed the course of the civil rights movement, and laid the groundwork for the 1960s student movement. These activists often saw themselves and were perceived by others through the prism of their age. Theirs was a new generation that would step outside of expectations and challenge authority. "I remember realizing that with what we were doing, trying to abolish segregation," Nash later commented, "we were coming up against governors of seven states, judges, politicians, businessmen, and I remember thinking, I'm only 22 years old, what do I know, what am I doing?"[3] The actions of Nash and others provided some of the most important building blocks for an emerging generational identity that crossed racial and regional boundaries. But this identity, which emphasized the importance of challenging authority, was intermingled with a separate but related vocational identity. These activists not only were young but also were students, and the fact that their actions grew from a particular educational environment was also significant. The sit-in movement had important implications not only for what became the 1960s generation but also for the South's and the nation's college and university campuses. The introduction of nonviolent direct action opened up new possibilities for student political mobilization on black southern campuses while prompting students to ask new questions about what it meant to be a student and what should constitute a college education.

Nonviolent direct action was not new in 1960. The kinds of actions that fall under its umbrella — boycotts, marches, and an array of physical challenges to segregation that included what would be known by late 1960 as sit-ins — had occurred sporadically since at least the era of Reconstruction. The Fellowship of Reconciliation (FOR) had explored the use of nonviolence to achieve social change since its founding in 1914, and its affiliate, the Congress of Racial Equality (CORE), had been experimenting with forms of nonviolent direct action since its inception in 1942. In 1947, an interracial team of FOR and CORE activists that included Bayard Rustin and James Peck embarked on the Journey of Reconciliation, an interstate bus trip through the Upper South to test a recent Supreme Court ruling ordering the desegregation of interstate bus terminals. During the 1950s, a number of nonviolent challenges to segregated establishments occurred, including lunch-counter demonstrations in Washington, D.C.; St. Louis; Baltimore; and Oklahoma City.[4]

So when four black students from North Carolina Agricultural and Technical College in Greensboro sat down at the city's segregated Woolworth's lunch counter on 1 February 1960, their actions were far from unprecedented. Nevertheless, this episode was different. In contrast to similar demonstrations, this one ignited a movement driven by students and unleashed a host of forces that affected southern politics, culture, and education throughout the decade. The sit-in movement introduced college students as independent political actors capable of altering the region's political landscape and provided a vocabulary and a cache of tactics that drove the movement for years. But the sit-ins also had a tremendous impact on the institutions that housed the foot soldiers of the nonviolent assault on segregation. The sit-in movement drew a national spotlight to the college and university campuses that served as the staging grounds for the student assault on segregation, highlighting these institutions as breeding grounds for idealistic young people seeking to nudge the South toward living up to national ideals of freedom and equality. On individual campuses, the sit-in movement was often a galvanizing event that was at times even celebrated in school yearbooks and alumni publications. But it also at times was a divisive force that set in motion a process that eventually shone a spotlight of a different sort on the South's Negro colleges. The sit-in movement initiated a period of student activism that eventually took aim at the institutions themselves and in the process raised fundamental questions about the connections between politics and education as well as the role of segregated colleges in a desegregating South.

Origins of the Movement

Franklin McCain, one of the four students whose actions initiated the Greensboro movement, later recalled the deep imprint made by the 1957 Little Rock school desegregation crisis. Watching on television, he saw the Arkansas National Guard protecting the black students while angry whites screamed epithets. The scenes planted the seeds of a desire for change.[5] Ezell Blair Jr., another of the Greensboro Four, was influenced by the activism of Mohandas K. Gandhi. "I've never forgotten a television show I saw last year called 'The Pictorial Story of India,'" Blair stated a little more than a month after the demonstrations began. "Gandhi was shown time and time again leaving jail, only to be arrested again."[6] Other students were motivated by a FOR comic book that dramatized the Montgomery Bus Boycott before offering a step-by-step primer from Martin Luther King Jr. in the philosophy and practice of nonviolent direct action. "First, decide what special thing you're going to work on," King said. "In Montgomery, it was buses, somewhere else it might be voting, or schools, or integrated churches. . . . When you are ready, then go ahead and *don't turn back* no matter how hard the way or how long the struggle."[7]

The numerous forces that generated the sit-in movement had deep roots, but the proximate cause occurred halfway through the 1959–60 academic year. On 1 February 1960, at about 4:45 P.M., four black students from North Carolina Agricultural and Technical College entered F. W. Woolworth's, bought some supplies, and sat down for service at the whites-only lunch counter. After being rebuffed by a waitress, they waited for service at the counter until the store closed at 5:30. At that point, concerned about the possibility that they would be prosecuted, the students went to the executive committee of the local chapter of the National Association for the Advancement of Colored People (NAACP) for advice and support. That evening, the four students met with about fifty others from A&T and formed the Student Executive Committee for Justice. The next day, they returned to Woolworth's with twenty-three more students from A&T and four students from Bennett College, a black women's school. All sat at the lunch counter, but no one was served. The demonstrations expanded in the following days, with the group of nonviolent demonstrators growing to include not only other students from A&T and Bennett but also a few white women from the Women's College of the University of North Carolina in Greensboro.[8]

The first national news stories were small. "A group of well-dressed Negro college students staged a sitdown strike in a downtown Woolworth store today and vowed to continue it in relays until negroes were served at the lunch counter," a 3 February United Press International story picked up by the *New York Times* reported. No students were named, though a "spokesman for the group" was quoted as saying, "We believe since we buy books and papers in the other part of the store we should get served in this part." The store's manager declared, "They can just sit there. It's nothing to me."[9] During the next week, North Carolina students launched additional "sitdown strikes," as they initially were called in the press, in Durham, Winston-Salem, Charlotte, Fayetteville, Raleigh, Elizabeth City, and High Point. In Durham, four white students from Duke University joined black participants at the Woolworth's lunch counter. The demonstration was cut short when the store's manager, C. L. Storm, closed the store at midday after receiving a bomb threat. The forty demonstrators moved on to the S. H. Kress and Company store, which also closed soon after their arrival, and then across the street to a Walgreen's drugstore, where they found the lunch counter already roped off and closed. This cat-and-mouse game between student demonstrators and store managers was replicated in other cities. In Greensboro, stores reopened on 8 February only after students agreed to a two-week cooling-off period.[10]

Sit-down demonstrations spread to Hampton, Virginia, on 11 February and to Rock Hill, South Carolina, the following day. There, demonstrators faced white counterdemonstrators, who shoved the protesters, threw eggs, and tossed a bottle of ammonia. On 13 February, students in Nashville, Tennessee, and Tallahassee, Florida, conducted sit-ins. By this time, not quite two weeks after the initial Greensboro sit-in, observers were beginning to detect the development of something more than a handful of isolated demonstrations against segregation. Skeptics had initially tended to view the sit-ins in light of college students' previous, more frivolous, mass actions—as what journalist Claude Sitton called "another college fad of the 'panty-raid' variety." But, as Sitton noted on 15 February, even skeptics could not summarily dismiss the sit-ins as they spread throughout the region.[11]

By April, seventy-eight cities in thirteen southern states had experienced sit-ins. That month, representatives from college campuses throughout the South gathered in Raleigh, North Carolina, to form an organization, eventually dubbed the Student Nonviolent Coordinating Committee (SNCC), to facilitate communication among the demonstrations. The sit-ins tapered off around the time of spring examinations but picked up again during the summer with the help of high school students. In addition to expanding geographically, the demonstrations also grew in scope. The movement expanded its list of targets to include all types of public accommodations—parks and swimming pools, museums and art galleries.[12]

The sit-ins initiated a reconsideration or in many cases a discovery of black colleges. College campuses that had been criticized as breeding grounds for apathetic, materialistic students became almost overnight sources for a new militancy that breathed life into the movement for racial equality. "Not long ago the Negro collegian imitated the white collegian," suggested King in a September 1961 article in the *New York Times Magazine*. "In attire, in athletics, in social life, imitation was the rule. For the future, he looked to a professional life as in the image of the middle-class white professional. He imitated with such energy that Gunnar Myrdal described the ambitious Negro as 'an exaggerated American.' Today the imitation has ceased. The Negro collegian now initiates."[13] That same month, a Southern Regional Council study was just as grandiose in its assessment of the impact of the movement: "A solitary instance of spontaneous rebellion has now become a movement of truly massive proportions which has stirred the conscience of the South and of the nation." By then, more than one hundred cities in southern and border states had experienced direct-action demonstrations, with seventy thousand participants and an estimated thirty-six hundred arrests.[14]

The sit-ins were locally organized but were nevertheless connected to others throughout the South by student personnel, tactics, the language the demonstrators used to describe their actions, and the philosophical and religious ideas that provided the demonstrations' foundation. Many people, including student leaders, viewed the sit-ins through a generational lens—that is, as a rejection of older, slower methods of opposing segregation and racial exploitation. At times, the rejection appeared as a function of the practical difficulties faced by older African Americans who showed signs of aggressiveness. "You see, what we call the old Negro has always had to comply with everything in the South because of his economic status," declared Blair. "As new Negroes, we can speak up loudly now and without fear of economic reprisals."[15] But, at other times, the rejection was more explicit — an indictment of the gradualism, even meekness, of adults.

A number of material and psychological factors contributed to the advent of the sit-in movement. The 1954 *Brown* ruling had inspired many black southerners to hope that segregation would end — if not soon, then someday. But progress toward that day was slow, and it became even slower with the rise of massive resistance. Many African Americans became frustrated. By 1960, that frustration was especially intense among black college students. Only the wealthiest African Americans had access to a college education. Usually hailing from urban areas with comparatively benign race relations and more likely to have seen or read about the world, black college students often were sensitive to the ceiling that segregation placed on their potential advancement. In short, their frustration and impatience grew out of a sense of relative deprivation. "*Impatience* was the mood of the young sit-in demonstrators," wrote historian and activist Howard Zinn, "impatience with the courts, with national and local governments, with negotiation and conciliation, with the traditional Negro organizations and the old Negro leadership, with the unbearably slow pace of desegregation in a century of accelerated social change." But their frustration did not consume them. Instead, despite their awareness of their deprivation, African American students who participated in demonstrations tended to be optimistic about race relations and tolerant of whites. The sit-ins represented their claim on their right to participate in mainstream American middle-class life. But the sit-ins also provided a way for black students to express their pent-up frustration. Prior to the Greensboro sit-ins, SNCC leader Cleveland Sellers recalled, "we had no effective means to express our discontent with segregation and other forms of racial discrimination."[16]

One commentator suggested that intercollegiate basketball games served as an early conduit for the spread of sit-ins. In the weeks after the Greensboro sit-ins began, five schools that played North Carolina A&T became involved in sit-ins.[17] Atlanta activist Julian Bond later noted the competitive nature of the movement: "People in Atlanta said, 'What are they doing in Nashville?' 'How many people did they get arrested last week?' 'How many restaurants did they hit?'"[18]

The Greensboro sit-ins and those that followed were neither as solitary nor as spontaneous as accounts often suggest. Throughout the South, organizations such as the Southern Christian Leadership Conference (SCLC), CORE, and the NAACP's youth councils had been organizing black communities to engage in nonviolent protest during the 1950s. The tactical vehicle of the 1960 movement, the sit-in, was itself not a new idea. CORE had experimented with the tactic for years, and in the late 1950s, NAACP youth councils in Oklahoma and Kansas had employed direct action. Nor, according to sociologist Aldon Morris, were students quite the independent actors indicated by some portrayals. Instead, students often worked in concert with movement leaders to spread the sit-ins, and adult leaders often organized student protesters.[19]

But many of the early student sit-in participants acted as if they had invented something new. Their buoyant enthusiasm and — from the perspective, perhaps, of a more cynical time — naive embrace of ideals such as freedom and equality created the energy that helped generate a movement that quickly touched much of the Southeast. Nevertheless, all locations that experienced this wave of nonviolent direct action did not experience it in the same way. As would be true later in the decade when southern students demonstrated against the Vietnam War or in loco parentis restrictions, local conditions always played an important role in shaping the way protests developed and the response they received from campus officials and community leaders.

The geographical distribution of sit-ins was neither random nor uniform. While the student-led demonstrations spread throughout the South, many parts of the region — even areas in which black colleges were located — did not experience sit-ins. As a rule, the Upper South and urban centers throughout the region were the most likely locales for direct-action attacks on segregation. The climate of race relations in these areas tended to be more benign than that of the Deep South. As Zinn noted at a 1963 SNCC meeting, the rural areas of Mississippi, Alabama, and Georgia represented a qualitatively different problem from that posed by Nashville. The former areas, Zinn suggested, resembled a police state. Moreover, urban areas provided the kind of targets necessary for a challenge to segregated public accommodations. Rural areas lacked the commercial establishments that often were at the center of student demonstrations.[20]

Differing college characteristics also helped determine the presence or absence of activism. One 1962 study found that the manner in which a college was supported and its quality significantly affected protest. Public colleges, more vulnerable to external pressures because of state control, were less likely than private institutions to produce demonstrators. At public colleges, 19 percent of students participated in sit-ins, whereas 37 percent of denominational private-college students and 30 percent of secular private-college students participated. Moreover, students at public colleges were more likely than were students at private colleges to perceive administrators as failing to support activism.[21] But as historian Joy Ann Williamson has pointed out, it is possible to overstate this dynamic. Presidents of private institutions often found themselves pressured by powerful segregationists and sometimes responded with attempts to curb demonstrations. Conversely, vibrant movements sometimes developed at public institutions with politically skillful administrators who found ways to protect their students.[22]

Sit-ins in more repressive areas of the South were also less likely to wipe out segregation. One study of early sit-ins found not only that the Upper South provided the setting for many more sit-ins than did the Deep South but that Upper South campaigns were much more likely to succeed. Martin Oppenheimer's study of sixty-nine communities found fifty-two sit-in campaigns in Arkansas, Florida, Kentucky, Maryland, Missouri, North Carolina, Oklahoma, Tennessee, Texas, and Virginia, of which thirty-nine were successful. In Alabama, Georgia, Louisiana, Mississippi, and South Carolina, however, only seventeen sit-in campaigns took place, and all failed to defeat segregation, at least in the short run.[23] Where no sit-in movement occurred, the implications for later student activism could be significant. For example, the sit-in movement bypassed Tuscaloosa, Alabama, home of historically black Stillman College and the University of Alabama, and serious civil rights activity did not develop in the city until 1964, when one of King's protégés, the Reverend T. Y. Rogers, led demonstrations aimed at prompting enforcement of the new Civil Rights Act. Only then did students at both schools find a focus for civil rights activism.[24]

Other variables, such as the organizing abilities of the student activists themselves and the presence of encouraging or discouraging faculty members and administrators, also played a role. On campuses where effective student movements developed, leadership frequently came from nontraditional students. Some had entered college after serving terms in the military or working. Others had previous political experience that gave them insight into mobilizing people. At many schools, student government leaders helped organize demonstrations, thereby hastening mainstream acceptance within the student body. Sympathetic faculty members lent additional support when student movements developed. Finally, the response of an institution's president often played a central role in determining whether a movement died in its infancy or had room to grow. While no college presidents joined the sit-ins, some administrators took a more sympathetic view than did others.

The Nashville Movement and Nonviolent Direct Action

Though the story of the sit-in movement usually begins in Greensboro, Nashville exerted the larger influence on the southern student movement of the early 1960s. The events in Greensboro helped nudge many students toward involvement in demonstrations against segregation, but the Nashville movement would have occurred even if the Greensboro Four had not staged the first sit-in. In the months leading up to February 1960, Nashville had a local movement led by, among others, Kelly Miller Smith, pastor of the First Colored Baptist Church, and James M. Lawson Jr., an African American graduate theology student, who were already engineering an assault on segregation.[25] A field secretary with FOR, the thirty-one-year-old Lawson brought years of experience in nonviolent social change. In the early 1950s, he had served a prison term for refusing induction into the army. After getting out of prison, Lawson had spent three years in India, where he nurtured an admiration for Gandhi. He came back to the United States just as the Montgomery Bus Boycott had initiated the heroic phase of the civil rights movement, and the developing movement spurred him to set aside his plans for a career that included advanced theological study followed by a pastorate. Instead, he signed on with FOR and headed for the South. After considering Atlanta as a possible base of operations, Lawson chose Nashville, a moderate city in a border state with a fairly liberal newspaper (the *Nashville Tennessean*) and a vibrant array of colleges and universities.[26]

The best known of these institutions were Vanderbilt, a private university for white students that had recently begun admitting blacks for graduate study, and Fisk, a respected private black college. But other institutions — Meharry Medical College, Tennessee Agricultural and Industrial State University, and American Baptist Theological Seminary for blacks; Peabody Teachers College and Scarritt College for whites — also provided activists who ultimately made Nashville an important locale for southern student activism. Fisk, Meharry, Tennessee A&I, and American Baptist reflected color and class divisions within the African American community. Fisk was one of the country's most prestigious black universities and, not unlike Morehouse and Spelman Colleges in Atlanta, tended to draw students who were wealthier and lighter skinned. In some senses, the Fisk students of the 1950s were far removed from their predecessors of the 1920s who had driven Fayette MacKenzie out of office. While the university continued to operate near the center of African American intellectual and cultural life, its dominant student culture discouraged political activism. Fisk students could be expected to be better prepared educationally than members of their collegiate cohort at other institutions in Nashville, but social expectations often prevented them from participating in political activity. Thus, when Lawson began the nonviolence workshops, few Fisk students participated. One who did, Marion Barry, was a chemistry graduate student who came from a modest background and who had already tasted activism, having challenged a white segregationist member of the board of trustees of his undergraduate institution, Memphis's LeMoyne College. Barry found little in common with the young members of the black aristocracy who gravitated to Greek societies and seemed to see political activity as beneath them. Another participant was the Chicago-raised Nash, a transfer student from Howard University who was surprised at the extent of Nashville's segregation.[27]

During the movement's initial stages, Tennessee A&I also seemed an un-friendly environment for activism. Although the public A&I was the state's largest black school, Curtis Murphy, an early organizer, initially had difficulty convincing fellow students to join. But as the sit-ins attracted publicity, Murphy became something of a campus hero.[28] Some of the most captivating of the Nashville sit-in leaders came from American Baptist, a seminary supported by the white Southern Baptist Convention. According to journalist David Halberstam, American Baptist "was a place filled with political ferment and passion. Its faculty was gifted and its students, many of them diamonds in the rough, were hungry to learn."[29]

These institutions provided the foot soldiers for the attack on segregation in Nashville. For its part, white Nashville nurtured the movement. The city had more benign race relations than could be found in the Deep South, and Mayor Ben West had a record of moderation. But Nashville remained a segregated city capable of directing violence at those who challenged segregation. "Nashville at that time was an odd mix of racial progressiveness on the one hand and conflict and intolerance on the other," observed John Lewis. Though African Americans wielded some political clout, holding seats on the city council and positions in the police force, much of the city's public space—libraries, theaters, schools, hotels, and restaurants—remained segregated. By April 1960, Nashville stu-dents had become among the most battle-worn in the South.[30]

Lawson provided Nashville's students with a galvanizing ideology that mixed the Gandhian philosophy and tactics of nonviolence with Christianity. At a practical level, this approach to social change used noncooperation to fight corrupt power under the assumption that political power depends on the co-operation of the subjects of that power.[31] But as Lawson taught his pupils in Nashville, nonviolent direct action was more than a tactic; it was a way of life. According to Lawson, activists not only should resist the inclination to respond to violence with violence but also should love those using the violence. "It was not enough to resist the urge to strike back at an assailant," Lewis later recalled. "'That urge can't *be* there,' he would tell us. 'You have to do more than just not hit back. . . . You have to *love* that person who's hitting you.'" Christian love also bound together the members of the activist community. Members of Lawson's troupe believed they were creating the ideal of the Beloved Community, which in Lewis's later recollections was "nothing less than the Christian concept of the kingdom of God on earth." This community would not be structured like other communities; it would not be dominated by a strong leader. Instead, the Nashville Student Movement adopted a practice of rotating leadership, an ap-proach that initially repelled some traditional campus politicos.[32] Finally, the Nashville Student Movement was avowedly and intentionally interracial. Paul LaPrad, a white Fisk student who recently had transferred from a school in the

Midwest and who had strong Quaker roots, became a regular participant in the Lawson-led seminars of the fall of 1959. Indeed, when the Nashville movement hit the streets in early 1960, LaPrad, viewed by militant anti-integrationists as a traitor to his race, became a prominent target for violent reprisals.[33]

The Nashville Student Movement's insistence on nonviolence not just as a tactic but also as a philosophy and its intentional and provocative interracialism came into play as the movement kicked into gear in February 1960. Major operations began on 13 February, when 124 people, most of them black, made their way in the snow from a downtown church to several lunch counters. "The demonstration was orderly," reporter James Talley noted in an article in the next day's *Tennessean*. "There were no incidents. Some of the students wandered about the stores, purchasing candy and other items, then returned to the counters. Some read books; other studied their school homework." Store owners responded by closing the lunch counters. This pattern continued off and on over the next two weeks.[34]

However, events elsewhere in Tennessee indicated the possibility of more violent confrontations. On 23 February, rioting broke out in the midst of sit-ins at an S. H. Kress and Company lunch counter in Chattanooga. Screaming, shouting, and pushing between white counterdemonstrators and students led police to give orders to vacate the store, which in turn led to a fifteen-minute fight. "Flower pots, dishes, bric-a-brac and other merchandise in the store were thrown as the Negroes started for rear exits," a news report stated. "Some fought back." White youths involved and some police officers claimed that some of the black participants were armed with knives. Nevertheless, according to the *New York Times* account of the melee, the white participants appear to have been the more aggressive: "After the fighting had subsided, white youths walked through the aisles of the stores, jeering at Negro customers and frightening many into leaving. Some of the leaders said their purpose was 'to run the niggers out.'"[35]

Similar violence reached Nashville on 27 February. Police overlooked attacks on the student demonstrators and then arrested eighty-one students. The next day, the front page of the *Nashville Tennessean* showed LaPrad doubled over on the floor as a white counterdemonstrator beat him. *Tennessean* reporter James Talley described jeering whites, whose anger seemed to increase when their insults provoked no response from the black students. At the first-floor Woolworth's counter, the students "were not talking. They were looking straight ahead. One or two were reading magazines." A group of white boys moved in behind the students and, with no policemen around, began harassing them — "kicking them, spitting on them, calling them vulgar names, and putting cigarets out on their backs." At the second-floor counter, a group of white boys taunted two black demonstrators, "Go home, nigger" and "What's the matter, you chicken?" When the whites' comments provoked no response, they attacked, and one black demonstrator was pushed down a flight of stairs.[36]

Despite their preparation, the violence seemed to take some of the students by surprise. "I really wouldn't expect this type of thing in Nashville," Luther Harris, a Fisk student, told the newspaper. "The police just pulled out and left us unprotected. Something's got to be done." In a phrase that would resonate with late-1960s' militancy, Harris added, "The Negro in the South has taken a lot but there is just so much he can take." Harris's rhetoric reflected the fact that he had not been part of the core of Lawson's seminars on nonviolence; rather, Harris was one of the "campus politicians" whom Lewis described as "maneuver[ing] themselves into position" as committee chairs. In Lewis's view, however, Harris and another campus politico, Earl Mayes, were uncomfortable with the Nashville Student Movement's power-sharing philosophy, and they soon resigned their positions.[37]

The violence of 27 February neither spiraled out of control nor weakened participants' or supporters' resolve. In fact, the violence seemed to give the Nashville movement momentum, galvanizing the black community's support for the students. At Fisk, President Stephen J. Wright announced his approval of the movement at chapel meeting the next day: "From all I have been able to learn they have broken no law by the means they have employed thus far, and they have not only conducted themselves peaceably, but with poise and dignity." The students, Wright stated, "have been exposed all their lives to the teachings of the great American scriptures of democracy, freedom and equality, and no literate person should be surprised that they reflect these teachings in their conduct."[38]

Activist students viewed Wright's support as significant. Faced with pressures from the community, from Fisk's board of trustees, and from worried parents, Wright had previously been cautious. Those forces were powerful, even if Wright, as the president of a private university, did not work under the same constraints encountered by public university presidents. Nevertheless, Wright's public stand put him in the vanguard of college presidents who supported the sit-in movement, and it effectively opened the doors for widespread participation from Fisk students. On other occasions, Wright served as a force for moderation, encouraging students not to let their participation in the movement interfere with their attendance at classes. "It has come to my attention that class attendance has been erratic over the past several days as a result of the lunch counter demonstrations," read a statement from Wright posted on campus bulletin boards. "This is to call your attention to the fact that University regulations require attendance on a regular basis, and that all students except those involved in the actual litigations of the cases are expected to attend classes as usual." However, as spring term continued, the sit-ins at times took on the feel of a sanctioned activity. Alongside the regular reports about mundane campus activities (a new photographic display in the library, "sons and daughters planning to go to the altar this summer"), the spring issues of the normally staid campus publications offered detailed summaries of the sit-ins.[39]

The apparent widespread unity that the Nashville Student Movement inspired belied fissures that existed beneath the surface. One split existed along generational lines and surfaced later in the spring as younger and older activists clashed over the movement's pace. Another breach existed along campus subcultural lines that had previously seemed to dissolve. Lewis later described a November 1961 encounter on the Fisk campus, where he had matriculated after finishing at American Baptist, between demonstrators and a group of fraternity men, "wearing dog collars around their throats and carrying their Greek paddles. They ran past us, barking like hounds, hollering and whooping and going through their fraternity ritual." Lewis recalled being stunned at the behavior, "to see these young black men swept up in this trivial silliness at the very moment that people their own age . . . were risking their lives . . . standing up for the future of all of us." Such incongruities existed on many campuses but were especially pronounced in Nashville, where the committed core of the movement had undergone such intentional and intense schooling in nonviolence.[40]

Moreover, as the Nashville movement's influence spread, activists such as Lewis, Nash, and James Bevel found themselves drawn away from the city. Nashville continued to serve as a movement center, and direct-action attacks on segregated public establishments continued through the early 1960s, winning victories, expanding from lunch counters to other kinds of public accommodations, and attracting a growing contingent of white students from Vanderbilt and Scarritt. But the workshops that had generated the Nashville Student Movement and made its participants the best schooled in the theory and practice of nonviolent direct action ended by the spring of 1961.[41]

Nevertheless, Nashville essentially defined the southern student movement of the early 1960s. When SNCC was formed in April 1960, Nashville's vision and more specifically that of Lawson animated the organization's founding statement:[42]

> We affirm the philosophical or religious ideal of nonviolence as the foundation of our purpose, the presupposition of our faith, and the manner of our action. Nonviolence as it grows from Judaic-Christian traditions seeks a social order of justice permeated by love. Integration of human endeavor represents the crucial first step towards such a society.
>
> Through nonviolence, courage displaces fear; love transforms hate. Acceptance dissipates prejudice; hope ends despair. Peace dominates war; faith reconciles doubt. Mutual regard cancels enmity. Justice for all over-

throws injustice. The redemptive community supersedes systems of gross social immorality.

Love is the central motif of nonviolence. Love is the force by which God binds man to Himself and man to man. Such love goes to the extreme; it remains loving and forgiving even in the midst of hostility. It matches the capacity of evil to inflict suffering with an even more enduring capacity to absorb evil, all while persisting in love.

By appealing to conscience and standing on the moral nature of human existence, nonviolence nurtures the atmosphere in which reconciliation and justice become actual possibilities.[43]

The Atlanta Student Movement and the City Too Busy to Hate

Farther South, another movement center was developing in Atlanta. Like Nashville, Atlanta had a history of black protest and political action. The cities also shared a reputation for featuring relatively moderate racial environments and for being centers for African American education. In Atlanta, moderate white leaders made some space for black input, and the city's reputation as "too busy to hate" stood in stark contrast to cities such as Birmingham, with more rabid administrations. Over the years, a coterie of black leaders had gained some bargaining power with Atlanta's moderate white leadership, trading support from black voters for concessions. Some elements in Atlanta's established black business community opposed the developing sit-in movement, favoring their long-practiced methods of behind-the-scenes negotiation. In fact, the *Atlanta Daily World*, the city's established black newspaper, refused to cover the demonstrations, prompting proponents of the sit-ins to start a competing newspaper, the *Atlanta Inquirer*. But the student movement cast doubt on both the city's racial enlightenment and black leaders' emphasis on negotiating progress.[44]

The first push for large-scale demonstrations occurred shortly after the initial Greensboro sit-ins, when Morehouse student Lonnie King, a Korean War veteran, spearheaded an assault on segregated lunch counters. Atlanta University president Rufus Clement then suggested that the students draft a statement outlining their concerns, presumably in hopes that doing so would encourage students to move more slowly. The students created "An Appeal for Human Rights," drawing on an article by Clark College humanities professor Carl Holman, "A Second Look at Atlanta," that outlined the inequalities beneath the surface of what appeared to be a glistening New South city. The "Appeal" appeared in full-page, paid advertisements in Atlanta's daily newspapers on 9 March. Six days later, students from the Atlanta University Center conducted their first coordinated sit-ins, targeting various lunch counters and cafeterias. Police immediately arrested seventy-seven students.[45]

The Atlanta University Center included Morehouse, Spelman, Clark, and Morris Brown Colleges as well as Atlanta University and the Interdenominational Theological Seminary. While the histories of the six institutions had been tied together intimately, each had its own identity. Morehouse, a male college, and Spelman, a female college, had reputations for drawing from the more elite segments of African American life. Both were Baptist institutions founded with money from the Rockefeller family, and both had an aura of prestige. Less prestigious were Clark College, founded by the Freedman's Aid Society of the Methodist Episcopal Church, and Morris Brown, which was affiliated with the Colored Methodist Episcopal Church. Atlanta University was the center's graduate institution; its students were thus older.[46] "Atlanta is the center of Negro higher education in the United States," noted the *Atlanta Journal-Constitution* in the midst of the sit-in movement. In early 1960, 3,781 students were enrolled at the Atlanta University Center schools: 823 at Clark College, 756 at Morehouse, 896 at Morris Brown, 513 at Spelman, 701 at Atlanta University, and 92 at the Interdenominational Theological Seminary.[47]

Despite the deep pool of students, crosscurrents of conservatism at all of the institutions as well as in Atlanta's black community made launching the student sit-ins a complicated effort. Morehouse's president, Benjamin Mays, a legendary academic leader who had long been involved in the struggle for racial equality, provided tacit support for the movement. In talks to the student body, Mays had always encouraged students "to accept only the segregation that they had to accept." But Mays's position, he later recalled, prevented him from participating actively in the movement, even if he embraced its goals: "I was president of Morehouse, and I couldn't be marching and in and out of jail without resigning from Morehouse. And I thought my job was to build Morehouse."[48] Bond later recalled Mays as a revered but distant figure to students: "We had his blessings and support, but he was almost an unreal figure." If Mays represented an element of resistance to racial discrimination embedded within Morehouse's campus culture, then the school's student leadership represented a contradictory impulse — the dominance of Greek society leaders who viewed campus political power as an outgrowth of their social power. Bond later described Morehouse's student government as "a tradeoff between fraternities"; the Clark College student government, in contrast, was more functional and representative of the entire student body. And Lonnie King later noted the gap that existed between the established student leadership at Morehouse and those, like King and Bond, who represented "a different kind of leadership. . . . Some of the students at Morehouse really kind of wondered — some of the leaders — why were some of us in charge rather than them?"[49]

Conservatism took on gendered contours at Spelman, where administrators and faculty prided themselves on their ability to train their students not only in matters of the intellect but also in manners and morals. The participation of Spelman students in the 1960–61 demonstrations complicated that picture. The seventy-seven students arrested in the first sit-ins included fourteen Spelman students, and their participation, according to Howard Zinn, then on the Spelman faculty, "brought some bewilderment to the conservative matriarchy which has played a dominant role in the college's history."[50] Spending time in jail violated traditional conceptions of ladylike activity. Moreover, the regulations that circumscribed outside activities could make involvement difficult. The college did not allow students to leave campus in the evenings without special permission. One student, Gwen Robinson, became frustrated with these limitations and complained loudly. Albert Manley, the institution's president, responded by demanding to know if Robinson was a communist. Manley was not completely unsupportive, however: he commended the members of the graduating class of 1960 "for demonstrating that college students are not apathetic, but can become involved in great causes when the moment arises."[51] Bond later described Manley's attitude toward the student activists and students in general as being both patronizing and supportive.[52]

The sit-ins resurrected fundamental issues regarding the nature of the Negro college's educational mission. Students had raised the same questions during the 1920s, and they remained unanswered. Manley's acceptance that students could legitimately act on social concerns in an overtly political way led to other questions: What kind of activity was proper, and how much of it? And what did this activity have to do with the educational enterprise? Despite Spelman's finishing-school reputation, student political activity was not new at the institution. In 1957, Zinn had taken one of his classes to visit the Georgia state legislature, where the students decided to sit in the main gallery rather than in the "colored" section. After the speaker of the house shouted at them, "You nigras get over to where you belong! We got segregation in the state of Georgia," they moved. In 1959, students and teachers in the Social Science Club (for which Zinn served as adviser) decided to "undertake an experiment in deliberate, organized social change," visiting the segregated Carnegie Library and requesting books. The library had policies that enabled employees to deal with this situation while maintaining the facade of segregation, but the action put library officials on notice that African Americans needed the facilities. The next step was a lawsuit, but before it was filed, officials desegregated the city's public libraries, a decision that caused little commotion.[53]

As these examples suggest, Zinn saw educational value in student political activity. "The young people who leave college to join the movement have not deserted education. In an important sense, they are getting the best education in the country today," Zinn wrote in his book on SNCC. Not all faculty members, however, shared Zinn's enthusiasm for the educational value of sitting-in. In fact, the possibility that activism could intrude on classroom responsibilities lay at the heart of much of the Atlanta University Center faculty's opposition to the sit-ins. Morehouse student Alton Hornsby recalled that the chair of the history department advised Hornsby not to participate because of the possible risk to winning scholarships. Arthur C. Banks Jr., a political science professor at Morehouse, declared in a reply to an article by Zinn in the *Nation* that the students' activism, while noble enough, "may have been carried on at the expense of legitimate classroom activity." He added that picketing was a good activity, "but reading the Great Books can yield greater profits."[54]

At a more visceral level, the Atlanta University Center administrators' reservations grew out of concern for student safety. Operating under what was still the legitimate framework of in loco parentis, college presidents feared having to inform parents that their children had been hurt in the demonstrations. "We had a responsibility for these students," recalled Clark College president James Brawley. "Not only just the responsibility of not wanting to see anything happen to them, but we had a legal responsibility to the students. They had come here, and their parents were expecting us to not let anything happen to them, if possible."[55] Similarly, Mays recalled being "concerned about their safety. Any president would have to be concerned about his students' safety." However, Mays later attributed some of the impetus of the Morehouse movement leadership to his exhortations in chapel: he knew that the movement "couldn't be stopped, and I wasn't going to try. Because here these kids were doing what I had been doing alone since the turn of the century, fighting against injustice and discrimination."[56] This point apparently was not lost on students. In the days before a planned march on the Capitol in the late spring of 1960, Mays asked students not to march, apparently out of fear for their safety. Hornsby saw Mays's request as hypocritical — "all these years telling us we had to be men" and then asking the students to back down.[57] Nevertheless, the march occurred, with no injuries, and the Atlanta movement continued to draw widespread student participation.

Despite restrictions from several sources — administrators' desire to protect students from physical assault, an emphasis on maintaining the integrity of traditional academic objectives, and the presence of some faculty and administration members who were skeptical of or even opposed to the sit-ins — the Atlanta University Center schools apparently provided a supportive environment for the sit-in movement. Morehouse, Spelman, and Clark provided the largest share of participants and leadership. Atlanta University, with its preponderance of graduate students, some of whom had families, contributed fewer leaders and foot soldiers. And Morris Brown, which functioned more as a commuter institution than a residential college and drew from a more economically marginalized student base, also funneled fewer students into the movement.

But these institutions' location in a city with some history of black political power and with a moderate leadership somewhat insulated them from the vicissitudes of white segregationist power. And even with a segregationist governor in the same city, their status as private institutions, outside the direct influence of the state, provided cover.

But the limitations were not insignificant. The tensions between Atlanta's established system of black political power and student activists' impatience with the slow pace of change and with the ambiguity of compromise emerged in full force at a spring 1961 meeting in which a compromise agreement between black negotiators and city leaders was announced. According to the agreement, lunch counters would be desegregated only after city schools were desegregated in the fall of 1961. Though student leaders reluctantly agreed to the compromise, they later backed away after intense opposition emerged at the meeting. Though Martin Luther King Jr. temporarily muted the opposition, student leaders Lonnie King and Herschelle Sullivan subsequently resigned from their positions as chairs of the Committee on the Appeal of Human Rights. If anything, the anger at the compromise energized the student movement: "We gave up too much," Sullivan later wrote. "Yet because of it the community is united as it has never been . . . . The older leadership which has been a hindrance has been denounced."[58]

Thus, the Atlanta sit-ins uncovered political, generational, and educational tensions. In time, those tensions would become more focused on the Atlanta campuses as a split emerged between the traditional conception of education in operation at the Atlanta University Center schools and the imperatives of social action, which, some participants argued, had its own educational value. These tensions resurfaced throughout the decade, not only in Atlanta but at colleges and universities throughout the South.

A Regional Movement and Local Dynamics

The sit-in movement generated a regionwide mobilization of black college students. SNCC's formation in April 1960 represented one effort to harness and direct that movement. The organization's founding conference attracted 120 black student activists representing fifty-six colleges and high schools in twelve southern states and the District of Columbia. Topics addressed at the convention reflected concerns that emerged in the early days of the sit-ins. Though Nashville students had received intensive training in the philosophy and practice of nonviolent direct action, few students in other parts of the region had received such schooling, even if basic information about how to conduct a nonviolent campaign filtered rapidly throughout the South. Bond later described the news coverage of the Greensboro movement as a virtual primer: "The students walked in.

The students were well dressed. The students sat down. The students asked for service. The students were courteous. I mean, it was just as though it was an instruction manual on how to do it."[59] But sessions at SNCC's founding conference reflected an effort to provide more depth in training student activists. A session on techniques of nonviolence, for example, provided an opportunity for the discussion of such questions as how much negotiation should precede sit-ins or demonstrations and whether students should agree to cooling-off periods. Other sessions discussed whether students who were arrested should post bail or pay fines, what kind of help from white supporters was desirable, and how the movement should respond to expulsions of students?[60]

Throughout 1960, SNCC remained, in Clayborne Carson's words, "a loosely organized committee of part-time student activists."[61] The nature of the organization changed dramatically and quickly, however, in early 1961. In January and February, SNCC became involved in student demonstrations in Rock Hill, South Carolina. Diane Nash; Charles Jones of Johnson C. Smith University in Charlotte, North Carolina; Ruby Doris Smith of Spelman College; and Charles Sherrod of Virginia Union University traveled to Rock Hill and soon were arrested and jailed. Although the protest collapsed because few local students were willing to join the activists in jail, Rock Hill represented the new organization's determination to confront segregation wherever a challenge surfaced. A group identity began to emerge; the Freedom Rides of the following spring and summer continued the process of identity formation. SNCC members risked life and limb to challenge segregation in southern transportation. Through the Freedom Rides and subsequent activities in McComb and other parts of Mississippi, SNCC transformed itself from a coordinating committee into a cadre of full-time organizers and protesters.[62] At the same time, CORE struggled to gain a foothold in the South, eventually establishing beachheads in Florida, Louisiana, and South Carolina.[63]

Local student movements developed along several trajectories that were determined by a complex array of factors, including the white community's response to demonstrations, the response of administration and faculty at colleges and universities, the unfolding dynamic between student activists and black community leaders, and the makeup of the student body and its leaders. These factors, in turn, correlated with other considerations, such as individual college or university institutional type and the region's political geography.

Greensboro and the Politics of Moderation

Despite their limitations, the relative moderation of the racial climates in Nashville and Atlanta gave activist students free space to challenge segregated public establishments.[64] Such free space existed on some other southern campuses, though it was by no means universal. It was always connected with the policies of a school's president, which themselves developed from a combination of personal beliefs and professional autonomy. For example, when Martin Luther King Jr. visited Greensboro in 1958, North Carolina A&T refused to host him because officials feared reprisals. But Willa B. Player, president of Bennett College, a private, black institution supported by the Presbyterian Church, offered the school's chapel. Bennett was somewhat more insulated from white retaliation than administrators at the state-supported A&T. Less than two years later, when the sit-ins began, Player not surprisingly supported the Bennett students involved. She and the members of the faculty decided that the students "were carrying out the tenets of what a liberal education was all about, so they should be allowed to participate," Player recalled.[65] But perhaps more surprisingly, A&T's president, Warmoth T. Gibbs, also supported the 1960 sit-ins. Gibbs had assumed the school's presidency in 1955, succeeding the recently deceased F. D. Bluford, just a few days after A&T students booed North Carolina governor Luther H. Hodges when he repeatedly used the word *Nigra* in an address at the college. Gibbs, a Harvard-educated teacher of history and government who had come to the college in 1926 and had served as dean of the School of Education and General Studies, had been a disciple of Bluford. But when the demonstrations broke out, Gibbs resisted pressure from Hodges to rein in the students.[66] That Gibbs was able to take such a position without threatening his job or the college's state appropriation (which was larger in 1960 than in 1959) illustrates one of the ambiguities of North Carolina's "politics of moderation."[67] If white moderation offered African Americans something far less than full equality, it at least provided more security than black southerners in the Deep South enjoyed.

According to William Chafe, the Greensboro movement was characterized by swings between open rebellion and quiet negotiation. Thus, the sit-ins initiated negotiations and a quieting of movement activity, only to be followed by another round of demonstrations in late 1962 and early 1963. Tying these periods together were the continued activities of a small group of students — chiefly picketing campaigns at downtown movie theaters. In the summer of 1962, A&T student William Thomas established a local CORE chapter, which joined other chapters in challenging segregation at interstate restaurants. A quiet and disciplined organizer, Thomas had participated in the 1960 demonstrations while still in high school. He was joined in the 1962–63 efforts by A. Knighton (Tony) Stanley, a black minister and Greensboro native who began serving at A&T in 1962, and Jesse Jackson, a South Carolina native who had transferred to A&T from Chicago. Jackson was charismatic, even flamboyant, and had established himself as a traditional campus leader — football star and Student Council president — and Thomas and Stanley apparently saw Jackson's involvement as an opportunity to mobilize large numbers of rank-and-file students. By the fall of 1962, a substantial number of Bennett and A&T students took part in two mass marches on successive weekends in October. Student-led demonstrations reached a high point in the spring of 1963, as hundreds of students from Bennett and A&T targeted segregated restaurants, cafeterias, and theaters.[68]

These demonstrations exposed a growing generational cleavage, with students and adult black leaders disagreeing on strategy and methods. *The Candle*, a student-movement newspaper, lampooned black employees' accommodating attitudes toward their white bosses:

> MR. CHARLES: A really educated Negro like you doesn't want integration, does he?
>
> TOM: No, Sir.
>
> MR. CHARLES: You'd rather be with your people, wouldn't you?
>
> TOM: Yes, Sir.
>
> MR. CHARLES: Tom, I always enjoy talking to you because I like to find out how you people feel about things. Wait 'til I tell ole Dave how you people really would talk if those communists didn't get you all confused.[69]

But not all African American adults played this role. When mass arrests resulted in the jailing of hundreds of Bennett and A&T students in May, Player responded with stunning support for the students. Her in loco parentis role might have dictated that she intervene to get the Bennett students out of jail or to expel them. Instead, Player mobilized faculty to distribute mail and assignments to jailed students, lobbied for better conditions in the jail, and managed the concerns of the jailed students' parents. A&T's acting president, Lewis Dowdy, was more vulnerable. North Carolina governor Terry Sanford instructed Dowdy to seek the return of the jailed A&T students to the campus. Dowdy appeared to sympathize with the students but was forced either to comply or be insubordinate. He failed in his initial efforts to convince the students to return with him to campus, but he ultimately succeeded in removing some seven hundred students to the campus, some of them forcibly. Nevertheless, A&T continued to serve as a base for dramatic demonstrations into June, when Greensboro city officials endorsed desegregation of public accommodations. This significant victory, as Chafe suggests, seemed to throw into high relief the limits of white moderation in Greensboro. Whites would move toward a more substantive engagement of racial inequality only when forced to do so by the continued mass mobilization of the black community.[70]

Centers of black-student activism also developed, albeit sometimes haltingly, in other parts of the South. New Orleans, the South's most cosmopolitan city, with six universities, might have seemed to hold strong potential for a vibrant black student movement. But a small, insular, and atavistic power elite controlled New Orleans, and though the civil rights movement would force concessions in the early 1960s, "these were men," as historian Adam Fairclough puts it, "of small compromises rather than strategic vision."[71]

For generations, white students had attended two private New Orleans universities, Tulane and Loyola, as well as St. Mary's Dominican College, while black students attended Dillard and Xavier, also private institutions. Dillard, affiliated with the American Missionary Association, was headed from 1941 to 1969 by Albert W. Dent, a graduate of Morehouse College and a "self-conscious member of the city's black elite." In the late 1970s, Dent described himself as an adamant opponent of segregation, but he was more a negotiator than a protester, accustomed to fighting behind the scenes and working the levers of power.[72] Across town, Xavier University, administered by the Sisters of the Blessed Sacrament, was the only Catholic institution of higher education for African Americans in the United States. Administrators closely monitored Xavier students' lives: "The control here is tight," noted U.S. National Student Association President Harry Lunn Jr. in 1955. "When you combine the normal strict control of a Catholic institution with that generally exercised at a Negro school, you have something."[73] Nevertheless, challenges to segregation emanated from Xavier. In 1952, recent graduate Norman Francis became one of the first two black law students at Loyola, and three years later he became the school's first black graduate. Quiet interracial contact developed throughout the 1950s between Xavier and Loyola students through the Southeastern Regional Interracial Committee, in which Francis participated.[74] Indeed, Xavier and Dillard manifested the same cross-currents of conservatism and activism common to black institutions, to varying degrees, throughout the South.

Public institutions added to the contours of New Orleans student life. In the late 1950s, thanks in part to the initiative of Governor Earl K. Long, the state of Louisiana opened New Orleans branches of historically white Louisiana State University and historically black Southern University. These commuter campuses appealed to white and black city residents from working-class backgrounds. But their opening at precisely the moment when the state's dual system of higher education was coming under legal attack raised the full range of questions that clouded the future of southern higher learning. Indeed, Louisiana State University in New Orleans (LSUNO) opened as a desegregated institution in 1956 as a result of a federal court order. And when Southern University in New Orleans (SUNO) opened two years later, it faced the opposition of the Louisiana NAACP, which saw the institution as an attempt to prevent the true integration of LSUNO.[75]

The first stirrings of student activism in New Orleans developed against this backdrop. The wave of direct-action protest that swept the South after February 1960 did not reach New Orleans until a few months later, but groundwork had already been laid during the winter of 1959, when the Consumers League of Greater New Orleans formed and began targeting stores in predominantly black neighborhoods that refused to hire African Americans. At the same time, the aftereffects of a late-1950s assault on the NAACP's right to exist in Louisiana left a vacuum that younger activists, operating through CORE and the NAACP Youth Council, seemed primed to fill. By August 1960, spurred in part by students from Southern University in Baton Rouge who had conducted sit-ins in the spring, a handful of black and white New Orleans students formed a local CORE chapter. On 9 September, five black students and two white students conducted a sit-in at one of the Woolworth's stores on Canal Street. The next day, members of the NAACP Youth Council picketed both Canal Street Woolworth's stores. In the following months, students from all six New Orleans–area universities took part in nonviolent direct-action protests. Participation from the city's private black campuses was limited. Rudolph Lombard, one of the leaders of the New Orleans CORE chapter, later recalled that he was the only participant from Xavier; other students stayed away for fear of expulsion. A few white students came from Tulane and Loyola. But LSUNO and SUNO played particularly important roles, providing leaders for both CORE and the NAACP Youth Council.[76]

LSUNO became an NAACP stronghold, thanks in part to the participation of student Raphael Cassimere, who was president of the Youth Council throughout the early 1960s. A native New Orleanian who had attended segregated institutions all his life, Cassimere was part of the second freshman class at LSU-NO. Though he had earned a scholarship to attend Southern in Baton Rouge, Cassimere relished the excitement of attending a desegregated institution; a tuition of thirty-five dollars a semester also enticed this resident of the working-class Ninth Ward. In those early days, campus administrators quelled incipient disturbances by white students who opposed desegregation, and LSUNO avoided the violence that plagued other southern institutions when they desegregated. LSUNO was not burdened by a past of racial violence, though tensions did surface. Moreover, the number of African Americans in each class was considerably larger than the handful that desegregated other southern institutions.[77]

Unlike Xavier and Dillard, officials at LSUNO offered little resistance to the participation of Cassimere and his cohort in demonstrations. In fact, Cassimere later recalled an institution that in some ways supported his movement activities. Though the faculty included some segregationists, it also contained a number of young, liberal northerners. Nevertheless, LSUNO was not free of segrega-tionist impulses. A private company, Morrison's, operated the campus cafeteria and refused to admit black students, though the company offered them a snack bar, which black students began to boycott in early 1960. That action prompted the university to ask Morrison's either to desegregate the cafeteria or to vacate its lease, and a desegregated cafeteria opened under new management in the spring of 1961. This boycott both preceded and reinforced the more publicized Canal Street activities. Their action against the cafeteria acquainted LSUNO students with the concept and practice of on- and off-campus student activism.[78]

New Orleans student activists focused on segregated establishments on Canal Street and in other parts of the city. During a brief fall 1960 school deseg-regation crisis that received national media coverage, the direct-action move-ment faltered. But it picked up momentum again in 1961, despite the reluctance of the NAACP's old guard, and won the quiet desegregation of the city's lunch counters in 1962. Just as the New Orleans student movement was experienc-ing some degree of success, however, internal disputes weakened it. In early 1962, the New Orleans CORE chapter expelled fifteen members, most of them white, after the publication of an article in the Louisiana Weekly criticizing CORE members for participating in interracial social activities. Leading the charge was Oretha Castle, who later asserted that male white students from Tulane had joined the movement organization primarily to get dates with black women. "The word was that the CORE chapter was where you could come into contact with black women without any problem," Castle later declared. Though she saw her actions as a necessary response to activities that were "not what CORE was about," others involved, including Hugh Murray, a white Tulane student who was among those expelled, saw the incident as an early step in the eventual emergence of black nationalism. Whatever the motivation, the move reflected racial tensions in New Orleans's CORE chapter and was followed quickly by a de-cline in the organization's activity and effectiveness.[79] Though the NAACP Youth Council, led by Cassimere, continued its activities, the New Orleans student movement fell behind that of Nashville and Atlanta in the mid-1960s.

Castle later argued that "New Orleans never really had a student movement or a real overall mass movement." Though she overstated her point, she cited several factors, among them religious, class, and color divisions, that indeed impeded the development of activism in the city.[80] To that list of inhibiting factors might also be added recalcitrant city leaders and the loss of key lead-ers to the larger movement. Lombard departed New Orleans in 1961 to attend graduate school at Syracuse University, while several others took over signifi-cant leadership roles in CORE. August Meier and Elliott Rudwick later compared the influence of New Orleans activists within CORE with the Nashville Student Movement's impact on SNCC.[81]

Deep South Struggles

The sometimes intense resistance that the city's student movement met in the early 1960s hinted at the kinds of conditions that students in the Deep South would face as the sit-in movement spread. Student movements sputtered for want of basic ingredients — a degree of protection from campus administrators that would partially mitigate the risks of participating in direct-action campaigns, a sense among a critical mass of students that the possibilities of progress made the risk worth taking, and support from "adults" in the black community. Nevertheless, the Deep South did not remain completely insulated from the new wave of nonviolent direct action, although the sustained mobilization of black students in much of the Deep South would have to wait until late in the decade. Events in Orangeburg, Tallahassee, Montgomery, and Baton Rouge suggested, however, that as difficult as generating a movement in the face of militant opposition could be, maintaining the movement was even more challenging.

In Orangeburg, South Carolina, spring 1960 demonstrations, led by students from South Carolina State College and Claflin College, were part of a pattern of ongoing activism that dated at least to 1955, when student activism had emerged as a corollary to a movement led by local NAACP leaders to end segregation in public schools. At one point, an NAACP leader approached South Carolina State's student government president, Fred H. Moore, about securing student support. However, when Moore went to the college's president, Benner C. Turner, about the matter, Turner warned Moore to avoid the controversy. Moore nevertheless organized student support for a campaign to convince African Americans to avoid patronizing companies that would not hire blacks; the college continued serving food from companies targeted by the campaign. South Carolina's governor subsequently sent law enforcement officials to campus to maintain control, and students responded by going on strike. "This is not a mental institution nor a penal institution but an institution of higher learning attended by free people in a free land," declared Moore.[82]

South Carolina officials were more hostile than their North Carolina counterparts toward any perceived threats to segregation. Members of the South Carolina State board of trustees made it clear to Turner that they would tolerate no integrationist sympathies. Turner thus instituted a profusion of rules designed to keep potentially dissident students and faculty in line. Shortly after the 1956 student strike began, students shifted their ire from South Carolina government officials to Turner and his administrative policies. Student demands included reforms in the conduct of disciplinary hearings, the selection of students to serve on campus committees based on merit rather than presidential prerogative, and a revised publication policy for the campus newspaper.

The boycott ended after six days, and the board immediately expelled Moore. Turner then expelled other student participants and fired sympathetic faculty members. In the end, both the selective-buying campaign and the student movement against Turner failed. Orangeburg's schools remained completely segregated, and Turner maintained his power.[83]

Another wave of student sit-ins began in late February 1960 and took place against this backdrop of opposition to segregation that soon translated into opposition to repressive campus policies. The high point came on 15 March, when some one thousand students marching in Orangeburg were met with fire hoses and tear gas. Police arrested nearly four hundred students. This time, Turner kept a lower profile, but he remained unpopular with students and faculty. Considering the restrictive environment, the mass participation of students from South Carolina State and Claflin was impressive. But the repression made it difficult to keep the movement going when students returned from summer break. Sit-ins continued sporadically during the 1960–61 academic year, but success was elusive and solidarity difficult to maintain.[84]

This pattern was replicated at other state-controlled institutions for African Americans in the Deep South. In most cases, the cast of characters remained the same: an all-white state governing board, a black president forced to answer to that board, and a critical mass of protesting students. Some of the most dramatic confrontations occurred in Montgomery, Tallahassee, and Baton Rouge. The showdown in Montgomery began on 25 February 1960, when thirty-five students from Alabama State College conducted sit-ins at local lunch counters. Governor John Patterson, who also served as chair of the state board of education, threatened to expel demonstrating students and, more seriously, warned that he would close down the institution if more protests took place. The next day, students held another demonstration and threatened to enroll at white schools if the governor closed Alabama State. On 1 March, more than one thousand students marched from the campus to the State Capitol, where they sang the national anthem and the Lord's Prayer. Alabama State remained open, but Patterson insisted that the school's longtime president, H. Councill Trenholm, expel nine student leaders or risk losing state funds. The expulsions prompted further demonstrations and a student strike beginning on 5 March. The student boycott was effective, but a heavy police presence and the threat of white mobs limited student demonstrations. On 7 March, about three thousand African Americans, mostly students, began a march to the State Capitol, only to meet a group of some ten thousand white citizens. Police broke up the white gathering and sent the black demonstrators away before any violence occurred. By 9 March, police armed with tear gas and submachine guns had cordoned off the Alabama State campus in an effort to prevent further demonstrations. Six of nine expelled students sought readmission, and a state district judge upheld the expulsions, although an appeals court eventually overturned them.[85]

The expulsions indicated the state government's power over college affairs. Alabama State fell under the jurisdiction of the state board of education, which also set policy for white institutions in Normal, Florence, Jacksonville, Livingston, and Troy. (Alabama's other state institutions — the University of Alabama, Auburn University, and Montevallo College — had separate boards.) Trenholm's letter to the expelled students listed grounds for which an Alabama State student (or any student at an institution governed by the state board) could be expelled, including "willful disobedience to the rules and regulations," "willful and continued neglect of studies," "conduct involving moral turpitude," and "For Conduct Prejudicial to the School and for Conduct Unbecoming a Student or Future Teacher in Schools of Alabama, for Insubordination and Insurrection, or for Inciting Other Pupils to Like Conduct." Court documents indicate that Trenholm reported to the state board that the demonstrations were disrupting the college's operations and that he could not control the students' activities. But testimony by board members demonstrates that they, not Trenholm, exercised ultimate authority.[86] Faculty members who sympathized with the sit-ins were also vulnerable. In June, the board fired history department chair L. D. Reddick, whom Patterson accused of having communist connections.[87]

A similar story unfolded in Tallahassee, where sit-ins mobilized by students from Florida Agricultural and Mechanical University resulted in student expulsions and the failure to extend a contract for one faculty member, Richard Haley, who went on to serve as a CORE organizer. In Tallahassee, as in Montgomery, a bus boycott loomed in the recent past, though the Tallahassee City Commission had sidestepped integration with a "seat assignment plan" and the 1956 boycott had collapsed. But in late 1959, two Florida A&M students, sisters Patricia and Priscilla Stephens, organized a campus chapter of CORE and began testing segregation on buses and in bus terminals. Thus, when the sit-in movement broke out in early 1960, a contingent of Florida A&M students was already primed for action. The first lunch counter sit-in, at a Woolworth's, occurred on 13 February, and within weeks the Tallahassee movement included not only black students from A&M but also white students from nearby Florida State University. Arrested activists chose to stay in jail rather than pay bail, the first use of this tactic, and although Florida governor Leroy Collins took a moderate stance, threats of local violence and tepid support for direct action within the Tallahassee black community resulted in a diminution of the sit-in movement by early 1961.[88]

In Baton Rouge, Louisiana, some of the forty-seven hundred students at Southern University, the nation's largest black school, launched direct-action attacks on segregation throughout the early 1960s. The all-white state board of education warned that students who participated in protests would be subjected to "stern disciplinary action," but students ignored the announcement and demonstrated beginning on 28 March, when seven students sat in at a local five-and-ten. On 30 March, thirty-five hundred students marched through the city's center, with one, Major Johns, openly attacking segregation and discrimination in his speech to the crowd. He and sixteen other students were "suspended indefinitely" the same day, a tactic longtime university president Felton Grandison Clark used throughout the 1960s to quell dissent. The Southern student body voted to boycott classes until all seventeen students were readmitted, but the boycott ultimately collapsed, in part because Clark, who in a very real sense had inherited control in 1937 from his father, Joseph S. Clark, limited faculty and staff participation by declaring that their jobs depended on a quick end to the boycott. Felton Clark feared that the unrest threatened the university's future, telling students, "Like Lincoln who sought to preserve the Union, my dominant concern is to save Southern University."[89] Moreover, Clark justified his actions by declaring that political activity fell outside the bounds of Southern's mission: "We at Southern are interested in 'education' and nothing else."[90]

Divisions within the black community over direct action limited the effectiveness of the student demonstrations. CORE activists complained that Baton Rouge's black community had not provided sufficient support for the boycott at crucial points — for example, when boycotting students were unable to go home because they lacked the money for bus fare.[91] Administrators' forced resistance to demonstrations also caused Southern's students and faculty to turn a critical eye toward the university itself. Clark's actions met with opposition from many blacks and the American Association of University Professors, which eventually censured the university for violating academic freedom. Clark and his opponents had different definitions of *education*. One opponent, Adolph L. Reed, a member of Southern's history and political science department, took aim at Clark's handling of the sit-ins in an open letter to the president: "Can education really exist in the abstract?" Reed asked. "Can there be 'education' that exists apart from people and issues?" Even the Southern catalog, he argued, outlined a broader view of education: "A central concern of Southern University is that of making students individually sensitive to community problems, and through a foundation in liberal and vocational education, helping them to develop practical procedures for coping with these problems." Reed also questioned Clark's autocratic treatment of faculty and students, his tendency to see his destiny and that of the university as one and the same, and his poor response to the sit-ins.[92]

Reed broadened his criticisms in an article published in *The Nation*: "On the whole, Southern University may be thought of as typical of the 'Negro college' — and particularly typical of the 'Negro college' that receives the major portion of its sustenance from public resources," he wrote. He acknowledged that the presidents of such colleges occupied an awkward position that was not of their own making. He identified the larger problem as the federal government's unwillingness to enforce the law in the South.[93]

By the time Reed's article appeared in February 1962, another wave of demonstrations had roiled the Southern University campus. In October 1961, about ten Southern students formed a campus chapter of CORE. Workshops and negotiations with merchants the following month led to sit-ins and pickets in December, with dozens of students and local CORE leaders arrested. After a clash with police and the arrests of some fifty activists and students on 15 December, student body president D'Army Bailey led about three thousand students to Clark's home. According to Bailey, Clark pledged "that no student would be suspended or expelled as a result of his or her participation in anti-segregation demonstrations." The next day, the state board of education ordered the presidents of all Louisiana universities to ban student demonstrations and automatically suspend any students who were arrested. Clark responded by closing Southern for Christmas break four days early. When classes resumed in January, Clark responded to continued student restiveness by expelling eight students, including Bailey, who had supposedly violated Rule 16 in the Student Handbook:

LACK OF UNIVERSITY ADJUSTMENT
The university reserves the right to sever a student's connection with the university for general inability to adjust himself to the pattern of the institution. This may be done without prejudice to his attendance at another institution.

Bailey had served as president of the freshman class at Southern, as assistant managing editor of the student newspaper, and as a member of the Student Disciplinary Committee. "I was never subjected to any form of disciplinary action while matriculating at Southern University," Bailey noted. Bailey's expulsion revealed the significant gap between Clark and Southern students. During one faculty convocation, Clark denounced Southern students as hoodlums, anarchists, and "culturally void." Although activists later used campus administrators' intransigence to mobilize significant demonstrations, in the context of an assault on segregation, the turn to campus issues was a distraction. By late February, CORE activist David Dennis lamented the change in the Baton Rouge movement's focus from segregation, which he described as "the real source of the problem," to "its instrument" — that is, the university.[94]

Activists who fell outside the arena of university punishment also experienced harsh consequences for their actions in Baton Rouge. SNCC activists Chuck McDew and John Robert Zellner found themselves charged with "criminal anarchy" and experienced jailhouse conditions that Zellner later described as torture. The tactics employed by administrators and local law enforcement had their intended effect, dramatically reducing the level of student activism for the next several years and preventing the Baton Rouge movement from regaining real momentum until 1969.[95]

Pockets of Activism on Private Campuses: Tougaloo and Talladega

Despite the Deep South's repressive atmosphere, pockets of activism survived. In particular, two private colleges, Mississippi's Tougaloo and Alabama's Talladega, had administrations whose political views and educational philosophies allowed them to permit and in some cases protect students who employed nonviolent direct action.

A creation of the American Missionary Association, Tougaloo was known as the Oasis because, as one of the few white students at the school noted in the early 1960s, "it is the one place in Mississippi where people of all colors, nationalities, and religious persuasions live and work together as people."[96] Many black people saw Tougaloo as a college for light-skinned members of the black middle class. Anne Moody, a Mississippi native who had spent two years at the Baptist-affiliated Natchez College, transferred to Tougaloo in the fall of 1961. When she told one of her Natchez friends her plans, her friend responded, "Baby, you're too black. You gotta be high-yellow with a rich-ass daddy." Moody nevertheless followed through with her plans and was initially alarmed to find that she had only one black teacher. Fearful that white instructors would not treat her fairly, she confided her concerns to a dormitory mate, who replied that Tougaloo's white teachers "are all from up North or Europe or someplace. We don't have one white teacher here from the South. Northern whites have a different attitude toward Negroes."[97]

Later in the decade, white faculty members came under fire from black students for practicing a paternalistic, "benevolent" racism. Some white faculty members acknowledged an element of truth in this accusation, but Tougaloo's most conspicuous feature in the early 1960s was the presence of whites who were willing to challenge discrimination. Two of the most passionate white activists were social science professor John Salter and chaplain Edwin King, who helped spearhead demonstrations. Salter, who coordinated the campus NAACP activities, regularly hosted a group of activist students and faculty at his home for what came to be known as the Salter Coffee House. Protest-oriented Tougaloo students also benefited from the permissive attitude of Adam Daniel Beittel, a white former president of Talladega College who became president of Tougaloo in 1960. Beittel supported students' civil rights activities. In 1961, Tougaloo housed Freedom Riders when they arrived in Jackson, an action

Beittel described as providing "hospitality to human beings who needed a place to sleep." Tougaloo never expelled anyone for civil rights activities and enrolled some students who had been expelled from other schools as a consequence of activism.[98]

Nevertheless, the intensity of white resistance to integration held off demonstrations at Tougaloo until an April 1961 "study-in" at which nine Tougaloo students attempted to sit down in the segregated Jackson public library. They were arrested and tried, and two dozen policemen used clubs and dogs to break up a gathering of some one hundred blacks who ventured to the courthouse to observe the trial. By the summer of 1961, a cadre of young activists who had cut their teeth in Nashville in 1960 and with the Freedom Rides had come to Jackson and helped organize the Jackson Nonviolent Movement. Student activists at Tougaloo subsequently fed off the burgeoning Mississippi movement, participating in sit-ins at a drugstore, bus and train stations, and the state office building. In December 1962, activist students and faculty threw their support behind a boycott of downtown Jackson stores that practiced discrimination. And in the fall of 1963, the Tougaloo student movement, under the leadership of two women, Joyce Ladner, who was black, and Joan Trumpauer, who was white, decided to concentrate on two areas — live entertainment and white churches. The entertainment committee devoted its attention to nearby all-white Millsaps College, where some students were embarrassed that police and dogs had been used to prevent Tougaloo students from participating in the college's cultural programs. After negotiations in which Beittel participated, the two institutions agreed to hold cultural events in Millsaps's Christian Center auditorium. However, implementing the agreement brought problems, and when city officials continued to enforce segregation, the Tougaloo Cultural Committee encouraged several entertainers to cancel rather than perform before segregated audiences.[99]

At times, whites fired shots while driving through the Tougaloo campus, but authorities failed to investigate the incidents. Moreover, the State of Mississippi occasionally targeted Tougaloo, which many whites saw as a nest of communists and rabble-rousers, with legislative efforts to curtail integration activities. In June 1963, state officials won an injunction preventing Tougaloo's trustees, Beittel, the NAACP, CORE, and other groups from "engaging in, sponsoring, inciting or encouraging demonstrations," including kneel-ins at churches. The college appealed the injunction, which was overturned. In 1964, Beittel suddenly resigned as president, an action for which members of the Mississippi State Sovereignty Commission, a state agency established in the wake of *Brown v. Board of Education* and given broad powers to fight racial integration, subsequently claimed credit. Commission members had met privately with three of the college's trustees and suggested that Tougaloo could avoid a potential "collision" with the Sovereignty Commission by dismissing Beittel and hiring a new president who "was more concerned with education than agitation." Beittel went on to serve as director of the American Friends Service Committee in Mississippi and neighboring states.[100]

The Sovereignty Commission's power to force out the president of a private institution demonstrates why campus activism had little room to grow elsewhere in Mississippi. Although activists occasionally emerged from other Mississippi schools, including Jackson State College, they feared reprisals from school administrators. Moody recalled that after one early 1960s sit-in, "there were a couple of girls in [jail] with us from Jackson State College. They were scared they would be expelled from school. Jackson State, like most of the state-supported schools, was an Uncle Tom school. The students could be expelled for almost anything. When I found this out I really appreciated Tougaloo." On 12 June 1963, the day that Medgar Evers, the head of Mississippi's NAACP, was shot, Moody and another SNCC worker, former Jackson State student Dorie Ladner, went to the Jackson State campus to organize protests. They received a tepid response, prompting Moody to complain, "I felt sick, I got so mad with them. How could Negroes be so pitiful? How could they just sit by and take all this shit without any emotions at all? I just didn't understand."[101]

The city of Talladega, located about an hour east of Birmingham and known as "an interracial community in the heart of the rural South," had always bucked the region's racial trends to some degree. Talladega College, a Congregationalist school with an enrollment of about four hundred students, had often been in the forefront of subtle but significant challenges to racial orthodoxy. During Beittel's tenure as president of Talladega, he had adopted the same open attitude toward interracialism he later showed at Tougaloo, allowing interracial conferences to meet on campus and speaking out against discrimination. Beittel's successor, Arthur Gray, continued such practices. Talladega's first black president, Gray was an outspoken opponent of segregation, which he once called "harmful to the growth of personality and . . . a violation of the spirit of Christianity and democracy." The college hosted several conferences of the Alabama Council on Human Relations in the late 1950s, and in April 1956, the Alabama Student Ecumenical Conference met on campus. During this meeting, white students from the University of Alabama, Auburn, Jacksonville State, Birmingham-Southern, and Southern Union College lived on campus with black students from Talladega, Stillman, Alabama State, Tuskegee, and Miles.[102]

Students also occasionally took stands against segregation before the advent of the sit-in movement. In 1952, the *Talladega Student*, the student newspaper, returned payment for an advertisement because the employees of the advertiser, a local store, refused to use courtesy titles when addressing college faculty and staff. In 1954, Alabama policemen attacked a white student at the college when he tried to sit in the same section of a bus with black students. And in March 1960, the student body sent a telegram to Governor Patterson protesting his role in the expulsion of Alabama State students who had participated in demonstrations against segregation. Nevertheless, that support did not immediately translate into direct action in Talladega. The first demonstrations there came in early January 1961, when whites beat student Arthur Bacon and a college staff member after Bacon lingered in the interstate waiting room of the Southern Railway Station in Anniston. In response, students voted to march in protest on 5 January. When rented buses failed to appear, the students commandeered campus and community cars and taxis and traveled to Anniston, where about four hundred people paraded two abreast while hecklers threatened and spat on them.[103]

Despite this march and a June 1961 statement by the faculty and staff deploring the violation of civil rights of the South and commending the Freedom Riders, students waited until April 1962 before beginning direct-action demonstrations in Talladega. Sentiment had been building since the advent of the sit-in movement more than a year earlier. The Student Action Committee (SAC), a group operating within the framework of the Student Government Association, provided the organizational mechanism to mobilize students. But when the movement finally hit the streets, its leaders already had direct-action experience. Dorothy Vails, a Tuscaloosa native who had transferred to Talladega from Southern University in Baton Rouge, was the pivotal actor in the unfolding drama. Vails, a senior, had participated in the 1960 Baton Rouge protests and had been expelled for her actions. Seeking to generate a similar movement in Talladega, Vails turned to CORE and SNCC for help. SNCC, with its small staff already stretched thin, sent Zellner, a white field secretary whose primary duty was to translate the movement to students on white campuses throughout the South. The Alabama native arrived on 3 March, spoke at a student rally, and met with the SAC executive committee. Two days later, he met again with students and taught them freedom songs. Zellner returned two weeks later with Joan Browning, a white student from Emory University who had participated in the Freedom Rides and like Zellner a veteran of the U.S. National Student Association's Southern Student Human Relations Seminar. Zellner and Browning passed on nonviolent techniques.[104]

But the Talladega students, who conducted negotiations with city officials and ran the nonviolent workshops that were held in preparation for the sit-ins, generated the movement that followed. Talladega mayor J. L. Hardwick hoped to stave off a confrontation until after a planned 6 April visit by former Alabama governor James E. Folsom, but when Hardwick refused to accede to the students' demands for desegregation of lunch counters, city restrooms, drinking fountains, and the public library and the establishment of a biracial mayor's committee, the students set the rallies in motion. As Folsom spoke in the town square, a crowd of between 150 and 300 students, faculty, and local blacks demonstrated with signs demanding desegregation, justice, and equality. On 9 April, the action moved to three drugstores. The SAC had been negotiating for the desegregation of the stores' lunch counters, but when the negotiations failed, a group of eighteen students and college chaplain Everett MacNair conducted sit-ins and were arrested. Talladega had no segregation ordinances, so the demonstrators were charged with trespassing. Adopting a tactic pioneered by demonstrators in Rock Hill, South Carolina, in early 1961, most of the students refused bail.[105]

The SAC and the community-wide Talladega Improvement Association soon raised their sights from desegregation to equal employment opportunities, including the hiring of black police officers, firefighters, and clerks. Perhaps not coincidentally, the goals resembled those of students in nearby Birmingham; the tactics were also similar, as black Talladegans began an Easter boycott of stores. The Talladega movement met stiff opposition, not only from white city officials but also from President Gray, whose opposition to segregation did not imply support for the use of nonviolent direct action to end it. On 16 April, some 150 students planned a march from the campus to the town square to coincide with the trials of the students arrested earlier in the month. When he became aware of the march, Gray called the assistant police chief and asked him to intercept the marchers and tell them they were "headed for jail." Addressing the faculty a few days earlier, Gray had declared that the objective of integration was sound but expressed concerns about some of the students' tactics, particularly the decision to refuse to post bail. "Jail without bail means academic suicide," he said.[106]

A temporary injunction ended Talladega's spring demonstrations. The injunction named not only Zellner, Vails, and other activists, but also Gray. SAC organizers had difficulty maintaining any semblance of the spring activity despite MacNair's support, and Gray discouraged further action by the committee, believing that sit-ins posed a threat to the college's future that superseded any imperative to resume the demonstrations. "To lose the accreditation of the college and to have a number of students in jail," Gray stated, "would only defeat the purposes of the freedom movement." When the temporary injunction became permanent in June 1962, Gray encouraged students to obey it and encouraged them to look to other worthy issues, such as voter registration and illiteracy. Gray's limited support resulted in some criticism that he was too cautious, although other observers noted that he had offered more substantial support than had other southern college presidents who "were either denouncing student movements or failing to comment." When Gray resigned in June 1962 to become pastor of the Congregational Church of Park Manor, Chicago, some attributed his resignation to the spring demonstrations, though tense relations with the college's board of trustees seemed to play a greater role.[107]

But even if the movement temporarily stalled after the injunction, activity continued sporadically and bore fruit. In the spring of 1962, Talladega's public library integrated "to the extent that it now admits Negro citizens who are listed in the Talladega phone book." And in 1963, a year before the passage of the Civil Rights Act, Talladega merchants agreed to desegregate lunch counters.[108]

SNCC and the Student Movement

By 1963, seemingly contradictory tendencies were evident in the student movement. The movement had won important victories over segregation, chiefly in the Upper South. SNCC, which many people throughout the nation saw as the public face of the black student movement, had established a reputation as the shock troops of the movement and in so doing had captured the imagination of a nascent New Left taking shape among progressive white students outside the South and manifesting itself in the emergence of Students for a Democratic Society. Writing in September 1961, Martin Luther King Jr. trumpeted the "double education" offered by the movement — "academic learning from books and classes, and life's lessons from responsible participation in social action." Activism was invigorating black campuses, King suggested, offering a new democratic vision for education and learning in which colleges "become a tool shaping the future and not devices of privilege for an exclusive few" and allowing black student activists to set the tone for progressive white students throughout the country.[109]

But King's assessment was too glowing. By 1963, mass actions of the type that materialized in the spring of 1960 were rare, and campus "movements" were now more likely to be the purview of a small group of rebels. In part, this development resulted from a failure to replace the first generation of activist leaders. Some, such as Xavier University's Lombard, had graduated and moved on to graduate school or careers. Others, like much of the leadership at Southern University in Baton Rouge, had been expelled. And finally, some, like Nash, had left school for full-time activism. Nash left college after her stint in jail in Rock Hill gave her the feeling that a gap existed between the "real world" and the make-believe version that existed at Fisk and that this gap was complicit in the maintenance of segregation. If she stayed at Fisk, she could envision a future in which she would, as David Halberstam put it, "marry some black doctor, and live a black life parallel to the life of the wife of a white doctor." Indeed, Nash came to believe that real education about humanity and ethics occurred off the campus; college was more about credentialing.[110]

It is not clear how many in Nash's cohort felt similarly about higher education, but SNCC largely removed itself from southern campuses after 1961. Members of the organization occasionally played important roles in local campus movements, as Zellner did at Talladega College in 1962. But even in that case, Zellner's involvement suggested the tenuous connection between SNCC and black southern campuses, since he had been hired as a campus traveler to interpret the movement to *white* college students. Thus, as members of the small cadre immersed themselves in a confrontation with segregation in Mississippi, the state that held to it most fiercely, the movement began to wane on black southern campuses. As one SNCC staff member said in March 1962, "We must get around the 'misnomer' of SNCC being a student movement."[111]

Even if SNCC's focus shifted from campus to community, black students still looked to the group for leadership. They read the *Student Voice*, the primary connection between SNCC and the South's black campuses during the early 1960s. SNCC's leadership, however, never developed a comprehensive plan for how black campuses should fit into the movement. Answering this question would have required a careful consideration of the relationship between higher education and social change.

Some movement leaders saw a connection between higher education and activism and recognized a weakness in SNCC activists' departure from the campus. Zinn, fired in 1962 from his tenured job at Spelman as a result of his activism, proposed an educational program for full-time civil rights workers in the South. "About 200 young people have interrupted their education at various levels — high school, college, graduate school — to devote their energies full-time" to the movement, he noted. Those activists were receiving an education that was not possible in a traditional academic setting, but "to be involved in social action without utilizing its stimulation for intellectual growth, is to leave unrealized a great potential, for the individual and for society." Drawing in part on a program at Antioch College that combined education and social concern, Zinn proposed the creation of an "educational system" for field workers in the southern movement that would offer "educational refueling" in blocks of five or six days three times a year or ten-day or two-week periods twice a year. The curriculum would include literature, such as novels by James Baldwin, Ralph Ellison, and Richard Wright; historical works by C. Vann Woodward, John Hope Franklin, W. E. B. Du Bois, and others; and works on the American political system, including Walter Lippman's *The Public Philosophy* and C. Wright Mills's *The Power Elite*. On civil liberties, Zinn proposed Plato's *Apology and Crito*, Henry David Thoreau's *Civil Disobedience*, and Arthur Miller's *The Crucible*. "The books to be used should not be text books, but works of quality which are interestingly written and intellectually challenging," Zinn suggested.[112]

Zinn's proposal was not enacted, but it nevertheless suggests something about both the connections and the disconnect between the movement and the campus. The advent of nonviolent direct action had breathed new life into the civil rights movement and provided students with a new method of political expression. Indeed, the sit-ins' signal contribution had been the incorporation of black students into the civil rights movement and of students in general into a southern Left that had been severely limited by massive resistance and cold war politics. But the sit-ins also created a generation gap within the movement, as younger activists resisted calls to go slow and negotiate. Student activists saw wrong and believed that it needed to be righted, and they carried this tendency to see moral and political questions in such stark terms throughout the decade. This mode spoke more to the students' generational identity than to their identity as students. Membership in a young cohort that saw itself as more able and more willing to recognize and confront evil loomed larger during the early 1960s. In this context, *student* often meant *young*.

However, even if young activists' student identities were often submerged, they remained important. The tensions created by the emergence of nonviolent direct action on black college campuses had exposed the contradictions inherent in southern higher education. The South's segregated system of higher education purportedly offered black southerners equal opportunity, but black colleges were usually poorly funded and academically deficient. The sit-ins exposed black campuses' limits — both externally enforced and self-imposed — on intellectual curiosity. And while administrators such as Felton Clark repressed students who crossed the boundaries of "proper" behavior, the administrators' actions underscored their ultimate inability to preserve their institutions' integrity in the face of far more powerful segregationist politicians. Driven to act by their generational identity, young activists found that their identities as students mattered.

Of course, the problems plaguing the South's Negro colleges were not unique. Writing in the mid-1960s, Zinn noted the tendency of black and white students working together in the movement to compare notes about their collegiate experiences and to learn, "somewhat to their surprise, that both white and Negro colleges suffer from the same disabilities." These problems included "pallid middle-class ambitions," the paternalistic attitudes of administrators and faculty members, a "hierarchy of authority" that put disproportionate power in the hands of administrators, and the resulting restrictions of both faculty and student academic freedom. "That these qualities are exaggerated in Southern Negro colleges (and in Southern white colleges) is due to the fact, easily overlooked, that they are products of a segregated society," Zinn concluded. Indeed, as the sit-in movement spread throughout the South, it created similar tensions on white campuses while opening up new possibilities for political action for white students.[113]

CHAPTER THREE

White Students, the Campus, and Desegregation

IN THE EARLY DAYS of the Atlanta student movement, Constance Curry, Southern Project director for the U.S. National Student Association (NSA), tried to recruit students from Atlanta's white colleges for sit-ins. "Somehow or other I scraped up a white representative from every college, even Georgia Tech," she later recalled. "They only came to one meeting because they were terrified. . . . [T]hey took one look at [Morehouse student] Lonnie King and all those students and never said a word and went home that night and we never heard of 'em again."[1] Curry's failed effort was not an isolated event. The vast majority of white southern students sat on the sidelines, either because they did not sympathize with the cause or because they feared the potential price of involvement in terms of entanglements with the law or consequences imposed by college officials or parents.

But nonviolent direct action nevertheless had a profound impact on the political mobilization of white students and the political culture of southern campuses. A handful of white southern students crossed the most fundamental line of regional orthodoxy by acting to support integration. The controversies of the desegregation era presented all white students with choices, even if they did not participate in the movement. Most remained silent, but some publicly supported integration, airing their opinions in campus newspapers or associating with black students on recently desegregated campuses. When white students publicly supported integration, under whatever circumstances, they set in motion processes of personal and regional change. For individual white southerners, the decision to reject segregation could be the first step on a political journey that would lead some to involvement in the southern New Left. For the colleges and universities they attended and for the region as a whole, desegregation in all its guises served as the linchpin of a political awakening that expanded the political spectrum and opened up new possibilities for mobilization.

The politics of the desegregation era cut in more than one way. Since the mid-1950s, opposition to integration had manifested itself on many white campuses, generating what might be considered informal college chapters of the massive resistance movement. The campus politics of massive resistance manifested itself in a number of ways. Riots against the matriculation of Autherine Lucy at the University of Alabama established one model that would be followed in the early 1960s at the Universities of Georgia and Mississippi. But the early 1960s also saw conservative students refine their arguments against the disruptions caused by nonviolent direct action and an intrusive federal government that stepped in at key points to secure the end of segregation in higher education.

As was the case with the emergence of activism from black campuses, white students' responses to desegregation affected both southern politics and southern college campuses. White students who participated in sit-ins, wrote editorials encouraging the acceptance of integration, or visibly associated with black students played a role in wrenching southern liberalism away from its traditional embrace of gradualism and toward immediatism. At the same time, student participation in on- and off-campus clashes over desegregation exposed the limits on academic freedom that blighted southern higher education and laid the groundwork for a more thoroughgoing critique of higher education later in the decade.

Southern Students and Academic Freedom

In the early 1960s, the University of Alabama remained both under judicial order to admit black students and segregated. Moreover, the Lucy episode continued to cast a pall over the university. In 1961, Asa Carter, national grand wizard of the Ku Klux Klan, told the campus newspaper, "If anyone can stop integration at the university, the Klan can do it." A prominent figure in John Patterson's 1959 gubernatorial campaign, Carter embodied the power of militant segregationists in Deep South politics, and his comment underlined the vulnerability of colleges and universities to reactionary forces, which prompted some faculty to depart the South for friendlier surroundings. Most, however, stayed. "The place to fight for a principle is where it is a living issue, not where it is an accomplished fact, and still less where it has become a mere object of sanctimonious self-congratulations," declared Iredell Jenkins, a philosophy professor at the university.[2]

Clashes over race were not new to southern college campuses, but they appeared with greater frequency in the late 1950s and early 1960s as the wave of reaction against integration clashed with the black freedom struggle. As on black campuses, the reverberations from the collision between these two movements demonstrated the weaknesses in the structure of segregated higher education. By 1962, historian C. Vann Woodward bemoaned the assaults on academic freedom, including dismissals of faculty members and reprisals against students. In that year, twenty-three of the fifty-five outstanding cases of academic freedom and tenure in the files of the American Association of University Professors were in the South, as were the majority of the institutions censured by the association. "The colleges have felt the wrath of the resistance to the movement and the fury of the Radical Right because they are vulnerable targets and because they have sometimes furnished enlightened opposition to the reactionaries," Woodward argued.[3]

Black institutions were the region's most vulnerable and thus provided the most egregious examples of violations of academic freedom. But a similar dynamic existed on white campuses. Particularly at weaker institutions — Woodward cited cases from Sam Houston State Teachers College, West Texas State College, and the University of Tampa — faculty members who ventured controversial opinions, especially regarding race, could be exposed to pressures from politicians as well as from White Citizens Councils, the John Birch Society, and the Ku Klux Klan. Even the University of Florida and Louisiana State University suffered intrusions. In 1959, a committee of the Florida legislature held hearings for seven months, during which hundreds of witnesses, including students, testified against professors. In 1960 and 1961, Louisiana State narrowly avoided such an inquiry by sacrificing a professor who had tangled with members of the legislature over school desegregation. "The bleak and frightful truth," mourned one professor at the University of Alabama, "is that . . . it is dangerous for an educator to stand openly, actively, and vigorously for decency and moderation."[4]

No state and no institution better demonstrated the costs of massive resistance to academic freedom than Mississippi and its flagship school, the University of Mississippi. In the decade after World War II, Ole Miss had seemed to one of its most prominent professors to be "on the verge of living up to the dreams and hopes of its founders and directors of exactly a century before." As historian James Silver noted, the immediate postwar years had seen an expansion of libraries and laboratories, new departments, and "the gathering together of an excellent faculty dedicated to good teaching and solid research." Law school dean Robert J. Farley discussed the possibility of admitting black law students, a small number of liberals appeared on campus without repercussions, and legislative charges of communist sympathies among some faculty members brought none of the hysteria that appeared later. By the mid-1950s, however, the university's administration increasingly appeased conservative politicians with professions of ideological purity.[5] Silver, who later wrote of the state of Mississippi as a "closed society" and was chased from the university for his outspokenness, challenged the reactionary Right's ill effects on the campus, as did Baptist minister Will D. Campbell, who suffered the same fate in the late 1950s. If anything, the pressure at Ole Miss on even racial moderates grew after Campbell's departure, especially during the months surrounding the university's desegregation in 1962. Like its home state, the University of Mississippi was always a problematic representative of universities in other parts of the South. The university's repressive atmosphere from the mid-1950s into the next decade offers a somewhat extreme example of what happened on many campuses throughout the South.

Thus, when white students and faculty responded to the emergence of the sit-ins, they often did so in an environment that constricted not only overt political activity but any kind of speech or action that hinted at the desire to remake the South's social arrangements. These restrictions raised the stakes for any student participating in the movement and no doubt discouraged many whites from becoming active. However, the period was a time not only of intellectual repression but also of ferment. Even as segregationists fought to stem the tide of integration, they helped define race as the preeminent moral issue of the day. In so doing, they forced white students to make conscious choices about the morality of segregation and the racialist assumptions that undergirded the system. Whites had increasing difficulty in maintaining a casual and unthinking acceptance of the received wisdom about race. Moreover, the ongoing progress of desegregation, combined with the emergence of interracial nonviolent direct action, provided white southern students with new opportunities to interact with African Americans, furthering a process in which black people ceased to be an abstraction.

Vanderbilt: Race and Politics in the Early 1960s

In February 1960, Vanderbilt University was a culturally and politically conservative institution. Its undergraduate programs were segregated, and though the numbers had dropped in previous years, most of its students were members of Greek societies, where the labels *southern* and *conservative* were profoundly connected. "Vanderbilt is a Southern university," observed undergraduate Roy Blount in a column in the *Hustler*, the student newspaper, in the early 1960s. "The majority of the people here come from people who have tried to make lazy Negro field hands work, have seen many Negroes and not many white men in knife fights, have given extra money to the yard man because he has spent all the rest on something he shouldn't and his children are hungry, and who remember fondly the old colored folks at home and are angered by Martin Luther King."[6]

Vanderbilt was, however, in transition. Though no African Americans had matriculated as undergraduates, its graduate programs had desegregated in 1954. One of the handful of black graduate students at Vanderbilt was James M.

Lawson Jr., who was responsible for making Nashville the philosophical ground zero for the sit-in movement. The rise of the Nashville movement and Lawson's central role in it shook up Vanderbilt, challenging the university's student political culture, opening the door to a new form of political mobilization, and initiating a wave of student examination of the institution.

Lawson's involvement in the Nashville movement prompted the university's administration to expel him in early March 1960 after local newspapers labeled him "the leading organizer" of the demonstrations. Citing a section of university regulations dealing with student conduct at the scene of mob action or disturbance, divinity dean Robert J. Nelson asked Lawson whether it was true that he had made statements urging Nashville students to continue their demonstrations regardless of the law. Lawson responded with a two-page statement in which he declared that he endorsed not "defiant violation of the law" but civil disobedience "within the context of a law or a law enforcement agency which has in reality ceased to be the Law." University officials responded by asking Lawson to withdraw. When he did not comply, university officials expelled him, aware that their actions would make the university appear repressive. "It is ironic," the *Hustler* quoted one anonymous administration official as saying, "that something like this should happen to Vanderbilt after we were among the first to admit Negroes, after we held to a liberal policy. Now those who didn't will be saying 'I told you so.' The whole cause of better race relations in Southern education has been set back." Publicly, chancellor Harvie Branscomb attempted to head off criticism that the university was abridging freedom of thought or conscience: "The issue is whether or not the University can be identified with a continuing campaign of mass disobedience of law as a means of protest."[7]

The university's actions found support in the pages of the *Hustler*. "Compared to other Southern schools," the paper's editors wrote, "Vanderbilt has bent over backwards in attempting to make its educational facilities available to qualified men and women, regardless of race. In view of this rather liberal (for the South) attitude, it is ironic that in the immediate future Vanderbilt will probably be vilified by critics in other sections of the United States for its handling of the case of James M. Lawson." To the editors, Lawson's actions resembled two other recent violations. In one episode, two students had been expelled for staging an impromptu "broadcast" through carillon horns atop Kirkland Hall on campus. In another episode, a group of female students had been suspended for inciting a panty raid. "The 'sitdown' affair, in which Mr. Lawson has admitted a part, is of a far more serious nature," the *Hustler* concluded.[8]

In the following days, student and faculty groups on the campus took up the issue. The Vanderbilt student senate soon overwhelmingly approved a resolution endorsing Lawson's expulsion. But although conservatives controlled the establishment channels — the student newspaper and student government — Lawson's supporters found other outlets. Small American flags marked by a large black splotch and accompanied by a statement protesting the expulsion appeared throughout the campus. Divinity School students picketed Kirkland Hall in protest. Lawson's expulsion clearly initiated discussion on campus, and the *Hustler* agreed that students needed to engage the issue: "The Lawson case has proved at least one thing to us: that it is time for every Vanderbilt student to debate, with himself and with his fellows, the entire issue of segregation. As the South's future leaders, these students will likely be called upon to give an answer, and for the sake of everyone concerned, it had better be a good one."[9]

The Lawson case in particular and the sit-in movement in general provided the backdrop for a renewal in the spring of 1960 of a long-standing debate over Vanderbilt's NSA membership. The group's national leaders endorsed and actively supported the sit-in movement, adding fuel to those who complained that the organization was too liberal, even radical, for Vanderbilt. According to one April *Hustler* editorial, the NSA's views "on the question of racial segregation are much too radical for most southerners — and most of the Vanderbilt student body is from the South." The editors continued, "Vanderbilt is not a hotbed of rabid segregationists by a long shot; neither, however, is it as liberal as most of the schools" in the NSA.[10] In early May, Vanderbilt students voted overwhelmingly to end the university's affiliation with NSA; however, the referendum was not binding. Thus, Vanderbilt sent representatives to the National Student Congress, the NSA's annual gathering, held at the University of Minnesota in the summer of 1960. The sit-in movement divided the congress and produced considerable tension, at one point pitting two white southerners — one from Vanderbilt, the other from the University of North Carolina — against each other. Vanderbilt student Joe Roby spoke for conservatives, arguing that the NSA's position on the sit-ins neglected the views of the majority of Vanderbilt's student body: "We wake up one morning and read that NSA supports the sit-ins, and in the same article, 'Vanderbilt University is a member of NSA,'" Roby complained. "I know that NSA has a mandate on civil liberties, but does this mean that your membership wants you to go to Nashville, Tennessee, and support the violation of civil law?" Roby's speech won applause from many of the students in the hall, but the debate was not over. In response, Curtis Gans, a former editor of the University of North Carolina's *Daily Tar Heel* who was serving as an NSA vice president, explained, "I made a tour of the South, and then I had a decision to make in conscience. Some people said the South was moving gradually toward integration, but we realized there had been only a little, mostly token, desegregation. If we were going to live up to the NSA Constitution, and mandates, we had to act." Gans admired the courage of "the southern Negro college student" and believed that "the overwhelming sentiment of the nation" was behind the sit-in movement. As Gans sat down, applause ensued.[11]

By September, when the *Hustler* reported on the National Student Congress, the paper's new editors had changed the publication's stance to favor continued NSA membership. The editors thus staked out a moderate position that decried the careless charges of communist influence sometimes levied against NSA and acknowledged the inevitability of desegregation without endorsing the black freedom struggle. An editorial argued that the spring referendum had been voted down "mainly because of two loaded words — integration and communism — which its opponents brandished so frequently and slung so widely that hardly anyone bothered to look or think very deep into the real issue." The editorial pointed out that NSA's endorsement by both the Democratic and Republican presidential candidates demonstrated its lack of communist ties. The editors acknowledged the unpopularity of NSA's support for integration but argued that membership in the group was crucial to Vanderbilt's continued relevance in the national debate on race relations. "It is true that NSA urges the accomplishment of racial integration in education with all possible 'deliberate' speed," the paper noted, adopting the language of the *Brown v. Board of Education* decision. "This, as we sometimes forget here, is the official position of most of the American nation. Though it be anathema to some Southerners, it cannot be wished away or ignored out of existence. NSA may not represent the South in this area, but it does represent a substantial majority of the American educational community, of which Vanderbilt is inevitably a part. This fact will be the same, whether we stay in NSA or get out. The only difference is that out we have no voice, no influence in the decisions NSA makes in behalf of the American College Student."[12]

The Vanderbilt student senate continued the school's NSA membership during the 1960–61 academic year. Roby, now the senate president, and other conservative members pushed the body to adopt positions that would act as a conservative counterbalance within NSA. In February 1961, a bill that would have criticized the NSA for attempting "to legislate the conscience of American college students" and condemned sit-ins as a "mass, organized violation of existing statutes" narrowly failed, in part because of the opposition of senate vice president Lamar Alexander. Although Alexander had played a role in the bill's formulation, he opposed its passage because "it doesn't express as intelligently a position on our NSA's stand." Weeks later, the senate unified behind a bill opposing the sit-ins and their endorsement by the NSA. Wrangling over wording — for example, whether the senate should call on the NSA to "cease" or "rescind" its actions — dominated much of the debate, and in the end, the *Hustler* suggested that the senators, though united in their support of the resolution, "were not of a united opinion as to what they were opposing." But Roby probably spoke for most when he took aim at the tactic of the sit-in, which he argued was "explosive" and represented an undesirable way to solve "an essentially legalistic question."[13]

In January 1962, Senate debate turned from sit-ins to the desegregation of Vanderbilt after junior senator John Sergent proposed a bill establishing a student committee to investigate the admittance of qualified black applicants to all Vanderbilt schools. The discussion pitted opponents of any desegregation or of any movement toward it against those who believed that integration was inevitable and that resistance would damage Vanderbilt's national reputation. Few opponents seemed willing to follow the lead of one anonymous student who argued, "Vanderbilt is one of the institutions of higher learning that still preserves the purity and superiority of the white race and I am definitely against integration." Instead, opponents argued about timing and process. Integration would proceed more smoothly in six years, when student attitudes would provide for a more welcoming environment and segregationist alumni would be less likely to withdraw financial support. Few proponents argued that segregation was immoral, more commonly taking the position that segregation was destined to end and that maintaining it would prevent Vanderbilt from being "a truly great university." In February, the student senate organized a campuswide student referendum on integration. Students voted against the idea 862–661, with about 60 percent of the student body casting ballots.[14]

Over the ensuing months, however, the *Hustler* took a more assertive stand in favor of integration, led by editors Blount and Alexander. Blount's columns, peppered with sarcasm and colorful language, moved as close to an indictment of segregation as any writer in the paper had come: "'There ought to be a place,' students say, 'for people who believe in segregation.' There also ought to be a place for people who believe in going naked, but it ought not to be a university. We take our places around with us, and we have no right or power to impose them on other people or things. The Negro has been given his place, and he doesn't want it or deserve it." In the same April 1962 issue of the paper, Alexander warned that Vanderbilt was falling behind other southern universities in ending segregation.[15]

The decision to end undergraduate segregation came from Vanderbilt's board of trustees the following month. The *Hustler*, now edited by Blount, celebrated the decision as a step forward but cautioned against "quick token integration" and warned that accepting Negro applicants over more qualified white applicants "just so that we can be integrated and our consciences can be salved and our critics silenced" would amount to reverse discrimination. The primary purpose of ending segregation was to realize the goal of true university, and this ideal resided somewhere between the vision of a segregated "social club" on the one hand and a progressive "social crusader" on the other. The university should be "a community of scholars that welcomes other scholars. In this way Vanderbilt will do its job as a University, and in the process will help the Negro to gain his rights as a man."[16]

The *Hustler's* evolving embrace of desegregation suggested significant movement at a university that still had a self-consciously conservative student body. But coming in 1962, more than two years after the advent of student sit-ins, what was perhaps just as significant was the editorial's dismissive reference to the university as a "social crusader." The stance suggested discomfort with if not outright opposition to nonviolent direct action. Both responses to direct action soon became evident as a small group of Vanderbilt students began sit-ins and picketing against segregated restaurants. This wave of direct-action activities started in November 1962, when a national conference of the Student Nonviolent Coordinating Committee (SNCC) meeting in Nashville led to demonstrations against two restaurants. In mid-December, physics professor David Kotelchuck attracted local attention when a photograph of him dodging a punch from a restaurant employee at a sit-in ran in the *Nashville Tennessean*. The university took no action against Kotelchuck, but the continuing demonstrations and Kotelchuck's involvement unleashed debate on campus and in the *Hustler*. The Vanderbilt Senate voted in December to denounce the demonstrations as "injurious to the law-abiding citizens of the community." The *Hustler* responded with an endorsement of the sit-ins that was less than full throated: "Sit-ins aren't good, but the discrimination they show up is worse, and that discrimination is what must be either opposed, or rationally defended by responsible people." Three years after the beginning of the sit-in movement, Vanderbilt students appeared to be hovering on its periphery, offering commentary for or against but not conspicuously involved. Indeed, in January 1963, Blount described a sit-in that he and several student senators had observed at the B&W restaurant. Blount was uninspired by the demonstrators.[17]

Not until late spring, when a new "campus liberal organization," PROD, was formed, was any kind of movement toward student involvement in direct action was evident. The *Hustler* first mentioned PROD in May 1963, when the group sponsored a speech by Fisk professor Vivian Henderson, a politically active scholar who was working to mobilize black voters through the Tennessee Voting Council. Henderson endorsed the use of nonviolent demonstrations, but his comments were more focused on the potential for black voters to change electoral outcomes. PROD advertised itself as a club for liberals, though its president insisted that "responsible moderates and all others who feel a need for a forum to express their ideas" were welcome.[18]

By the fall, PROD was poised to move from discussion to action. The organization, led by Ron Parker, a psychology graduate student, focused its attention on the Campus Grill, a segregated restaurant situated in the middle of the

Vanderbilt, Peabody, and Scarritt campuses. Some Vanderbilt divinity students had already begun to boycott the restaurant. In October, PROD announced a picketing campaign, prompting the student senate to pass a resolution favoring restaurant desegregation in Nashville but qualifying the resolution with a statement that government had no right "to force a restaurant manager to alter the management of his business in regard to whom he shall or shall not serve." The *Hustler*, now edited by the more conservative Dick McCord, lampooned the proposed picketing campaign as a "self-righteous and slightly ridiculous" move that "smacked . . . of children playing games," though the paper continued to endorse the goal of desegregation.[19]

PROD's life as a campus organization was shortened by a split between moderates and what one *Hustler* writer termed "vociferous radicals." But the Campus Grill campaign led to contacts among students from Vanderbilt, Scarritt, and Peabody. From Vanderbilt, graduate and divinity students were the most visible participants in the nonviolent crusade for desegregation. They eventually joined colleagues from the neighboring colleges to form the Joint University Council on Human Relations. Members of the organization quickly developed a camaraderie based in part on a perceived set of common experiences as southern whites. They held meetings or parties almost nightly.[20]

At the center of this group of white activists was Sue Thrasher, a native of rural West Tennessee who had grown up a devout Methodist and had come to Scarritt College to prepare for a career in the ministry. Run by the General Conference of the Methodist Church, Scarritt College for Christian Workers began with the junior year and had a substantial number of graduate students preparing for careers in "Christian service." The college fell within the tradition of American Protestant liberalism, and though it was a predominantly white institution, the student body included a few African Americans. Moreover, one-fifth of the student population came from outside the United States. A friend of Thrasher's who was a native of the Fiji Islands had helped initiate the demonstrations against the Campus Grill when the manager of the restaurant refused to allow her to eat there, and this confrontation helped propel Thrasher toward activism. She soon met Archie Allen, a Virginia-born Scarritt student upset by the Campus Grill incident, and the two gradually immersed themselves in the Nashville movement by attending meetings of the Nashville Christian Leadership Conference, the local affiliate of the Southern Christian Leadership Conference (SCLC), headed by Kelly Miller Smith. Through the Nashville movement, Thrasher and Allen met John Lewis, Bernard Lafayette, Bob Zellner, Sam Shirah, Carl and Anne Braden, and Ed Hamlett. Hamlett, also a native of West Tennessee, had attended several colleges before joining SNCC in early 1964. His baptism into the movement had come in 1962 in Knoxville, where as a student at the University of Tennessee he served as cochair (with Marion Barry) of Students for Equal Treatment, a group that desegregated several business establishments.[21]

By April 1964, just as Vanderbilt was preparing to admit its first black undergraduate students, sit-ins at three Nashville restaurants had not only attracted the participation of Vanderbilt students but resulted in the arrests of four students. The *Hustler* continued to editorialize against the "misguided" demonstrations, and conservative students continued to flex their muscles in the student senate, but the political spectrum at Vanderbilt had widened to include direct action.[22] Moreover, activists from the city's white colleges had developed into a vanguard that would play a prominent role in the formation of the southern New Left, underlining Nashville's role as an important center for student activism.

The Politics of Moderation: North Carolina

Some 470 miles to the east, another movement center was developing in North Carolina. Geography played a role in generating and sustaining the student movement there. Greensboro, where the first sit-ins occurred, is about an hour's drive west of Durham, home of historically black North Carolina Central University and Duke University. Durham is a little more than eight miles from Chapel Hill, home of the University of North Carolina, and Chapel Hill is about twenty-five miles from Raleigh, the home of North Carolina State University as well as some smaller colleges and where SNCC's first meeting took place in April 1960. The concentration of black and white students and the interaction and competition among them helped to make this area among the most active in the South during the 1960s. North Carolina's renowned moderation provided another ingredient. The political environment in Piedmont North Carolina offered sufficient free space for organization while providing a foil against which students could act. Nowhere was this truer than at the University of North Carolina, whose liberal reputation came under attack. Early in the decade, a small group of campus rebels embraced nonviolent direct action and provoked controversy both in the town and on the campus.

Pat Cusick was an outsider at the University of North Carolina in 1962. An air force veteran who had served in the Korean War, Cusick, a Deep South native with a Catholic upbringing, arrived in Chapel Hill at age thirty. He had taken courses part-time at Belmont Abbey College, a Benedictine institution in Belmont, North Carolina, but he was looking for an institution with more prestige, and he was taken with the Chapel Hill campus. "It looked like a university was supposed to look, and most of them don't," Cusick later noted. "I went up in the summer and said, 'Ahh!' I rushed and transferred to Chapel Hill." Cusick took a full load of classes while working as a janitor at the student center,

Graham Memorial, named after liberal UNC president Frank Porter Graham. Cusick occasionally hauled portable pianos in and out of fraternity houses for parties. And fraternity members occasionally called Cusick derogatory names as he worked.

Soon after his arrival, the outsider became a rebel. Having seen a leaflet describing the Student Peace Union (SPU), Cusick went through the steps to form a chapter on the UNC campus. It was the group's first chapter in the South, and it was "the only thing left, if you want to put it in left-right terms, of the Young Democrats," Cusick recalled. Cusick and his SPU colleagues questioned President John F. Kennedy's Vietnam policies, thereby raising the ire of the Young Democrats, and debated the campus chapter of the Young Americans for Freedom. But the SPU's activities received only minor attention until early 1963, when members began to direct their attention toward race relations. By the spring, SPU had begun picketing the College Café, a segregated establishment on the town's main thoroughfare, Franklin Street. The picketing campaign threw cultural and political divisions on campus into high relief. "Certain fraternities made it a requirement of the pledges that they had to break the picket line," Cusick recalled; the Naval Reserve Officers Training Corps also required its members to cross the picket line. But liberals also had problems with the demonstrations. In fact, SPU's move from discussion to action produced a rapid evolution in Cusick's beliefs, which initially included an opposition to "radical" tactics such as picketing. According to Cusick, "When we started picketing, I wasn't that much in favor of marching. When we started marching, I was not in favor of civil disobedience." But "the events swept us along."[23]

The Chapel Hill movement had started in January 1961 with a picketing campaign targeting segregated theaters. A combination of community activists, operating under the auspices of a local chapter of the National Association for the Advancement of Colored People (NAACP), and black student activists generated the movement, which soon opened up avenues for white students. However, UNC faculty members initially were more prominent participants, and some 350 pro-integration faculty eventually took out an advertisement in the student-run *Daily Tar Heel* in which they took the student body to task for its inactivity: "Where are our brave, intrepid students, fighters for right and leaders in the battle for equality? It seems that they are hiding behind the rock of self-indulgence and fear, refusing to commit themselves lest they suffer reprisals." The ad then moved on to larger questions: "What has happened to youth? Has it become so concerned with its own well-being that it leaves social action to minority groups and its elders? Has it lost the courage and daring that marked the 1920's and 1930's and the post-war period?" Finally came a somewhat sarcastic call for students "to support *anything at all*. We ask them to find the courage to have an opinion, whether it be segregationist or integrationist."[24]

The critique of student apathy, which resonated with the "silent generation" label of the 1950s, was not uncommon on southern campuses, black and white, at the time. And to some extent, the criticism of students at UNC was apt. The "planned frivolity" of college life continued to thrive in Chapel Hill. In March 1961, a series of *Daily Tar Heel* editorials assessed the status of the university's faculty, student body, and intellectual climate. Students placed too much emphasis on high grades rather than intellectual activity. The library was more a social center than a research center. Chapel Hill lacked a really good bookstore. Theaters did not show good movies. Students were "far more involved with athletic teams and fraternity parties than they are with books and what is contained within books." Moreover, "a cult of masculinity has arisen which finds people who seem to derive pleasure from intellectual endeavor considered just a little bit 'fruity.' This is to no one's credit."[25]

But UNC's student culture also fostered pockets of rebellion. Harry's, a café near campus, provided comfort for a diverse group of campus rebels that included "the rag-tag end of the Beats . . . proto-hippies, aspiring writers and painters," and people interested in drugs and Eastern religions. The people who gathered at Harry's were, in short, a counterculture. "An interesting and special group of people passed through Chapel Hill in the years from 1962 to 1967," explained a 1985 newsletter, "but they aren't the ones you'd see if you looked in" yearbooks "or at pictures taken during the class reunions more recently. To the fraternity and football set or to the administration of the University, we were inconvenient, scruffy, and contentious. To Jesse Helms of WRAL-TV, we were a godsend of good copy — outside agitators stirring up the Negroes and demanding free speech!"[26]

Moreover, UNC's campus political scene was larger and more diverse than any other in the South. Campus politics were serious business for members of the Student Party and the University Party. Membership and significant involvement in the NSA further leavened the campus with a sense that what happened in the Student Senate could have national importance. On the right, a campus chapter of Young Americans for Freedom maintained a visible profile, sponsoring, for example, a showing of the House Un-American Activities Committee film *Operation Abolition* in October 1961. At the other end of the spectrum, the New Left Club advertised itself as "left of Kennedy," with a membership that included several liberal Democrats, several democratic socialists, and two or three Marxists but no Trotskyites, Stalinists, or Communist Party members, "though such people would be welcome at our meetings insofar as they would enliven the discussions. Anyone is welcome to join the group so long as he shares enough of the basic assumptions of the political Left to make discussion possible — such assumptions as that all political action should be grounded on a belief in humane values and in egalitarianism."[27]

Nevertheless, as an outpost for radical political action, Chapel Hill left something to be desired. In the spring of 1962, the fledgling Students for a Democratic Society (SDS) held a conference on "the integration movement in American politics" designed "to bring together student integration leaders to discuss wider implications of the movement for racial equality." It was a failure. Members of the SDS executive council blamed UNC graduate Curtis Gans for poor planning. Gans had not written a conference prospectus, had not met with the Chapel Hill arrangements committee, and had not prepared working papers. Others complained that only about half of the seventy attendees were from the South and that organizers had spent too little time listening to what southern students wanted and needed. Nicholas Bateson, a UNC graduate student, an SDS member, and a leader of the New Left Club, noted that conference organizers had not facilitated local participation and that Chapel Hill people thus felt shut out.[28] More significantly, the failed conference illustrated SDS leaders' difficulties in fashioning an effective approach to organizing southern students. The conference may also have indicated the limits of Chapel Hill's reputation as a liberal haven. Even locals complained at times that the reputation was unmerited. "It is time for Chapel Hill to wake up," the *Daily Tar Heel* editorialized in 1961. "This comfortable, complacent little center of liberal thought is, in reality, as steeped in prejudice as any southern hamlet. The only difference is that there are more men and women here who believe in equal rights for all and are determined to see them obtained."[29]

The challenges to comfort and complacency sought by the editors of the *Daily Tar Heel* came from forces within and outside Chapel Hill. In the spring of 1963, John Dunne, a Morehead Scholar at UNC who had attended Connecticut's elite Choate boarding school, traveled to Birmingham, at the time the epicenter of the civil rights movement. Dunne, a member of SPU who had participated in the picketing campaign against the College Café, went to Birmingham at the invitation of a *Daily Tar Heel* staffer and quickly became deeply involved in the Birmingham movement, at one point serving time in jail. The trip transformed Dunne. An excellent student who had been voted "straightest arrow" by the Choate senior class, Dunne's participation in civil disobedience represented an abandonment of the track record he had established and eventually led him to relinquish his coveted scholarship and drop out of school. On 1 May, he wrote to his parents from Birmingham, "The compelling factor in my staying here has been the fact that I am, to my knowledge, the only white man actively in the movement."[30]

Civil rights activities continued in Chapel Hill under the guise of several organizations, including chapters of the NAACP and the Congress of Racial Equality (CORE). An assault on segregated public establishments occurred through a coalition group, the Committee for Open Business, whose demonstrations culminated in the arrests of hundreds of people, including UNC students, in December 1963. The committee was succeeded by Citizens United for Racial Equality and Dignity (CURED), which was joined by other groups including SNCC and the SCLC. By early 1964, tactics were more confrontational, and in February dozens of people were arrested after activists blocked downtown intersections. Dunne and Cusick were sentenced to one-year prison terms in April 1964. The *Daily Tar Heel* offered supportive editorials throughout this time, including an endorsement of a student boycott of all segregated establishments. But the rising level of activism belied divisions within the local movement. CORE, led by Floyd McKissick, who had desegregated UNC's law school, set the tone for the more militant wing of the movement. Older leaders within CURED, including the Reverend Charles Jones, worried "that the young leaders were talking about using peace as if it were a missile, of using love as if it were a weapon — admittedly a nonviolent weapon, but a weapon of coercion, nonetheless."[31]

In the short run, the weapon failed to win the day. Activists had sought a local ordinance forbidding segregation, but Chapel Hill leaders failed to enact such a measure before Congress passed the Civil Rights Act of 1964. Cusick later suggested that it had been a tactical mistake not to pressure the university, which exercised tremendous power within Chapel Hill, to put its weight behind a local public accommodations ordinance. But in the immediate wake of the demonstrations, John Ehle reported "considerable dissatisfaction" with university leaders' aloofness. "Young people reach decisions not on the basis of what is told them, but on the basis of what they feel is so," Ehle suggested. "It was all very well for the university hospital to say it was not segregated, but it was. It was all very well for the chancellor to say the university did not practice segregation, but in some ways it did, and in other ways, one feels, it wanted to but could not because of laws."[32]

Ehle's comments were published in 1965, the aftermath of the Free Speech Movement, a major series of demonstrations at the University of California in Berkeley. Many people perceived those demonstrations as embodying a new generational identity; thus, it was perhaps natural for Ehle to look at Dunne and Cusick as well as the other young people who drove the direct-action wing of the Chapel Hill movement through a generational lens, as an indication of "what the young people of America are up to." The members of the Chapel Hill group shared a number of characteristics with "young people in the North," Ehle argued: they were optimistic, tough, interested in self-improvement, moderate and controlled in social habits, and committed to a mission for a limited period of time. They were also "almost always late for an appointment" and "always broke." In sum, they were committed if a bit flighty. But perhaps the most revealing characteristic that Ehle saw was a motivation that was moral rather than political: "Therefore they are serious, dedicated, self-sacrificing, un-compromising, but they are politically naïve." As a result, though Ehle laid the blame for the Chapel Hill movement's failure largely on the community's apathy and intransigence, he also criticized the young civil rights activists for their refusal to work strategically with older, more moderate leaders. Projecting out from Chapel Hill, Ehle was ultimately optimistic about a new "sense of mission" emanating from young activists who aimed at a "fulfillment of the American democracy." Though young leaders such as Dunne had "almost wrecked Chapel Hill," Ehle believed that "if the schools and other institutions across our country come to understand them, the prospects for good are immense. I believe they offer us our greatest opportunity in several generations."[33]

The student movement in Chapel Hill was on the cusp of a dramatic ex-pansion, but that expansion was prompted by resistance to the movement from state legislators in Raleigh. In 1963, motivated in large part by civil rights activi-ties in Chapel Hill, the legislature passed a measure controlling who could speak on the state's college and university campuses. The Speaker Ban generated a massive backlash among UNC students from across the political spectrum.

Nonviolent Direct Action and the Development of Movement Centers

In Nashville and in central North Carolina, sit-ins had provided a new kind of political mobilization for small numbers of white students. The same dynamic replicated itself in other locales throughout the South, initiating a process that would result in the development of movement centers that dotted the region. When one activist with extensive knowledge of the South's college campuses surveyed the region in 1963, most of the locales he cited as the most active had experienced the first wave of the sit-ins.[34] By then, Nashville, Atlanta, Tallahassee, Gainesville, Chapel Hill, and Austin had fairly well developed centers of white student activism. Black student activists, in conjunction with community leaders, had set the standard by initiating nonviolent direct-action movements. White student activism had then developed in conjunction with, in sympathy with, or as a continuation of the sit-ins. Local conditions modified the form and content of this emergent activism, but in all cases, the white student activists of 1963 and 1964 owed a great debt to black students and community activists for providing organizing issues and tactical models.

Tallahassee

What would become Florida State University started as West Florida Seminary in 1857. It was a military institute for a time in the late nineteenth century and a college for women in the first half of the twentieth century before it was reconstituted as the coed Florida State University in 1947. Strict rules governed the lives of all students, female and to a lesser extent male. Moreover, campus life played out against a backdrop of the social conservatism of Tallahassee, a Deep South city that was, as one historian notes, "governed by a close-knit group of white men . . . who controlled its economy, determined its politics, and guarded its social mores."[35] But from the 1950s through the 1960s, a series of campaigns against segregation shook up this "small southern enclave." Black students had undertaken serious political activity in the Florida capital since 1956, when students from Florida Agricultural and Mechanical University initiated a boycott of the city's segregated bus system. By early 1957, the local movement attracted a handful of white students from Florida State University.[36]

In the late 1950s and early 1960s, the nexus of white activity on the Florida State campus was Canterbury House, an interdenominational residence sponsored by the Chapel of the Resurrection. The brainchild of an Episcopalian minister, Canterbury House was designed as a communal living situation for young college men who wanted to be involved in "transforming the world, not hiding from it." Located off campus, the house was somewhat insulated from scrutiny accorded on-campus organizations, and it was one of the few places that hosted interracial gatherings. Consequently, white FSU students first learned of the local CORE chapter from A&M students at Canterbury House.[37] After the fall of 1959, CORE was the most important organization driving student activism in Tallahassee, providing a vehicle for interracial nonviolent direct action. Students from FSU were present for Tallahassee's largest and most dramatic sit-in, which occurred on 12 March 1960. Police at one point used tear gas against black and white demonstrators, and six FSU students were arrested.[38] FSU students' involvement in civil rights activities subsequently ebbed and flowed, as did the actions of the Tallahassee CORE chapter, which largely depended on its cofounder, Patricia Stephens, a Florida A&M student. In September 1961, Stephens left Tallahassee, first to study at Howard University and then to live in New York, although she returned to Tallahassee in 1962. FSU student activists also struggled to maintain their status at the university, which at one point required students who had been placed on academic probation as a result of their involvement in demonstrations to sign affidavits promising not to participate in further acts of civil disobedience.[39]

Florida State admitted its first black students in 1962, and the following year, activists launched another round of nonviolent demonstrations aimed at segregated public establishments — restaurants, bus stations, the airport, the courtroom, the city pool, and theaters. This time, FSU students were more prominent participants, and the unfolding campaign originated in a manner that resembled Nashville's 1963 Campus Grill campaign. In Tallahassee, four restaurants adjacent to the campus continued to deny service to African

Americans, and the University Religious Council and the Liberal Forum, which was affiliated with the Unitarian Church, took the lead in pushing the restaurants to desegregate. By October, failed negotiations had led to picketing, which prompted counterdemonstrations by conservative students who hurled insults such as "Nigger-lover" and "Go home, Yankee." After a violent showdown between a couple of dozen picketers and several hundred counterdemonstrators was narrowly averted on 14 October, university officials forbade student participation in mass demonstrations and placed five students who were arrested in September 1963 demonstrations at segregated theaters on "administrative probation" until they graduated. The students also were confined to the campus for the remainder of the semester. FSU president Gordon Blackwell seemed to focus primarily on separating the university from the demonstrations rather than on stopping them. He insisted that the students acted as "private citizens" and suggested that they "were motivated by humane considerations." Similarly, the *Flambeau*, the student newspaper, took what one historian has termed a "moderately pro-integration position," trumpeting FSU's peaceful integration and expressing concern that violence would tarnish the university's "mature" and "clean" image. Pro- and anti-integration students traded arguments in the pages of the *Flambeau*, but a student government poll suggested that student attitudes were evolving as the reality of desegregation set in. Nearly two-thirds of the 225 respondents favored allowing black students to use off-campus eating establishments, and more than three-quarters would continue to patronize restaurants that served black patrons.[40]

Gainesville

The Gainesville student movement developed in the wake of and was influenced by events in Tallahassee. In 1960, Gainesville was a sleepy college town on the cusp of significant growth. The home of the University of Florida, Gainesville doubled its population over the ensuing decade, largely as a consequence of the university's expansion. Perhaps in keeping with this growth, race relations in Gainesville had a veneer of moderation. "This town clearly is not an 'open society,' but it is unbelievably difficult to pinpoint actual segregation, albeit it is ubiquitous," wrote Mike Geison, an early leader of Gainesville's CORE chapter, in May 1964. "The 'White' and 'Colored' signs are now few and far between in the city proper, most restaurants and both downtown theatres are open to negroes, the city government claims it does not discriminate in hiring, and you have to listen closely sometimes even to hear the word 'nigger.'"[41]

The University of Florida shared in the facade. The school had quietly desegregated in 1958 but in other respects resembled other Deep South public universities, with a campus culture and political system dominated by Greek societies. According to faculty member Marshall B. Jones, "The fraternity-sorority system at Florida was extremely developed. Fraternity row looked like so many country clubs set end to end. These houses were quarters for the rich and socially aspiring students on campus, and the motivation that flowered among them was opportunist, cynical in the most self-serving way, and endlessly pliant to the administration; the fraternities and sororities were so many stables of the establishment."[42] Within this environment, a small group of students and faculty became involved in civil rights activities, first under the leadership of a local NAACP Youth Council and subsequently through a local chapter of CORE founded in May 1963. University students and faculty were central to Gainesville CORE's activities, and some of those students and faculty were instrumental in founding a campus organization, the Student Group for Equal Rights. In addition to Jones, key players in this early period of mobilization included another faculty member, Ed Richer, and students Judith Benninger and Dan and Jim Harmeling, who were brothers. In the fall of 1963, Benninger and Dan Harmeling were arrested at antisegregation demonstrations in Tallahassee, and the University of Florida subsequently suspended them. Benninger, a graduate teaching assistant who also lost a Ford Fellowship, later won reinstatement as a result of the intervention of her father, a professor at Florida who had lost his job at the University of Alabama after supporting Autherine Lucy's application for admission. This core made the University of Florida a center of significant and creative activism. Benninger was also a key figure in the founding of Gainesville Women for Equal Rights and worked with Jones's wife, Beverly, to make the city a center for the women's liberation movement. A significant university-reform movement also emerged at the University of Florida in the mid-1960s.[43]

Atlanta

Atlanta's numerous white campuses included two private schools, Emory University and Agnes Scott College, and two public institutions, the Georgia Institute of Technology and Georgia State College. Business moderates worked with mayor Ivan Allen to promote the city as more concerned with economic growth than with racial conflict, while Governor Ernest Vandiver accused black student demonstrators of communist sympathies and promised that no blacks would enter the University of Georgia. During the 1960s, the public institutions experienced only moderate amounts of activism. Georgia State was one of a growing number of urban institutions that also included Louisiana State University in New Orleans (now the University of New Orleans) and the University of Alabama at Birmingham. Georgia State had no on-campus housing and thus little in the way of campus life. Many of the school's students also held jobs and consequently had little time for activism. Georgia Tech was dominated by engineering students, a group that throughout the country showed little inclination toward activism.

Emory and Agnes Scott were hardly hotbeds of radicalism, but they allowed some free space for activist students. Agnes Scott had been one of the few southern white colleges to affiliate with the NSA, the result at least in part of the efforts of Constance Curry, a student in the 1950s who later directed the NSA's southern organizing efforts. Emory, for its part, had a conservative student body drawn largely from the South and did not integrate until 1963. But the Methodist-affiliated university had been the home institution of a number of southern liberals, among them Atticus Greene Haygood, Emory's president from 1875 to 1884 and an early proponent of a "New South" with improved race relations.[44] By October 1960, the university's position on race relations was vague enough that when a handful of white students, faculty, and clergy met to discuss how to support the sit-ins, they considered starting with an effort to provoke some sort of stand by the university administration. No written policy existed regarding interracial meetings or the admission of black students. In fact, some students noted that interracial meetings had occurred on the campus, although individual organizations rather than the university had invited the black guests. The twenty-eight students, four faculty members, and three ministers at the meeting, held at the Emory Christian Association Office on campus, eventually concentrated their first efforts on an Election Day project spearheaded by Atlanta University Center activists. This decision led to picketing of polls by a handful of Emory students, an action SNCC's Jane Stembridge later called "the first all-white student demonstration for civil rights in the Deep South." The students at the meeting knew they were in the minority. "There was concern that probably 95% of the students at Emory were apathetic," Stembridge noted. Though the students decided not to "engage in a campus-wide educational program at this time," they hoped that if a few people took action, they would pave the way for "discussion and enlightenment."[45] The November 1960 demonstration indeed provoked discussion: the editors of Emory's student paper, the *Wheel*, expressed disapproval of the tactic. "Being an educational institution and not a training center for sit-ins, we must move slowly — with the tide of public opinion, not in front of it," the *Wheel* declared in a front-page editorial.[46]

The cadre of Emory activists remained small. By January 1964, some students had joined Georgia Students for Human Rights, a new organization designed to connect the handful of activists on Georgia campuses, who suffered from the isolation, as was frequently the case for like-minded students throughout the South. Led by Georgia Tech's Richard L. Stevens, Georgia Students for Human Rights started in Atlanta and eventually made halting efforts to encompass institutions throughout the state. Georgia Tech might not have been the home to many student activists, but Stevens was not a typical student. A Florida native, he had served a military stint in Germany before returning to school to study industrial management. His inclination toward activism eventually drew him from the campus to the NSA's Southern Project, for which he served as assistant director in the mid-1960s.[47] Georgia Students for Human Rights was "an attempt to give the students on the white campuses in Atlanta an outlet through which to express their concerns about the problems that confront us today." The group's 1964 activities included holding mass meetings, picketing restaurants, distributing leaflets urging a boycott of downtown stores during Lent, organizing campus groups, conducting "hit-and-run" sit-ins, and training in nonviolence by C. T. Vivian.[48]

Austin

In Austin, activism grew from student religious organizations in response to the burgeoning civil rights movement. The University of Texas was in many ways a conservative place. The members of the board that governed the university were closely linked to the oil and gas, construction, real estate, and finance interests that held the preponderance of power in the state. In 1944, they had used that power to fire liberal UT president Homer Rainey, prompting a student strike. But the University of Texas desegregated well before the rise of massive resistance, admitting its first black graduate student, Heman Sweatt, in 1950 under court order and the first black undergraduates in the middle of the decade. By 1960, the nineteen-thousand-person student body included some two hundred African Americans. When UT's black students joined the sit-in movement, they concentrated not only on segregated public facilities in Austin but also on discrimination in campus activities, including athletics, drama, and housing. These actions demonstrated the difference between the admission of black students and the full integration of the campus, but they also placed the university farther along than students at other southern white campuses in developing activism.[49]

Two religious organizations, the Christian Faith and Life Center and the University YMCA/YWCA, nurtured progressive white students. In the spring of 1959, an interracial group of Y activists had begun sitting-in at segregated restaurants. When the 1960 sit-ins began to spread, white students involved in the two groups launched demonstrations, working within a new group, Students for Democratic Action (SDA). A coalition of mostly black students from the University of Texas and another Austin school, historically black Huston-Tillotson, provided the model; by May 1960, sit-ins conducted by these students had resulted in the desegregation of more than thirty lunch counters and cafés. These successes whetted the appetite of UT's white student activists. One of them, Sandra (Casey) Cason, attended the NSA's National Student Congress that summer and gave a rousing speech challenging students to be willing to risk their own security to end racial inequality. In the fall, white students in the SDA initiated "stand-ins" at two segregated theaters in Austin. Accompanied by black friends, they attempted to buy tickets; when refused, they went to the back of the line to try again. They continued this tactic for six months, until the theaters promised to integrate the following September. During the campaign, SDA mobilized between forty and two hundred people each night.[50] The formation of a community of activists from within the ranks of campus religious organizations and that community's mobilization around desegregation provided the foundation for what historian Doug Rossinow has called "the largest center of new left activism in the American South, one of the biggest in the United States and probably the most important in all the vast spaces east of Berkeley, west of Morningside Heights, and south of Chicago."[51]

New Orleans

In New Orleans, picketing and sit-ins by black students provided a model for students at the city's white (Tulane) and predominantly white (Louisiana State University in New Orleans [LSUNO] and Loyola) universities. A boycott of white-owned establishments on Dryades Street, a shopping district patronized by New Orleans blacks, began in April 1960 and served as the precursor for a full-scale student movement that gathered momentum by the fall.[52]

On the city's white and predominantly white campuses, the implications were different. Officials at still-segregated Tulane watched the fallout from the Lawson situation at Vanderbilt while a handful of students joined early sit-ins. For years, university policy had required the suspension of any student accused of a crime until the student's trial was completed. However, the case of graduate student Sydney Langston (Lanny) Goldfinch posed special problems. Goldfinch's participation in a lunch counter sit-in at McCrory's brought an arrest and a charge of "criminal anarchy," along with a bail that was ten times higher than that of the three black students arrested with him. Given the severity of the charge, Tulane president Herbert E. Longenecker worried that the university would appear to be persecuting Goldfinch for his activism if it took action against him. In part because of the events at Vanderbilt, Longenecker and Tulane charted a cautious course. When Goldfinch, evicted from his apartment because of his legal troubles, applied to live in Tulane's dormitories, the university allowed him to move in with only a warning that he not "bring his problem into the dormitory," thus setting aside the long-standing suspension policy. Though hardly an endorsement of student activism, the university's position emboldened the small number of liberal students on campus. During late 1960 and early 1961, a few Tulane students joined the ranks of the New Orleans

CORE chapter, which coordinated the local movement. By the following fall, that trickle, augmented by whites from LSUNO and Loyola, had turned into a steady stream.[53]

By 1962, a small number of Tulane students participated in sit-ins at the University Center Cafeteria as well as other eating establishments in the city. One article in the student newspaper, the *Hullabaloo*, quoted four sit-in participants, three of whom were graduate students. Their activities prompted criticism from the Louisiana Branch of the National States Rights Party but received tentative support from the *Hullabaloo*. In a front-page editorial, the newspaper argued that the protesters had not shown how sit-ins would force the university to do anything but nevertheless encouraged "non-violent peaceful demonstrations" if Tulane was not integrated and criticized the university's "fence straddling" policy.[54]

By the time of the editorial, however, a rift had already developed between black and white participants in the New Orleans student movement. Beginning in the fall of 1961, the city's CORE chapter had received an influx of new members, including many students from Southern University in New Orleans and a fair number of students from Tulane. Some of the group's founding members were troubled by the new members, and in February 1962, the chapter suspended white males and black females responsible for local criticism of "interracial social activities."[55] Tulane students and faculty nevertheless continued to participate in protest activities. In the fall of 1963, drama professor Richard Schechner led a Tulane contingent in demonstrations at the mayor's office and the city hall cafeteria.[56]

At the forefront of Tulane student activism was the Liberals Club. In late 1962, the club requested permission to invite socialist Michael Harrington and historian Herbert Aptheker, a communist and later at the center of the controversy surrounding North Carolina's Speaker Ban, to speak on campus. Tulane's Major Events Committee approved Harrington but rejected the request for Aptheker, drawing protests from the Liberals Club. Members of the Liberals Club also joined students from Xavier, Dillard, LSUNO, and Loyola in a late-1964 protest of a segregated restaurant located near the Tulane campus.[57]

The proximity of the Loyola and Tulane campuses facilitated cooperation between activists at the two schools. A Jesuit institution, Loyola served a student body dominated by city residents throughout the first half of the twentieth century. Thanks in part to a faculty that included Father Louis J. Twomey, founder of the Institute of Industrial Relations, and other clergy oriented toward social justice, the university fostered more progressive action than might have been expected from a "streetcar school." An affiliation with NSA, which was unusual for white schools in the Deep South, also provided a level of cosmopolitanism within the campus political culture. Loyola's student council had voted to affiliate with NSA in 1960 as a consequence of the prodding of Bill Caldwell, a sophomore business administration major. Council president Bill Hammel had opposed the proposal, charging that the association had a "pink tint." Nevertheless, the student senate approved the affiliation by a 22–4 vote.[58] For the next couple of years, Loyola's liberal activists benefited from the connections afford by NSA. Father Thomas H. Clancy, who served on Loyola's history faculty and as an adviser to NSA's Southern Project, recalled, "It was heady business for students from such schools which were generally removed from the mainstream of Southern higher education to be addressed by NSA national officers from the Ivy League and Big Ten Universities." Every Holy Week between 1962 through 1965, the NSA sponsored a Deep South Human Relations Seminar at Xavier. Well-known activists such as Al Lowenstein, Barbara Jordan, and Aaron Henry spoke at the seminar, and visitors included movement activists Stokely Carmichael and Bob Moses.[59] The connections facilitated a sense of adventurousness among Loyola's small group of activists. Curry later described Loyola's students as "always pretty far out. You could always count on them to be among the more active."[60]

But the NSA affiliation and perhaps the activism it engendered produced a backlash. In 1962, the university's Student Council voted to disaffiliate from the organization. In 1961, Loyola's dean of students had called the NSA "a dangerous organization composed of atheists, agnostics, and some who would not even salute the flag." Such comments accurately reflected NSA opponents' sentiments, and in early May 1962, Loyola students voted by a two-to-one margin in favor of withdrawal.[61]

A small number of black and white students continued to participate in direct-action demonstrations even after the passage of the Civil Rights Act of 1964. In early 1965, the Tulane Liberals Club spurred students from Loyola, Tulane, LSUNO, Dillard, and Xavier in a series of sit-ins and picketing at Phillip's, a restaurant several blocks from Tulane that had continued to deny service to African Americans by claiming to be a private club. When group members sat down at the restaurant, proprietor Rose Phillip asked Adam Weber, an African American student from Loyola, for his membership card. He had borrowed one from another Loyola student, and when he presented it, Phillip tore up the card while a waiter grabbed Weber by the ear, presumably to lead him out of the restaurant. She then called her lawyer and the police, who instructed her that the integrated group had a right to stay in the restaurant, although she had a right to deny them service. Phillip instead closed the restaurant. "All we wanted to do was integrate the place," said John Joerg, a Tulane English instructor. The demonstration came three years after most of CORE's white members had been expelled but demonstrated the continuing power of interracialism.[62]

Activism without a Sit-In Movement

On a rainy Monday in October 1962, Helen Davey posed outside the Gorgas House at the University of Alabama. A sophomore transfer student from Columbia College and pledge of the Delta Delta Delta sorority, Davey was being photographed for the following Thursday's edition of the *Crimson White*, the UA student newspaper. She had earned the title of "Bama Belle," a regular feature of the newspaper that offered glimpses of attractive female students. The photo ran in the top left-hand corner of the *Crimson White*. Next to it but below the fold was a story about rumors of a demonstration "relating to the Mississippi situation" that was scheduled to occur at a pep rally for the university's vaunted football team. The "Mississippi situation" was the desegregation of Ole Miss, and the reference reflected the nervousness with which Alabamians — especially those at the state's still-segregated flagship university — looked at events to the west. At the rally, Coach Paul (Bear) Bryant, who was not on the schedule, spoke for ten minutes, "hitting constantly on the theme of 'togetherness' and 'oneness' of the student spirit." President Frank A. Rose delivered a similar message of unity, a call for students to ignore those who "every year try to use us to riot us . . . to destroy our institution." No riot occurred, and within a year the University of Alabama was desegregated with plenty of spectacle but with no violence.

The top story of the 11 October 1962 *Crimson White* described an upcoming student government program on "the Cuban situation" featuring two congressmen and a Latin American historian from the university. Events in Cuba had not reached crisis proportions, at least in the public mind. Public awareness of the Soviet offensive weapons in Cuba did not come until 22 October, when President Kennedy delivered a televised address announcing an American "quarantine" of Cuba. But a week and a half earlier, articles in the *New York Times* detailed ongoing repercussions from the April 1962 Bay of Pigs debacle, negotiations with Soviet Union regarding both Cuba and Berlin, and a new radio program, *Radio Free Dixie*, broadcast by Havana's Radio Progresso. The program's mixture of jazz music and commentary was targeted at blacks in the U.S. South, encouraging them to revolt against their country's treatment of them.[63] The front page of the *Crimson White* thus reflected regional, national, and international tensions filtered through the "planned frivolity" of a college campus. Those tensions, the responses of students who lived with them, and the efforts of some students to build a progressive movement out of them provided the context for student politics at Deep South universities.

The crises that unfolded at the Universities of Georgia, Mississippi, and Alabama were significant events in the story of white southern student activism, although, as historian Peter Wallenstein notes, the tense and sometimes violent episodes that occurred at Georgia in 1961, Ole Miss in 1962, and 'Bama in 1963 were unrepresentative of the manner in which desegregation occurred in the South. In most institutions, "the drama was of a far more subtle sort," developing in court cases whose resolution sometimes spanned years.[64] But these dramatic incidents held great meaning for contemporary and subsequent students at those universities. The desegregation crises provided the foundation on which subsequent progressive campus movements were built, politicizing these campuses in ways that forced students to respond. Some responded by embracing desegregation, thereby setting in motion a chain of events that expanded the possibilities for political mobilization on campuses where W. J. Cash's "savage ideal" persisted. For many students in other parts of the South, the events constituted an embarrassment, something to be avoided. For some, the distaste or even repulsion generated by these episodes led to a search for a third way, something between intransigent opposition to integration on the one hand and nonviolent direct action in support of it on the other. For others, it led inexorably toward an embrace of desegregation.

But the politicization prompted by the desegregation crises should not be exaggerated. Desegregation provided a foundation for activism, but it was not a firm foundation. Students at Georgia, Ole Miss, and Alabama found that even the most cautious affirmations of integration often brought on hostile reactions that choked out meaningful expressions of support for racial equality and limited the possibilities for students who sympathized with the black freedom struggle. In a real sense, "activism" at the Universities of Alabama, Georgia, and Mississippi could be as simple as expressing support for the nonviolent acquiescence to federally enforced integration. The forces of reaction on the campuses and in the surrounding communities often were powerful enough to prevent anything more substantial from occurring.

The University of Georgia

The University of Georgia was central, at least symbolically, to the lives of many Georgians. "Almost every family in Georgia has some connection with the University of Georgia," Governor Ernest Vandiver once noted. "A father, mother, brother, sister, uncle, or aunt, somebody in the family group had attended." This reality not only made the desegregation of the university important but also reduced the likelihood that legislators would close the school rather than see it desegregated. Located seventy-five miles east of Atlanta, Athens seemed at one level like an idyllic college town. But it was also the home of a poor white working class employed by textile mills and resentful of black advancement. And it was seedbed of Klan activity, most conspicuously the murder of Lieutenant Colonel Lemuel Penn in 1964.[65]

After years of legal wrangling, Atlantans Charlayne Hunter and Hamilton Holmes won the right to matriculate at the university in January 1961. On the night of 11 January, Hunter's and Holmes's first day of classes, a crowd of students gathered outside Hunter's Myers Hall dormitory room after Georgia's basketball team suffered a narrow defeat at the hands of in-state rival Georgia Tech. A riot ensued. Campus lore later contended that the melee was not as bad as national media made it seem and that TV reporters had encouraged students to look more menacing to make students who were as agitated about the basketball game as they were about desegregation fit the mold of the reactionary, violent white southerner. But historian Robert Pratt has argued persuasively that the episode's danger was serious and that it represented more than an impromptu venting of steam after a losing basketball game. Ku Klux Klan members were present, and several students displayed a large banner that read, "Nigger go home." Members of the crowd started fires and lobbed bricks into Hunter's room. The Georgia State Patrol failed to respond to a call, and Athens police used tear gas and water hoses to break up the gathering. Hunter later declared, "Believe me, it was a nasty riot, and any assertions to the contrary are absolute bullshit." Moreover, evidence suggests that the riot was planned, the result of collusion between state officials and student leaders who sought to replicate the 1956 events at the University of Alabama that had resulted in Autherine Lucy's expulsion as a threat to public safety.[66]

In the short run, the effort to block desegregation through riots worked and thus underlined mobilized students' potential ability to affect outcomes. University officials withdrew Hunter and Holmes from the university, and state troopers took them back to Atlanta that night. The violence prompted responses from many faculty and students in the following days. About 80 percent of the faculty signed a resolution condemning the violence.[67] In The Red and Black, editor Terry Hazelwood criticized organizers of the riot as well as "curious onlookers." "Ladies and gentlemen of the University, you made history last night. Are you proud of the manner in which you did so? We hope not."[68] On 13 January, federal judge William A. Bootle ordered the university to readmit the two black students. By that time, more moderate white students had begun to recoil at the media coverage of the violence. Nevertheless, white proponents of integration and black students often met with resistance at the newly integrated university. Joan Zitzelman, a white student who befriended Hunter, later recalled sitting down on the first day of a journalism ethics course for which she knew Hunter had registered and seeing "Nigger Go Home" written on the blackboard. Zitzelman erased the message before Hunter arrived. Dean John E. Drewry designated a seat for Hunter, and Zitzelman "tried to concentrate on his words and make helpful notes, and I tried not to look over at

Charlayne Hunter, sitting in a side section of the auditorium, with empty seats all around her."[69]

As late as 1964, the environment remained unfriendly for black students and their white supporters. When Nelson Blackstock, a white student who would represent the University of Georgia at the founding meeting of the Southern Student Organizing Committee, posted pro-integration flyers on his dormitory door, some of his neighbors hurled epithets at him, and the dean of housing asked Blackstock to explain his actions.[70] Religious organizations provided the most conspicuous safe havens for UGA students who supported integration. When Hunter looked for camaraderie, she found it, in varying degrees, in the Catholic Newman Club and the Presbyterian Westminster House, which was one of the first safe havens for racial liberals and moderates and served as the headquarters for Students for Constructive Action, a pro-integration group. The Westminster House also served as the outpost for a campus minister, Corky King, who eventually lost his job because of his outspokenness.[71] By the spring of 1964, the students at Westminster were "the most actively involved in the movement," although the Methodist Wesley Foundation and the Jewish Hillel House were also friendly to civil rights activism. By this time, the university's small community of liberals was making contact with Atlanta activists operating under the aegis of Georgia Students for Human Rights. In Athens, however, progressives struggled not only against hostility but also against indifference. "General impression from faculty, ministers is that the students 'don't give a damn,'" an NSA report concluded.[72]

The University of Mississippi

If liberal students at the University of Georgia battled a mixture of belligerence and indifference, then their counterparts at the University of Mississippi seemed to face a combination that was heavier on the hostility. The two universities shared some characteristics: picturesque campuses in quaint towns, emphases on gridiron excellence, student cultures dominated by Greek social fraternities and sororities, and tight connections between campus and state politics. "Ole Miss was to prove to be a fine launching pad for my career beyond campus," U.S. senator Trent Lott, an Ole Miss undergraduate during the early 1960s, later wrote. "In the 1950s, all of the governors and statewide officials were graduates of the University of Mississippi."[73] But as Harry Lunn of the NSA observed of other southern schools at the time, a campus political system with wide participation was not necessarily healthy. Indeed, according to a devastating *New York Times* article, the Ole Miss student culture was barren of intellectual vibrancy or political diversity: "The university has no active debating society, no student organizations of even faintly liberal hue and no humor magazine. . . . No magazine of even middling quality is available on the campus, and few are sold in Oxford. In fact the cultural life of the city is as barren as that of the university appears to be." Politically, the campus brooked practically no dissent from orthodoxy. In this respect, the *Times* article suggested, Ole Miss mirrored its home state, in which, "with minor exceptions, the range of political opinion is from Y to Z." The College Characteristics Index, devised by a professor of higher education at the University of California at Los Angeles to measure educational institutions as seen by their students, found that University of Mississippi students placed a high value on possessions, status, and the material benefits of higher education but little emphasis on ideas.[74]

In this light, it is plausible, as Lott has asserted, that James Meredith's "imminent enrollment at Ole Miss was not a dominant issue on campus in the immediate days" after courts ordered the university to accept its first black student. Meredith entered the university on 30 September under the protection of federal marshals. Students and nonstudents, appalled by the presence of the marshals, rioted. After a night of gunfire, rock-throwing, and clashes between rioters and troops, a French reporter and a maintenance worker were dead, and the campus looked like a war zone. According to Lott, the forces that gave rise to the riot came from outside — from Mississippi governor Ross Barnett, who tied his political fortunes to the issue and who essentially encouraged segregationists to flood the campus, and from a federal government that forced integration on the university. Indeed, for months before September 1962, Barnett had fanned the flames with defiant promises that he would never allow integration. Still, even if most students approached the issue of integration with a mixture of apathy and unquestioning acceptance, some were more actively involved in fighting to preserve segregation. In fact, Lott notes the existence of the Rebel Underground, a "disreputable, segregationist organization" operating "in the shadows of Ole Miss," and describes the organization's efforts to get Lott to accept a slate of Rebel Underground cabinet members in exchange for the group's support in an election for student body president. Lott turned them down and lost the election by a narrow margin. When Bob Zellner, a white SNCC field organizer, visited the Oxford campus immediately after the riots, he saw evidence that Rebel Underground was more than a peripheral, "disreputable" organization. Its flyers, which called on Mississippi students to unite in opposing integration, were printed on expensive paper, and he heard members of the campus community speculate that the Rebel Underground was funded by the White Citizens Councils. He perceived that the organization's cause had widespread support: "I don't see why they have to call themselves the 'Rebel Underground,'" one undergraduate said, "because most everybody's in favor of them anyway."[75]

University officials met with student leaders the night of the rioting and them to encourage their fellow students to remain calm rather than join in the violence. Among those present was Sidna Brower, editor of the campus newspaper, the *Mississippian*, who wrote an editorial for the next day's paper, "Violence Will Not Help." Chancellor J. D. Williams also used the paper to urge students to avoid congregating in large groups, to identify "agitators" to campus police, and to "cooperate fully" with them.[76]

In subsequent weeks, Brower wrote editorials that called for calm, criticized demonstrators, and faulted the administration for its failure sufficiently to discipline students. Her editorials won her a Pulitzer Prize nomination, but they also garnered the opposition of students who thought she was sending the wrong message. One student, George Monroe of Newton, Mississippi, led a drive in the student senate to censure Brower for failing to represent the students who elected her editor. A compromise motion eventually passed, reprimanding but not censuring Brower. Conscious of the need to preserve free speech, some participants worried that *censure* might be confused with *censor*.[77]

The decision to acknowledge Meredith's presence by speaking to him or by sitting with him became a fundamental line of demarcation on the University of Mississippi campus. "If a white student sat down and drank a cup of coffee with me or walked with me across the campus, he was subjected to unhampered intimidation and harassment," Meredith later wrote. Taking the lead in this organized ostracism was the Rebel Underground. Meredith noted that "many students" visited his dormitory room in the immediate days after his entrance to the university, but the number of visitors declined after the Rebel Underground began publishing the names of the visitors.[78] Zellner described a sheet circulated by the "Rebel Resistance" that urged students to "banish from them ANY white student" who tried to befriend Meredith. Continued the flyer, "Such warfare, which is of the mind and of the spirit, is far beyond the control of the U.S. Supreme Court. Such warfare was used by the South during Reconstruction, and the South eventually triumphed. Let us strike while the iron is hot!"[79]

Some Ole Miss faculty members hoped that the episode would initiate a cultural transformation on campus. While they acknowledged that a temporary "turning inward" might occur among students who sought calm in the wake of chaos, these professors hoped that the events would force white students "to think seriously for the first time about the racial issue and their attitudes toward it." Nevertheless, as the *New York Times* article noted, "The speed with which the students appeared able to forget what had happened make[s] observers doubt that the riots would bring about any substantial awakening." Zellner hoped to encourage just that sort of awakening: "As a recent student in a Southern institution of higher learning and as a victim of the trauma that befalls a Southerner when he goes against his fa[s]cist-like background, my heart is with these brave young students, members of the emerging creative minority."[80]

The University of Alabama

Members of the University of Alabama community watched the "Battle of Oxford" with trepidation from a campus that was still segregated. The University of Alabama was a provincial institution: the vast majority of students came from within the state, and the faculty, though solid enough, as historian E. Culpepper Clark suggests, was undistinguished. Newly minted high school graduates often spent four years in Tuscaloosa and then returned home to lead lives that resembled those of their parents. Some students were more ambitious, however; as was true at the Universities of Georgia and Mississippi, 'Bama's system of student politics was a training ground for men, among them Governor George Wallace, who sought careers in state politics, teaching them how to build coalitions and win elections.[81] Student politics at the University of Alabama more often produced demagogues and mediocre timeservers than it produced genuine leaders.

Alabama still operated in the shadow of the Lucy episode. In the aftermath of her expulsion, the little free space that had been available to the campus's few moderates and liberals disappeared. Though desegregation remained an important issue, faculty and students did not discuss it openly, least of all in campus publications.[82] Thus, when the student sit-in movement erupted, it bypassed Tuscaloosa. A handful of students, at one point aided by SNCC's Zellner, arranged clandestine meetings with black students at nearby Stillman College, but these meetings had only limited effects on the university, at least in the short run.[83]

In 1956, students and faculty had expressed support for obeying the law as it related to integration only at their own peril. By late 1962, a little more latitude was apparent. In the immediate aftermath of Meredith's enrollment at the University of Mississippi, editors of the *Crimson White* argued that "morally, there is no justification for his rejection." This editorial and a few other stances that offended staunch conservatives earned the paper's editor, Melvin Meyer, death threats from the Klan and prompted the university to hire a detective to protect him.[84]

In the academic year leading up to 'Bama's eventual desegregation, dread of another explosion existed side by side with the more mundane events and concerns that animated most American college campuses — the lack of school spirit and student apathy. In November 1962, a *Crimson White* editorial issued yet another call for "law and order." Citing calls from the university's board of trustees, the faculty, and a Tuscaloosa businessman to avoid reenacting the

Battle of Oxford, the editorial declared, "It must not happen here. It matters not what your personal views are on segregation, integration, state sovereignty, or the Kennedys. What is of the utmost concern is that we profit from the mistakes of others."[85]

Two black students, Vivian Malone and James Hood, finally entered the university in June 1963. Though Wallace stood in the doorway of Foster Auditorium to prevent Malone and Hood from registering, the resistance was only symbolic. The presence of hundreds of city police, state troopers, and National Guardsmen ensured that the violence of 1956 would not recur. Desegregation played out as an orchestrated event, allowing the governor to act as if he had mounted a noble defensive effort against a federal government that ultimately forced him to step aside from the schoolhouse door. Though the national press portrayed Wallace as the clear loser in the episode, his supporters in Alabama drew a different conclusion.[86] Tensions continued to grow between Wallace and a university administration that sought institutional advancement, which could come only through meeting national standards. For the university's president, Frank A. Rose, and his staff, the primary goal through the desegregation crisis was order. Avoiding a Battle of Tuscaloosa would position the university to continue its expansion.

F. David Mathews, a student at the University of Alabama during the Lucy episode, had subsequently left to pursue graduate studies at Columbia University but returned to help Hood get settled in his dorm and to work with the dean of students, John Blackburn, "in getting the support of the student leadership." To Mathews, avoiding the mistakes of 1956 was at the top of the agenda in 1963, and student leaders at Alabama performed that task admirably: "For me, this generation defined student activism at its best. These young people, only a few years my junior, were involved in the larger world and the great issues of their time. They avoided political drama (having seen it for what it is) and exhibited quiet courage. Though often stereotyped as self-indulgent, follow-the-crowd students only interested in the next party, they were anything but that. They understood responsibility and embraced it. As much as the integration itself, they still stand out in my mind. Perhaps more than the adults," Mathews suggested, "the students sensed that the future was going to be different from the past."[87]

Even so, the theme for these students and for Mathews, who became the university's president during the late 1960s, appeared to be "law and order." In the November 1962 editorial, the *Crimson White*'s editors cited as cautionary tales the examples not only of Oxford but also of Alabama's response to the Freedom Rides — evidence that violent opposition to racial change only resulted in embarrassment in the national spotlight. "A unified movement of mature leadership to accept the inevitable has taken place within the state," the editorial stated. The tone of resignation is clear, as it is in the *Crimson White*'s statement shortly before desegregation occurred that the "courts have ruled that integration must come, that segregation is illegal. We disagree with these rulings on a states' rights basis, although we are in favor of desegregation on moral ground."[88] In the end, ameliorative gradualism and a desire to see the "best people" managing gradual change won out.

Hood may have been trying to sing the same tune as moderate student leaders when he penned a guest editorial for the *Crimson White* that eventually led to his abrupt withdrawal from the university. In "Needed: More Students, Less Pickets," Hood argued that "the protest movements have resulted in, literally, a big unnecessary mess." Instead of "sit-ins, lie-ins, swim-ins, etc.," he suggested, African Americans should focus their energies on the classroom to "meet the demands of society. In order for one to be accepted in a society he must meet certain standards and possess certain values in accordance with that society in which he is seeking a position." But rather than engaging in such constructive action, Hood argued, too many blacks sought the excitement of protest. And the central civil rights groups — Hood had "made a careful study of three major organizations" — were stirring up conflict that benefited only the organizations' leaders.[89]

Hood thus made a textbook argument against nonviolent direct action. And, as E. Culpepper Clark suggests, some segments of the black middle class might have listened to his argument. But it was surprising coming from Hood, who as a student at Atlanta's Clark College had regularly attended SCLC, SNCC, and CORE meetings and who had helped organize demonstrations in Gadsden, Alabama, the preceding summer. The *Birmingham News* picked up Hood's article, and Hood quickly realized how it would be received outside the University of Alabama community. He began backpedaling, suggesting that he had not written the piece. Wallace and other segregationists took advantage of the situation, setting in motion the machinery that would produce Hood's departure. By August, Hood had withdrawn from the university for "health reasons." In retrospect, Hood appears to have been seeking some common ground with moderate student leaders who had shown him some sympathy. But in building a cultural bridge, he started "from the middle of the stream toward his new white friends, rather than from the shore he so recently left."[90] In the aftermath of 'Bama's desegregation, there was no liberal Left organizing on campus. In fact, nothing public on campus existed to the left of the idea that order needed to be maintained in the face of forced integration. Not until the aftermath of events in Selma, Alabama, in March 1965 did University of Alabama students begin to mobilize in a way that even remotely resembled the early 1960s sit-in movement.

Evolving Racial Attitudes

A similar political dynamic held at other campuses in the Deep South where no local sit-in movement had developed and where institutional desegregation was delayed. At times, other southern colleges and universities have celebrated their relatively quiet desegregation, absent the tumult at Georgia, Mississippi, and Alabama. The phrase "integration with dignity" is often associated with the January 1963 matriculation of Harvey Gantt at Clemson. At Auburn University (known more formally at the time as Alabama Polytechnic Institute), the January 1964 enrollment of Harold Franklin was, in the words of the student newspaper's Hunter Smith, "just another day on the Plains." But a quiet desegregation process did not imply a welcoming atmosphere for African American students: Franklin found himself ignored by students and faculty alike. Jerry Gainey, among the first white students to visibly associate himself with Gantt, was the subject of ridicule and worse in conservative underground newspapers. A front-page editorial supporting the Freedom Riders brought all sorts of difficulties for Auburn's J. R. Bullington, editor of the *Plainsman* during the 1961–62 year. Segregationists burned a cross in front of his fraternity house and sent hate mail to his parents in Chattanooga. Students verbally assaulted him. The university president personally reprimanded him. The university's Publications Board demanded that he submit future editorials for censorship. And some state legislators threatened to cut Auburn's funding unless something was done to curb his "un-Alabama" agitation.[91] These examples suggest the existence of an unfriendly or even hostile atmosphere not only for the first generation of black students at previously white universities in the Deep South but also for "liberal" students, regardless of the tumult associated with desegregation. More precisely, they suggest the infertility of the ground tilled by Zellner and others who sought to mobilize white southerners in support of the civil rights movement.

That infertility in large part reflected white student racial attitudes that were decidedly opposed to integration. But those racial attitudes evolved rapidly during the 1960s. Historian Robert Cohen's study of thirty-five student essays written for University of Georgia math professor Thomas Brahana on 17 January 1961, in the midst of the university's desegregation, found only three essays that condemned Jim Crow. The rest contained "absurd ideas about black skull size, jungle rhythm, and shiftlessness," all expressed with great seriousness. Such ideas reveal a mind-set that enabled many students to participate in the riots that greeted Hunter's and Holmes's enrollment. "If you believe, as some of Brahana's students did, that the subversive NAACP together with a dictatorial federal government were victimizing white southerners by forcing them to integrate with members of an inferior race, there is a logic to rioting against such oppression," Cohen argues.[92] The essays' greatest significance lies in their status as an intellectual exercise that took place during dramatic confrontations. Brahana forced his students to articulate their racial assumptions; even when they reached absurd conclusions that supported rioting against integration, they indicated a process in which many other students were participating. Desegregation was forcing a consideration — if not a *re*consideration — of racial assumptions.

Those racial assumptions were slow to change, but they nevertheless did so. A series of surveys at the University of Alabama provides evidence of both the persistence of racial prejudice among white students and the tendency for prejudice to diminish. Shortly before the university's desegregation, two Alabama sociologists found that 56.4 percent of the students sampled would have no objection to attending class with black students. As the level of interaction became more intimate, however, the objections increased. Only 39.1 percent had no objection to sitting next to black students, while 27.7 percent did not object to walking on campus with them, 18.2 percent had no objection to eating at the same cafeteria table, and 5.8 percent did not object to sharing a room. Interracial dating prompted the most objections, with less than 1 percent approving. Subsequent surveys, however, found that white students' resistance to social interaction with black students slowly dissipated. In 1966, for example, 55.3 percent had no objection to sitting next to black students in class, with that number rising to 80 percent in 1969 and 88.3 percent in 1972.[93]

Farther north, a questionnaire that Allard Lowenstein gave to thirty-two students at North Carolina State illustrates the variety of ways in which white students responded to desegregation. Lowenstein's surveys, completed two years after the Georgia student essays and in a more moderate part of the South, indicate the ways in which time and local variation could lessen white students' racist ideas and opposition to integration. Lowenstein asked whether the integration of the Varsity Theater had influenced students' attendance at movies and whether the opening of restaurants to African Americans would cause white students not to patronize those establishments. Only three students said that they would not attend integrated theaters, while ten said they would not eat at integrated restaurants. The responses ranged from ardent opposition to integration ("I definately [*sic*] would not eat in restaurants that subject me to close relations to negros") to support for ("I believe in the rights of all people"). Such principled declarations were in the minority, however. Most students answered without comment. A few answers reflected internal divisions: one student stated that he would not object to patronizing a desegregated theater under some circumstances, but "with a girl I would not want to go in a full theater of Negroes because something unforeseen might arise."[94]

Such surveys offer a tantalizing but incomplete picture of white southern racial attitudes in transition, leaving unanswered questions about what caused some students to moderate their racial views while others held onto old ideas. However, these questionnaires show white southern students in the process of responding to the challenge of desegregation. The forces that pulled some white students toward more moderate racial views and in some cases toward activism came from both within and outside of campuses. Major episodes in the civil rights movement — the sit-ins, the Freedom Rides, anti-integration riots at the Universities of Georgia and Mississippi, George Wallace's "stand in the school-house door," the 1963 Birmingham crusade, the 1964 Freedom Summer, and the events at Selma in 1965 — often prompted discussion and action. On relatively open campuses on the region's periphery and in more cosmopolitan locations, activist groups formed to agitate for racial equality and to a lesser extent for other issues such as disarmament and free speech.

At the same time, regional and national organizations — chiefly, the NSA, SNCC, and after 1964 the Southern Student Organizing Committee — tried by various means to nudge white students to support racial equality. If these efforts failed to produce the groundswell of left-liberal student activism that organizers hoped to inspire among white students in the South, they at least created more room in which activists could operate. Optimists could point to a number of pockets that featured the beginnings of a student "movement" — the Universities of North Carolina, Texas, and Florida as well as multicampus communities in Atlanta, Nashville, and New Orleans. Conversely, predominantly white college campuses in the Deep South — most notably, those in Mississippi and Alabama — remained strongholds of segregation and conservatism.

By 1965, the New Left was beginning to get some attention in the national press. In late 1964, students at the Berkeley campus of the University of California who opposed restrictions on speech generated the Berkeley Free Speech Movement, which received national coverage and created a sense that Berkeley students might have created a template for mobilization that other campuses could employ. "What has happened at Berkeley is merely a taste of what may happen in the future if other university administrations fail to stand firm against" right-wing elements, declared Berkeley Free Speech Movement leader Mario Savio in December 1964.[95] The Berkeley movement revolved around a critique of American higher education, but it was directly inspired by the southern black freedom struggle. Savio had participated in the Freedom Summer, a program that attracted some one thousand college students to Mississippi to register voters, and he attributed his commitment to the Free Speech Movement to that experience: "I spent the summer in Mississippi. I witnessed tyranny. I saw groups of men in the minority working their wills over the majority. Then I came back here and found the university preventing us from collecting money for use there and even stopping us from getting people to go to Mississippi to help."[96]

As the Free Speech Movement was winding down, American military involvement in Vietnam was escalating. President Lyndon B. Johnson ordered bombing strikes on North Vietnam in February 1965 in response to a Viet Cong attack in South Vietnam that resulted in American deaths. The first bombing raids and the first commitment of American ground troops followed in March. At the same time, violence exploded in Alabama's Black Belt. On 7 March, Alabama state troopers violently broke up a march in Selma, Alabama, at which the demonstrators included SNCC chair John Lewis. "I don't see how President Johnson can send troops to Vietnam — I don't see how he can send troops to the Congo — I don't see how he can send troops to Africa and can't send troops to Selma, Ala.," said Lewis, who was injured in the clash. A week later, Johnson asked Congress to pass voting-rights legislation, telling the members assembled in a joint session, "Their cause must be our cause too. Because it's not just Negroes, but really it's all of us who must overcome the crippling legacy of bigotry and injustice. And we . . . shall . . . overcome."[97]

Against this backdrop, a 15 March 1965 *New York Times* article described a "new, small, loosely bound intelligentsia that calls itself the new student left and that wants to cause fundamental changes in society." The piece focused on white students who, motivated by the civil rights movement, poverty, and "the possibility of nuclear extinction," sought fundamental change in American society. Most were members of the middle class, and they wanted "to create an alliance between the millions of American whites and Negroes who have no economic or political power." They were also decidedly in the minority on their campuses: "Now, as before, the great majority of their fellow students are primarily interested in marriage, a home, and a job."[98]

The article's author, Fred Powledge, had interviewed various southern students, and he quoted the University of Texas's Jeffrey Shero. But though Powledge mentioned the relatively new Southern Student Organizing Committee, he provided little indication of the extent to which he saw visible evidence of the New Left in the South. Events in the first half of the 1960s had enabled the development of centers of activism in Chapel Hill, Nashville, Atlanta, Tallahassee, Gainesville, New Orleans, and Austin. In all cases, these locales had experienced some direct-action protest; in all cases, black students' activism had provided a model that white students — at first in ones and twos, eventually in larger numbers, but always a minority on their campuses — followed.

Outside of these areas, however, progressive white student activism remained inchoate. White students in less cosmopolitan locales and especially in the Deep South generally only read about direct-action protest or watched it on

TV. Housed in institutions still in the first stages of desegregating, students who might have sympathized with the New Left agenda lacked a firsthand model for nonviolent direct action and had access only to a rather more modest model that defined *activism* as interaction with African Americans or declarations of support for the concept of integration. Students in the Deep South's most conservative locales faced the challenge of getting from these forms of politicization to direct action.

CHAPTER FOUR

Building a Southern Movement

IN OCTOBER 1963, Anne Braden was wondering why Samuel C. Shirah Jr., the campus traveler for the White Students Project operated by the Student Nonviolent Coordinating Committee (SNCC), was late with an article for the *Southern Patriot* on the reaction of Birmingham-Southern College students to the Sixteenth Street Baptist Church bombing on 15 September. Perhaps, she mused, Shirah had not contacted her because he was disappointed with the response he had received. Shirah might have believed that Braden, editor of the *Southern Patriot* and field secretary for the Southern Conference Educational Fund (SCEF), would be disappointed in his inability to goad white students in Birmingham to action. Braden hoped that this was not the case. "I'm not going to be critical if he didn't set the world on fire with the Birmingham-Southern students," she wrote in a letter to a mutual acquaintance. "Actually, I was rather amazed that he even *thought* he might get them to move. It is not the place I would expect the revolution to start." Braden believed that an apathetic reaction by Birmingham-Southern students was newsworthy: "It reminds me of that old, old story about the cub reporter who went to cover the wedding and came back and told his editor there was no story because the groom didn't show up." Even if students at the small, all-white, Methodist-affiliated college showed no inclination toward action, it was important to know why. Did fear prevent them from acting? Was there some other reason?[1]

Shirah, a former Birmingham-Southern student, had faced a number of difficulties in his attempt to organize Birmingham students. After hitchhiking from Atlanta to Birmingham on the afternoon of the bombing, Shirah found it difficult to navigate safely in the city. On the first night, he slept in a closet at the Birmingham-Southern radio station, where he had worked as an undergraduate. He met with some students, but on his second day in town a dean at the college ordered him to leave the campus and never to return. He spent most of his time attempting to set up a program that would bring Birmingham-Southern students together with students from nearby Miles College. However, fear of reprisals suppressed the number of interested students, and those who were interested wanted to do so without Shirah's help, since his affiliation with SNCC made him dangerous.[2]

Shirah's experiences illustrate some of the obstacles that full-time activists faced when trying to mobilize students in the Deep South. Even though Shirah was a native Alabamian, his relationship with SNCC made him an "outside agitator" in Birmingham and other places where resistance to social change was strong. His predecessor in the White Student Project, Bob Zellner, another Alabamian, later called attention to the obstacles that prevented organizers from reaching southern students by drawing a comparison with the Soviet Iron Curtain. "For two years, I worked to cut through the cotton curtain to the minds of Southern white students," Zellner declared in a January 1964 *Southern Patriot* article.[3]

SNCC was not the only organized effort to spread the movement throughout the region. Starting in the late 1950s and continuing throughout the 1960s, a number of organizations — the U.S. National Student Association (NSA), the Congress of Racial Equality (CORE), liberal religious groups such as the YMCA/YWCA and the American Friends Service Committee, Students for a Democratic Society (SDS), and the Southern Student Organizing Committee (SSOC) — sought to pull together the strands of activism that had appeared in the South as a result of the sit-in movement. Their halting efforts revealed the challenges inherent in organizing a regionwide student movement. Conservatism and apathy, racial divisions, and strategic and philosophical difficulties presented obstacles to the new student movement. Nevertheless, by the middle of the decade, activists had achieved some successes, most notably the development of a loosely connected network that lessened the sense of isolation often felt by student activists on individual campuses.

"Sandlot Politics" and Social Change: The NSA

Even before the advent of the sit-in movement, the NSA had made the elimination of segregation and racial discrimination one of its foremost goals, a stance that made the organization controversial in the South. The NSA had been formed in 1947 as a confederation of student governments, and most white schools in the South refused to join because of the group's liberalism. Nevertheless, some black colleges and universities maintained NSA membership, and a few white institutions, including the Universities of North Carolina and Texas, bucked the trend and at times wielded a significant amount of power in the national organization. Participation in NSA activities, particularly the annual National Student Conference, which was held each summer on a different university campus, allowed students to make contact with their counterparts in other parts of the country and to deal with important educational, social, and political issues.

These contacts could, in turn, bring a somewhat more cosmopolitan tenor back to campus politics. For example, the involvement of UNC students — particularly Allard Lowenstein, who served as the NSA's president in 1950 and subsequently played a prominent role in the association — affected campus politics throughout the 1950s and early 1960s. The *Daily Tar Heel* frequently served as a forum for reports and debates regarding the NSA.[4] The South, in turn, played an important role in NSA politics. As it did for Cold War liberalism, the South came to symbolize the flaws that kept the United States from reaching its potential as a great nation. NSA liberals often focused their most passionate rhetoric on the South's segregation and disfranchisement.

In fact, the NSA was itself a product of Cold War liberalism. The association grew from the 1946 founding congress of the International Union of Students in Prague. An American student delegation attended and was impressed by the power of European student unions, which emphasized student services and rejected a purely political role. Members of the delegation returned and vowed to start a union in the United States. The founding convention was held the following year on the campus of the University of Wisconsin in Madison; 800 delegates from 351 colleges and universities and 20 national organizations attended. The crowning achievement of the convention was the Student Bill of Rights, which stressed academic freedom and freedom for students to organize and bring speakers to campuses.[5]

In the South, these ideals would have stirred controversy, but the convention's statement on racial discrimination proved even more contentious. With Europe seemingly the prize in an ideological tug-of-war between the United States and the Soviet Union, liberals saw racial discrimination in the southern United States as the nation's one glaring violation of what Gunnar Myrdal had called the "American Creed of liberty, equality, justice, and fair opportunity for everybody." Jim Crow thus undermined the fight against communism. But at the NSA's founding convention, such arguments failed to resonate with white southerners, most of whom adamantly opposed a strong stand against segregation. In the end, a white liberal from the University of Texas, Jim Smith, helped engineer a compromise statement that supported the "eventual elimination" of discriminatory education. But most white southern students found even that statement too liberal, and southern representation in the NSA subsequently remained small.[6]

Notwithstanding white southerners' lack of participation, the NSA became "the most important political forum for American students" during the 1950s. Despite occasional challenges from conservatives, the organization's leadership was characterized by moderate liberalism. Its officers tended to be somewhat left of center and concerned with social issues, but as historian Philip Altbach notes, they also "tended to be basically moderate in their view of the political system, since they were willing to engage in the 'sandlot' politics of the local campus in order to rise to the top of the NSA bureaucracy."[7]

In 1957, a white liberal from Texas, Ray Farabee, was elected president of the NSA. Farabee supported integration and believed that the NSA could play a role in furthering it through education. He petitioned the Marshall Field Foundation to support such an initiative, and in 1958 the foundation provided funding for the Southern Student Human Relations Project, which would conduct conferences and other activities in the field of race relations. The centerpiece of the program was a summer seminar to be held on a northern campus in the two weeks before the annual National Student Congress. The first two seminars, coordinated by Farabee, brought together an even mix of southern students from all-black, all-white, and desegregating schools. These seminars were fairly moderate affairs in that they preached communication and discussion over confrontation. During the 1958 seminar, participants role-played a meeting between students and their college president in which the students threatened to boycott classes and publish articles in the student press. The organizers intended the exercise as an example of how not to behave, encouraging participants not to "demand student rights without realizing that there are also administrative rights and student responsibilities." Other scenarios took an ambiguous approach toward activism. In one, a white student and a black student enter a segregated restaurant and hold an impromptu sit-in. The owner calls the white student aside and explains that he cannot serve blacks because "he has a family to support and cannot let his business be ruined."[8]

After February 1960, this ambiguity regarding the use of nonviolent direct action disappeared. In 1959, the NSA had received funding for an expansion of the southern seminars in the form of a year-round Southern Project to be headquartered in Atlanta. In addition to the annual seminars, the project would also conduct conferences on southern campuses and build a network in the South of former seminar participants and students who favored integration. The NSA hired as the new program's director Constance Curry, a graduate of Agnes Scott College in Atlanta who had been one of the few white southern students active in the NSA. When the Greensboro sit-ins broke out a couple of months after Curry took control of the project in December 1959, Curry, a Greensboro native, was in town visiting her family. She began meeting with the demonstrators, arranged for the NSA's vice president for national affairs to come to Greensboro, and became one of the more important "adults" involved in developing the regionwide sit-in movement. In fact, Curry was the only white person on SNCC's executive committee.[9]

The NSA's Southern Project attempted to bridge a gap between apolitical and conformist student government officers and the few white southern student activists who more often than not were motivated by religious ideals.

While the NSA was the preeminent organization of student governments in the United States, the Southern Project drew less from white campus politicos than it did from those who participated in religious organizations, such as chapters of the YMCA/YWCA and the Methodist Student Movement. Among the black participants, the dynamic was somewhat different, with student government leaders much more prevalent. Curry drew on her contacts within the South's small network of liberals to find participants for each year's summer seminars. After 1960, the curriculum was geared more directly toward activism, with sessions such as "Techniques of Action," led by James M. Lawson Jr. Zellner, for one, chose to become a SNCC organizer after participating in the 1961 seminar, spending the next two academic years traveling from campus to campus encouraging white students to embrace integration. For many white students, however, the central experience revolved as much around interracial contact as it did the curriculum. "I think that the white students were a lot more frightened and in awe of the 'interracial experience' than black students," Curry recalled. "It was doing something that was illegal and that they'd been taught was bad and wrong, and of course with the black students that was never the case."[10]

Some white students had more experience than others in dealing with African Americans. In his application to participate in the 1962 seminar, Clifford Hewitt, a student at Berry College in Rome, Georgia, candidly acknowledged his lack of interracial experience as well as his stubborn prejudices. Hewitt, from Jennings, Florida, was, like most of his fellow Berry students, "reared in the typical southern atmosphere of 'white supremacy.'" He had begun questioning his racial assumptions in high school, and college had provided additional opportunities "to think in a freer atmosphere. Even so it is not truly free here as most of the students are rabid segregationists and to express your ideas means quick and complete condemnation." Nevertheless, Hewitt had attended group meetings with students from the Atlanta University Center institutions. He felt freer with each contact but admitted that something kept holding him back, and he wanted to change. Hewitt also had intellectual reasons for wanting to attend: "My college at present *seems* to be rather dead intellectually and academically. I need to meet other students and see what the rest of the world is like." Moreover, Hewitt's attitude toward activism was at best ambiguous: "The problem of successful cooperation and mutual acceptance between Negro and white will come only by love and consideration. Pushing too fast will bring bloodshed and other serious consequences. Moving too slow or being too meek will likewise cause the movement to become stagnant."[11]

For Hewitt and others like him, activism was secondary to the desire to experience the wider world, and contact with African Americans, whom white students had been taught simultaneously to fear and ignore, represented an important step in venturing outside the parochialism of the traditional

South. Located in Rome, a small town in northwest Georgia, in the southern Appalachian Mountains, Berry College had been founded by Martha Berry at the turn of the twentieth century and in its earliest years was devoted to the education of students from rural backgrounds and to the regenerative power of work. After Martha Berry's death in 1952, the school increasingly emphasized its liberal arts curriculum and gradually phased out its requirement that all students work on campus, although it drew many students from modest socioeconomic backgrounds and allowed them to earn their education through manual-labor jobs on campus. Berry College was fairly far removed from the major racial conflicts of the day, and Rome, which had a small black population, did not experience the sit-in movement. In selecting Hewitt to attend the seminar, Curry and others probably hoped that he would return to the college and serve as a moderating influence.

Other seminar participants came from less isolated campuses, including the University of Alabama and the University of Mississippi, both of which were in the midst of desegregation crises. Miles Lovelace, a graduate student at Ole Miss studying ancient history, participated in the 1962 seminar and was subsequently one of the few students who ate with James Meredith after he enrolled. Lovelace, who had been an undergraduate at Memphis State, was so upset with the Meredith episode and its aftermath that he quit the graduate program and moved to Arizona.[12]

Another 1962 participant, University of Alabama junior Robert E. Roberts, was so moved by the events in Oxford and experiences at the seminar that he took a public, albeit anonymous, stand against segregation in an editorial for the Alabama student newspaper, the *Crimson White*. The piece criticized Mississippi governor Ross Barnett's actions, not just because integration had become inevitable and violence reflected badly on the South or because integration was the law of the land. Instead, Roberts rejected segregation as a dangerous idea that ultimately threatened anyone who did not enjoy the security of being in the majority: "If the bigot or the demagogue can muster a majority to turn on the Negro, will he necessarily stop there? Or will he next turn to the Catholic and the Jew, or the member of any other minority group?"[13] Roberts attributed his willingness to express such views to his participation in the summer seminar. Though he saw his actions as "hardly an act of moral courage," he told Curry that they were "perhaps an indication of fruit which the seminar" had borne.[14]

From Human Relations to Direct Action: The Campus Travelers

At various times during the 1960s, a cadre of southern movement leaders that included Bob Zellner, Mary King, Sandra (Casey) Cason (who married SDS leader Tom Hayden in 1961 and was subsequently known as Casey Hayden), and Sam Shirah visited college campuses throughout the region looking for potential activists. It was not an easy job. Students and faculty members hesitated to stake out even moderate positions on the racial issues that dominated activism in the early 1960s.

In part, this attempt to encourage the student movement from outside the campus emerged from established liberal organizations. The SCEF, which descended from the long-defunct Southern Conference for Human Welfare and for two decades had been on the front lines in an effort to liberalize the South, actively encouraged the nascent student movement in the early 1960s. SCEF published the *Southern Patriot*, which for thirty years chronicled any sign of activity that might fall under a broad heading of liberalization. When the sit-in movement broke out, SCEF stalwarts Anne and Carl Braden were at the center of the efforts to build on it. For some, SCEF's battles with the House Un-American Activities Committee tainted the progressive organization; its opponents labeled SCEF a communist-front organization, and any activist who associated with the Bradens ran the risk of receiving the "fellow-traveler" label.[15]

The Marshall Field Foundation, which funded the NSA's Southern Project, also sponsored campus travelers for several years through the National Student YWCA. Casey Hayden was the traveler in 1961 and 1962; the following year, Mary King, a white woman who would go on to work with SNCC, and Roberta Yancey, a black woman who recently had graduated from Barnard College, visited campuses. The stated purpose of the Field Foundation's grant was to examine academic freedom, but as Hayden noted to King in 1962, "academic freedom" provided a convenient cover to talk about race. According to King, "In university after university, academic freedom had been sacrificed on the altar of racial segregation. . . . Casey described social-science professors afraid to discuss race and the effects of segregation, and white students and professors feeling abysmally alone when they questioned the validity of racial segregation. She told of how the fear of being labeled communist, a tangible threat, kept scores of professors from speaking out on southern campuses on the issue of race."[16]

Given these conditions, the idea of mobilizing students to act against segregation often seemed unrealistic. King and Yancey tended to take a practical approach aimed at broadening the outlook of provincial students, focusing on the creation of interracial experiences along the lines of the NSA's Southern Project. "As a result of speaking with each other about race relations, the participating students, we hoped, would be more likely to overcome their fear and exert some influence when they returned to their campuses," King recalled. The similarities with the NSA seminars were not coincidental and did not simply reflect their common funding source. The network of people interested in southern social change was fairly small. Hayden, King, and Yancey were based in a building at 41 Exchange Place in Atlanta that also housed the offices of Curry and the NSA; Jean Fairfax and the American Friends Service Committee; and the World University Service. The Georgia Bureau of Investigation, which frequently monitored the building, considered it a hotbed of dangerous radicals.[17]

The activities of Hayden, King, Yancey, and Curry constituted a classic example of what at the time was called "human relations" work. According to this philosophy, bringing black and white people together to talk would cause stereotypes to fall by the wayside. The approach found its fullest expression in the actions of the Southern Regional Council (SRC) and its state councils on human relations. The SRC had been created in 1944, largely by white and black educators, journalists, and religious leaders; most of its members were white and moderately liberal. In its early years, it sought to improve race relations within a segregated society through research and education, but when this approach produced few results, the council's board of directors endorsed desegregation.[18] In some Deep South states, involvement with the state human relations council, which usually took a mild approach to social change, represented a fairly radical position. Nevertheless, the new possibilities for activism initiated by the sit-in movement redefined the work of southern campus travelers.[19]

Although the human relations model informed the efforts of early campus travelers, the sit-in movement opened up new possibilities and approaches, which were apparent in Zellner's work. During his two years as a campus traveler for SNCC's White Student Project (funded in part by SCEF), Zellner was as much a soldier in the direct-action challenge to segregation as he was an initiator of interracial meetings. In fact, while Zellner devoted considerable attention to setting up contacts between black and white students, his frequent arrests for involvement in demonstrations compromised his ability to serve as an effective human relations facilitator. By the middle of the decade, Zellner expressed his preference for "action" (presumably of the sort that tended to lead to arrests) over "talk" (as embodied in the human relations work of the late 1950s). "You get people in the habit of talking, and they do it the rest of their lives," he groused in a 1965 critique of the Southern Project.[20]

The son of a Methodist minister and former Ku Klux Klan member who had undergone a conversion to racial liberalism, Zellner grew up sharing his parents' liberal racial assumptions. But Zellner's movement baptism came during the 1960–61 academic year, when he was a senior at Huntingdon College in Montgomery, Alabama. Assigned to study the "race problem" and then write a paper presenting a solution, Zellner and four other students researched the topic by attending an annual workshop on nonviolence sponsored by the Montgomery Improvement Association, which had led the 1955–56 bus boycott. Their participation in interracial meetings, along with their decision to take up a collection for Ralph D. Abernathy and other ministers who were defendants in a lawsuit, caused a controversy at Huntingdon, which announced a policy against attending interracial meetings.[21]

Zellner's actions created friction with Huntingdon's administrators, but he nevertheless graduated in the spring of 1961 and assumed his new responsibilities as the campus traveler for SNCC's White Student Project in the fall. With funding from SCEF, Zellner was to contact white students on southern campuses and interpret the civil rights movement to them, with a goal of interesting them in taking some sort of constructive action. During the first year, Zellner visited fifteen white or predominantly white schools and thirteen black schools, all in the South. He had some success in setting up contacts between white and black students. In Alabama, he arranged secret meetings between students at white Birmingham-Southern College and black Miles College and set up contacts between the University of Alabama and Stillman College and Alabama State and Huntingdon Colleges.[22] While these contacts did not produce much interracial action against segregation, they were no doubt significant experiences for participants on both sides of the color line. Nevertheless, as Zellner acknowledged in a May 1961 report, his desire to participate in the movement ultimately compromised his ability to reach white students. First in McComb, Mississippi, and then in Albany, Georgia; Baton Rouge, Louisiana; and Talladega, Alabama, Zellner's participation in the movement resulted in arrests and an increasingly high profile as a proponent of integration. He believed that he could not explain the movement to white students "unless I myself became an integral part of it." However, "of course my personality make up and psychology also tended to draw me into the area of action." But his high profile made it hard for him to enter college campuses without attracting attention. In one instance, Zellner's presence at Huntingdon College prompted a "mob" of forty-five to fifty students to threaten physical harm if he did not leave the campus.[23]

Zellner's experiences demonstrated the dramatic gap between movement activists and even moderate white students. More important, his relative success in organizing black students, as in the Talladega College movement in the spring of 1962, suggested the gap between black students and most white students. A traveler who was less inclined to throw himself into the thick of the movement might have had more success in coaxing white southerners toward some level of involvement. Zellner's entanglement with southern law enforcement officials certainly prevented him from devoting his full attention to white southern students. In 1962, Zellner devoted three pages of his ten-page year-end report to his efforts to find a white lawyer in Mississippi who would represent him. However, in much of the South, the level of tolerance for even the slightest identification with the goals and tactics of the civil rights movement was low. Given that the traveler's job description included reaching "that 'significant minority' of white students who potentially will join the Negro students in *ac-

tion," even the most skilled of emissaries would have had difficulty not calling attention to his or her actions. Zellner later acknowledged that some members of the SSOC, an effort to encourage southern student activism, mainly among white students, that emerged in 1964, "thought that I was maybe a little stand-offish from the white student organizing because of my 'special position' inside SNCC," but he defended himself by noting that "my dedication to organizing white southerners lasted much longer than my association with SNCC."[24]

In the fall of 1963, Zellner moved to Massachusetts for graduate study (and continued activism) at Brandeis University. His successor in the White Student Project was Shirah, whose style of campus traveling closely resembled that of Zellner. Shirah was the son of a Methodist minister at whose church George Wallace served as Sunday school superintendent. Shirah often found that the fields were not ready for harvest when he visited campuses but by early 1964 could point to some progress: "No longer is it one or two white students active; often there are hundreds. For example, Nashville, Atlanta, Tallahassee and Gainesville, Fla., and Chapel Hill, N.C., are spots where large movements of white students have developed." Although the black freedom movement had inspired the actions of white students, "at this point there is actually more motion on predominantly white campuses than on Negro ones."[25] Shirah's comments in part demonstrate the greater deprivation of academic freedom on black campuses than on white ones. But his remarks also illustrate trends in the black student movement. After 1961, SNCC increasingly turned its attention to community organizing, specifically voter registration and education in Mississippi.

The Movement and the Black Campus at Middecade

SNCC and CORE were the two most important organizations in the spread of the sit-in movement in the early 1960s. They disseminated information, trained activists, and provided guidance that was crucial in making the movement a regional and national phenomenon rather than a handful of isolated local actions. Nevertheless, both organizations struggled at times to develop an effective approach to organizing students and campuses. Despite its name, SNCC's primary purpose after the end of the most active phase of the sit-in movement was organizing communities, not students or campuses. SNCC continued to draw from a pool of student activists as well as to serve as an important — perhaps the most important — conduit between the movement and the campus throughout the early 1960s. But its campus organizing efforts remained more a byproduct than a driving force. Similarly, although CORE had a substantial presence on campuses in Florida, Louisiana, and the Carolinas, such efforts were always means to a larger end, never an end in and of themselves. Southern campus organizing waxed and waned in the early 1960s, and inconsistent attention from the two main organizations promoting the southern student movement of the early 1960s played a role in that process.

SNCC's internal struggle to define itself has been well documented. Initially a loosely connected network designed to facilitate communication among local movements, SNCC developed into a vanguard organization whose members developed a reputation for bravery for their willingness to move into the most dangerous parts of the South to organize local people. Though progressive black and white southern students continued to look to SNCC for guidance, group leaders' attention was divided. A debate between proponents of direct action versus proponents of voter registration consumed much of the organization's energy, and by 1962, SNCC organizers were increasingly drawn to rural communities in the Deep South — Mississippi and southwestern Georgia, for example — rather than the urban and Upper South locales where the sit-in movement had been most effective. In 1964, SNCC again began directing attention at black campuses in the South, assigning Stanley L. Wise to travel to the institutions to locate and train potential activists. By then, activism on many black campuses had ebbed, just as more significant numbers of white students in some pockets of the South were beginning to experiment with direct-action techniques.

The connections between SNCC and black campuses in Alabama were tenuous. Wise spent part of the fall of 1964 investigating a possible work-study program for students, a topic on which he conducted numerous meetings with university administrators. But he also investigated possibilities for activism, and at times the prospects looked dim. In Tuscaloosa, home of Stillman College, Wise found "very definite interest but apparently no effective directions or means of expression. Organization here is very stagnant. The will to demonstrate has been stymied because of the failure of the boycott and thus many persons appear discouraged."[26] At other times, he experienced the kinds of false starts and dead ends that regularly challenged campus travelers. He arrived in Mobile after most students had been evacuated for a hurricane. He arrived at Alabama State on a weekend and found few people since the school had no dorm facilities. Noted Wise, "It is paramount that we return there during the week." Wise also found some promising leads. In Talladega, the community seemed "ready for some types of action." However, the city's civil rights structure appeared "leaderless and without adequate direction in any area and as a result many of their projects are stifled before they get off the ground."[27]

SNCC subsequently devoted more attention to black campuses, a renewed focus that coincided with the rise of Black Power in the mid-1960s as well as with the emergence of a sharpened critique of the Negro college that emerged from within the black freedom movement and a vision of a black university that could act as a tool of African American liberation.

"SNCC's Brother in the North" Comes South: SDS

Similar visions of the university as a tool of liberation and social change eventually emerged from within the New Left, in large part as a result of SDS. SDS evolved in the early 1960s from the Student League from Industrial Democracy but broke with the "adult" organization by refusing specifically to exclude communists. This organizational and ideological openness helped make SDS the symbol of the New Left, and its widely circulated Port Huron Statement became one of the scriptures of the 1960s student movement. Indeed, "participatory democracy" became one of the defining ideals of the New Left, filtering to southern campuses and helping to inform the activism that developed in the region. Nevertheless, while the South played an important role in the early years of SDS, the region always posed problems for the organization.

In the fall of 1961, Tom Hayden, a midwestern student activist, gained renown for taking a beating in a small southern town. Hayden was a University of Michigan student whose political evolution had brought him to McComb, Mississippi, where SNCC was attempting to register African Americans to vote. On 11 October, an assailant dragged Hayden and another northern student, Paul Potter, from a car and beat them. An Associated Press photographer captured the episode, and the resulting photo, showing Hayden on the ground, protecting himself from blows, ran in newspapers throughout the country. Hayden became a symbol for white students who were willing to lay their bodies on the line for social change. In later years, Hayden's career as an activist came to symbolize for many the rise and fall of the New Left and its best-known organizational manifestation, SDS.[28]

Hayden's trip to McComb was an important step in his political evolution from thoughtful student journalist to activist. The previous summer, Hayden had hitchhiked to California to cover the Democratic National Convention for the *Michigan Daily*. While there, he had encountered an intense group of politically minded student activists at the University of California in Berkeley. Later that summer, he traveled to the National Student Congress at the University of Minnesota, where he connected with a number of southern civil rights activists, among them Casey Cason, whom he later married. In early 1961, Hayden traveled to Fayette County, Tennessee, where he reported for the *Daily* on the plight of sharecroppers who had been evicted for attempting to register to vote. The experience offered a preview of what he would see in McComb, where SNCC organizers faced hostility as they attempted to educate and register voters. To Hayden, now serving as the SDS liaison to the southern civil rights movement, SNCC activists who risked their lives for the movement offered a stirring model for young people to escape "the middle-class emptiness of alienation."[29]

Thanks in part to Hayden's influence, civil rights became the first issue that SDS emphasized. The choice allowed the organization, which was casting about for an issue to ignite student activism, to make a real impact. Other issues resonated with the SDS leadership, including anti-atomic-bomb activity, peace research, academic freedom, poverty, and university reform. Moreover, as SDS evolved, it adopted a multi-issue orientation that incorporated all of these concerns. But civil rights had the greatest moral power and eventually achieved the greatest national publicity.[30] Thus, the South played a key role in SDS's development. SDS, in turn, emerged as a powerful force in the student movement, though historians have perhaps overemphasized its importance and thus minimized the significant roles played by other student and movement organizations, especially in the South. By the end of the decade, SDS — as a symbol if not always as an organized presence — loomed large on southern campuses. Even at its height, however, it was always just one of a number of influential movement organizations seeking to leave their imprint on southern college campuses

Although the southern civil rights movement had played an important formative role in SDS, the organization's leaders had trouble building a base in the South. From the beginning, SDS identified itself with and sought ways to support SNCC. As SDS's southern liaison, Hayden wrote dispatches on SNCC's activities in Mississippi to publicize and interpret the group's efforts to the rest of the country. In this sense, SDS became a sort of northern affiliate of SNCC — as one member phrased it, "SNCC's brother in the North." But by 1962, SNCC was beginning to make a name for itself apart from Hayden and SDS. At the same time, while SDS was beginning to establish chapters in the Northeast and Midwest, it seemed to lack direction regarding how to deal with the South and its campuses, as the failed 1962 Chapel Hill conference indicated.[31]

The disappointment at Chapel Hill seemed to reflect more general uncertainties regarding a proper approach to organizing in the South. A late-1962 analysis by Robb Burlage, a former undergraduate student and campus newspaper editor at the University of Texas and founding member of SDS, brought a series of difficult questions: "What is our exact relationship with SNCC now? We sometimes advertise ourselves as SNCC's brother in the North . . . but just how close are we . . . ? We must seriously ask the question: what can we *do* for organizations now working in the South? What can we *do* for campuses now organizing local action or discussion groups?" Burlage also noted a more practical problem — the lack of a staff person in the region who was working to connect SDS with southern campuses. "We have NOONE in the REAL SOUTH right now who is full-time or even 'part-time' SDS," Burlage declared. The solution, Burlage suggested, was opening the lines of communication within the region.[32]

But subsequent progress was slow. As of December 1963, the University of Texas and North Texas State had the South's only SDS chapters, though the

Universities of Tennessee and South Carolina showed "good potentialities for chapter organization."[33] Prior to 1968, only a handful of SDS chapters operated in the South.[34]

"What Is the Role of the Southern White?": The SSOC

One night in January 1964, a conversation among a group of white student activists in Nashville turned to the dilemma of white students in the South. In the previous weeks, they had been involved in a direct-action campaign against a segregated restaurant, efforts that had brought them contacts within both the black freedom struggle and the student movement developing outside the South. "We were talking about the problem of white Southern students, how isolated they were," one of the participants, Sue Thrasher, recalled. "We didn't feel they could be reached through the Northern white students who were beginning to come South then." Northern students' tendency to make facile, often uninformed judgments about the South irritated the Tennesseans. No supporters of segregation, they nevertheless believed that students with a firsthand view of the complexities of the South could best reach white students in the region. What was needed, they concluded, was some sort of effort to combat the isolation by creating a network of white student activists throughout the South.[35]

With the help of Shirah, whose campus travels brought him the most complete knowledge about white student activism, the Nashville group invited all of the region's activist groups to attend an April 1964 conference in Nashville. Some forty-five students from fifteen predominantly white institutions in ten southern states responded — representatives from the Universities of North Carolina, Georgia, Florida, and Tennessee; Duke, Tulane, and Emory Universities; and Millsaps (Mississippi), Maryville (Tennessee), Lynchburg (Virginia), and Clemson Colleges. Some had been participating in their local movements for months, even years. Others had only recently become acquainted with the concept of activism. One common thread, however, seemed to be a sense of isolation as rebels against southern orthodoxy. The Nashville meeting provided many participants with an opportunity to chip away at that feeling of being alone. Thrasher recalled the excitement among people who "had gone through some of the same things white southerners went through when they got involved, which is this immediate isolation from your peers and possibly from your family."[36]

The formation of SSOC provided a new focus for white student activism. The meeting itself consisted of a series of presentations, workshops, and discussions. Ed Hamlett, who had been with SNCC's White Southern Student Project for three months, gave a keynote address that encouraged students who had discovered activism through the civil rights movement to look beyond that movement and "embrace broader issues to meet the many problems of Southern politics and economy." Hamlett also urged the students to return to the campuses ready to fight not only for desegregation but also for civil liberties and academic freedom. At the same time, however, he suggested that the students should not dwell solely on campus issues; instead, they should be willing to move into the community with antipoverty, open-housing, and voter registration campaigns.[37]

ssoc's founding document, "We'll Take Our Stand," reinforced this expanded view of activism. The statement was designed to be for ssoc what the Port Huron Statement was for sds — a manifesto that would capture its audience's imagination. But while similarities existed between the two documents — not surprising, since the author of "We'll Take Our Stand," Burlage, wrote the economics section of the Port Huron Statement — the ssoc paper was designed specifically to reach white southern students. As an undergraduate at the University of Texas in the late 1950s and early 1960s, Burlage and his wife, Dorothy Dawson Burlage, had participated in civil rights demonstrations. But Burlage's concern with the South and its problems predated his undergraduate activism. His father had been a pharmacy professor at the University of North Carolina, home of Howard Odum and other regionalists, and Burlage admired their approach to regional change. The regionalists had defined themselves in opposition to the Nashville agrarians who published a 1930 collection of essays, *I'll Take My Stand*. The essays argued for a rejection of modernization and industrialization in its various guises in favor of a return to the ideals of the southern agrarian life.[38]

In the ssoc founding statement, Burlage explicitly played off the agrarians' ideas. He rejected their backward-looking efforts to re-create a feudal society that included the subjugation of African Americans but seized on the agrarians' refusal to embrace industrialization and their corresponding willingness to see the South as a region with distinctive traits that separated it from the rest of the nation. In other writings, Burlage, who spent some time in graduate study in economics at Harvard, had explored the idea of the South as an "underdeveloped country."[39] In the ssoc manifesto, Burlage again emphasized the region's distinctive problems: "Our Southland is still the leading sufferer and battleground of the war against racism, poverty, injustice and autocracy," he declared. "It is our intention to win that struggle in our Southland in our lifetime — tomorrow is not soon enough." The manifesto proclaimed that ssoc students would return to their colleges and their communities "to create non-violent political and direct action movements dedicated to the sort of social change throughout the South and nation which is necessary to achieve our stated goals." These goals included the abolition of segregation, "an end to personal poverty and deprivation," and the transformation of the

South into a place "where industries and large cities can blend into farms and natural rural splendor to provide meaningful work and leisure opportunities for all."[40]

Burlage's device of using a thirty-year-old document written by agrarian conservatives as a jumping-off point for a manifesto of progressive reform was at best awkward. The difficulties inherent in such an endeavor symbolize the problems that plagued ssoc during the next five years. Grappling with the agrarians' legacy was part of a larger project to embrace the parts of southern history and regional distinctiveness that could be employed to support social change while rejecting those parts that were problematic. In practical terms, ssoc wrestled with the question of how to mobilize a population of white students that remained largely apolitical and conformist. During the next few years, ssoc activists as well as those in other organizations debated strategies for reaching the white South. Should they concentrate on students or attempt to organize within other groups, possibly labor? Should they concentrate on those white students who were already inclined toward left-liberal activism, or should they set their sights on drawing a broader array of moderates into the activist fold?[41]

The final problem was particularly thorny. By concentrating on the small number of radical students, ssoc risked alienating the moderates. But if the organization zeroed in on moderates, it risked watering down its program to the point that it would produce little substantive change. The dilemma was not new for southern activists, but the politics of the early 1960s made it particularly prominent. As Anne and Carl Braden noted in a position paper written for sds's 1962 Chapel Hill conference, the gap between "militant Negro movement of the South and the *liberal* white Southerner" had widened with the emergence of nonviolent direct action. White southerners who considered themselves liberal — and who fell decidedly within the tradition of southern liberal gradualists — still often insisted that direct action was dangerous and should be rejected in favor of a more cautious approach. Meanwhile, leaders in the black freedom struggle argued that the time for action had come. The Bradens believed that more white southerners needed to commit themselves to action, writing, "It may not always be immediately obvious, but two white people on an otherwise Negro picketline may bring a more profound influence in a white community than 50 white people at a discussion session on 'race relations.'"[42]

But if ssoc faced the same sort of dilemma outlined by the Bradens, then the organization's existence suggested the changes that had occurred over the two years between when they wrote the discussion paper and the ssoc's founding convention. ssoc's formation represented the culmination of activist ferment among white students in pockets throughout the South. White students had responded to the Bradens' and others' calls for action, indicating that southern liberals had begun to reject the idea of slow, careful social change. If a left-liberal/moderate gap still existed in the South, it had at least begun to narrow.

SSOC's founding conference also revealed that the still inchoate white southern student movement would be about more than civil rights. Hamlett's keynote address demonstrated this desire to move beyond a concern with racial inequality to a deeper analysis. "As students in the South, are we not questioning our entire system which oppresses the white as well as the Negro?" Hamlett asked. He went on to outline an array of southern problems that should concern white students, including inferior education, the one-party political system, the lack of civil liberties, and the priorities of the federal government. "Is there a significant body of students, who are interested in seeing that half of the national budget which goes for weapons of mass destruction directed instead toward weapons for a real war on poverty — for potential living power instead of killing power?" To Hamlett, this list of broader concerns flowed naturally from the black freedom struggle, which had been the point of entry for most white southern students. "The civil rights movement, in a sense, has freed the Southern white. It has allowed him to get outside himself, and to think about new ideas."[43]

In many ways, Hamlett's vision was fulfilled as a growing number of white southern students seized on the full range of issues he had outlined. The SSOC conference had signified a transition in the political mobilization of white students in the South. A broader base of student activists would now address not only civil rights but other issues.

By middecade, SSOC's emergence signaled new possibilities for student political mobilization. In 1965, the Field Foundation received four applications for a total of one hundred thousand dollars' worth of student programs in the South. The applications presented a quandary for Leslie Dunbar, the foundation's executive director and a former executive director of the Southern Regional Council. Funding them all was not an option. How could the foundation maximize its investment? The two most significant proposals came from the NSA (for the continuation of its Southern Project, which the foundation had funded since 1959) and the SSOC. And Dunbar believed that those two proposals contained too much overlap. In late November, Dunbar asked NSA president Philip Sherburne some pointed questions about the relevance and effectiveness of the Southern Project's approach. Dunbar suggested that NSA focus its southern efforts on supporting SSOC: "Isn't a movement like SSOC's what the Southern Project of NSA always wanted and worked to see created?" Suggesting that NSA's proposal to recast and enlarge the Southern Project lacked definition, Dunbar wondered whether the human relations approach had become "somewhat outmoded."[44]

Sherburne responded by attempting to differentiate the NSA's and SSOC's organizational strategies in the South. SSOC focused on locating "liberal to radical students" on southern campuses, bringing them together around some issue, and then connecting them with other like-minded groups "to form a liberal Southern student voice" that could produce "organized confrontation of issues." But, according to Sherburne, this approach made it difficult for SSOC to work with leaders of student organizations: the group's liberal-radical focus made it "very suspect" with members of the campus establishment. NSA offered a greater ability to reach "students of moderate or nonpolitical orientation" as well as technical expertise on a host of issues, including education, academic freedom, and poverty. "The South needs an organization that can accomplish the objectives of SSOC," Sherburne argued. "It also seems to me that the South cannot afford to be without a group that accomplishes the goals that I do not feel that SSOC can accomplish. . . . We have the experience, the credibility and the backup resources to accomplish the job." Nevertheless, Sherburne conceded that the human relations approach was outmoded: "It was certainly our feeling that the day of inter-racial gatherings over tea and crumpets (or an RC [Cola] and a Moon-Pie) is past, or that we should at least speed it on its way," Sherburne stated. Activists needed to get students engaged in the issues that troubled the South: "The way in which you provide students with a better understanding of the other race and its implications, is by focusing on issues which most clearly bring problems of racial discrimination to the fore. Poverty, Southern political structures, secondary school reform, cycles of Negro education, unemployment cycles, and civil liberties are just a few areas of issues that need to be explored."[45] The NSA modified its request, dropping the seminars, and Field provided a two-year grant of seventy thousand dollars, twenty thousand less than the NSA had requested.[46]

The exchange reflected not only the evolution in approaches to student political mobilization but also some level of frustration with the slow pace of the organization of southern students. At the same time that Dunbar and Sherburne corresponded, students at Berkeley were in the midst of the Free Speech Movement. While neither correspondent mentioned Berkeley, those images could not have been far from either Dunbar's or Sherburne's mind. Dunbar drew an implicit contrast between southern students and the "radical" editors of the University of Michigan student newspaper, with whom he had met in October. Ironically, Dunbar noted, two of the members of the paper's editorial board were from the South, an indication of the potential that existed on southern campuses. Nevertheless, Dunbar seemed to suggest that the southern student movement in 1965 was all potential, raising "these questions out of my concern for the student movement, if that can be the correct word, in the South. It is weak."[47]

CHAPTER FIVE

From the Community to the Campus, from University Reform to Student Power

IN THE SPRING of 1965, Berkeley Free Speech Movement (FSM) veteran Steven Weissman toured the South. He visited twenty-seven colleges in ten southern states, and twenty-five hundred students heard him talk about the recent demonstrations at Berkeley and the idea of "university reform," a phrase that was beginning to gain currency. Sponsored by the Southern Student Organizing Committee (SSOC), Weissman's tour represented an effort to export the Berkeley movement to southern campuses. "Berkeley came to UNC Sunday night," the University of North Carolina's *Daily Tar Heel* reported. "Free Speech Movement leader Steve Weissman excited wild applause from a small audience, many of them student activists, as he called for student-faculty control of universities." If anyplace was ready to become a southern Berkeley, it was Chapel Hill. In June 1963, the North Carolina State Legislature had passed a law denying communists or fellow travelers the right to speak on state-supported campuses. A swipe at civil rights activity in Chapel Hill, the Speaker Ban's limits on campus speech had already ignited some opposition at UNC. Weissman called on students to "organize and force the faculty to speak as a body," suggesting that if the faculty were collectively to invite a communist speaker to the campus, legislators would be unable to enforce the law. The *Daily Tar Heel* opposed what it called the "we want everything or we'll keep demonstrating until we get it" attitude: "The only result of 'collective student action' here against, say the Speaker Ban, would be a further alienation of the General Assembly and a loud cry from many North Carolinians that UNC has fallen prey to communists."[1]

Despite the *Daily Tar Heel* editorial, a movement against the Speaker Ban attracted a broad spectrum of support from self-styled New Leftists and main-

136

stream student leaders during 1966. Like other movements against speech restrictions and for student rights, UNC's opposition to the Speaker Ban suggested the potential of campus issues to mobilize southern students. Less polarizing than civil rights or Vietnam, these campus issues sometimes attracted students who otherwise might have stayed on the sidelines. Organizers thus sought to use such issues to jump-start campus movements. But organizing around campus issues reflected more than a potential route to activism. Debates over limits on speech and academic freedom, the rights of students within an academic community, and the meaning and relevance of education grew from the local soil. On campuses still sorting out the rubble left by clashes over student participation in nonviolent direct-action campaigns and institutional desegregation, these questions had particular relevance. In this respect, although the FSM can be seen as an influence on southern free-speech and university-reform movements of the second half of the 1960s, the roots in the South were deeper, and the movements were homegrown.

University Reform and Southern Student Organizing

Writing in late 1964, the new Southern Project director for the U.S. National Student Association (NSA), Hayes Mizell, noted the problems encountered by any progressive organization seeking to organize southern students, the majority of whose politics remained conservative. Mizell's central concern was SSOC, which was struggling with its identity. After noting that the SSOC's stated purpose was to reach "students of minimum commitment" as well as "students of maximum commitment," Mizell further defined these two groups. Students in the first group, whom Mizell labeled "moderate/new liberal" students, usually had "only recently become concerned with social and political questions." They tended to come from middle-class backgrounds, to have a religious orientation, and to fear creating controversy. The only thing separating members of this group from their "Goldwater-supporting classmates," Mizell argued, was a social conscience and a need to find an outlet for this concern. Despite the obvious limitations, Mizell argued that people in this category were important because they could provide a link with the "campus power structure." Students in the second group, "the more committed/radical members of the Left," often rose from the ranks of the moderate/new liberals, but "they have long since become more knowledgeable, more sophisticated, and even more articulate." They were more willing to act than new liberals but also had more difficulty reaching their fellow students, who regarded them with suspicion. Mizell concluded that the SSOC needed to make a "renewed and stronger" attempt to reach out to moderate/new liberal students. To do so, however, would require playing down issues and strategies that were likely to alienate these students, including U.S.

involvement in Vietnam, peace, and massive student political action. Instead, Mizell argued, the ssoc should concentrate on issues with which moderate/new liberals were familiar: civil rights, poverty, education, politics, and academic freedom.[2]

Academic freedom and related campus issues were especially potent because it was possible to envision a broad-based coalition of students united behind the goal of freeing students to question and learn. Postadolescents enjoying their first taste of freedom away from home and parents can find limits especially distasteful. But the context of the 1960s made this tendency even more pronounced. Rebellion against campus limits of all types coincided with other national forces, including a revolution against existing sexual mores and the retreat of American colleges and universities from the doctrine of in loco parentis. Both forces were slower to reach the South than other parts of the nation. Beyond these broad forces, however, lay more specific questions about the roles that students could and should play on campus and in society and more fundamentally about what higher education should look like in the South and the nation. As the southern student movement broadened its base, it engaged these issues in the guise of university reform and what by 1967 became known as "student power." These issues ultimately became productive ones for southern student activism. In terms of concrete results, the southern student movement's drive to reform higher education was arguably its most effective project. By the end of the decade, in loco parentis had been crippled and students had won an increased role in the decision-making processes on many campuses. Moreover, the student movement for university reform produced a number of changes in curricula and pedagogical practices. Demands for relevance brought new courses as well as a greater flexibility for students to determine their own course of study.

Berkeley and the South

Many accounts portray the FSM as the key event in the development of 1960s campus activism. In 1970, the President's Commission on Campus Unrest, which investigated student activism in the wake of deaths at Kent State University and Jackson State College, labeled Berkeley students' employment of civil rights tactics on the campus the "Berkeley invention."[3] Scholars subsequently have emphasized the FSM's catalytic role in 1960s student activism. "FSM was critical," Winifred Breines has argued, "because, as the first major white student rebellion, it laid down the terms for many others during the rest of the Sixties." Berkeley, according to Breines, provided the "ideas, demands, and experiences" that resurfaced "time and again" on other northern college campuses. Indeed, coming after years of fermenting civil rights protest, Berkeley's mobilization seemed to provide an exciting new model of action for white students outside the South.[4]

The FSM and the politicized Berkeley campus more generally were also important symbols for southern students. These images contributed to a process, already in motion, in which students questioned the morality of southern society and the university's proper role in addressing these questions. The FSM provided a blueprint for action for activists on some southern campuses and helped refine the vocabulary with which students addressed the university's role in larger societal issues. For their part, more conservative students saw Berkeley as representing the dangerous possibilities of a campus out of control. And administrators sought to prevent "another Berkeley." The mid-1960s witnessed the slow construction of a southern student movement, made possible in part by the breakdown of legalized segregation, which dissolved that requirement of the South's rigid orthodoxy. The ranks of committed participants in the "campus Left" remained small, and these students continued to struggle to find issues that would increase participation without diluting the agenda.

The FSM was an uprising of University of California students against regulations that forbade political activists from passing out literature, soliciting money, or organizing support from card tables set up on the edge of the Berkeley campus. At one level, it represented a movement for academic freedom; at another level, it represented a student indictment of Cold War restrictions on political discussion as well as a condemnation of the impersonal education of the modern "multiversity," a term coined by University of California president Clark Kerr. Berkeley students turned Kerr's description on its head. Kerr had seen the modern university as more useful to society, whereas students argued that it had become more vulnerable to outside forces and had lost sight of its responsibility to its students. If, as Kerr had suggested, knowledge was now an industry and universities were now factories, complete with managers and employees, then students must be the raw materials in the equation. Universities had "become factories to produce technicians rather than places to live student lives," FSM leader Mario Savio declared. "And this perversion develops great resentment on the part of the students."[5]

In time, the student movement that Berkeley helped move forward addressed a long list of issues, from the war in Vietnam to women's rights. Indeed, Berkeley students had deliberately extended their critique beyond the campus. Drawing on the language of the Beats and cultural critics of the 1950s, they complained about the simultaneous blandness and vulgarity of modern American society, of which the university was only a part. But despite these tendencies toward a broader analysis of U.S. problems, the FSM's primary contribution was to popularize scrutiny of the university's role in society and the student's role in the university. Students' discontent with their role was nothing new. Students had previously expressed this discontent and its corresponding antiauthoritarianism in rebellions against professors, which occurred with special frequency in nineteenth-century southern colleges. What was new in the 1960s was the political content that usually was connected to these rebellions. The dissemination of the FSM's rhetoric gave northern, middle-class, white students a way to place themselves in the social movements of the time. Activists engaged freely in the practice of making connections, and student critics of higher education had no problem finding the similarities between their oppression and that of black people.

The relationship between Berkeley and the South was multifaceted. If Berkeley was a catalyst for the student movement in the 1960s, then the southern civil rights movement was a catalyst for Berkeley. In the spring of 1960, the NSA had coordinated efforts to involve northern students in sympathy protests. Civil rights had also been crucial in formative years of Students for a Democratic Society (SDS), which went on to follow patterns established by the Student Nonviolent Coordinating Committee (SNCC) throughout much of the 1960s.

The most important event in the exportation of the civil rights movement to campuses throughout the United States was importation of a thousand or so white student volunteers to Mississippi in the summer of 1964. They came south for a large-scale voter registration project that included an education component called Freedom Schools and community centers. Looking for volunteers, SNCC recruited heavily from the country's most elite colleges and universities. Harvard, Yale, Stanford, Princeton, and their ilk accounted for nearly 40 percent of the applicants.[6] The presence of these volunteers, most of whom were white and were not from the South, was important for a number of reasons. The Freedom Summer students brought with them attention from media outlets and federal law enforcement officials, and the attention only increased when two white volunteers and a black SNCC worker were murdered. Some of the volunteers also brought with them paternalistic attitudes, which increased racial tensions and helped to move SNCC toward its eventual policy of excluding whites from membership. Tensions also developed around the gendered division of labor, beginning discussions by female volunteers that eventually led to the development of the women's liberation movement. Freedom Summer also played a crucial role in disseminating the tactics and philosophy of the civil rights movement to elite private and public campuses in the East, Midwest, and West Coast. For many of the participants, Freedom Summer was the central event in a process of political radicalization and personal movement away from various aspects of mainstream society and toward an alternate vision of America and themselves.[7]

At no institution was the impact of Freedom Summer more direct than

Berkeley. Of the twenty-one Mississippi summer volunteers known to have returned to the university for the fall semester, twelve showed up on the list of those arrested in connection with the 2–3 December sit-in at Sproul Hall. Both Weissman and Savio, two of the most important leaders of the FSM, were Freedom Summer participants. Tactically and philosophically, the contributions of the southern student movement and of Freedom Summer to the FSM also were tangible. They included the use of the sit-in; SNCC's anarchic, consensual style of decision making; "freedom classes" as an alternative to regular university offerings; freedom songs; and, most important, a general identification with the civil rights movement. "Last summer I went to Mississippi to join the struggle there for civil rights," said Savio. "This fall I am engaged in another phase of the same struggle, this time in Berkeley." To Savio, the right to participate as citizens in democratic society and the right to due process of law lay at the heart of both movements. Moreover, the enemy was the same: "In Mississippi an autocratic and powerful minority rules, through organized violence, to suppress the vast, virtually powerless, majority. In California, the privileged minority manipulates the University bureaucracy to suppress the student's political expression."[8]

University Reform, Southern Style

Ironically, though Freedom Summer happened in the South, its effects on southern campuses were muted. About 11 percent of the applicants for Freedom Summer were from southern schools, and almost half of these southerners were black.[9] Not surprisingly, then, the narrative of idealistic white students stunned by their first encounter with segregation and disfranchisement does not work for southern campuses. The Berkeley movement, however, caught the attention of some southern students, eliciting reactions that ranged from awe to anger. Carlton Brown Jr., editor in chief of the University of Georgia's *Red and Black*, lamented the effects of the Berkeley revolt, which he characterized as a "revolution against law and order," and described the subsequent wave of protests that Berkeley had spawned as a "malignant disease." "If students in our institutions of higher learning haven't got anything better to do than conjure up demonstrations, they might as well leave," Brown declared. "But, then they'd get drafted."[10] Others found some aspects of the FSM admirable, although they had some difficulty endorsing the movement in its entirety. Emory's E. Culpepper Clark, who served in the school's student senate, represented the opinions of many traditional student leaders when he declared that the ideals represented by Berkeley were fine but the means that the students employed were wrong.[11] At the University of North Carolina, a *Daily Tar Heel* reporter who set out to discover what his fellow students thought of the Berkeley movement found a mixture of opinions. "I would generally defend their right to demonstrate," said

Charles Nash, a sophomore economics major from High Point, North Carolina, "but I question whether the demonstrators want political freedom or just want to raise a lot of cain."[12] The headline from an article in Emory University's *Wheel* after Weissman's April 1965 speech at the Atlanta university more succinctly captured the perception of many southern students of the FSM: "Bearded Radical Hits Suppression."[13]

Some were more sympathetic. The University of Georgia's Frank White celebrated the intense questioning that Berkeley had unleashed among American students: "There are many of us who have grown very weary of the old ways that have been fed to us by the carefully stylized 'propaganda mills of conformity' that some of our bureaucrats refer to as our educational and social systems."[14] In fact, this image of the Berkeley student as questioner of orthodoxies and seeker of truth seemed to resonate more than any other in the southern student press. "Universities exist to search for truth and to pass that truth on to new generations," wrote Vanderbilt student Frank Allen Philpot in October 1965. "They have no other legitimate purpose. The search for truth brings forth ideas that may sometimes clash with the existing ideology or methods of doing things. . . . This campus will never be another Berkeley, and that's probably a very good thing. But that doesn't preclude the possibility of revolutionary ideas and concern appearing here sometime in some form. Vanderbilt will never be a great university until it does."[15]

Activist students' tendency to compare and contrast their campuses with Berkeley was natural, as was the desire to replicate such a monumental movement. Yet replicas were uncommon. The FSM was a rare mass campus movement that united students from across the political spectrum, drew the attention of people from throughout the nation, and served as a catalytic event for many other campus movements. The FSM did not recur in the South — at least not on the same scale as in Berkeley — but it was a part of a transitional period in the southern student movement. By 1964, the sit-in movement was over as a coherent phenomenon, but individual antisegregation demonstrations continued on throughout the South. Participation in these demonstrations now reached further into the mainstream of the student body, and campus activist organizations became more established. At the same time, ideas about weaknesses and problems in southern higher education as well as about students' role in society were incubating.

In taking up university reform and student power, southern students drew on a variety of sources, many of them from outside the region. The NSA had long been working on student issues and university reform. SDS, which had made a critique of higher education an important part of the Port Huron Statement, continued to entertain ideas about reforming or remaking the university. Campus speakers, including Paul Goodman, who criticized what he saw as university expansion gone wrong, left an imprint on many southern students. But the region's continuing distinctiveness forced them to adapt these sources to their particular circumstances. They were aided by ssoc publications that offered analyses of the problems of southern higher education as well as by seminars from the NSA's Southern Project. But, in general, rank-and-file southern students were less concerned with fashioning a regional analysis than with changing the arrangements on individual campuses to make education meaningful in a world of controversy and chaos.

Students' scrutiny of their campus roles transcended racial boundaries. The critiques of the university that emerged on black and white campuses had much in common. Both groups demonstrated a growing willingness to challenge previously undisputed authorities. Both sought goals such as student involvement in the campus decision-making process, an end to restrictions on nonacademic life, and curricular changes. Nevertheless, racial politics modified campus protest. On predominantly white campuses, black students were rarely in the vanguard of movements for university reform and student power. Slow-growing black enrollments on white campuses made racial identity primary for most black student activists on such campuses. On historically black campuses, the emergence of student power was intimately tied with the emergence of Black Power. The two concepts were often difficult to separate, as black students saw demands for more campus power as part and parcel of an emerging consciousness of and pride in racial identity. Put more simply, on historically black campuses, a revolt against the university president's rules and regulations was often a revolt against Uncle Tom.

For black as well as white students, however, the skirmishes of the early 1960s prepared the ground for a thorough questioning of all sorts of assumptions and orthodoxies. At the ssoc's founding meeting in early 1964, Ed Hamlett had called on students to use the civil rights movement as a springboard to think about new ideas. Southern students increasingly did so, in the process beginning to question whether the educational enterprise in which they were involved was accomplishing what it should accomplish, and if not, why not?

The North Carolina Speaker Ban

In June 1963, the North Carolina General Assembly passed a statute that denied speaking privileges on state-supported campuses to Communist Party members, anyone who was "known to advocate the overthrow of the Constitution of the United States," or anyone who had pleaded the Fifth Amendment with respect to communist activities. With no real communist threat in the state, the new law was a not-too-cleverly concealed attack on the flagship university in Chapel Hill, which had a reputation — inside and outside the state — as a haven for liberals. In fact, despite its reputation, the university had excluded communism since the late 1940s. Nevertheless, anxiety concerning an uprising of black North Carolinians in the spring of 1963 stirred up enough anticommunist sentiment to get the bill passed. University officials, especially President William Friday, opposed the Speaker Ban and worked behind the scenes to get it repealed.[16]

The issue remained dormant until the FSM developed in California and cast the legislature's actions in a new light. UNC students soon made the connection between the Speaker Ban and the events in Berkeley, although important differences existed between the two conflicts as well as between the two universities. Unlike the clash over restrictions at the University of California, the Speaker Ban controversy did not pit students against the administration: neither group was happy with the conservative legislature's actions. Moreover, student discontent with the university itself had not been brewing at UNC to quite the extent that it had at Berkeley.[17] Thus, in February 1965, when UNC graduate student James W. Gardner attempted to capitalize on the connections by forming a local FSM and organizing a rally on the campus, the results were less than impressive. The initial mobilizing issue for the rally was not the Speaker Ban but a fraternity's racial insult of an African student who was visiting the campus for a Model United Nations assembly. At the rally, Gardner played down the racial insult and played up the Speaker Ban, but his arguments did not resonate with the estimated fifteen hundred spectators. Hecklers were vocal and visible, and Gardner, along with fellow organizer Timothy Ray, judged the forum a failure.[18] Later that spring, Weissman, touring the South under the SSOC's auspices, tried again to generate activism around the Speaker Ban issue, encouraging students and faculty to resist the law and create controversy. In response, the *Daily Tar Heel* called for students to eschew conflict in favor of quiet negotiation. Students and representatives of the university's administration already were seeking a discreet repeal or amendment of the Speaker Ban.[19]

The *Daily Tar Heel's* response to the Weissman speech demonstrated traditional student leaders' difficulties with direct action. And traditional student leaders flourished in Chapel Hill. The campus had a vibrant student government in which two parties, the University Party and the Student Party, competed year after year for dominance. Participants in the student government system often pointed with pride to the fact that their budget was in the neighborhood of $125,000.[20] This tradition initially militated against an activist student response to the Speaker Ban. When the ban threatened to cost UNC its accreditation, a commission chaired by state representative David M. Britt proposed and the General Assembly enacted a revised statute that gave the university's board of trustees power to oversee speakers on campus. Both student body president Paul Dickson III and the *Daily Tar Heel* expressed support for the Britt compromise. In May 1965, however, a campus SDS chapter formed. The following January, looking for a mobilizing issue, the chapter invited Herbert Aptheker, a historian and Communist Party member, and Frank Wilkinson, who had taken the Fifth Amendment in connection with his opposition to the House Un-American Activities Committee, to speak on campus.[21]

The episode did not represent the first time that Aptheker had caused controversy on a southern campus. In November 1962, the Liberals Club at Tulane University sought permission to invite him and socialist Michael Harrington. The university approved Harrington but rejected Aptheker "because of the delicate position in which the University finds itself at the present time." Members of the Liberals Club, who a few months earlier had been leaders in a cafeteria sit-in on the still-segregated Tulane campus, protested, but to no avail. Previewing calls for student power, the editors of the campus newspaper asked whether students should control student activities, "or should the control rest in the hands of the faculty and the administration?"[22]

Aptheker was also a controversial speaker outside the South. In the spring of 1963, in the midst of a free-speech battle at Ohio State University, Students for Liberal Action invited Aptheker, but the administration banned him from the campus. The move prompted picketing and Ohio State's first sit-ins. A month later, Aptheker came to the Ohio State campus, but he did not speak. Instead, he sat silently on a stage while between twenty-five hundred and three thousand people watched faculty members read excerpts from his books, all of which had been checked out from the Ohio State library. The event received national attention. Others who had already been banned from the campus included Wilkinson and Anne Braden.[23]

To a great extent, the free-speech battles on southern campuses constituted an outgrowth of the Cold War and an indication of its impact on higher education. On the surface, controversies over inviting speakers such as Aptheker and Wilkinson looked the same at Ohio State, Tulane, and UNC. Ohio State was, in fact, a relatively conservative midwestern institution. Some 90 percent of its students came from within the state, and a powerful and conservative board of trustees controlled the university's affairs. But racial issues differentiated the southern cases from that of Ohio State. In the South, it was not uncommon for the most vocal student proponents of free speech to come from the ranks of civil rights activists. Such was the case with the Tulane Liberals Club.

In North Carolina, SDS's move to invite Wilkinson and Aptheker proved to be the key event in turning the Speaker Ban into a mass-mobilizing issue. Key members of the UNC board of trustees balked at inviting controversial speakers so soon after the compromise had been approved and consequently instructed the president to deny the two men speaking privileges. This move pushed mainstream student leaders, who had initially been satisfied with the compromise, to the side of SDS. First, the Carolina Forum, a student organization that sponsored outside speakers, and the *Daily Tar Heel* endorsed the invitations. Then, on 3 February, Dickson announced that the student government was officially sponsoring Aptheker's visit, now scheduled for 9 March. Dickson, a twenty-four-year-old Vietnam veteran, provided centrist leadership. His military service made it more difficult for proponents of limitations on speakers to raise the communist specter. To Dickson, the issue was less the danger of what Aptheker might say than "the right to hear this man, and all others who would speak of the broad and dangerous world in which we live." Speaking to the trustees in late February, Dickson argued that by restricting the invitation of speakers, the board would hurt the university's competitiveness in attracting good students and faculty: "We cannot compete with such institutions as Duke University solely on a financial basis because we are not as rich. We are able — or have been able in the past — to compete because of our high regard for academic freedom, free inquiry, and free speech."[24]

Dickson's statement revealed why restrictions on academic freedom, especially bans on communist speakers, would be so important in mobilizing college students throughout the South who might otherwise have stayed on the sidelines. Indeed, limits on speakers and the censorship of student publications provided one of the most common avenues through which southern students became activists, at least briefly. Even when they were indifferent or hostile toward the specific ideas that a controversial speaker or publication might disseminate, early student activists still cared intensely about their right to hear such ideas. The possibility that restrictions on this right might hurt the standing of the university — and, in the process, the value of a degree awarded by that institution — magnified this concern. However, the motivations of such students, who under normal circumstances might have heartily endorsed the status quo, simultaneously explain the successes and limitations of activism based on such civil libertarian issues. A small cadre of campus activists tried to use these issues as a jumping-off point for activism that was based on a deeper, more radical critique of the university and society. But most students were not ready to make the step from a liberal issue to a radical political orientation.

In the short run, the North Carolina Speaker Ban produced confrontations that pitted students against conservative legislators and trustees. Administrative officials — primarily Friday and chancellor J. Carlyle Sitterson — were caught in the middle. Like the students, they opposed the Speaker Ban, but because UNC was a public institution, they faced the difficult task of maintaining a viable political position while simultaneously supporting the academic ideal of free inquiry. Friday thus denied Wilkinson and Aptheker permission to speak on campus. Both men came to Chapel Hill and spoke separately to large crowds in early March 1966, but they did so off campus. Friday met regularly and secretly with Dickson to discuss the situation, and the two developed a good working relationship. In fact, Dickson at times informed Friday of student actions before they occurred. In return, Friday offered advice, although Dickson did not always follow it. The conversations with Dickson ultimately caused Friday to realize that North Carolina's political leaders were incapable of resolving the Speaker Ban controversy. As a result, he encouraged Dickson to take the matter to court, even if it meant suing Friday himself. "In effect," William J. Billingsley argues, "Dickson became an agent for Friday, doing what the president could not do for himself."[25]

Despite SDS's impact on the trajectory of the Speaker Ban controversy — the group had turned the tide of student opinion against the Britt compromise — maintaining the momentum proved difficult. By November 1966, Gary Waller, the cofounder and chair of the campus chapter, was complaining that the university was "a very provincial, backwater school" and that UNC students were "more conservative and more provincial in their orientation" than their counterparts at Berkeley, Chicago, and Columbia. Waller, a doctoral candidate in sociology from Versailles, Missouri, noted that most of the chapter's thirty or forty members came from outside the South. Since the Speaker Ban episode, SDS had pressed the UNC administration to investigate racial discrimination in off-campus housing, prompting Sitterson to issue a policy statement against such bias. The chapter also had been publishing an alternative newspaper, the *Left Heel*, which students had read with interest, even if they were not joining the chapter in droves.[26]

The Speaker Ban controversy contributed to a heightened level of political consciousness on the campus and played some role in pushing the student government to the left. The Student Government Association soon led a drive for university reform through the creation of an experimental college. The Speaker Ban controversy thus represented primarily a response to internal developments rather than to events in Berkeley.

Free Speech and Other Southern Campuses

Similar dramas played out in other parts of the South, but in more conservative areas, these controversies did not produce the same coordinated student action. In Alabama, legislators debated proposed speaker-ban bills from 1965 to 1967. The first attempt, which would have prohibited speakers who were members of the Communist Party or otherwise advocated overthrow of the government, prompted concern from some attendees at a University of Alabama student-leader retreat. University officials responded by creating a set of procedures for approving potential speakers. Proposed invitations would go to the university's Student Life Committee before they could be issued. The goal, according to

Dean of Men F. David Mathews, was for the university rather than governmental officials to retain the power to determine who would speak on campus.[27]

The 'Bama campus, while more open than it had been in the days between the desegregation crises of 1956 and 1963, nevertheless remained politically tentative. When SSOC traveler Gene Guerrero visited Tuscaloosa in February 1965, he described the campus political spectrum: "No liberal groups apart from the campus religious groups. Even the [Young Democrats] are defunct."[28] Guerrero, a student at Emory University in Atlanta, first approached the leaders of campus religious organizations before moving on to fraternity and sorority houses. Sympathetic but cautious students might have been alarmed by SSOC's self-described "radicals" and the causes they supported, including the abolition of capital punishment, the seating of the Mississippi Freedom Democrats in place of the regular party, and university-distributed contraceptives. The *Crimson White* noted that some students had rejected SSOC but were investigating the possibility of forming an independent organization.[29]

Only after Alabama state troopers attacked civil rights activists in Selma in March 1965 did moderate to liberal 'Bama students begin to organize publicly. On 11 March, a meeting took place, involving about twenty students and faculty members who "felt compelled to do something of some nature in order possibly to effect a more constructive understanding and meeting of the problem."[30] The next day, black leaders in Tuscaloosa organized a sympathy demonstration in the downtown area. A few white students and faculty members joined the crowd. Though the march prompted hecklers to turn out along the parade route, no violence accompanied the demonstration. But one anonymous student described other negative effects of his participation: "Many students with whom relations had been quite friendly now ranked us just beneath snakes and lizards."[31] A *Crimson White* editorial also alluded sarcastically to the ostracism of the participating students: "Next thing you know they might be saying, 'I'd rather go read poetry than stuff crepe paper in chicken wire for our homecoming decorations.' Or 'It is spring and I'd rather go look at trees than to volleyball practice.' Or, 'I just don't know if marrying a cute boy from a top fraternity will guarantee happiness.' Such people are indeed dangerous; they destroy the most [sacred] of our institutions."[32]

Nevertheless, with the state government, especially Governor George C. Wallace, serving as a foil, a coterie of activist students continued to organize more overtly under the banner of academic freedom. In April 1966, six demonstrators, including two University of Alabama students, picketed Wallace's appearance at the university's annual Governor's Day ceremonies. Carrying signs that read "The U of A is *not* George Wallace High" and "Stand Up! For Academic Freedom," the students passed out press releases that stated, "We are Alabama students and concerned with the detrimental effects George Wallace's actions have had on academic quality and freedom on campuses across the state." Campus police arrested one student, William Palya, on charges of disorderly conduct, but university officials later recommended that the charges be dropped after Student Government Association president Ralph Knowles and his predecessor, Zach Higgs, urged university administrators to clarify the policy on student picketing. These events illustrated that dissent would not stay within established channels for long. Knowles emerged as a voice for "moderation and reason." The picketers were part of what one observer called "a splinter group of liberals." Palya claimed that the Governor's Day demonstration opened up possibilities for students: "We feel that students should have a more effective voice in the social and academic environment in which they live."[33]

Only in 1967 did another attempted speaker ban prompt a significant number of 'Bama students to mobilize. And even then, university president Frank A. Rose seized the high ground by leading a campaign against the proposed limits. Rose declared that he would resign before selling out to "people with political ambitions." In the short run, he became a hero to students, some of whom staked signs into the ground at the president's mansion that read "Freedom is a Rose" and then sat down on the lawn to show their support. But Rose's liberalism had limits. When students proposed inviting William Sloane Coffin to speak in the spring of 1968, Rose rejected the invitation, arguing that a campus appearance by controversial Yale University chaplain would harm the 'Bama's strained relationships with the governor's office and the state legislature. In response, the student editor of the *Emphasis* magazine resigned, complaining, "I think it's time the administration started dealing with students as adults."[34]

In the following months, University of Alabama students continued to clash with administrators over the right to hear any speaker they chose to invite. In the fall of 1968, the Democratic Students Organization (DSO) initiated efforts to invite to campus four controversial speakers — Black Panther Eldridge Cleaver, Aptheker, yippie Jerry Rubin, and SDS leader Tom Hayden. In accordance with the 1966 regulations, the DSO submitted the names of the proposed speakers to the Student Life Committee for approval with the stipulation that the invitations would be issued if no response was forthcoming. With the Coffin episode still fresh in their memories, DSO members apparently expected the invitations to be rejected. Law student and DSO leader Jack Drake told the committee that the invitations represented an effort to test free speech on campus. In October, Rose notified Drake that the speakers could not be invited. The DSO responded by filing suit in federal court to enjoin the university from barring the speakers.[35]

A few days later, the DSO demonstrated its opposition to Rose's refusal and to further limitations by staging a rally on the steps of the Alabama Union building. The DSO had intended the gathering to focus on the Vietnam War, but Rose instructed the group that it could only assemble on the Union steps for ten minutes before moving in silence to Foster Auditorium. DSO held a meeting at which its members voted to cooperate, prompting the group's president, Mike Stambaugh, to resign. As the DSO suit wound its way through the court system, another speaker controversy erupted. In March 1970, Mathews, now the university's president, vetoed an invitation to Abbie Hoffman to be part of an Emphasis '70 program with Wallace because the Chicago Seven defendant represented a "clear and present danger" of unrest. In response, the program chair and several other students and faculty filed suit against the ban, and about 250 students staged a sit-in outside Mathews's office. Mathews argued that he supported the presentation of diverse viewpoints on the campus, citing his previous opposition to the speaker-ban bill, but suggested that the public "feels we want to hear what is sensational rather than sound."[36]

A speaker ban also created controversy in neighboring Mississippi, where the Board of Trustees for Mississippi Institutions of Higher Learning took the lead in implementing the ban. Young Democrats chapters at the University of Mississippi and Mississippi State University assumed the role of defenders of civil liberties. In 1966, following speeches by Robert F. Kennedy at Ole Miss in March and by Aaron Henry, president of the National Association for the Advancement of Colored People in the state, at Mississippi State in November, the board required that the names of all speakers be furnished to each trustee before invitations were extended. University of Mississippi chancellor John D. Williams invoked the policy when the university's Young Democrats invited Henry to speak in May 1967. When Williams announced that Henry would not be allowed to speak, the Young Democrats, along with the Ole Miss chapter of the American Association of University Professors and Henry, filed suit demanding that the speaker ban be set aside. The federal district court ruled that the policy was unconstitutional and ordered the board to write a new one.[37]

But the matter did not end there. The board's revised policy was also rejected by a three-judge panel, which subsequently wrote a new policy that gave the power to review speakers to the president, with the advice of a campus review committee. This policy received a test in February 1970, when the Mississippi State University Young Democrats invited Charles Evers, a black civil rights leader and mayor of Fayette, Mississippi, to speak. The board directed school president William Giles to withdraw the invitation, citing Evers's role in demonstrations at Alcorn Agricultural and Mechanical College in 1966. Giles, who had followed the stipulations of the new policy, disregarded the directive. The board then invoked its power as the university's governing authority and ordered Giles to rescind the invitation. When he complied, the Young Democrats sued, winning a restraining order permitting Evers to speak. M. M. Roberts subsequently wrote a vitriolic and racist letter to his fellow board members that revealed how far to the right politics in Mississippi were skewed. Noting that a luncheon had been held for Evers, Roberts commented, "I hope he smelled like Negroes usually do." Roberts subsequently led an unsuccessful drive to have Giles fired.[38]

Similar conflicts occurred elsewhere in the South, though often with less visceral racism in evidence. A 1968 College Press Service story found speaker-ban controversies brewing in Louisiana and Kentucky and speech limitations of other types in Tennessee and Florida. The controversies reflected significant gaps in the assumptions about the meanings of order, academic freedom, and education. Tom Ethridge, a columnist for Mississippi's *Jackson Clarion-Ledger*, reflected the conservative viewpoint: "With due respect for zeal and academic freedom, it would seem that students automatically agree to accept the authority of a college administrator when they enroll. If, and as that authority becomes unacceptable, students should leave — and good riddance."[39] But throughout the South, when politicians or administrators intervened to prevent students from inviting controversial speakers, they often set in motion a process in which students who might otherwise have stayed on the sidelines became activists.

From Academic Freedom to Student Power

Battles over free speech and academic freedom provided one important portal through which student activism entered campuses throughout the South. But these issues, which had broad appeal and the potential to energize significant portions of the student population, were only the starting point for a movement that ultimately pushed for fundamental reforms. Mobilization against limits on free speech tapped into the currents of generational revolt as well as vague but common ideals about the university as a sanctuary for free thought without necessarily threatening the power distribution on the campus or in society. However, more radical activists usually attempted to use these relatively moderate issues as launching pads for more thoroughgoing critiques of education and society. On southern campuses, this critique concentrated on two separate but interrelated areas. One area was the role of the student on campus. Drawing from the university-reform ideas that circulated within the NSA as well as from the concept of participatory democracy that was a fundamental tenet of the New Left, activists sought to expand students' power in campus decision making. After 1967, calls for student power became common on southern campuses. But student activists' efforts to reform southern higher education entailed more than empowering students. Activists also charged that education was stale and disconnected from the most pressing issues of American life. To this end, they called for curricular changes that would make education more relevant and for pedagogical changes that would facilitate an atmosphere of learning.

The individual issues that made up the call for university reform were not new. Indeed, many of the ideas sprang from progressive educators' early-twentieth-century critiques of traditional education. Student critiques that classes were stultifying and irrelevant recalled these earlier complaints against education as a matter of teachers handing down fixed truths for students to learn.[40] More direct inspiration came from the NSA, which had always included university reform among its primary domestic goals. At the first National Student Congress, it passed a Student Bill of Rights, a highly publicized document that stressed academic freedom, freedom for students to organize and bring speakers to campuses, and the right of every young person to a college education.[41] On those few white southern campuses with direct and prolonged connections to the NSA, the university-reform efforts had a direct impact. But even on campuses that lacked ongoing, formal relationships with the NSA, university-reform ideas seeped in. The Collegiate Press Service distributed editorial columns that presented some of these ideas, and these columns ran in student newspapers throughout the South. Moreover, the NSA's Southern Project periodically organized seminars on university-reform topics and invited students from member and nonmember schools.

During the 1960s, the NSA's concept of university reform accepted the broad outlines of American higher education but sought to modify some of the specific arrangements. In 1966, NSA representatives joined with representatives from nine other educational organizations under the auspices of the American Association of University Professors to draft a "Joint Statement on Rights and Freedoms of Students." The document covered such topics as the classroom, student records, student affairs, students' off-campus freedom, and procedural standards in disciplinary proceedings. In general, the "Joint Statement" advocated a framework in which students had greater control over their nonacademic and academic lives. It became the starting point for numerous efforts to revise individual campus codes.[42]

The following summer, education reform was one of the central issues at the NSA's National Student Congress, held on the campus of the University of Maryland in College Park. The congress passed a resolution calling for an increase in student power on campuses — in particular, for universities to give students complete control over chartering student organizations, financing student activities, determining dormitory hours, setting social and housing rules, and meting out disciplinary actions concerning the violation of student regulations. The gathering also demanded joint control with administration and faculty over curriculum decisions, admissions policies, the hiring and dismissal of faculty members, college services, and grading systems.[43]

One of the delegates was Edward Schwartz, a graduate of Oberlin College who served as president of NSA during the 1967–68 academic year and became the group's most articulate and well-known proponent of student power. In an October 1967 column distributed by the Collegiate Press Service, Schwartz argued for more student power based on the educational premise that "people learn through living, through the process of integrating their thoughts with their actions, through testing their values against those of a community, through a capacity to act." While he allowed that faculty members and administrators needed to advise and even "attempt to persuade" students, Schwartz argued that students should bear the ultimate burden for a whole range of noncurricular regulations, including those related to dormitory hours, student fees, clubs, and newspapers. Schwartz also contended that students should "co-decide" curricular policy, admissions policy, and other issues, including university investments. He acknowledged that "most students don't want student power" because they are "too tired, too scared, or too acquiescent to fight for it" but argued that this acquiescence resulted in a limited education: "Students who accept other people's decisions have diluted their desire to question, to test themselves, to become through being. They create walls between their classroom material and their lives, between their inner and outer selves." Schwartz ultimately was calling for education to prepare people to be citizens by providing them with the opportunity to be fully participating academic citizens.[44]

Schwartz's vision of student power was consistent with the view that emanated from SDS. The 1962 Port Huron Statement, authored primarily by Tom Hayden, criticized college campuses as a breeding ground for apathy and zeroed in on four ills within academia. First, colleges operated within the framework of a "let's pretend" theory of extracurricular activities, embodied in the student government, that discouraged initiative "from the more articulate, honest, and sensitive student." Second, the doctrine of in loco parentis extended to the classroom, where the teacher-student relationship resembled the parent-child relationship. Third, the treatment of subjects in college tended to be sterile and to remove them from reality. Finally, a cumbersome academic bureaucracy limited the possibilities for meaningful education. The reverse of these ills was an ideal education, in which students were actively engaged in issues of tremendous importance to themselves and society. Indeed, the Port Huron Statement viewed the university as the lever for change, "an overlooked seat of influence." Before universities could serve this purpose, however, students and faculty needed to "wrest control of the educational process from the administrative bureaucracy" and "import major public issues into the curriculum. . . . They must make debate and controversy, not dull pedantic cant, the common style for educational life." Once properly reformed, universities would serve as the "base and agency in a movement of social change."[45]

By 1967, SDS's approach to educational issues had changed, reflecting the radicalization of the organization's leadership. One aspect of this transformation was a shift in leadership from an old guard made up of alumni of elite universities to representatives of nonelite campuses, especially in the Midwest and

Southwest. Carl Davidson, the product of a working-class family in Aliquippa, Pennsylvania, and an activist at Penn State University, helped to generate and reflected this transformation. At the 1966 SDS national convention in Clear Lake, Iowa, Davidson was elected vice president and Greg Calvert, an Iowa State University activist who also had a working-class background, was elected president.[46] Davidson played a crucial role in the emergence of SDS's souring vision of higher education. He authored a working paper for the Clear Lake convention, "Toward a Student Syndicalist Movement; or, University Reform Revisited," that was widely distributed. The essay began with a harsh assessment of campus movements, almost all of which, Davidson suggested, had failed "to alter the university community radically or even to maintain their own existence." They had failed because they had not fully acknowledged the university's role in supporting "corporate liberalism," the system that ultimately was responsible for carrying out repression within the United States as well as the war in Vietnam. Universities trained the oppressors, and activists who failed to recognize this fact fell into a number of traps. They formed single-issue groups that died after their goal was achieved. They attempted to work through existing channels, including student government, which often put off substantive change. They waited for faculty support, which was "like asking Southern Negroes to wait for White moderates." Real change would come only when students began to promote a "syndicalist" movement, which he defined as a movement that sought student control rather than better conditions — that is, better rules — for students. The student syndicalist movement should take as its central goal the abolition of the grade system, since grades were harmful to real education and an issue with which all students could identify. Abolishing grades would radically alter the shape and purpose of education, promoting contact between students and faculty. Secondary issues would emerge from the idea of participatory democracy. Students might, for example, demand at the beginning of the semester that a professor allow them to participate in shaping a course's structure, format, and content. They might "sign up for, attend, denounce, and then walk out of and picket excessively large classes." Women students might organize a decentralized federation of dormitory councils that would formulate their own rules.[47]

Davidson authored a more concise statement of these ideas the following year that was published in a column, "Student Power: Radical View," distributed by the Collegiate Press Service in tandem with Schwartz's column. For the column, Davidson shed the analytical tone he had adopted in the student syndicalism working paper, replacing it with a rambling, conversational style. He began by lampooning the idea that students were oppressed: "Bullshit. We are being trained to be oppressors and the underlings of oppressors." Given the seriousness of the war in Vietnam and exploitation at home, protests over impersonal class sizes and dormitory regulations were frivolous. What, then, should activists do with a student movement that clearly was making waves? "We have no blueprints," Davidson suggested. "Only some guidelines. Administrators are the enemy. Refuse to be 'responsible.' . . . Refuse to accept the 'off-campus–on-campus' dichotomy." Most important, Davidson called on students to "demand seriousness by dealing with serious issues — getting the U.S. out of Vietnam, getting the military off the campus, enabling people to win control over the quality and direction of their lives." "In short," he concluded, "make a revolution."[48]

Davidson's emergence as an SDS leader did not reflect the group's widespread acceptance of his ideas, even if chapters frequently distributed copies of "Toward a Student Syndicalist Movement."[49] On southern campuses, the individual issues that provided the fodder for Davidson's radical view and Schwartz's liberal view of campus organizing — free speech, dormitory regulations, irrelevant curricula — began to emerge with greater frequency after 1967. Even if most students on southern campuses did not cite Schwartz or Davidson chapter and verse, their clashing perspectives on university reform were reflected in the developing campus movements.

By 1967, a broad consensus emerged that restrictions on student speech should be curbed or eliminated. But did this goal constitute an end unto itself or merely an entry point into a more radical critique of the university? Should university reform occur for educational reasons, or should it represent one aspect of a broader societal revolution? Indeed, could the university be reformed at all? By the late 1960s, some activists concluded that universities, as reflections of American society, were beyond repair and that the only solution was to create alternative institutions.

Experimental Colleges and Free Universities: Alternative Routes to Change

Often implicit in calls for student power was a rejection of the educational value of higher education as it existed. But while advocates of student power sought to win students the right to make the decisions that affected their lives, other activists worked explicitly to change the content and practice of education. Experimental colleges and "free universities" represented one version of these efforts. Free universities were part of a larger trend to create "parallel institutions" that would avoid the exploitation inherent in existing institutions. The idea of the free university emerged from a marriage of university reform and the civil rights movement. In 1962 and 1963, as it was seeking out issues that would mobilize students, SDS sponsored several university-reform groups and meetings. The civil rights movement then intervened, contributing a new approach to education reform. In the summer of 1964, in addition to registering voters, Mississippi Freedom Summer volunteers conducted freedom schools, which sought to teach basic skills and training. Aimed at both children and adults, freedom schools were a necessary response to a system in which the state spent four times as much money on white schools as on black schools. However, the movement schools did not simply offer black students an approximation of white education. Led by Staughton Lynd, who had taught for a period at Atlanta's Spelman College, educators and activists developed a program that built on the progressive idea that the best classroom was not one in which the teacher merely passed down knowledge to the student. Rather, in freedom schools, teachers would learn along with students, who also possessed valuable knowledge and culture that should be preserved. Freedom schools also offered significant variations on traditional curriculum, with classes in black history supplementing more traditional subjects. The schools represented an early attempt at parallel institutions, an idea that resonated not only in the black freedom struggle but also in other social movements.[50]

In fact, some form of this concept surfaced in late 1964 on the Berkeley campus of the University of California, as spontaneous seminars and teach-ins further suggested the possibility of alternative rather than reformed universities. The following March, the first Vietnam teach-in was held at the University of Michigan, kicking off a wave of similar events throughout the nation. The teach-ins further demonstrated the possibilities of educational ventures outside the established institutional framework. About the same time, SDS created a Free University Committee to push the idea of alternative universities. In the summer of 1965, at SDS's annual convention at Kewadin, Michigan, participants hammered out the essential features of free universities, which included open admission, "relevant" courses, unrestricted curricula, community service, and radical development. By the fall of 1966, several free universities had opened, including a Free University of Florida in Gainesville. Others followed. But SDS soon soured on the idea of free universities because, as Davidson noted, they pulled the best people from the campus, allowing the university to function more smoothly. Nevertheless, the concept of free universities had been important within the evolution of SDS, a sign of the decline of reformism and the emergence of revolutionary alternatives.[51]

In the South, the formation of alternative institutions took two forms. Free universities tended to be the creations of campus activists working outside the established mechanisms of the existing university, although activist faculty members and graduate students often provided most of the courses. But in a few universities, student government officers created experimental colleges that were, in concept at least, sanctioned by the university. The best-developed example of this form occurred at the University of North Carolina.

In announcing the creation of the UNC's experimental, noncredit curriculum in December 1966, the *Daily Tar Heel* connected the new curriculum to free universities. Specifically, a staff writer compared the proposed experimental college to alternative institutions at the Universities of Pennsylvania, Texas, and New Mexico.[52] To the extent that UNC's Experimental College drew on the growing educational ferment throughout the country, it resembled these alternative institutions. In the preceding months, discussion of education reform had appeared frequently in the pages of nearby Duke University's *Chronicle*. The discussion at Duke was quite structured, consisting of university-sponsored symposia featuring professors as well as columns in the *Chronicle* by student government leaders. As such, it seemed to lack much potential — at least in the short run — to spark overt political activism on the campus. In November, Duke's annual symposium, which attracted speakers of national renown to discuss a particular topic, brought a slate of speakers that included Paul Goodman; Berkeley English professor Charles Muscatine, coauthor of a post-FSM study that proposed increased experimentation at the university; and David Harris, a Stanford University student body president and Vietnam resistance leader who later served time in prison for draft evasion. The symposium, on "Concepts of a University," featured several days of freewheeling criticism of American higher education.[53] An even more important influence for reform-minded students at UNC, however, was the 1967 National Student Conference in College Park, Maryland. "When the UNC delegation returned," said student David Kiel, who provided early leadership for the Experimental College, "we began to talk to students interested in educational reform and formed three groups to discuss what could be done to make education better at Chapel Hill." Out of this group came proposals for an experimental college and a pass-fail option for students.[54]

Adopting as its slogan "Not to be taught, but to learn," the Experimental College offered thirty-two noncredit, nongraded seminars in the spring of 1967. Course titles included Attempts at Comparative Mythology, Genetics of Pet Animals, the Meaning of Faith, and the Alternative of Conscientious Objection. More than five hundred students registered for the courses, most of which rejected a lecture format. Surveys conducted in twenty-five of the courses found that full-time faculty members led nine of the courses, while graduate students led eleven and chaplains led five. "All but one of the 25 reported courses used seminar-discussion formats, and of these 16 used techniques which emphasized freedom, student participation, and student direction," noted one report.[55]

To the extent that the UNC Experimental College encouraged free thinking and addressed such topics as conscientious objection, it had the potential to serve as liberalizing and possibly even radicalizing influence. But organizers of the college never suggested that they intended such results. Instead, these liberal members of the UNC student government sought reform; indeed, the Experimental College operated under the auspices of the Student Government Association, a dynamic possible only at a university in which one could be both a liberal and a viable participant in established student politics. The 1966–67 student government president, Bob Powell, gained renown — and some opposition — for signing an open letter to Lyndon B. Johnson in late December 1966 that expressed concern about the Vietnam War.[56]

In contrast, the Free University of Florida, which offered a similar menu of experimental, noncredit, nongraded courses to students at the University of Florida, arose from an activist group that not only operated outside the established boundaries of student government but also represented a challenge to it. Civil rights had provided the entry point for activism at the University of Florida during the early 1960s. In 1963, students and faculty interested in civil rights formed the Student Group for Equal Rights and mounted a number of demonstrations. In late 1964 and early 1965, however, some of those activists increasingly turned their attention to campus conditions, partly in response to administrators' efforts to limit off-campus activism by group members. By January 1965, this redirection of interest to the campus had taken the form of a new student political party, the Freedom Party. In previous years, campus politics had been the domain of politically minded members of Greek societies who often used student politics as a stepping-stone to state politics. The inherent organization of fraternities and sororities made it difficult for students outside the Greek fold to mount an effective challenge. Members of the Freedom Party offered Jim Harmeling, who had participated in civil rights activities sponsored by the Student Group for Equal Rights, as its presidential candidate, and the party's ticket included more than twenty candidates for various student offices. The idea of a "student-centered university" provided the foundation for the party's platform. Harmeling and his fellow party members called for "an institution in which the education of students is the first concern of the university" and "attacked the existing order for its preoccupation with physical plant, grants, appropriations, publications, degrees, and image-making." The platform called for abolition of compulsory participation in the Reserve Officers' Training Corps, the creation of a student-led antipoverty program, the elimination of all vestiges of racial discrimination on campus, and a formalization of university disciplinary procedures. "This statement of objectives transcends Homecoming and football seating," the preamble to the platform stated. "It reaches for projects that will liberate the contemporary student's idealism and natural and youthful ambition to help others who need his help."[57]

Activist faculty member Marshall B. Jones later noted, the "Freedom Party was the local civil rights movement come home." As such, its appeal was limited to those with similar political orientations — and at the University of Florida in the mid-1960s, such people were decidedly in the minority. Harmeling polled 879 votes, about 10 percent of the total, which supporters viewed as a moral victory of sorts. "For a campus in the heart of cracker Florida," Jones concluded, "it was an extraordinary performance." Indeed, according to Jones, the Freedom Party's showing loosened conservative fraternities' hold on the student government system. Two years later, the student newspaper sponsored a party comprised of independent (that is, non-Greek) students that won with a reform platform.[58]

The Freedom Party's brief challenge to established student politics served as a precursor to the formation of a free university in the fall of 1965. Another necessary precursor was the firing of the university's leading activist faculty member, Edward Richer. A charismatic instructor — "a born teacher and talker," according to one former colleague — Richer nevertheless was vulnerable. With no publications, only a master's degree in journalism, and apparently no intention of earning a doctorate, Richer operated on year-to-year contracts. In the spring of 1965, university officials notified Richer that they would not renew his contract because of his lack of a terminal degree. Richer and his supporters claimed that Richer's political activism, not his academic limitations, had prompted the university to fire him. He requested a hearing before a faculty senate committee on academic freedom and tenure, but the hearing, which convened in August, ended abruptly when the administration's lawyers refused to participate.[59]

Richer remained in Gainesville in the fall of 1965 and participated in the creation of the Free University of Florida (FUF), a project of the same band of activists who had spearheaded both the integration demonstrations and the Freedom Party challenge. FUF drew its inspiration from Paul Goodman, whose trenchant critiques of American education — *Growing Up Absurd, Community of Scholars*, and *Compulsory Mis-Education* — greatly influenced the New Left's ideas on university reform. In these books as well as in countless campus appearances, Goodman argued that universities had expanded too rapidly and were too much at the mercy of bureaucrats and administrators. The overrationalization of education took the focus away from the essential relationship in education — between student and teacher. "If a teacher wants to teach something, he must think it worthwhile; and students want either to learn something particular or find out what it is they want to learn," Goodman wrote in *Community of Scholars*. "This is enough for a school." This quotation appeared at the top of an FUF fund-raising pamphlet.[60]

FUF's first slate of courses during the 1965–66 academic year included

"The Young Christian Conscience and Its Problems," "African Government," "World Political Awareness in Twentieth Century American Literature," "Race, Segregation, and Intelligence," "The Engineer as a Moral Decision-Maker," and "How to Read the Daily Newspaper." Faculty members, all volunteers, came from in and around the University of Florida community. The university maintained no criteria for instructors: "A teacher's worth will be proved in the classroom or in the field," the pamphlet declared. Richer, no longer connected with the university, served as FUF's chancellor and was the only salaried employee. FUF's founders intended the university to complement rather than compete with the University of Florida by "attracting the latter's students and teachers as voluntary scholars in search of something that is missing where they work."[61]

Some within Gainesville's community of activists expressed doubts about the FUF from the beginning. "It seemed to us that we needed to contend for control in the existing places, not go elsewhere and do better," recalled Jones, who reasoned that despite FUF's best efforts, "higher education in America would continue as it was and more easily, if our energies were diverted into utopian educational experiments." He did not have to worry about FUF as a drain on activist energies for long. Richer, whose reputation as a rabble-rouser often preceded him, had trouble finding a physical home for FUF; no one would rent space to him. Moreover, according to Jones, university officials threatened to fire at the earliest opportunity anyone who taught in FUF. The experimental university thus collapsed in 1966.[62]

Nevertheless, Gainesville activists' efforts began to bear fruit in early 1966, when two Freedom Party members challenged university regulations prohibiting the on-campus distribution of materials published by noncollege organizations. The two activists, Alan (Nik) Levin and Lucien Cross, handed out a college humor magazine, the *Charlatan*, and an antiwar periodical, prompting university officials to bring charges against the two students. Jones, who attended the students' hearings as an advocate for them, wrote in the campus newspaper of the harsh and condescending tone that administrative officials had used in dealing with the students, prompting an outcry from students and faculty. The university later issued a policy guaranteeing free-speech rights to students. But in February 1967, university officials placed a female student, Pamme Brewer, on probation for "indiscreet and inappropriate conduct" after she appeared nude in the *Charlatan*. After news of Brewer's punishment spread throughout the campus, students organized an impromptu demonstration in the Plaza of the Americas, a gathering spot at the center of the campus. The protest eventually moved to the lobby of the administration building, Tigert Hall, where 150 students spent the night. Shortly thereafter, an anti-Greek student political party, the Apathy Party, captured the student government presidency by making the revision of the student code that informed Brewer's probation its central issue. By then, the staff of the campus newspaper, the *Alligator*, which had previously opposed the efforts of the Gainesville activists and the Freedom Party, supported the Apathy Party. To the paper's editors, student government provided the proper forum for campus change. Revision of the student code, the *Alligator* argued, "won't be accomplished by 150 students who elected to spend a night tossing and turning on the hard floors of Tigert. Instead it will be the result of hard work by responsible student leadership and not the uncertain tactics of a few seekers of martyrdom."[63]

Other efforts at experimental colleges and free universities met similar fates. As institutions, these experiments were usually short-lived failures. But they sometimes inspired other, more successful, efforts at activism or social criticism. In Jackson, Mississippi, Millsaps College student David Doggett and anthropology professor William Peltz attempted to form a free university in the fall of 1967. The Millsaps administration, in the midst of a drive for a matching-funds grant from the Ford Foundation, resisted the effort, announcing that Peltz would not be rehired. In response, Doggett and others started a mimeographed satirical newspaper, the *Unicorn*. After graduating, Doggett started an alternative newspaper, the *Kudzu*, which was one of the first underground newspapers in the South.[64]

In Georgia and Alabama, organizers with the NSA's Southern Project attempted to organize integrated free universities in 1968 but also met with limited success. In Alabama, one Birmingham organizer attempted to involve predominantly black and white institutions in the community Free School, while another organizer worked in Tuscaloosa with students at the University of Alabama and Stillman College. But the organizers encountered a lack of interest on the part of students — especially black students, who no doubt were less inclined to participate in integrated efforts at a time when Black Power was ascendant — along with transportation difficulties and "other practical problems." The Alabama organizers soon moved to other causes, most notably the National Democratic Party of Alabama, that state's equivalent of the Mississippi Freedom Democratic Party. The Georgia organizers launched the Free School of Atlanta, although black students again hesitated to participate. The greatest success of the Southern Project's efforts in Atlanta, however, was another spin-off underground publication, the *Great Speckled Bird*, which became a well-regarded alternative newspaper.[65]

University Reform and Southern Higher Education

Southern students' efforts to reform or remake higher education revealed a willingness to raise basic questions about the nature of education. To what extent did activists address university reform as a specifically southern problem? On individual campuses, student efforts to eliminate in loco parentis, win more power to determine policy, and modify curricula and pedagogy were rarely formulated in a region-specific manner. At times, southern students compared restrictive campus policies with more liberal policies on campuses outside the region. The University of California at Berkeley often served as a point of reference against which people at both ends of the political spectrum measured their institutions. Thus, students sometimes implicitly placed their institution — if not their region — in a comparative framework. But overall, the rhetoric of university reform and student power on individual campuses rarely dealt explicitly with educational problems peculiar to the South.

This is not to say that southern activists did not treat university reform as a southern problem. ssoc and Southern Project activists grappled with the issue during the late 1960s. Within ssoc, an emphasis on university reform emerged in late 1966, at roughly the same time that some of the organization's members began formulating a southern-nationalist interpretation of the region's problems. This analysis increasingly emphasized the South as an exploited colony of an imperialistic corporate capitalism headquartered in the Northeast. Within the framework of ssoc's analysis, southern universities were merely outposts of corporate capitalism. As was true with other New Left treatments of higher education, the process of uncovering the ties between southern universities and corporate capitalism began with an analysis of the corporate roles of members of a school's governing board. By revealing the university's power structure as well as how it connected with that of the community or state, ssoc members hoped to demonstrate the need for radical social change. But this analytic approach posed problems for southern radicals, as it did for radicals outside the region. If, as they argued, corporate capitalism so completely controlled the universities, then how could the minority of campus radicals wrest control? Were universities simply lost causes? Would the dramatic social changes ssoc sought require starting again from scratch? Alternative institutions, efforts to create ideal universities from scratch, largely failed, and by 1969, ssoc's answer seemed to be that radical students and faculty members should organize and bore from within individual campuses. But this answer did not lack ambiguity. ssoc included a number of activists who were no longer in school either because their activism had earned them expulsions from conservative administrators or because they believed that their social consciences required them to abandon their student identities to be full-time organizers.[66]

In part, the question was whether southern students' political orientation had changed enough since the early 1960s to allow for the kind of activism that would produce fundamental campus and community change. ssoc struggled throughout its existence with precisely this issue. Thanks in part to university-reform and student-power issues, more and more students who, as Constance Curry phrased it, "weren't all the way there yet" could tap into the currents of activism.[67] ssoc played a role in encouraging these developments, but its leadership was always more radical than the students who provided the backbone for campus activism.[68]

The nsa's Southern Project also grappled with this issue during the mid- and late 1960s. In general, the Southern Project approached the problem by aiming at a broader segment of the student population, those students whose political orientations remained fairly moderate. Through seminars on education and social issues, project organizers hoped to meet students where they were and nudge them to the left. An example of this dynamic can be seen in the organization's Southwide Conference on Educational Reform, held in Atlanta in late February 1968. The conference had its origins in the influential 1967 National Student Congress, during which Edward Schwartz had been elected president and student power had become a rallying cry. During the congress, a caucus of southern schools instructed their representatives to organize a regional conference for educational reform. Gene Guerrero, ssoc's founding chair and a former activist at Emory, coordinated the conference, aided by a committee of students from Clark College, Emory University, Agnes Scott College, Spelman College, and the Universities of Alabama and North Carolina. More than two hundred students attended the conference, which included workshops on student legal rights, educational reform, black consciousness, experimental colleges, and student government services. The emotional high point of the conference came during a speech by black comedian Dick Gregory, who declared that revolution was necessary and justified unless America changed quickly. "The student audience, predominantly white, moderate southern middle-class students, stood and cheered for a full five minutes," Southern Project director Howard Romaine later reported. "Four years ago only a small, a very small minority of white southern students would have shared this emotion — most were in sncc or ssoc." To Romaine, the reaction to Gregory's speech indicated that "the white southern student community is liberal enough to allow nsa to press vigorously on controversial issues such as student legal rights, educational reform, racism, the war and the draft" without alienating most students. In the liberalization of white southern students, Romaine saw a process in which the South was "gradually being integrated into the spectrum of national student life and politics. Pushing this process along is one of the most important roles nsa can play at present."[69]

As Romaine suggested, the transformation of the political views of white southern students was part of a larger process in which southern campuses were

Americanizing. Some activists perceived this transformation as occurring too slowly. Where it did occur, however, it fed a corresponding trend toward liberalizing southern campuses. Student activism during the 1960s incorporated drives to eliminate restrictions on speech and social restrictions as well as efforts to modify pedagogy and curricula. The curricular challenges arose primarily over the issues of race and the war in Vietnam, but the impulse came from a desire for an education that was more relevant to the issues of a politically tumultuous time.

University of Alabama students after police blasted them with tear gas and smoke bombs on 7 February 1956 in an attempt to break up a demonstration against the enrollment of Autherine Lucy. The image of campus riots continued to resonate at Alabama into the 1960s. F. David Mathews, a student during the Lucy episode who served as president of the university in the late 1960s and early 1970s, suggested that when students mobilized in the late 1960s, he sought to prevent the kind of unrest he had seen while a student. AP/WIDE WORLD PHOTOS.

The front page of the 26 April 1957 edition University of Richmond's student newspaper, the *Collegian*, provides a glimpse of college life on a segregated white campus of the 1950s. The article on the left focused on the oddity of student Lovey Jane Long's academic interests: "Thoughts of elections and politics — not love and marriage — are uppermost in the mind of the girl selected as the most beautiful senior at Westhampton College." *Richmond Collegian*, Virginia Baptist Historical Society, University of Richmond Archives.

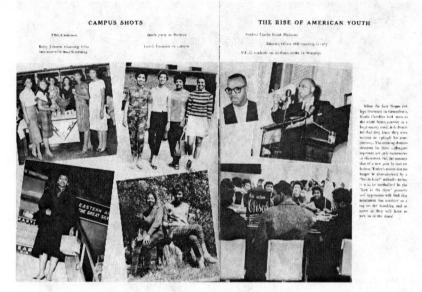

Two pages from *L'Annee*, the 1960 Virginia Union University yearbook, capture the dissonance evident on many predominantly black college campuses as the sit-in movement developed. Virginia Union University Archives.

Participants in a lunch counter sit-in in Richmond, Virginia, February 1960. The sit-ins in Richmond began on 22 February 1960, three weeks after students from North Carolina A & T in Greensboro, held their first demonstration. Anderson Collection, Valentine Richmond History Center.

Students from Alabama State College in Montgomery speak to a reporter during the March 1960 sit-ins. A public college under the control of the state board of education, which was chaired by Governor John Patterson, Alabama State was vulnerable to the intervention of segregationist politicians. Nine students involved in the Montgomery sit-ins eventually were expelled. U.S. News and World Report Magazine Photograph Collection, Library of Congress.

The front page of the 11 April 1968 issue of the *Red and Black*, the University of Georgia student newspaper, details a student sit-in in opposition to regulations that controlled many aspects of women students' nonacademic lives, including appropriate attire, curfews, and social functions. *The Red and Black*, University of Georgia Archives, Hargrett Rare Book and Manuscript Library, University of Georgia.

Duke University students gather in the quadrangle in front of the chapel, April 1968. The Silent Vigil after the assassination of Martin Luther King Jr. occurred in the wake of growing debate over race relations at Duke. Duke University Archives.

Students react to police use of tear gas outside the Allen Building at Duke University, 13 February 1969. Between fifty and seventy-five black students had took over the building and renamed it the building Malcolm X Liberation School before leaving after school officials threatened punishment. Duke University Archives.

An antiwar demonstration on Franklin Street in Chapel Hill, North Carolina, October 1969. Antiwar activism in Chapel Hill took a variety of forms, including demonstrations, dorm talks, guerrilla theater, and draft resistance. North Carolina Collection Photographic Archives, Wilson Library, University of North Carolina at Chapel Hill.

Father Joseph Tetlow, an assistant professor of history, conducts a memorial service for the Louisiana war dead at Loyola University in New Orleans, 15 October 1969. Some two hundred students participated in the service. A relatively quiet place through much of the 1960s, Loyola became increasingly divided by the war, issues of campus governance, and other questions, leading to the May 1970 student takeover of the Danna Center. AP/WIDE WORLD PHOTOS.

CHAPTER SIX

Student Power and Black Power at the South's Negro Colleges

THE SIT-INS of the early 1960s opened the black campus up to criticism. When the presidents of these institutions responded to the threat or reality of student-led demonstrations by attempting to limit student and faculty involvement, they invited questions about the limits of academic freedom. From this opening grew a more detailed critique of the black college or university. In many respects, this critique resembled the calls for university reform and student power that developed on predominantly white campuses. The South's black colleges and universities often maintained social rules that were, if anything, more restrictive than those on white campuses. These rules and regulations, along with limits on speech and political activity, often were the first targets for activist black students, just as they were for white students. But the rapid emergence of Black Power in the summer of 1966 modified the direction that activism on black campuses took.

"Like a Black Midas' wand, this movement imbues everything it touches with an ebony hue," reported Robert Goodman, an instructor at Morehouse College, in 1968. "A discussion of Descartes in Western civ is likely to wind up in heated debate over how Descartes would have analyzed Black Power or whether white philosophers are relevant to Black people anyway."[1] Goodman's comments provide a window into a period in which scholarly controversies and political turmoil fed off of each other. By the late 1960s, many radical black activists had rejected the philosophy of nonviolence, the usefulness of alliances with white liberals, and the virtue of integration. Instead, they argued for self-defense, the need for black people to form their own institutions, and the virtue of power — which they should take "by any means necessary." In their 1967 book, *Black Power*, Student Nonviolent Coordinating Committee (SNCC) activist Stokely Carmichael (who later changed his name to Kwame Ture) and political scientist Charles V. Hamilton argued that the black community should "redefine itself, set forth new values and goals, and organize around them." Rejecting assimilation into white society as surrender to co-optation by an exploitative white power structure, Carmichael and Hamilton instead contended that black people should identify with Africans and other Third World peoples who struggled against colonial domination. This reconfigured cultural identity would accompany a new political program that emphasized the need to "close ranks," controlling black institutions and participating in coalitions with other groups, such as white liberals, only when the conditions were right.[2]

Critics, a group that included not only whites but also moderate and conservative blacks, saw Black Power as counterproductive, violent, and even racist. At the very least, some observers argued, Black Power was a vague rhetorical tool that was short on specific political content. "I contend not only that black power lacks any real value for the civil rights movement, but that its propagation is positively harmful," declared Bayard Rustin in a 1966 *Commentary* article that is perhaps the best-known critique of Black Power from within the black community. "It diverts the movement from a meaningful debate over strategy and tactics, it isolates the Negro community, and it encourages the growth of anti-Negro forces."[3]

Black Power took on meaning in specific contexts; in the world of higher education, the movement informed scholars' efforts to explore the history and culture of African Americans and people of color throughout the world. Above all, Black Power was a cultural movement that sought the psychological liberation of African Americans. Black Power advocates worked to redefine terms. For too long, they believed, *white* had meant "right," while *black* was inferior.[4] On individual campuses throughout the South, black students of the late 1960s worked to modify curricula to reflect these developments. But curricular changes were only part of a larger agenda. Student activists on black campuses often wanted their institutions to become actively involved in the drive to liberate and empower African Americans. By the late 1960s, students on the South's black campuses were asking pointed questions about the racial assumptions that had informed the creation of the institutions that were supposed to be educating them. How could institutions that had been created by whites and that usually still answered to white trustees or politicians possibly serve the needs of the black community? In particular, how could such institutions serve as instruments of black liberation?

These questions would have been controversial at any time and in any place. But in the combustible atmosphere of the late 1960s and in a region still in the early stages of sorting out the meaning of desegregation, they were explosive. The level of activism in the late 1960s on southern black campuses was significant by any standard of measurement — the number of campuses that experienced clashes between students and administrative officials or the presence of actual or potential violence. The involvement of police sometimes heightened the tension. On several occasions, the showdowns turned violent. Protests at Texas Southern University in 1967, South Carolina State in 1968, North Carolina Agricultural and Technical College in 1969, and Jackson State College in 1970 resulted in deaths.

To a great extent, black campuses in the South mirrored the racial politics of the late 1960s. But the movements that developed on these campuses were also student movements. Activists in the South's historically black institutions drew on many of the issues that animated proponents of student power on predominantly white campuses. In fact, the movements on black campuses — as opposed to the movements of black students in the communities surrounding their campuses — began with an assertion of students' right to academic freedom and with rebellions against restrictions on nonacademic life. The mobilization of students on these issues occurred in some of the South's black college campuses before the rapid rise of Black Power in the summer of 1966. Nevertheless, Black Power modified the form and content of student activism on black campuses in important ways. At what were still called "Negro colleges," activists often sought to turn institutions that they believed were instruments of oppression into instruments of liberation.[5]

Late-Decade Fault Lines

Black student demonstrations of the late 1960s might have been creatures of the early 1960s sit-ins, but much separated the two entities. The sit-in movement of 1960–61 represented one of those rare moments in which a social issue produced great unanimity among students on many black campuses in support of political action. To be sure, differences of opinion existed within the black community, but these differences often were generational, as younger blacks favored a more militant approach and older blacks sought a go-slow philosophy. On the campus, however, traditional student leaders, often student body presidents, commonly served as the chief organizers of the sit-ins, and the crusades sometimes took on the feel of intercollegiate sports competition. This apparent unity contributed greatly to the success of the movement. In contrast, late-1960s protests on black campuses were more likely to exhibit divisions between campus rebels and traditional student leaders.

Other fault lines also divided black campuses. Longtime black presidents often stood at the center of these storms. The presidents might have been working for years behind the scenes for the gradual amelioration of the plight of African Americans in his community or state, but their precarious position forced compromises that militant black student activists now believed made these men Uncle Toms. In New Orleans, for example, Dillard University president Albert W. Dent spent years working for black equality, but the differences between Dent and his student body became pronounced by the late 1960s. A statement printed in the Dillard campus newspaper, the *Courtbouillon*, in April 1968 revealed Dent's impatience with rising protests elsewhere and the emergence of Black Power rhetoric. "Some of us want to be known as Blacks, others as Afro-Americans, some as Colored, and others as Negroes," Dent noted. "The assumption is, I presume, that what we are known as will have some dramatic effect on our participation in American and world society." After rejecting the use of drugs and the separatism of Black Power advocates, Dent argued that lasting solutions could come only from education — from the creation of minds characterized by understanding and intellectual discipline. "And where will we find such minds?" Dent asked. "My hope is that they will come from among Dillard students of today and tomorrow; and from others like you who have had the privilege of liberal education." By the fall of 1968, Dillard students were demanding a curriculum relevant to blacks, more and better black instructors and fewer white faculty members, better housing and food service, and extended curfews for women. That October, Dent, who had served as president for a quarter of a century, announced his decision to retire.[6]

The faculty at predominantly black colleges had also become divided along generational lines. Older black instructors, the backbone of most black college faculties, sometimes had trouble comprehending the behavior of campus activists. The activists believed that older teachers were concerned more about protecting the college and maintaining tradition than about meeting the needs of the black community. Moreover, activists sometimes complained that older professors were not competent teachers or scholars. "Most of them do not possess adequate training or educational backgrounds, having had little or no access to the scholarships and opportunities presently available to younger men," declared Robert Terrell, a Morehouse College senior who worked as a reporter for the *New York Post* from 1966 to 1968. "Many of them have been beaten down by racial discrimination and the lack of opportunity." Younger black instructors, conversely, tended to be more likely to identify with student activists' goals. In particular, the new generation of black teachers wanted to reform the decision-making processes on black-college campuses, where presidents still held disproportionate amounts of power. And they wanted to create a closer relationship between the campus and the black community. Terrell noted that although most younger black instructors had attended black colleges as undergraduates, they often had earned advanced degrees at predominantly white institutions. "They teach at Negro colleges because they want to and not because they have to," Terrell suggested.[7]

White faculty members at black institutions occupied the most precarious position. One of Black Power's central tenets was the need for blacks to control their own institutions. Such an outlook rendered the presence of white instructors inherently problematic. "Many Negroes and blacks are either suspicious of or openly hostile to white instructors," Terrell stated. "They do not believe that white instructors should be on Negro campuses." In fact, Terrell argued, most white faculty members were teaching at black campuses for "all the wrong reasons." Some were there because they felt guilty about American society's treatment of African Americans. Others saw their assignment as a sort of personal sociological experiment and were primarily interested in "learn[ing] about Negroes. And others needed jobs, and a teaching position at a Negro college was the first found."[8] A later analysis of white faculty on black campuses took an even more jaundiced view, breaking white professors down into four categories: the "moron," an incompetent professor who could not find a job on a white campus; the "martyr," who taught to expiate racial guilt; the "messiah," who was making an effort to "save the damned"; and the "marginal man," who occupied the only tenable position for white instructors. Members of this final category recognized their role as aliens in the black community and worked to create an accommodation between two different cultures.[9]

Ironically, at the same time that Black Power was calling into question the legitimacy of white teachers on black campuses, several programs, among them the Southern Teaching Program and the Woodrow Wilson Internship Program, were funding an influx of white faculty members. In another irony, white faculty members frequently encouraged student activism, inviting the enmity of administrators who wished to maintain quiet campuses. In 1965, the president of Bishop College in Dallas, Texas, dismissed a large group of white instructors who had come to the college through the Southern Regional Council's Southern Teaching Program. "They seem to have the idea they came down here for social revolution," the president complained. "Some of them must be sick, frustrated young fellows." A dean at Talladega College in 1966 voiced his belief that Woodrow Wilson teaching interns and other new faculty, encouraged by an older activist professor, were trying to foment rebellion on campus. In 1967, when South Carolina State College did not renew the contracts of three white Woodrow Wilson interns, students conducted a highly effective boycott.[10]

The timing of the growing controversy over white instructors reveals something of the uncertainty that surrounded black schools as desegregation proceeded. For decades, they had operated in relative obscurity, at least among white people. But the sit-in movement brought the South's black colleges and universities to the attention of a larger public. Because of the efforts to clamp down on student political activity, the weaknesses and shortcomings of black colleges received most of this attention. Observers such as C. Vann Woodward pointed out the political vulnerability of the leaders of Negro colleges and the numerous violations of academic freedom on black campuses, usually prompted by grandstanding, segregationist white politicians.[11] Accompanying the attention given to the violations of academic freedom was a heightened awareness of black institutions' educational and financial weaknesses. "The deadness, the stifling, the burden of Southern history press most heavily on the Southern Negro college," wrote Staughton Lynd, a white activist and history professor at Spelman College, in early 1964. "Generations of cultural deprivation have trained the Negro student, in [James] Baldwin's words, not to aspire to excellence but 'to make peace with mediocrity.'" Lynd went on to describe black college campuses with no bookstores, few student organizations, "a bare semblance of an independent newspaper," and poor laboratory facilities. Students, Lynd suggested, were poorly prepared when they entered school, having suffered through segregated and unequal primary and secondary schooling. And when they arrived on college campuses, they faced harshly restrictive environments: "Paternalism shows itself in the largely prescribed curriculum; in the absurdly restrictive social regulations; in the summary expulsion which student or faculty dissenters may expect."[12]

Lynd held out hope that the student movement was transforming black colleges. He also seemed to suggest, in relating the story of how he had decided to teach at a black college despite the contrary advice of his graduate program's vocational counselor, that one hope for black schools lay in the decisions of other progressive northern white teachers to come South.[13] In fact, the mid-1960s saw not only the advent of programs designed to send talented white instructors to black southern colleges but a trend in which elite nonsouthern institutions developed relationships with some black institutions.[14] At Miles College in Birmingham, President Lucius Pitts encouraged graduate students throughout the nation to take a year off to work at the college. John Monro, the dean of Harvard College, ventured to Miles for three summers in the mid-1960s to supervise and teach in a program designed to prepare recent high school graduates for college. In the spring of 1967, Monro resigned his position at Harvard to become director of freshman studies at Miles. Monro's program drew heavily on the missionary zeal of visiting professors and graduate students. One new Miles professor, Neil Friedman, a twenty-six-year-old with a doctorate from Harvard, came to Miles with "a zeal to right the wrongs he believes have been done to Negro students." Friedman acknowledged that his efforts were often experimental. "Nobody knows how to teach the culturally deprived," he said.[15]

By 1967, Friedman's well-intentioned if somewhat condescending words clashed with a rising tide of black consciousness. In August 1967, the Commission on Higher Educational Opportunity in the South, operating under the aegis of the Southern Regional Education Board, presented a report on predominantly Negro colleges that highlighted the institutions' major weaknesses. "In American society," the commission report stated, "a college degree is a badge of preparedness, but some graduates of Negro colleges have found it a hollow symbol because their preparation has been inadequate." Black educators rebelled at the blanket indictment of their institutions. The presidents of institutions within the Atlanta University Center were especially critical, arguing that the best black institutions were as good in their fields as the best white colleges. More significant, however, was the integrationist goal that the report presented. The commission called on southern states to develop long-range plans to eliminate "the South's dual system of higher education and create a single system serving all students."[16]

The rise of Black Power made this goal problematic at best. The ideas that comprised Black Power ideology were not new. They included racial separatism, a psychological and sometimes political identification with Africa, and the rejection of nonviolence and alliances with white liberals as effective tactics for black liberation. During the early 1960s, Malcolm X brought these themes together, only to see his militant posture become a foil for Martin Luther King Jr. and an implicit argument in support of nonviolent direct action. But time eroded King's hegemony. In 1966, "Black Power" entered the national lexicon as a political slogan when Carmichael used the phrase at an assembly of civil rights workers and reporters in Greenwood, Mississippi. "The only way we gonna stop them white men from whuppin' us is to take over," Carmichael declared. "We been saying freedom for six years and we ain't got nothin'. What we gonna start saying now is Black Power!"[17]

From that point on, one of the main challenges faced by Black Power's proponents was defining the term. Critics argued that it was a mere rhetorical device and was in fact devoid of meaning. The slogan certainly was subject to a variety of interpretations. Some activists used Black Power as a call for economic self-sufficiency, an idea that found favor not only with black business leaders but also with white conservatives such as Richard Nixon, who declared himself a proponent of black capitalism. Others saw more radical implications flowing from the phrase and called for a separate black nation within the United States. The diversity of meanings made Black Power a problematic political concept. But as a cultural impulse, the rise of Black Power was an important development. It was a broad movement encompassing many ideological orientations, but proponents of Black Power were united in the pursuit of the psychological liberation of African Americans.[18]

The Black Power critique grew from earlier demonstrations that focused on the stifling restrictions on students' intellectual and social lives and black institutions' educational shortcomings. These institutions began to serve as the target of organized protest activities around middecade. In these early demonstrations, black consciousness was often inchoate. With the rise of Black Power after 1966, along with several incidents of violent repression of demonstrations by law enforcement officials, black campus movements became more militant. A vision of a "black university," along with an implied rejection of integration as a primary goal, emerged along with more violent rhetoric. Activists continued to employ many of the tactics of nonviolent direct action but rejected the philosophy of nonviolence that James M. Lawson Jr. and the Nashville activists had championed.

Campus Activism and the Move toward Black Power

After the first two years of the 1960s, black college campuses temporarily became quieter places. In part, the ebb in activism resulted from the trajectory of the civil rights movement, although administrators' stiff resistance certainly played a role. In 1963, Sam Shirah, a white campus traveler for SNCC, noted that "at this point there is actually more motion on predominantly white campuses than on Negro ones."[19] By then, SNCC's goals were changing from integration to voter registration, while the organization's orientation was changing from the campus to the black community. When the predominantly white Southern Student Organizing Committee (SSOC) formed in 1964, one faction of the new organization envisioned it filling the campus-organizing void.[20]

However, SNCC did not completely lose sight of the campus. In the winter of 1964–65, SNCC sent organizers to Tuskegee Institute in search of participants for its Selma voter registration drive. SNCC had some success in mobilizing Tuskegee students, including George Ware, a graduate student in biological chemistry. In February 1965, Tuskegee students formed the Tuskegee Institute Advancement League (TIAL) in support of the Selma movement. They planned a march on the State Capitol for the following month, but the violence of 7 March at the Edmund Pettus Bridge in Selma threatened those plans. In fact, after a judge prohibited further marches, movement officials asked the Tuskegee students not to proceed. Nevertheless, more than seven hundred students, along with some faculty members and SNCC staff members, followed through with the demonstration on 10 March. They brought a petition to the Capitol protesting the denial of voting rights to black people as well as the brutal beatings of civil rights demonstrators at the Pettus Bridge. When Ware and another student leader attempted to read the petition, they were arrested. Frustrated, the students sat down on the sidewalk; many stayed for hours. By nightfall, about half of the students decided to leave, but the rest moved to a local church, where they spent the night. As SNCC veteran James Forman later wrote, the Montgomery episode represented the first time most of the Tuskegee students had participated in an organized demonstration against white supremacy, offering them a "cram course in civil rights." From these demonstrations emerged several students who went on to play important roles in the Tuskegee student movement, including Ware and Gwen Patton, a junior from Montgomery who won election as student body president a month after the Montgomery demonstration on a student-rights platform.[21]

More importantly, Forman suggested, the Montgomery experience prompted participating students to undertake a process of questioning that took them quickly from the violence in Selma to questions about their role as students: "What are my present goals as a black student? Is it enough for me just to get an education so that I can join (or remain in) the professional middle class? Does the administration of my school stand for progress or the status quo? Where do I stand in relation to that administration? What is the function of a student organization, and how do I relate to it? How far am I willing to go in order to end the oppression of black people? Who — to put it most basically — am I, and what is the meaning of my life as a black person in white America?"[22]

The mobilization of Tuskegee students during the winter of 1964–65 occurred as SNCC was becoming increasingly frustrated with older civil rights leaders and white liberals. It also occurred as a younger group was challenging the leadership of the Tuskegee movement by Charles Gomillion, chair of the institute's social science division. Younger activists increasingly rejected Gomillion's gradualist style, which had been the hallmark of Tuskegee blacks since the days of Booker T. Washington. One of these rebels was Charles V. Hamilton, a political science professor who had arrived at Tuskegee in 1958 at the age of twenty-eight. In early 1960, as the sit-in movement swept the South, Hamilton led a march of several hundred students from the campus to downtown Tuskegee. In April 1960, he was fired. Though Tuskegee president Luther Foster claimed that Hamilton's leadership of the march had nothing to do with his firing, Hamilton countered that Gomillion, chair of the institute's social science division, had told him that the march "figured in" the decision not to renew Hamilton's contract. Thus, the mobilization of Tuskegee students, who had been fairly quiet since 1960, represented a widening generation gap within the movement that corresponded with increasingly divergent views on the appropriateness of militant, confrontational tactics.[23]

Under the leadership of Ware and Patton, TIAL favored confrontation rather than Gomillion's usually quiet negotiation. In June 1965, the student organization launched an attack on segregated churches designed specifically to provoke a confrontation with whites. Whites responded as the TIAL members hoped, beating Tuskegee students who participated in the demonstrations. Racial tensions at Tuskegee increased, as did the gap between the activist students in TIAL and the Tuskegee administration, which had long exercised tight control over the institute. Led by Patton, students wanted to participate in campus decision-making bodies, to obtain better dormitory and cafeteria services, and to put an end to compulsory chapel. They marched on Foster's home, boycotted the vesper service, walked out of a mandatory chapel meeting, and conducted a cafeteria demonstration in which they turned over their plates.[24]

TIAL connected these on-campus goals with a voter registration drive. In this respect, the student organization represented a transitional stage between early and late 1960s activism. If black-student activism in the early 1960s focused primarily on the community, the later variety focused increasingly on the campus. In the winter of 1965–66, just a few months before Black Power became a rallying cry, the students who made up TIAL were blurring the lines between the campus and the community. Tactically, they rejected the gradualism of their elders. The January 1966 murder of Sammy Younge Jr., a Tuskegee student who had become an activist as a result of his participation in the Montgomery demonstration, pushed students toward greater tactical militancy and ideological radicalism. The student demonstrations that followed Younge's murder and then resumed in December 1966 after a jury acquitted Marvin Segrest, who had fired the shots that killed Younge, only widened the gap between students and administrators, setting the stage for a showdown in the spring of 1968.

Events at Tuskegee had great symbolic significance because of the institute's status as the living legacy of Booker T. Washington, the personification of the gradualism in pursuit of civil rights. Tuskegee students who chose to reject Gomillion and gradualism were, in effect, engaging in a personal battle with Washington, who was immortalized in a campus statue that depicted him as lifting a veil from the head of a kneeling black man. In Ralph Ellison's *The Invisible Man*, the protagonist notes that the statue can just as easily be read as Washington enshrouding rather than uncovering him the man. Does the statue represent "a revelation or a more efficient blinding"? One student activist, Wendell Paris, paraphrased Ellison's reading of the statue at a demonstration in the wake of Younge's murder: "We got this statue out here of that man who's suppose to be lifting up the veil. Man, he's putting it back on."[25]

Student activism at Tuskegee had more than symbolic importance. Several participants went on to play key roles in the spread of black student activism. Ware, the 1965–66 student body president who spearheaded much of the early TIAL activism, went on to work as SNCC's campus coordinator. In the fall of 1966, Ware traveled to Nashville to organize black students at Fisk and Tennessee Agricultural and Industrial State University. His work there played no small part in the Nashville student demonstrations of the following spring. In 1969, Ware participated in an effort to create a National Association of Black Students. Ernest Stephens, another Tuskegee activist, also went on to work with SNCC. And Patton subsequently signed on with the U.S. National Student Association's Southern Project and attempted to organize black students in the South along separatist lines.[26]

Nevertheless, if Tuskegee served as something of a nexus for black student activism in the 1960s, much also separated it from most black schools in the region. A high-profile, private institution, Tuskegee, though poor compared to white institutions, was wealthier than most of the region's other public and private black schools. In the spring of 1966, as Tuskegee students were organizing around the death of Younge and other issues, students at Alcorn Agricultural and Mechanical College in the southwestern Mississippi town of Lorman were engaged in their own struggle with a college administrator. In March 1966, students at Alcorn, one of the state's four public black colleges, asked Charles Evers, field secretary for the National Association for the Advancement of Colored People (NAACP), to help students organize against Alcorn's president, John D. Boyd. Boyd had suspended eight students for participating in civil rights activities and had fired the chief of campus security at Alcorn for his participation. On 4 March, campus security officers and local authorities arrested Evers and two hundred others in the midst of a march on the Alcorn campus to present a list of grievances to the president. A month later, students clashed with state troopers, who eventually used tear gas to drive brick-throwing students out of a dormitory. That same night, Evers tried to lead about three hundred African Americans who were not students onto campus, but seventy-five troopers barred the way. The next day was even more violent, with clashes between protesters and law enforcement officials producing what a *New York Times* reporter called a "wild, 15-minute melee that pitted bottles against rifle butts, nightsticks and tear gas." Alcorn students were not, however, part of the fight.[27]

Boyd, an Alcorn alumnus who had earned a master's degree at the University of Illinois before returning to his alma mater, answered to the all-white Mississippi state board of education. His freedom of action was severely limited, as he acknowledged to reporters when he said that he was "not opposed to civil rights," having "gone as far as a man in my position could go." Boyd added that he was not a member of the NAACP, "but I have contributed to it and I was working for better race relations before Mr. Evers even knew what they were." Nevertheless, Evers and the students made Boyd the primary issue. "J. D. Boyd has got to go," Evers declared. "We're going to get him sooner or later. He's only concerned with pleasing the white folks." The indictment of Boyd involved more than his restrictions on student participation in civil rights activities. The spring 1966 demonstrations also constituted a statement about Alcorn's quality as an institution of higher education. "This is my alma mater," Evers declared. "I went to school here four years, and right now I couldn't pass a sixth grade examination. They got teachers without degrees, students teaching. It's no wonder the Negro can't elevate himself." Students added complaints about the food, the infirmary, and the grading system. "They treat us like babies," one student told a reporter, adding that Boyd "won't even talk to us and we are students. The president dominates the whole school." Another student noted, "At the library they search you when you come out. And we have an infirmary that is not fit to take care of dogs."[28]

The Alcorn protests produced little substantive change on the campus. Evers took the case against Alcorn to the state board of education, which responded by praising Boyd for maintaining control on campus. ssoc attempted to carry the banner for Alcorn students by publicizing the demonstrations, assisted by the *New York Times*'s front-page coverage of the situation, and encouraging sympathy demonstrations on other southern campuses. But overwhelming white control prevented meaningful reform at Alcorn.[29]

The same might be said for Louisiana's Southern University, where Felton Grandison Clark had clamped down so harshly on student demonstrations in the early 1960s. Clark's actions had not killed student activism at Southern, which was less repressive than Mississippi's black colleges. Another wave of student activism developed at Southern in 1965, stimulated in large part by ssoc. In March 1965, seeking to position itself as the mobilizing instrument for all campuses in the South, ssoc elected an interracial slate of officers that included Herman Carter, a student at Southern, as its secretary.[30] Carter played a central role in demonstrations that developed at the Baton Rouge campus in November 1965 and authored a pamphlet that interpreted the movement to the rest of the region. The pamphlet began with a discussion of racial and economic inequality in the United States. Carter suggested that institutions reinforced this inequality and demonstrated how Southern University served this purpose by severely limiting its students' freedom of thought and action. "In essence," Carter declared, "Southern University perpetuates academic slavery, not freedom." He then connected problems on the Southern campus with problems in the community in which the university was situated. The residents of Scotlandville, where Southern was located, lived with open ditch sewers, unpaved roads, poor street lighting, unemployment, dangerous intersections, low water pressure, and bad storm drainage. Students at Southern suffered from inadequate dormitories, a limited library, a poor infirmary, overcrowded classrooms, a small student union building, and substandard classroom equipment. Students, Carter argued, needed to organize to address the problems not only on campus but also in the community.[31]

In November 1965, Carter led a movement of students on these issues. The demonstrations began on 15 November with a rally designed to galvanize students behind a direct-action crusade.[32] The following day, a march on the administration building by some five hundred students turned into an impromptu sit-in at a major campus intersection. That evening, a rally near the women's dormitories turned into a debate between activist leaders and representatives of the student government, who asked students to end the demonstration so that the student government leaders could negotiate with the administration.

Despite these entreaties, a 17 November rally attracted about fifteen hundred students and led to another march on the administration building. Southern's vice president then consented to negotiations, acknowledging that the students had some legitimate grievances and agreeing that the students should pressure state leaders to act. University officials subsequently removed the barbed-wire barriers that had prevented students from walking on the campus lawns and expanded library hours. Still, Carter noted, student government leaders continued to oppose activism.[33]

Like the TIAL's activities, the activism at Southern University represented a transitional stage in black-student activism. Activists merged community with campus issues, and while they highlighted the role that racial exploitation played in both sets of issues, they did not emphasize the need for black consciousness. In fact, the Southern movement was implicitly integrationist: its demands included the merger of all Louisiana schools to eliminate inequalities in state appropriations. In light of Carter's role in the SSOC at a time when the organization was purposefully interracial, this integrationist tendency is perhaps not surprising. Nevertheless, SSOC's interracial stage soon came to an end, and subsequent student movements on black campuses increasingly envisioned the improvement of black institutions of higher education through the lens of black consciousness.

The move toward black consciousness and its role in modifying student activism became apparent in a series of demonstrations in Nashville in early 1967. Ware had moved to Nashville in August 1966. The following spring, he organized a speaking tour for SNCC's Carmichael. In Nashville, Tennessee legislators and other white leaders attempted to prevent Carmichael from visiting, a move that angered students not only at Fisk and Tennessee A&I but also at Vanderbilt. On 8 April, Carmichael spoke to a predominantly white audience of more than five thousand at Vanderbilt before moving on to Fisk University. The speech at Vanderbilt was, according to the *New York Times*, "perhaps his first speech at a major Southern university." At Fisk, the SNCC chair urged students to "take over the administration" of their school. After the speech, an apparently unrelated altercation at a nearby restaurant between the establishment's management and a Fisk student quickly developed into a riot that lasted for three nights, with students from Fisk and A&I shouting, "Black power! Black power!" According to the *Times*, "That the disturbance started at Fisk surprised many community leaders here because the school was a leader in nonviolent protest during the sit-in here seven years ago."[34]

Nashville's white officials quickly blamed Carmichael for inciting the riots, while students complained that police had been unnecessarily zealous in their response to the initial conflict. In November, Fisk president James R. Lawson testified before a U.S. Senate subcommittee that only about fifty Fisk students had anything to do with the riots. Only six Fisk students were arrested, Lawson said. Nevertheless, Lawson also testified that the altercation between the student and the restaurant management, which precipitated the riots, seemed to have been prearranged; within five minutes of the dispute, students were at the restaurant with picket signs.[35]

Regardless of their origins, the riots nudged Fisk students toward Black Power. By the fall of 1967, they were calling for curricular changes that would focus more attention on black history and non-Western culture. *The Autobiography of Malcolm X* had become required reading. Expressions of hostility toward whites were aired with greater frequency. One Fisk professor, political scientist Paul D. Puryear, suggested that the class background of many Fisk students lent itself to activism. Newer members of the middle class, for whom upward mobility was more important, were less likely to engage in demonstrations for fear of endangering their chance at financial security. But Fisk, long a stronghold of the black elite, had a disproportionate percentage of students from more established families, Puryear argued. "Second- and third-generation middle-class Negroes are not willing to play the same game their parents played," he told the *New York Times*. "On the other hand, first generation Negro kids are like other first generation kids — they want jobs and security." If Puryear's analysis was accurate, then one manifestation of the tendency of financially comfortable students toward activism was their corresponding interest in less fortunate blacks. One professor declared that "the riots were beneficial because they taught middle-class Negroes that they were no different from any other Negro in the eyes of the police." Similarly, Gloria Anderson, the editor of the Fisk student newspaper, noted that since the riots, "for the first time Fisk was identified with the black community of Nashville."[36]

Such an explanation lends itself to a cynical and all-too-hasty conclusion that activism was merely a luxury for pampered offspring of the black middle class. Indeed, commentators at the time and since have reached the same conclusion about white activism. But such conclusions must be squared with the reality that activism touched not only the campuses of comparatively privileged black students but also campuses catering to students from farther down the socioeconomic scale. About the same time that Fisk students and faculty were grappling with the class implications of the emergence of black consciousness at their university, students at Grambling College in Louisiana were organizing their own student movement.

The differences between Grambling and Fisk were unmistakable. Like Alcorn and Southern, Grambling was a state-funded institution under the direction of an all-white state board of education. In this case, Ralph Waldo Emerson Jones played the role of the obedient (to his bosses) and autocratic (to his students) president. Located in rural northern Louisiana, minutes away from Louisiana Tech in Ruston and some thirty miles from Monroe, Grambling felt little impact from the early 1960s sit-in movement. By early 1967, the college still subjected students to a long list of rules: women could not wear pants, dormitories were locked at ten o'clock in the evening, and students were required to eat breakfast at six o'clock in the morning. Large signs hanging in the dining hall admonished students to "Take bite-size mouthfuls" and "Break bread before eating."[37] Student protests in the spring of 1967 brought an agreement from Jones to liberalize campus rules, but no changes had been implemented by the fall. In response, Grambling students, led by a group of men, the Informers, initiated a boycott on 25 October that quickly won widespread student participation.[38] The following morning, some twenty-five hundred students began a sit-in on the campus's main square. When administrators refused to negotiate, the demonstrators blocked the administration building's entrances; shouted, "Hell No, We Won't Go"; and sang songs. By 27 October, five hundred National Guardsmen had arrived in the area. College officials soon expelled the Informers, and the boycott collapsed.[39]

As at Alcorn, students at Grambling combined complaints about in loco parentis with criticisms of the college's inadequacy. They argued that Grambling's emphasis on athletics — the college funneled more players into the National Football League than did any other college or university in the country with the exception of Notre Dame — distracted from the mission of educating students. "It is true that basically Grambling is a college of athletics. It is true that the average student at Grambling reads on a 9th or 10th grade level. Percentage wise, the athletes make up only 4% of the college. It is true that this small group of athletes get more attention and consideration than the other 96% of nonathletes," the Informers declared.[40]

As the Informers saw it, one of the main problems with the situation was that it prevented the students at Grambling from competing with whites on an equal footing. These activists built their efforts around a desire to improve Grambling to better prepare its graduates. "OUR AIM IS ACADEMIC EXCELLENCY," they declared in one protest newspaper. "WE WANT A BETTER SCHOOL!!" Moreover, the Informers described themselves as good students who were nonviolent.[41]

While the students' goals centered on opening up the restrictive campus and improving the institution's quality, they announced those goals using some of the emerging language of Black Power. In one pamphlet published during the October demonstrations, the Informers placed their movement in the context of U.S. history. Beginning with the "honkie settlers" who realized that "something was wrong with their type of government" and organized to correct that wrong, the short history moved quickly through the Civil War and culminated with modern black leaders who emerged to free black people from bondage.

The leaders they cited did not, however, include Martin Luther King Jr. or others who espoused integration and nonviolence. Instead, the Informers cited Malcolm X, Stokely Carmichael, and H. Rap Brown.[42]

But despite such evidence of the emergence of black consciousness in the Grambling demonstrations, the essential problem these students were addressing, as at Alcorn, was the institution's quality as measured by an external — presumably white — standard. That is, students might have blamed the institution's problems on white people and their black accomplices but did not seem to question the assumptions that underlay the idea of the college or university. Rather, they complained that the white and black establishment was running the institution unfairly and/or poorly. Instructors were unqualified. Administrators placed too much emphasis on athletics and not enough on academics and put too many unnecessary and unfair restrictions on students. Such criticism fell well short of a full-fledged application of Black Power ideology to segregated higher education. Noticeably absent were calls for a black studies department or for the institution to take a more active role in alleviating the problems that plagued black Americans.

The Black University Comes into Focus

When it came to courses or programs that concentrated on the African American experience, black colleges and universities were no further along in 1968 than were predominantly white universities. In March 1968, in a special issue of *Negro Digest* devoted to the black university, North Carolina Agricultural and Technical College graduate dean Darwin T. Turner noted that aside from a few classes in history and literature, he knew of few courses "oriented to the Negro" in black institutions. "We can blame ourselves," Turner argued. "Nothing — to my knowledge — prevents predominantly Negro colleges from offering any course that is desired." While he acknowledged that black college presidents, at the behest of white officials, had in some instances clamped down on student demonstrations and that southern legislators had passed speaker bans, he contended that "white legislators scarcely knew or cared who spoke to the Negro students."[43]

Not surprisingly, considering its historic importance to black America, Howard University played a critical role in the development of a Black Power critique of the university and the emergence of the concept of the "black university," which provided a rallying cry on black campuses during the late 1960s and early 1970s. Founded in 1867 to provide educational opportunities to former slaves, Howard had subsequently been designed along lines of white colleges. Located in Washington, D.C., the university received half of its budget from the federal government. For years, the institution represented the pinnacle of success for African Americans in the academic world. During the early 1960s, students had mounted a significant sit-in movement. These students — including future SNCC stalwarts including Carmichael, Cleveland Sellers, Stanley Wise, and Courtland Cox — formed the Nonviolent Action Group and conducted demonstrations in Maryland and northern Virginia. However, activists complained that most Howard students were primarily concerned with attaining bourgeois status.[44] With the emergence of campus activism and Black Power, however, Howard became vulnerable to attack from student activists. Under the leadership of President James M. Nabrit Jr., the university maintained tight control over students' lives while offering them little power to govern themselves.[45]

In the fall of 1964, a group, Students for Academic Freedom, began demanding greater participation in setting admission standards, financial policies affecting students, and new curricular programs. These same sorts of student power concerns gelled again during the 1966–67 academic year, when two law students spearheaded a student-rights movement that initially centered on the lack of a written code of campus rules and the lack of student representation in the judiciary process. From this beginning came the Student Rights Organization, formed in late November. The group's grievances soon extended to compulsory participation in the Reserve Officers' Training Corps, restrictive curfews, and the lack of black awareness, which was becoming increasingly important with the emergence of the Black Power rallying cry. Campus events soon caused black awareness to resonate even more among Howard students.[46]

In September 1966, Nabrit announced his intention to raise admission standards to bring greater racial mixture to the student body. Black students who failed a proposed admission test might be admitted for a year of remedial work with a curriculum that would include a speech course as well as courses in reading skills, masterpieces of world literature, and the history of Western civilization. According to Nathan Hare, a sociology professor who would become the most vocal proponent of remaking Howard into a "black university," Nabrit's proposal had practically no support among students. "This curriculum would say to black students, who already were failures as individuals, that they had no ennobling ancestral roots: their kind had produced no civilization worthy of attention, no literary achievements, and indeed are guilty now of the wrong mode of speech," Hare complained in early 1968, after Howard had fired him.[47]

In early 1967, a group of students asked Hare to help them craft a manifesto in support of black awareness on campus. In February, this Black Power Committee issued a manifesto that called for "the overthrow of the Negro college" and its replacement by "a militant black university which will counteract the active white-washing black students now receive in 'Negro' and white institutions." The committee suggested that Howard be renamed Nat Turner or Garvey University and that the institution emphasize "subjects more pertinent to the present and future demands of the black struggle in America and the world."[48] By 1968, two black awareness groups had formed—Ujamma (Swahili for "togetherness"), a coalition of several groups, and the United Black People's Party, a more radical black nationalist student group. The combination of frustrated reform and black awareness set in motion events that led to a student takeover of the administration building. The outside impetus for the takeover in February 1968 came from Orangeburg, South Carolina, where a clash between students at South Carolina State College and police resulted in the shooting deaths of three students. The 8 February Orangeburg Massacre angered students at Howard, and eight days later, nearly five hundred students staged a sympathy demonstration that developed into an attack on Howard authorities for failure to provide leadership to the black community. Ujamma produced a pamphlet, *Spear and Shield*, that called for a number of reforms: the creation of a black university with more courses in black history and related subjects, the reinstatement of professors fired for political activism, the creation of a student judiciary committee and greater student control over budget matters, and Howard's redirection into an institution that was more relevant to the black community. The pamphlet, which became known as the Orangeburg Ultimatum, also called for the resignations of Nabrit and other administrators.[49]

The rising tensions came to a head in March, culminating in a three-day student takeover of the administration building that ended with trustees offering four concessions: student judiciary control, changes to make Howard "more attuned to the times and the mood of its people," a student-faculty board to work on student complaints, and amnesty for sit-in participants. After some debate, a majority of students voted to accept the concessions, though more militant students and Hare, who participated in the demonstration, called the agreement a sellout.[50] The events at Howard, intermingled as they were with events at South Carolina State, represented a watershed in black campus activism. In the short run, the well-publicized Howard demonstrations helped to generate subsequent demonstrations on other black campuses, including Fisk and Tougaloo, although none of these spin-offs lasted as long or received as much attention.[51] The spring 1968 Howard demonstrations represented the fullest development to date of a combined student rights and Black Power movement on a black campus. Thanks in part to the early participation of Hare, who went on to play a role in protests at San Francisco State, the Howard movement fleshed out the concept of a black university. Subsequent protest movements on black campuses throughout the South would employ varying interpretations of the black university.

At its most basic level, activists built their interpretations of the concept around two interrelated principles. First, proponents envisioned an institution whose curriculum was specifically geared toward African Americans' experiences. Black colleges as they existed in the 1960s, adherents of this view argued, were poor replicas of white institutions, with curricula designed to produce black graduates with no knowledge of their racial heritage. Black universities would correct this situation with a curriculum that would produce self-aware graduates. Second, black universities would be intimately connected with the black community. Community members would play an important role in university affairs, and the university in turn would work to alleviate the problems that confronted black Americans. At their worst, visions of the black university were both vague and utopian, not unlike the some of the parallel institutions envisioned by members of the New Left and the counterculture. But despite its excesses, the concept of the black university represented an important critique of higher education for African Americans. Drawing intellectual support from a rapidly expanding body of new scholarship in African American history and culture, the proponents of the black university joined a larger chorus of voices calling on Americans to recognize and eliminate the racial blind spots that had gone largely unquestioned on both white and black campuses.[52]

Through 1967, the Howard movement essentially constituted an institutional reform movement on two fronts. On one front, students and administrators battled over restrictions on the social lives of students and their right to govern themselves in nonacademic matters. On the other front, students argued for a restructuring of the curriculum and institutional purpose that would move Howard in the direction of the ideal of the black university. However, the Orangeburg Massacre raised the stakes, perhaps nudging the students toward a greater willingness to employ militant rhetoric and confrontational tactics. Indeed, if Howard served as a prototype for the black student movement that combined student rights and Black Power goals, then the clash between students and police in Orangeburg offered a prototype of another kind. The Orangeburg Massacre demonstrated that whenever black students in the South organized demonstrations, the possibility of violent clashes with law enforcement officials was never far away.

The Orangeburg Massacre and 1968 Campus Explosions

Orangeburg, a town of almost fourteen thousand located forty miles southeast of the state capital, had seen occasional outbursts of student activism in the preceding decade from the campuses of South Carolina State College and its next-door neighbor, Claflin College. In 1960, students on both campuses had staged sit-ins, prompting some violent clashes between demonstrators and police. In addition, an ongoing battle between students and the autocratic South Carolina State president, Benner C. Turner, was never far from the surface. In early 1967, this conflict erupted again when Turner refused to renew the contracts of the school's first two white faculty members. Both were Woodrow Wilson fellows and were popular, and the refusal to retain them initiated a student protest movement that eventually resulted in Turner's retirement in May 1967 at the age of sixty-one. His successor, former business manager M. Maceo Nance Jr., brought a more open administration. Moreover, in the aftermath of Turner's retirement, the chair of the state Commission on Higher Education created a committee to investigate the college's administrative operations. Its recommendations included the creation of a faculty senate, the adoption of a statement on academic freedom, and a revised policy on appointments, tenure, promotion, and dismissal. Thus, not unlike Howard, South Carolina State's student-led university reform movement had peaked in 1967. In fact, the South Carolina State movement had been more successful than its Howard counterpart.[53]

Evidence of the impact of Black Power began to emerge on the campus in 1967. In the spring, a few students organized the Black Awareness Coordinating Committee, while more moderate students organized a campus chapter of the NAACP. Cleveland Sellers, a veteran SNCC member, a native of Denmark, South Carolina, and a former Howard undergraduate, moved to Orangeburg and established a working relationship with the coordinating committee's members. However, the black awareness movement at South Carolina State did not zero in on the college's curriculum, as had the movement at Howard. Rather, blatant racial discrimination in Orangeburg provided a bigger target. The city boundary lines were gerrymandered to keep most blacks outside the city limits. For students, a particularly glaring example of continued discrimination was Orangeburg's only bowling alley, the All-Star Bowling Lanes, which was located about three blocks from the South Carolina State and Claflin campuses. In August 1966, a group of South Carolina State students went to the bowling alley, only to be turned away. The following fall, the new campus NAACP chapter discussed the possibility of taking action against the bowling alley. By December, almost any time a conversation on racism occurred on campus, someone mentioned the bowling alley. One student might suggest that things were getting better for blacks, only to hear, "Why can't we bowl then? Because we're black, that's why."[54]

On 5 February 1968, students from South Carolina State and Claflin, including members of the Black Awareness Coordinating Committee, visited the All-Star Bowling Lanes. Harry L. Floyd, the owner, would not allow the students to bowl and asked them to leave. When they refused to comply, Floyd called the police. Orangeburg's chief of police, Roger Poston, arrived and cleared out the bowling alley. The next night, another group of black students appeared at the bowling alley, and fifteen were arrested. Word spread throughout the two campuses, and by 7:45 P.M., about three hundred students had assembled in the parking lot, where they milled around with no apparent plan of action. City officials, alarmed at the gathering, decided to release the arrested students if they promised to urge those in the parking lot to return to campus. The detainees abided by the plan, and students began to leave, but the arrival of a fire engine, called presumably because its fire hoses could be used to quell any potential disturbance, angered the students. The situation escalated, and a brief melee ensued, during which some policemen beat the students, who responded by breaking the windows of businesses on the way back to the campus. After a late-night rally on the South Carolina State campus, the students decided to get a permit to march the next day. Male students were particularly enraged by the alleged beating of women in the crowd. Nance, South Carolina State's acting president at the time, picked up on this theme the next day, declaring that although he did not condone the destruction of property, "it happened after the young ladies were hit."[55]

The next day, students released a list of grievances, with demands that included a change in the bowling alley's discriminatory policy, an investigation of police brutality, a fair employment commission, changes in the city's discriminatory health care patterns, and complete enforcement of the 1964 Civil Rights Act. No response was immediately forthcoming, and on the night of 7 February, a group of mostly male students from South Carolina State and Claflin rampaged for several hours, at times tossing rocks at passing automobiles. That night, units of the National Guard, alerted the previous day by South Carolina governor Robert E. McNair, moved in.[56]

The climactic confrontation came the next night. During the day, Nance issued a memorandum requesting that students remain on campus. Some students, led by the Black Awareness Coordinating Committee, pushed for a more forceful response to events. During the evening, while an estimated two hundred students milled around the edge of the campus, someone suggested that they build a bonfire. Highway patrolmen, guardsmen, and city police were present, and tensions increased until a fire truck arrived. As firemen moved to extinguish the bonfire, the situation exploded. A banister pulled from a nearby building hit an officer. After a few minutes, a law enforcement official fired a shot. Other shots quickly followed during the next few seconds. The episode resulted in the deaths of three students, one of them from a nearby high school. Twenty-eight other students were injured.[57] As journalist Jack Nelson pointed out two years later, the entire episode bore a striking resemblance to May 1970 shootings at Kent State that resulted in the deaths of four students.[58]

The Orangeburg Massacre did not produce the same kind of national outrage and soul-searching, at least among whites, that Kent State produced two years later. Most mainstream media outlets accepted the official explanation that emanated from McNair's office: while regrettable, the shootings were the understandable response of law officers faced with sniper fire from the campus, which, in turn, had directly resulted from a minority of Black Power advocates on the two campuses. The chief culprit among these militants, according to the official story, was Sellers, who was eventually convicted of inciting a riot and sentenced to a year in prison. To South Carolina whites and some conservative blacks, Sellers came to personify the Black Power menace. Subsequent investigations by the Southern Regional Council and journalists Jack Bass and Jack Nelson demonstrated that Sellers had played a relatively small part in the escalating violence and that claims that the students had initiated the shooting were false.[59]

Over the next few months, McNair continued to hammer home the message that Orangeburg was a student-initiated, Black Power–inspired riot and that "the only way you can control it is to bring in maximum police power and immediately to isolate, control, and contain."[60] The governor's rhetoric reflected politicians' growing tendency to conflate urban and campus uprisings, especially when black students were involved, and to argue that both called for a renewed emphasis on law and order. Sellers's presence provided a convenient link to Black Power, which whites and conservative blacks found increasingly alarming. Other observers, however, found little connection between Black Power and the developments in Orangeburg and in fact likened the protests to the sit-in movement. One student, twenty-three-year-old Bob Haynes of Florence, South Carolina, told the New York Times that the Orangeburg protests revealed more than the influence of a few outside agitators espousing the idea of Black Power: "I don't think the supporters of black power played as great a part as the Governor thinks. I think the Governor is misinformed. If he had been at the meetings on the campus this week, he would have seen that the whole student body was concerned."[61] And in their report for the Southern Regional Council, Pat Watters and Weldon Rougeau emphasized the marginal roles played by Black Power rhetoric, the Black Awareness Coordinating Committee, and Sellers, concluding, "Black power was not the issue in Orangeburg." Indeed, the grievances outlined by the students after the initial confrontations at the bowling alley centered on white Orangeburg's failure to live up to the spirit of the Civil Rights Act of 1964. The students wanted to eliminate vestiges of segregation, not implement black separatism.[62] Nevertheless, some students' mood and demeanor as well as rhetoric revealed the imprint of Black Power. One crucial aspect of the emphasis on black consciousness was the rejection of deferential attitudes toward white people. In their clashes with police, the students showed a willingness at times to employ vulgar insults. Some threw bricks and bottles, while others took out their frustrations on the facades of business establishments. These were not the organized, nonviolent demonstrations of the early 1960s.

More than anything else, Orangeburg symbolized the potential violence that loomed any time black students organized on southern campuses. "Was it necessary that three people be killed because one hundred of them threw bricks?" asked Benjamin F. Payton, the president of historically black Benedict College in Columbia, South Carolina, a few days after the shootings. "I have difficulty conceiving in my imagination of the highway patrolmen firing point-blank at students at the University of South Carolina and Clemson on doing the same thing."[63] The presidents of the six institutions of the Atlanta University Center drafted an open letter appealing to President Lyndon B. Johnson and other public officials to prevent college and university campuses from invasions by "the American version of storm troopers."[64] As the news about Orangeburg filtered to campuses throughout the South, students responded with demonstrations. At Howard, the incident provided additional motivation for students to express grievances that were already present. At North Carolina Agricultural and Technical College in Greensboro, student activist Nelson Johnson led a group of students to a funeral home, where they obtained a coffin and took it to the A&T student union for an impromptu demonstration.[65]

The Orangeburg Massacre was soon followed by Martin Luther King Jr.'s assassination, which further signaled the emerging theme of violence in black student protest in the South. Throughout the nation, urban blacks rioted in response to King's murder. On campuses throughout the South, students organized demonstrations to memorialize King. The demonstrations were particularly intense on black campuses, where King's death often served as a flash point for students to express their dissatisfaction with both their school and the society. Students took over administration buildings at Fayetteville State in North Carolina and Virginia Union in Richmond; they boycotted classes and picketed at Virginia State in Petersburg and at Tuskegee. Demonstrations over King's death turned into clashes with police at Tennessee A&I in Nashville, North Carolina A&T in Greensboro, Florida A&M in Tallahassee, and Shaw University in Raleigh, North Carolina.[66]

The events at Tuskegee were particularly dramatic. There, students took over a building where members of the institute's board of trustees were meeting and held the trustees captive. The takeover represented the culmination of several years of student activism. By late 1967, campus issues loomed especially large. In December, engineering students issued a list of demands concerning the quality of their academic program. In February 1968, spurred in part by the events in Orangeburg, another group of activist students, aided by a contingent from Ohio's Central State University and intent on implementing the imperatives of Black Power at Tuskegee, created an organization, Unity. On 20 February, some of these students threw eggs during a program featuring representatives of the U.S. State Department. Unity's more immediate concerns, however, were campus issues. Members of the group wrote a set of demands, including restoration of the student judicial system, voluntary instead of compulsory participation in the Reserve Officers' Training Corps, longer library hours, student representation on policymaking boards, and athletic scholarships. A student boycott on 25 March prompted President Foster to reinstate the student judicial system and extend library hours, but he declined to act on the issue of military training, stating that the matter would have to go to the board of trustees. Students went back to classes.[67]

The student-administration conflict headed for a showdown on 7 April, Tuskegee's Founder's Day, when the institute celebrated its history and members of the board of trustees convened. In preparation, activist students prepared a twenty-page list of demands that centered on the concept of a black university and included a statement of general philosophy that called on the members of the institute community to "speak from a black experience and address themselves to black collective needs." Specific demands included courses in Afro-American history and sociology and African languages, a change in the emphasis in all social science disciplines to relate them to the black experience, the establishment of a student theater that could produce plays expressing black concerns, and the abolition of compulsory participation in the Reserve Officers' Training Corps.[68]

News of King's assassination came just as the conflict was approaching a boiling point. In response to King's death, activists decided to "stop all activities on campus so that the trustees would have to do some serious thinking about our demands," recalled Michael Wright, a Unity leader. Between twenty and thirty students locked all of the academic buildings, while other protesters marched. A student committee met with the trustees on 5 April, and the trustees responded to the demands with a promise to take seriously student concerns. The trustees cautioned, however, that making changes required time and recommended that the appropriate student-faculty committees begin working on the issues. Tuskegee's young activists deemed the response evasive.[69]

On 6 April, students took over Dorothy Hall, where the trustees were meeting. By the evening, school officials had obtained an injunction against the building takeover. Rumors spread that state troopers and the National Guard were on the way. With images of Orangeburg still fresh in their minds, students worried about violence, and the group's solidarity dissipated. Participants eventually voted to release the trustees but not Foster. Shortly before three o'clock in the morning, with between 100 and 150 students still in the building, the National Guard arrived. "There was nothing we could do — we were really in very pitiful shape," recalled Wright. The last of the students left.[70]

Foster subsequently announced that the entire school would close for two weeks and that all dorms must be vacated by 9 April. The institute required all students to file a statement of intent before receiving an application for readmission. Students were required to declare their "firm intention to abide by the rules and regulations of the Institute." School reopened on 22 April after 90 percent of students filed readmission applications. The institute fully admitted twenty-five hundred students, with an additional ninety on probation. Fifty-four students were not readmitted.[71]

Black Power at Its Height

Demonstrations continued throughout the South during the 1968–69 academic year. The Urban Research Council reported 292 "major student protests" on 232 campuses in the first six months of 1969. Although fewer than 6 percent of the students attending colleges and universities in the country were black, black students were involved in 51 percent of the protests, and seventeen tradition-ally black colleges saw major student protests.[72] By then, Black Power rhetoric suffused activism on black campuses, and violence loomed every time students organized. A new generation of black students helped generate this rising tide of Black Power activism. As a group, the younger activists were more willing to challenge authority and less likely than their predecessors to view integration as their primary goal. Divisions of course remained within the student popula-tion. One 1969 survey of the attitudes of black college students throughout the South found that those students concerned with black experiences and black consciousness constituted 20–25 percent of the student body. But an additional 23 percent of the student population expressed dissatisfaction with the admin-istration and were potential activists.[73]

Private campuses tended to foster the most militant versions of Black Power. Activists at privately controlled black institutions, especially those with reputations for higher academic standards and with a tendency to draw students from higher socioeconomic backgrounds, were more likely to pursue separat-ism and educational goals influenced by black nationalism. The drive for sepa-ratism often took the form of an effort to replace white faculty members with black professors. This issue was less pressing on public campuses, where whites were unlikely to teach, than at private colleges, whose facilities included many white instructors. Mississippi's Tougaloo College, for example, had acquired the nickname the "Oasis" in the early 1960s by virtue of its support for integra-tion and the presence of a few white students and faculty. But during the fall of 1968, freshman students demanded a black-oriented social science curriculum and more black professors. They also threatened to burn down a building that housed mostly white faculty and offices for white administrators. Not long after the demonstrations, which led to some curricular changes, an unexplained fire gutted part of that building.[74]

Clashes over the presence of white faculty members were especially heated at the institutions of the Atlanta University Center, in part because white instructors were especially visible. For example, Clark College had more whites than blacks on the faculty. The Atlanta University Center's shared art department faculty was all white, as was the psychology faculty. And in the general science project, where students from all six institutions took the same introductory courses, all of the faculty members were white. One student journalist, citing administrative sources, noted that white job applicants outnumbered black applicants by as much as forty to one. "To some, this may look like progress," reported Charlayne Hunter, one of the first black students at the University of Georgia, in a 1968 assessment of the mood of black students. "To the black students and some of the more activist black professors, this is cause for resentment."[75] That resentment boiled over in November 1968, when male students ejected Justine Giannetti, a white public-speaking teacher, from a Spelman College classroom after she allegedly called one black student a "jackass." Giannetti acknowledged using the word but insisted that it had no racial connotations. But the incident coincided with a rising tide of student activism, in which Atlanta University Center students were exploring the implications of black consciousness for the campus.[76]

The Atlanta University Center had been the scene of public debates over Black Power almost from the moment it emerged as a rallying cry in 1966. In July 1966, shortly after he was elected chair of SNCC, Stokely Carmichael participated in a public discussion at Spelman with Randolph Blackwell, head of the Southern Christian Leadership Conference, in which the two leaders discussed the merits and problems of Black Power.[77] The Atlanta University Center initially provided a platform for strongly worded critiques of the concept. In the summer of 1966, Atlanta University political science professor Samuel DuBois Cook publicly expressed his reservations in "The Tragic Myth of Black Power." Black Power, Cook argued, was "nonsense" and was destined to fail. "The Negro must form alliances and coalitions with liberal, progressive, and moderate whites," Cook contended. "Since he is a clear minority, constituting only about 10.5 percent of the total population, sheer arithmetic is against the success of any isolated program of action. There is no possibility of any black takeover of power. The Negro, therefore, must have allies and friends." Moreover, Cook suggested that Black Power's particularistic view of society was ethically inferior to the vision of the "beloved community."[78] Spelman president Albert E. Manley echoed Cook's thoughts in a fall 1966 series of lectures to the school's student body during which Manley employed the oft-cited criticism of Black Power as reverse racism: "It is absurd for radical exponents of black power to attempt to rip off the entire fabric of society as it exists and to substitute one form of racism for another."[79]

These public pronouncements did not prevent Atlanta University Center students from embracing Black Power and attempting to apply it to their campuses. At the beginning of the fall 1968 term, activist students formed the Ad Hoc Committee for a Black University. Organizers bypassed the established student governments of the individual schools, which were perceived as too conservative and as unable effectively to negotiate the committee's demands. Soon thereafter, the committee issued demands to each of the six college presidents. The demands combined student power and Black Power concerns and included 51 percent student representation on all committees, including the board of trustees; administrative support for student-sponsored community projects; disarming of the Atlanta University Security Patrol Force; elimination of administration-sponsored cultural events "which do not relate directly to the African or Afro-American culture — including appearances by Atlanta Symphony Orchestra"; automatic admission for any person active in the movement; and elimination of student-sponsored exchange programs that did not involve African, Third World, or black students. The demands seemed to have strong support. In fact, an activist-generated petition to ascertain the percentage of students supporting the goals found well over 50 percent in sympathy. A statement accompanying the demands characterized them as necessary steps in transforming Negro colleges into black institutions. The students connected the repression they faced as students with the repression that enslaved "the bodies and minds of Africans all over the world. . . . The so-called 'Negro College,' with the Atlanta University system high on the list, continues to function as one of the main tools used by our oppressors to perpetuate the cruel colonization of Africans in America."[80]

The incident involving Giannetti sparked many students to mobilize behind these general goals. At Morris Brown College, students held a vigil at the student center and presented a list of demands to President John Middleton, who subsequently announced the end of curfews for women, compulsory dress regulations, and compulsory class attendance. At Clark College, Student Government Association president James Mays led a drive that won similar concessions. At Spelman, administrative officials suspended all classes for a two-day cooling-off period, during which college officials organized a "speak out" to facilitate discussion among students, faculty, and administration. Following the break, Manley announced the abolition of compulsory chapel, curfews, and dress regulations. Manley also promised to consider the addition of more Afro-American courses to the curriculum. The concessions in all three cases dealt almost exclusively with in loco parentis regulations while leaving the larger, Black Power–oriented issues essentially untouched. Manley noted that although his administration supported student desires for more courses in Afro-American culture and greater involvement in community programs, "we cannot endorse a curriculum which is racially restrictive or a program which embarrasses teachers and students of other races or excludes them from our campus." But the concessions dissipated the tension on the campuses, at least in the short run.[81]

Radical students nevertheless continued to press a Black Power agenda. The issues emerged again in April 1969, when student activists took over a building where members of the Morehouse College Board of Trustees were meeting and held them for two days. The events began with a debate between Ralph Lee, Morehouse's acting dean, and Gerald McWorter, a Spelman sociology instructor, on "World Crisis in Black Unity: The Relevancy of the Black University." After the program, a group of students, most from Morehouse but some from Spelman, Clark, and Morris Brown, gathered to discuss the possibility of meeting with the governing boards of the Atlanta University Center schools. The students reached a consensus on a number of issues. Their institutions should not be named after "obscure white persons." The schools should be consolidated and should take a greater interest in the surrounding community. At least a majority of the governing board should be black. "Students should participate in the decision-making processes which govern their lives." And more and better courses on black history and life were needed. In the following days, graffiti appeared on the side of campus buildings declaring "Black Control of Black Schools" and "Martin Luther King University — Now."[82]

The activists adopted the moniker Concerned Students and arranged a meeting with the Morehouse College Board of Trustees in Harkness Hall on the morning of 18 April. During the meeting, other students began to gather outside the building. When some trustees attempted to leave, students sitting at the doors blocked them, while others chained the doors. The coordinators of the lock-in communicated with Joseph Price, vice president of the Morehouse Student Government Association, who presided over informational meetings in Sale Hall. At the top of the list of demands was the renaming of a newly consolidated university after Martin Luther King Jr. But confusion soon erupted on a number of fronts. First, although the Concerned Students included representatives of Clark, Spelman, Morris Brown, Atlanta University, and Morehouse (about fifty people in all), only the Morehouse board was meeting. Its ability to commit to consolidation was, at best, questionable. Morehouse president Hugh Gloster, one of the officials being held, announced from the balcony outside his office that "outsiders" with no interest in Morehouse were behind the lock-in. Gloster announced his resignation, declaring that he would not sign anything under duress. Moreover, one of the trustees, Martin Luther King Sr., quickly disassociated himself and his family from the actions and declared that he thought the name of his son was being exploited by people who despised the martyred civil rights leader. King was allowed to leave on the first day of the lock-in.[83]

Perhaps more important, it soon became apparent that the lock-in leaders' actions lacked the support of the majority of their fellow students. On the first night of the lock-in, Morehouse student government president Nelson Taylor led a student government meeting to determine the extent of support for the Concerned Students. Most students supported Gloster in his unwillingness to accede to demands under duress, although they also favored amnesty for the demonstrators if it would encourage them to release their hostages. At this meeting, a representative of the Concerned Students announced that the proposed name change was primarily a tactic and that the leaders had decided to drop it.[84]

The Concerned Students released the board members at 1:30 P.M. on 19 April. The members immediately proceeded to Sale Hall, where board chair Charles Merrill announced that the board had agreed to twelve proposals, including the revamping of the board to include more black members, support for the consolidation of the Atlanta University Center schools, a variety of student power proposals, and full amnesty for the Concerned Students. However, Taylor led a student movement to reject the proposals, and the agreement soon came apart. Student government leaders at Morris Brown, Clark, and Morehouse disassociated themselves from the lock-in. Taylor labeled the leaders of the lock-in "a minority that completely ignored the will of the majority." He accused them of fanning "the embers of strife and confusion. These are the people who are making the bomb threats. These are the people who are attempting arson on our campus." Despite the lock-in leaders' demand to rename the university in honor of Martin Luther King Jr., Taylor argued that they "had nothing but contempt" for King's principles when he was alive. The final blow came on 23 April, when the Morehouse board of trustees rescinded the agreements, with the exception of the amnesty provision, because they had been made under duress.[85]

However, most students may have opposed the Concerned Students' tactics but favored their goals. On 21 April, the Morehouse student body voted overwhelmingly for eight proposals that encompassed the essential elements of the Concerned Students' demands.[86] And student and faculty efforts to apply black consciousness to the university continued during the early 1970s at the Atlanta University Center, with increases in the number of courses that concentrated on African American history and culture. A comprehensive Afro-American studies program for the entire Atlanta University Center was created in 1969. According to its first director, Russell Spry Williams, the program focused on identity, relevance, and service to the black community. It provided some focus for the growing number of courses that dealt with black history and culture. By one contemporary count, the Atlanta University Center institutions offered thirty-four courses in the broad category of Afro-American and Third World classes, encompassing such subjects as "Black Power, Black Identity and the Third World," taught by McWorter, and "Comparative Slavery," a seminar taught by Melvin Drimmer, a white history professor at Spelman.[87]

Nevertheless, the advances fell short of the vision of a black university that animated many radicals. While younger, more militant students and faculty members worked to remake the Atlanta University Center schools into instruments of liberation, the commitment to a traditional liberal arts education remained strong. Manley later noted that he knew of no black college that developed a "distinctly black curriculum." Instead, most had included courses "in the curricular programs of study that deal with the black experience in the United States but not to the exclusion of other courses that provide a well-rounded liberal arts program." At Spelman, the incorporation of new courses on such topics as the sociology of black music, police in the black community, and Judeo-Christian beginnings in Africa accompanied a new, more flexible core curriculum instituted in 1968. The new curriculum permitted students to select from a menu those courses that would help them achieve more individualized goals.[88]

Several Atlanta University Center faculty members were behind an effort to create a new institution devoted to the study of African American life. In October 1968, Vincent Harding, Stephen Henderson, McWorter, A. B. Spellman, and Councill Taylor presented a proposal for the Institute for Advanced Afro-American Studies, which was to be part of the Martin Luther King Jr. Memorial Center. The proposal was an early version of what would become the Institute of the Black World. As its director, Harding embarked on an ambitious program that included historical studies, policy analysis, and development in the creative arts.[89]

Elsewhere in the South, black students at Duke University spearheaded the creation of Malcolm X Liberation University in Durham, North Carolina, in April 1969. Designed to "provide a framework within which black education can become relevant to the needs of Black people and the struggle for Black Liberation," Malcolm X combined courses on "nation building" with technical training geared toward community fieldwork. The new university drew much of its energy from the machinery put in place by the North Carolina Fund, an antipoverty program begun in 1963 and funded by the Ford Foundation. One outgrowth of the North Carolina Fund was the Foundation for Community Development, a statewide organization seeking to develop political activism among the poor. Under the leadership of Howard Fuller, the foundation increasingly became an advocate not only of community organizing but also of Black Power. Fuller, a central figure in the activism of black students at Duke and UNC, served as the director of Malcolm X Liberation University, which soon moved to Greensboro. By the early 1970s, Greensboro, also home to North Carolina A&T, had become, according to William H. Chafe, the "center of Black Power in the South."[90]

The Limits and Impact of Black Power

Despite Black Power proponents' accomplishments in modifying curricula and creating a few parallel institutions, the movement ultimately ran headlong into two difficult obstacles — violence and desegregation. When they occurred, the violent clashes were more likely to develop in or near public institutions than private ones. The confrontations that resulted in deaths — one in Greensboro, North Carolina, in 1969; two in Jackson, Mississippi, in 1970; and two in Baton Rouge, Louisiana, in 1972 — all occurred in or near state-supported institutions. As was true at the outset of the decade, these schools were less insulated from state politicians and more vulnerable to intervention.

The May 1970 killings at Jackson State College became the best-known example of violence aimed at students, in part because the shooting deaths of the two students in Jackson occurred shortly after the Kent State shootings. Although Jackson had been the scene for activism throughout the decade, the Jackson State student body had a reputation for apathy. And, in fact, the events that prompted Mississippi highway patrolmen to come to the campus were less about organized political mobilization than youthful shenanigans. Law enforcement officials arrived on 14 May in response to reports that students were throwing bricks at cars on Lynch Street. From there, the conflict escalated, until highway patrolmen opened fire into crowds of students and dormitories. By the time the chaos subsided, two students were dead and eight were injured.[91]

May 1970 represented the high point of massive student mobilization nationwide, but activism on many black campuses continued into the early 1970s. Black Power resonated with African Americans well into the decade, and radical black activists continued their efforts to realize the black university. But the threat of violence took its toll, and the ongoing process of institutional desegregation posed dilemmas for black colleges in the South. Predominantly white institutions now competed for black students, causing enrollment problems for some black schools. Both obstacles were evident in the activism that developed at a publicly supported black university in New Orleans.

As an institution, Southern University in New Orleans (SUNO) represented all of the ambiguities of southern higher education in the post-*Brown* era. The Louisiana State Legislature created New Orleans branches of Southern University and Louisiana State University 1956. But when Louisiana State University in New Orleans (LSUNO) opened in 1958, it did so as a desegregated institution. By the end of the 1960s, an open admissions policy enabled African Americans to make up one-fourth of the LSUNO student body.[92] But despite the school's desegregated status, SUNO opened in the fall of 1959 and in subsequent years remained essentially all black.[93] And while LSUNO grew rapidly, SUNO struggled with a small, underfunded campus.

The vast majority of SUNO's students came from nearby, largely as a consequence of the absence of dormitories. In 1969, only seven of the school's eighteen hundred students came from outside Louisiana.[94] On any campus, the lack of a resident student body made political mobilization difficult. Moreover, SUNO, like LSUNO, drew much of its student body from working-class backgrounds. Indeed, students at both institutions frequently took classes while working part-time or full-time jobs. Despite these limitations, students at SUNO began to express discontent. In 1966, students rebelled against the paternalistic policies of Dean Emmett Bashful, the highest-ranking official on the SUNO campus. But the rebellion did little to change an institution where power still resided at the top. Bashful took his direction from Felton Clark, Southern's longtime president, who had a disproportionate amount of power over faculty and students. In fact, the limits on academic freedom at Southern's Baton Rouge campus finally earned a censure from the American Association of University Professors in April 1968.[95]

Student discontent surfaced again at SUNO in the fall of 1968, when the university announced a fifty-dollar tuition hike. The tuition disturbed students who wanted more for the money they already were spending. SUNO had inferior facilities — four buildings for nearly two thousand people — and such a poor academic reputation that some referred to the institution as SUNO High School.[96] In early 1969, a small group of students attempted to block registration to protest the tuition hike. They were unable, however, to mobilize a significant number of their fellow students, and eleven students were arrested for participating in the demonstration. "It didn't go as well as we expected," said political science major Charles Williams. "I'd even call it a flop, and I think the reasons for this failure can be found in the complacency of the students and the incredible lack of interest in improving the standards of the university."[97]

Nevertheless, anger at the tuition hike grew slowly during February and March. Around that time, some students formed a group called the Afro-American Society and drew up a list of ten demands. On 31 March, the society's chair, Lynn French, presented these demands to students at an assembly commemorating the death of Martin Luther King Jr. The demands were wide ranging, addressing the university's poor physical facilities, its limited curriculum, and the need to reorient the institution as an instrument of black liberation. The group called for a department of black studies that offered a bachelor's degree; a noncredit course in black liberation to be taught by the director of the New Orleans SNCC chapter; fulfillment of the original construction plan for the campus, which called for a new building every year; increased hiring of faculty; a black draft-counseling center to be headed by Walter Collins, whose fight against draft-evasion charges made him "unofficially one of the foremost authorities on the draft"; immediate removal of the tuition hike; more books by black authors in the library; a revision of the university handbook to remove arbitrary rules and regulations governing student life; the creation of a department of education; and administrative changes to ensure "that there shall no longer be a Dean of the University to serve as Fuhrer and honky overseer of the campus."[98]

Two days later, several students walked up to the flagpole in front of the administration building, lowered the American flag, and replaced it with a black, red, and green black liberation flag.[99] The flag flew for several hours, drawing the attention not only of other students and the administration but also of the local news media. At three o'clock that afternoon, the students lowered the flag and carried it to a press conference, at which Afro-American Society leaders announced that they would raise the flag again and call for a boycott of classes if the demands were not met by 9 April.[100]

New Orleans police superintendent Joseph Giarrusso subsequently announced that the police would tolerate no more "desecration of the flag." Complaining that the "silent majority must quit being so complacent about these events," Giarrusso sounded chords that resonated with whites who had voted for Richard Nixon the preceding November: "Let no one mistake kindness and patience on the part of police officers for weakness."[101] Bashful attempted to calm the situation by mobilizing dependable students and faculty members. Shortly after the flag incident, the university's Faculty Association, led by political science professor George Haggar, issued a resolution that essentially supported the students' demands. By 7 April, however, Bashful had convened his own faculty group, without Haggar or others who sympathized with the students, which voted to deplore "many of the extreme methods used by the students, such as the removal of the American flag." Bashful also appointed a negotiating committee of students and faculty that was heavily stacked in his favor.[102]

Shortly before eight o'clock on the morning of 9 April, seven students approached the flagpole, unfolded the black liberation flag, explained its symbolic meaning, read off the list of ten demands, pulled down the American flag, gave it a military fold, and raised the new flag. Giarrusso was ready with a sizable police force. The officers allowed the students to raise the flag, at which point the chief stepped up to tell the students they were desecrating the American flag. Policemen then moved in to arrest the perpetrators, forming a circle around the flagpole. The circle was so large, however, that it included many of the estimated two hundred students who had turned out to watch the episode unfold. Police efforts to disperse the students only angered them; some began to fight back.[103]

Bashful had called an assembly for the same time to report on the administration's progress in responding to the demands. As news about the clash outside filtered in, many attendees left the assembly. During the next few hours, some twenty-five students took over the first floor of the administration building, while Bashful locked himself in his office. By the time quiet was restored, a female student at Delgado Community College and two policemen had suffered minor injuries, and police had arrested more than twenty people. No classes were held on that day, and students began a boycott of classes.[104]

Vallery Ferdinand III (later known as Kalamu ya Salaam), perhaps the most visible student leader of the spring 1969 demonstrations, later recalled the boycott with pride, referring to it as "one of the least well-known but best organized student strikes." The strike leaders met every day, reviewed the events of the previous day, and took suggestions regarding the next step. To prevent leaks, "the leadership never made a decision until it was time to make a decision." One student published a weekly newsletter, the *Black Liberation Express*, to air the striking students' opinions. Some students organized fund-raisers, while others made telephone calls to generate support. "We tapped the ability of people to work and created the context for people to do whatever it was they wanted to do," recalled Ferdinand.[105]

The activists faced some fundamental problems. The substance of the students' demands reflected the ambiguity that resulted when Black Power met desegregation as it stood in late-1960s Louisiana. Nominally, the students were concerned about poor physical facilities and a limited curriculum. However, they wanted more than increased funding. Drawing on student-power-oriented concerns, they called for the end of arbitrary campus rules and regulations. More importantly, they sought the remaking of SUNO as a black university, an instrument for black liberation.[106]

The SUNO activists essentially wanted state officials to increase funding so that students could create a university that would help liberate them from precisely those officials and the society they represented. And they sought this goal as Louisiana's white officials fought off federal efforts to enforce desegregation, which could have merged SUNO with LSUNO. SUNO students recoiled at the idea, which was eventually endorsed by the Louisiana NAACP. Moreover, despite their stated opposition to integration, the SUNO activists at one point during the boycott organized a demonstration in which five hundred students marched to LSUNO and threatened to register. The activists intended the demonstration as just that — a demonstration — rather than a serious proposal effectively to merge the two institutions. "Whether or not we registered wasn't important," Ferdinand later recalled. "The important thing was to put in the minds of the community the dichotomy of SUNO and LSUNO, LSUNO having all this and SUNO not having much." Regardless of intentions, the fact remained that the demonstrators were fighting for a black university by threatening integration.[107]

Louisiana governor John McKeithen came to SUNO twelve days after the boycott began and made enough promises to get students back into the classrooms. Negotiations began, but it soon became apparent that the only changes SUNO would see in the immediate future would be cosmetic changes, including the filling in of ditches that sometimes filled with rainwater and bred mosquitoes. University officials eventually addressed some of the students' other concerns by restructuring the administration, creating a department of education, hiring more faculty members, and creating an interdisciplinary black studies program.[108] Yet despite these developments, the SUNO student movement's larger goal of the creation of a black university remained elusive. In 1972, a new round of protests ensued on Southern's New Orleans and Baton Rouge campuses concerning issues that closely resembled those of the 1969 protests; in Baton Rouge, two students died in confrontations with law enforcement officials.[109] A year later, a retrospective article in the *Black Collegian* (which now employed Ferdinand as an editor) noted that most students at SUNO were "more interested in making up for the time they lost during the disturbance" than in continuing to fight for a black university.[110]

The trajectory of student activism on historically black campuses in the second half of the 1960s reflects the strengths and weaknesses of the southern student movement as a whole. At a number of schools, the list of accomplishments resembled those of university reform/student power agenda on predominantly white campuses — the end of regulations governing nonacademic lives, greater student involvement in campus governance, a more flexible and "relevant" curriculum. The emergence of Black Power dovetailed with demands for curricular relevance. But at historically black schools as well as predominantly white ones, the gap between utopian rhetoric and results is striking. The universities incorporated some elements of the black university agenda while maintaining their existing structures. At the same time, they drew on the currents of university reform and student power that were flowing through American and southern higher education. However, these changes occurred in a context of uncertainty about the meaning of the end of segregation. The same context informed the efforts of student activists, white and black, to address racial issues on predominantly white campuses in the South during the second half of the decade.

CHAPTER SEVEN

Black Power on White Campuses

ON CAMPUSES throughout the United States, black students and racial issues were central to the student unrest of the late 1960s. But racial issues were, if anything, more important in a region lurching toward a new, postsegregation society. What would integration mean in institutions for whose whiteness some southerners had so recently been willing to fight? What would it mean to black students who increasingly rallied around the cause of Black Power? In some respects, change came rapidly to now desegregating universities. Scenes that would have seemed unimaginable in the late 1950s occurred with regularity a decade later. At Vanderbilt, where James M. Lawson Jr. had been expelled for his involvement in sit-ins, Stokely Carmichael declaimed on Black Power in 1967 and black divinity students demanded the creation of a black studies institute in 1968. At the University of Georgia, scene of riots against the admission of black students in 1961, black students eight years later distributed a tongue-in-cheek flyer challenging members of the Kappa Alpha fraternity to a duel. And at Duke University, which admitted no black students before 1963, black students took over a building in 1969. Despite their still small numbers, black students throughout the South loomed large in activism on predominantly white campuses. For African American students, political activism formed part of a larger effort to define the scope and meaning of integration and to press for a kind of equality that would not require the abandonment of racial identity. In a profound sense, they challenged the culture of the white campus.

White students were forced to respond and adjust. Most in the early 1960s were slow to embrace integration and even more reluctant to participate in direct-action demonstrations. Nevertheless, white racial attitudes tended to moderate as time passed. After 1964, increasing numbers of white students awoke to the reality of societal racism and personal racial prejudices. Race continued to serve as the defining political issue — and the introduction to a larger world of political issues — for many students. But the emergence of Black Power, with its separatist impulse, challenged newly baptized white supporters of integration.

Some, especially older white activists who had participated in interracial demonstrations earlier in the decade, had difficulty accepting Black Power. Black and white activism increasingly moved along parallel lines. Nevertheless, by the end of the decade, more radical white activists usually incorporated black students' concerns into the agenda, even if joint actions were rare and sometimes awkward.

By the early 1970s, when the showdowns subsided, predominantly white, southern campuses had changed. Black students, now energized by racial pride, had hammered out more cultural space. Their efforts to lay claim to their rights as full campus citizens had paid dividends. Moreover, their activism had produced some curricular changes; classes in Afro-American history and culture now peppered the course catalogs of formerly segregated campuses. And in some cases, the activism of black students — sometimes supported by white students — produced commitments from universities to redouble their efforts to recruit black students and faculty members. Nevertheless, the changes had limits. Many whites continued to resist anything more than token integration. This reluctance, combined with the separatist impulse of Black Power, contributed to the emergence of campuses that were integrated but that nevertheless saw only a limited amount of racial interaction.

"Student Heroes": Deep South Universities and Desegregation

The roots of this late-1960s' activism lay in the immediate years after desegregation, as a handful of pioneers navigated their way through the often treacherous waters of formerly all-white campuses. These pioneers became some of the best-known students of the desegregation era. Indeed, the names James Meredith, Charlayne Hunter, Hamilton Holmes, Vivian Malone, James Hood, and Harvey Gantt still resonate on the campuses they entered in the early 1960s as well as throughout the South. They were, as journalist Calvin Trillin termed it, the Student Heroes.[1] Trillin employed the term with some irony, for after these heroes desegregated their institutions and after the initial media frenzy died down, they were left with the unenviable task of being students at institutions that had only reluctantly admitted them. In the words of Edwin Lombard, a black student at Tulane University in the mid-1960s, they were the "uninvited guests."[2] In most cases, this first generation of black students on newly desegregated campuses had only a small support group of black peers. In the most hostile environments, such as the state universities in Georgia, Alabama, and Mississippi, few white students were willing to risk the ostracism that might accompany a decision to associate with black students. Moreover, when these schools opened their doors to the first handfuls of African American students, all aspects of campus life were not available. Campus cafeterias sometimes remained segregated. Campus organizations, especially Greek societies, continued to resist integration. Isolated socially and facing intense academic pressure as "representatives of their race," these students had little opportunity to take bold positions on political issues. This task would fall to their younger brothers and sisters in the late 1960s. Admission was only the first of many firsts. Integration meant more than simply allowing one or two blacks to attend classes; an all-white campus culture had developed, and white students often hesitated to allow desegregation to disrupt that culture.

At the University of Alabama, as at other recently desegregated southern institutions, the number of black students increased very slowly. In the summer of 1965, when Vivian Malone became the university's first African American graduate, between twenty and thirty black students were enrolled in a total student population of fifty-five hundred. Malone noted slow changes in the attitudes of white students: "People are friendlier now. They walk along campus with you. At first they didn't." She recommended the university to other African Americans because "it is less expensive than going out of state."[3] African Americans at Alabama at least had a social outlet in Stillman College, a historically black college nearby. Many of 'Bama's first black students participated in dances and other social activities at Stillman rather than at Alabama, where they often felt unwelcome. As late as 1968, black students complained that the university had made no social room for them. Fraternities and sororities remained segregated, and other avenues for social life were similarly unwelcoming. "When we would go to a dance and start dancing, some people would just stop and start watching us," one student noted.[4]

The situation differed somewhat on campuses where initial desegregation had occurred earlier or in more moderate pockets of the South. Louisiana State University began admitting small numbers of black students into graduate programs in the 1950s, but the first twenty-five black undergraduates did not matriculate until the fall of 1964. One member of that group, Maxine Crump, a native of Maringouin, Louisiana, had always assumed that she would attend Southern University. But the opportunity to attend LSU enticed Crump, whose mother "had heard that some of the [Southern] teachers weren't competent, and that your education really wasn't valued once you got out of there." In fact, many of LSU's first black undergraduates came from Baton Rouge.[5]

Crump was the first African American to live in the LSU dormitories. She later discovered that university officials had handpicked the other women who lived on her hall and that none of them was from the South. Still, Crump developed friendships with white and black students and found enough breathing room to become an activist, participating in efforts to desegregate businesses around campus. The rise of black student activism, according to Crump, corresponded with an influx of students from Shreveport, Bogalusa, and New

Orleans, "where the blacks were more active in their own hometowns. Those from Baton Rouge and Plaquemine and where I came from, we didn't come from strongly activist communities." Students with activist backgrounds brought in a higher level of political consciousness, and after they began organizing, "the university started listening to us a little more."[6]

But Crump found herself in occasional disagreements with other black LSU students. After 1967, some black students began pressuring her not to continue associating with her white friends. She also did not keep pace with Black Power currents. Crump decided not to adopt two physical manifestations of black consciousness, the natural hairstyle, or Afro, and the dashiki, prompting some militant black students to give her trouble. Nevertheless, Crump continued to see herself as an activist, participating in the antiwar movement, in efforts to liberalize women's curfews, and in a black student group, Harambe.[7]

Crump's differences with her fellow African Americans illustrate some of the tensions within the small community of black students on predominantly white campuses. Age seemed to be one important dividing line, with the older students adopting a more conciliatory demeanor as well as a greater willingness to accept the established institutions of university life. Wesley Watkins, a black student at Tulane and executive officer of the Army Reserve Officers' Training Corps battalion, acknowledged that younger black students thought little of him: "I imagine I am considered one Uncle Tom, but I don't worry about it. The younger Negro today is not conservative like I am. He's a little bit more of an activist, he wants to see things done and he wants to see things done a little bit faster." Watkins suggested that he and a handful of other older black students on campus made up the "last of an old breed." He included in his list Marilyn Thomas, a senior, a member of the A Cappella Choir, and the first black woman to be elected to the Miss Pauline Tulane court. "Maybe it's wrong," Thomas noted, "but I'm not as conscious of being a Negro as some of the other kids are. I don't think people should be that conscious of being different in color or anything like that."[8]

Where political and philosophical differences existed among members of the black community, they rarely were aired overtly. At the University of North Carolina, however, the divisions emerged in the open and took the form of competing organizations of black students. In the fall of 1961, black students at UNC participated in the formation of a campus chapter of the National Association for the Advancement of Colored People (NAACP). Among the chapter's first actions was a "campaign against racial discrimination at UNC" that took aim in particular at segregation policies at North Carolina Memorial Hospital and at the Morehead Planetarium.[9] Five years later, the chapter protested discriminatory housing practices in Chapel Hill.[10] But in the fall of 1967, militant black students revolted against the campus NAACP leaders, who were perceived as too conservative, and voted to dissolve the chapter and form a new organization, the Black Student Movement (BSM). The leader of this revolt was a transfer student, Preston Dobbins, who had spent the previous year as a community organizer in North Carolina with Youth Educational Services.[11]

The leaders of the NAACP chapter did not back down quietly. The president was Kelly Alexander Jr., whose father was president of the North Carolina NAACP. The state organization investigated to determine whether the vote to dissolve had been unconstitutional. The younger Alexander showed up at the next BSM meeting and announced to the gathering, "I want you all to remember that there are now two Negro structures here." The two groups resolved to coexist and operate independently.[12]

By the time of the split, UNC had about seventy-five black students, enough to provide both a diversity of opinion and a certain amount of strength in numbers. Dobbins, whose political experience also included a stint as a student worker in a Chicago community-organizing project, provided the organizational skills and the black-consciousness rhetoric that put the BSM at the center of the campus activism for the next two years. In the days after the Orangeburg Massacre in February 1968, the BSM staged two protest marches, one of which included the burning in effigy of South Carolina governor Robert McNair. And in the aftermath of Martin Luther King Jr.'s assassination in April, the BSM sponsored a march that featured a burning of several Confederate battle flags and a one-day strike in which 95 percent of the black workers on campus stayed home.[13] The BSM's rhetoric contained the hallmarks of Black Power — affirmations of black consciousness and pride, the rejection of nonviolence, and the tendency toward separatism. Although white sympathizers participated in the demonstrations, the BSM was an all-black organization.

By the 1967–68 academic year, even casual observers throughout the South could see changes in black students' demeanor. A new militant posture reflecting the rhetoric of Black Power was beginning to filter onto predominantly white southern campuses at precisely the moment when black enrollment was surpassing the level of tokenism. Student organizations with names such as the Black Student Union or the Afro-American Association became the institutional symbols of a more assertive consciousness. Informed by cultural nationalist doctrines of the Student Nonviolent Coordinating Committee and the Black Panthers, these groups commonly pursued a set of goals that typically included some combination of a black studies program, increases in the enrollment of black students and the employment of black faculty members, the creation of an Afro-American cultural center or dormitory, and the elimination of such symbols of racism as the Confederate flag. At times, these organizations advocated on behalf of black campus workers by demanding higher wages or collective-bargaining rights. The groups used intentionally bold language and public demeanor to distance themselves from their ostensibly more deferential predecessors.

Black activists at times endorsed violence. The violent language was, however, more often a rhetorical tool than a real threat. For example, a 1969 Black Student Union (BSU) flyer at the University of Georgia took rhetorical aim at the members of the Kappa Alpha fraternity, which was noted for its veneration of the Old South. Members of the Georgia chapter had been particularly vocal in their opposition of desegregation in the early 1960s and had openly antagonized Hunter and Holmes.[14] Having already demanded that the university ban the fraternity from campus, male members of the BSU threatened to lynch Kappa Alpha brothers. "We niggers, being the gentlemen y'all try to be[,] challenge y'all honkies to a duel to the death," the flyer declared. "And Yeah, baby, if you can't get to that action, walk on like a chicken with your ASS plucked clean!"[15] Tactically, however, Georgia's BSU, like other black student organizations on predominantly white, southern campuses, stuck to nonviolent actions that looked more like early 1960s sit-ins than the riots of subsequent years.

In stark contrast, black students at Cornell University walked out of a building they had been occupying in April 1969 carrying guns and wearing bandoliers.[16] Though many people saw this episode as symbolizing late-1960s black student militance, it was not replicated in the South. The closest violence came to a southern university was in 1969, when black Duke University students took over an administration building for several hours before leaving peacefully. In the aftermath of the takeover, however, clashes broke out between white supporters and police that resulted in dozens of injuries.

"Remain Here and Continue the Struggle": Duke and the Allen Building Takeover

Black activism in North Carolina was extensive enough to earn the state the label "the center of Black Power in the South."[17] Regardless of the label's accuracy, black students at Duke and UNC unquestionably organized two of the South's most noteworthy movements of black students on predominantly white campuses. Both movements not only sought changes related to black students' academic and extracurricular lives but also made the concerns of black workers on campus a major part of their agenda. A vibrant activist community in Durham as well as the direct involvement of Durham activist Howard Fuller contributed to the ferment. Moreover, black activists on the two campuses fed off of each other.

Black undergraduate students entered Duke in the fall of 1963.[18] During the next few years, a campus chapter of the Congress of Racial Equality (CORE) provided an outlet for interracial demonstrations. When Samuel DuBois Cook, an Atlanta University political scientist who in 1966 had spoken against Black Power, became the first African American professor at Duke later that same year, the university still had fewer than twenty-five black students. In the fall of 1967, African American students at Duke, reflecting trends on predominantly white campuses throughout the South, formed the Afro-American Society (AAS), which provided both a social and political outlet for black students. The AAS almost immediately took aim at lingering vestiges of segregation. In November, group members supported an effort to forbid student organizations to use segregated off-campus facilities. The student government association passed the measure, but students voted it down 1,300–884 in a campuswide referendum. Thirty-five AAS members conducted a sit-in outside President Douglas Knight's office on 13 November, and seven days later, Knight barred university organizations from using segregated facilities.[19]

But Knight's membership in a segregated club soon provided fodder for black student disaffection. Knight's membership in the Hope Valley Country Club was already controversial with some students and a sensitive issue for the liberal president. A Yale-educated native of Cambridge, Massachusetts, Knight, like other college presidents, walked a tightrope between conservative alumni and donors and a student body that contained a growing number of vocal activists.[20] In April 1967, the student newspaper, the *Chronicle*, published a list of faculty and administrative officials who were members of Hope Valley. One graduate student in philosophy, Charles E. M. Dunlop, wrote scathingly to Knight that he was "personally offended by your willingness to slap [blacks] in the face with racial intolerance." The president was "acceding to a practice which is clearly immoral," and while Duke, as a Methodist institution, should have been in the forefront of civil rights, Knight's membership at Hope Valley symbolized "the many racial inequities apparent on this campus." Dunlop continued, "I have observed on Campus Drive the Southern custom of permitting Negro employees to patch the concrete, while a white 'overseer' lounges in the cab of his truck; I have talked to the maids who earned 85 cents per hour; I have seen the conspicuous absence of Negro cashiers in the cafeterias; I note that Duke will be able to say next fall that $1/600$ of its faculty is Negro; and I have a Negro friend who is barred from living in housing facilities listed by the Duke Housing Bureau. These and many other incidents add up to a despicable situation at what some students here so presumptuously call 'The Harvard of the South.'"[21]

Knight responded by drafting an equally scathing response, though he softened it before sending it. According to Knight, Dunlop knew "very well that" his letter was "impudent and insulting; you designed it so. What you may not know is that it was also immature and imperceptive." Knight excised this statement but left in a comment that he was returning the letter to Dunlop because it would embarrass the student in later years to know that he had written it. Knight pointed out that Dunlop was "heavily supported" by the same institution that he "flagrantly" scorned and argued that his decisions as president were "hardly timid" and often called "for some fairly complex analysis of problems which evidently seem simple to you."[22]

Knight's problems only became more difficult. A little more than a year later, the assassination of Martin Luther King Jr. turned thousands of Duke students into activists. On 5 April 1968, the day after King's death, some 350 students marched to Knight's house to press for racial reforms. About 200 students entered the house and spent the night. Another 150 stayed outside in a steady drizzle and debated their agenda with Knight. The students, along with a handful of faculty members, presented four demands: (1) that Knight sign an advertisement to appear in the Durham newspapers calling for a day of mourning for King and asking Durham citizens to do all they could to bring about racial equality; (2) that that the president resign from Hope Valley; (3) that he press for minimum wage of $1.60 per hour for nonacademic employees, a nearly 40 percent raise over the current $1.15 rate; and (4) that he appoint a committee of students, faculty, and nonacademic employees to make recommendations concerning collective bargaining and union recognition. By 7 April, the action had moved from the president's home to the main quadrangle on the Duke campus, where hundreds of students conducted a four-day silent vigil.[23]

Most of the one thousand participants in the silent vigil were white students, though a handful of blacks joined. To one Duke administrative official, the vigil took on the appearance of an "old-fashioned revival or camp meeting," with students playing the part of "new converts" who "saw their mission as that of converting others."[24] But the vigil represented more than an opportunity for white students to undergo racial conversion experiences; it had important institutional ramifications. During the vigil, the black, nonacademic employees — who were organized in Local 77, an unrecognized union — voted to strike, and vigil participants called for a boycott of all dining halls and classes.[25] Duke's trustees eventually agreed to establish an internal labor-relations board, and the chair of the board announced that the university would advance wages for nonacademic employees to $1.60 two years ahead of the legally required schedule. While the level of activism declined for the remainder of the academic year, the vigil helped push ahead a process in which students questioned campus decision making.[26]

Duke's seventy or so African American students stood on the sidelines during the vigil. "We didn't kill Dr. King," noted one student. "We had nothing to feel guilty about. Besides, it was [the white students'] thing and we wanted to let them do it."[27] However, black students' concerns continued to fester. During the week of 4 February 1969, black students participated in a symposium, "The

Beauty of Black," that included speeches by Fannie Lou Hamer, Dick Gregory, and Fuller. Knight closely watched these developments. On the day before the symposium began, he alerted members of the board of trustees to the unrest within the black student population. Among the planned events, he noted, was a program describing frustrations of black youth, including a ten-point program describing what Duke's black students wanted and why they wanted it. "Some may use language which will be offensive," Knight warned. "A careful reading will tell us a good deal about what these students feel, however, and we need to know."[28] The following day, Knight announced two actions designed to improve conditions on the campus for black students and other minority groups. One measure was an academic assistance program for "those who may need and desire assistance in their adjustment to Duke." The other action was the hiring of an adviser for minority groups. He and other administrators were "deeply" concerned about the attrition rate for black students. Moreover, he announced that he was resigning from the Hope Valley Country Club, finally meeting one of the leftover demands from the previous year's silent vigil, while simultaneously criticizing all forms of black separatism. "Forced separation of races can have no part in [the university], and we will not give our support to organizations and groups which would force separation on us," Knight declared.[29] The university also announced that the AAS would receive office space, that a black barber would be hired for the university barber shop, and that "Dixie" would no longer be played at school functions.[30]

Knight's move seemed to represent both a genuine effort to incorporate black students into the Duke community and a tactical move to placate the restive students. Shortly after issuing the announcement, he left for New York to seek funds from the Ford Foundation for a black studies program. Nevertheless, while Knight and other Duke administrative officials may have seen their efforts as evidence of real progress, black students later noted that the negotiations over their concerns, which had been ongoing since the fall, were more frustrating than productive. The events of the Black Week symposium emboldened them. On 13 February, about sixty African American students seized the first floor of the administration building, which they renamed the Malcolm X Liberation School.[31] They barricaded themselves in and issued a list of thirteen demands, including a black studies program controlled by black students, a black dormitory, more black professors, and an end to grading for African American students.[32] When Duke officials told the students that they were suspended and should leave the building or submit to criminal prosecution, they walked out, accompanied by white supporters who tried to shield them from identification. By then, Knight, who had received reports "of men in pickup trucks, shotguns in the window racks, driving slowly around the outer perimeter of the West Campus, waiting for dark," had called in a specially trained state police unit.

When a dispute broke out around a police car, police began using tear gas on the students, and an hour-long melee ensued. By nightfall, some three thousand students had gathered on campus. Some mocked the police with chants of "We surrender" and "Sieg Heil." As a result of the clash, forty-five people, including two policemen, reportedly required treatment at the university hospital's emergency room. The *New York Times* called the explosion "the first such protest at a major predominantly white Southern university."[33]

In the aftermath of the Allen Building takeover, the university apparently acceded at some level to almost all of the black students' demands. At the top of the list was the university's commitment to set up a black studies program, the first at a major southern university. Duke officials also agreed to create a dormitory — a "living-learning arrangement" — for black students and to hire an adviser for African Americans who was acceptable to both university officials and black students. On closer examination, however, the university's response to the demands appears to have been less a total capitulation than a decision to speed along developments already in the works. The decision to hire a minority adviser, for example, had already been announced. Officials had already signed off on the "living-learning arrangement" and were awaiting approval from the U.S. Department of Health, Education, and Welfare, which was involved in the fiscal support of the housing units. And a faculty committee had already been working on an African studies program. In fact, members of the faculty and administration had been meeting with AAS members on several of these issues since the previous fall. On other issues, especially those regarding the grading of black students and the recruitment and admission of black students, university officials agreed with the concerns of the black students but did not grant their specific demands. For example, Knight acknowledged that the general concept of grading was "a subject which can honestly be the concern of an academic community," but he expressed an unwillingness to eliminate grading for one group of students, which he said would be "unwise and insulting" to the group in question. And on the question of amnesty for protesting students, university officials simply announced that the students would be subject to the existing "pickets and protest" regulations, which had been implemented in early 1968.[34]

In fact, the peace soon proved fragile. The Allen Building takeover became Knight's undoing, reportedly because of a perception among conservative board members that he had caved in to the black students. Knight, who had been in poor health, resigned six weeks after the confrontation, declaring his desire "to protect my family from the severe and sometimes savage demands of such a career."[35] If conservatives were displeased with the outcome of the confrontation, so were black students, who soon became disenchanted with the ongoing negotiations regarding the black studies program. When the faculty supervisory committee rejected efforts to form a black studies supervisory committee with equal representation of faculty and students, some forty black students declared that they would withdraw from the university. A few days later, they changed their minds, declaring that "as revolutionary forces within one of the most conservative and oppressive institutions in America, we deem it necessary to remain here and continue the struggle." The revolutionary rhetoric belied crumbling solidarity among the students. Under pressure from parents and, according to one reporter, "torn by their own desire to get a degree from Duke or at least finish the semester," they seized on information that at least two of the faculty members were sympathetic to the kind of black studies program they wanted and decided to stay.[36] At the same time, radical white students under the guise of the Student Liberation Front attempted to capitalize on the ferment to push an agenda that increasingly focused on the war in Vietnam. Although the Allen Building takeover had radicalized a number of students — "the radical population at Duke went from 60 to 600," one movement journalist noted — the separatist trajectory of Duke's black students left little room for white activists to do anything more than sympathize.[37]

"We're Gonna Burn This Place Down": Black Students at UNC

Despite its somewhat ambiguous outcome, the Duke uprising encouraged similar protests in Chapel Hill. At UNC, the activity of the spring of 1968, when militant black students under the auspices of the new BSM generated several demonstrations, carried over into the fall. In November 1968, Stokely Carmichael visited the campus. The UNC student union director forbade the BSM from charging admission, and donations collected raised only seven hundred dollars of the fifteen hundred dollars Carmichael was supposed to receive for his appearance. Carmichael offered a provocative speech to his audience of sixty-seven hundred students, most of them white. "We are for revolutionary violence," he declared.[38] The following month, the BSM presented a list of twenty-three demands to UNC chancellor J. Carlyle Sitterson that included the concerns of students and campus workers. The group wanted significant revisions in the university's methods of admitting black students, including a new policy that no longer judged black students' standardized test scores, which were "based upon white middle-class standards." The BSM also called for the establishment of a department of African and Afro-American studies as well as an exchange program with black colleges and universities and an African university. In administrative matters, the BSM demanded the creation of a dean of black students and the placement of black representatives on the admissions committee and the athletic coaching staffs. Two of the demands sought the removal of administrative officials, including the replacement of Dean C. O. Cathey with "someone approved by BSM." Another demand called for black students to have "full jurisdiction over all offenses committed by Black students" or for students from BSM to represent the interests of black students on the existing judiciary courts. The BSM demanded seven thousand dollars repayment for the Carmichael address, with the money to be used for a scholarship fund, a tutorial program, and other community causes. The BSM also wanted university facilities and clinics to be opened to members of Chapel Hill's black community and for the university to take a more active role in alleviating the black community's problems. Finally, the BSM demanded that the university "begin working immediately to alleviate the intolerable working conditions of the Black non-academic employees."[39]

Some university officials found the demands difficult to swallow. "I believe most rational persons who are familiar with the facts and understand the nature of a University would agree that the demands of the BSM are, as a package, preposterous, and their manner of delivery rude and deliberately offensive," wrote graduate school dean James C. Ingram to Sitterson. "It is, therefore, tempting to reject them out of hand." Nevertheless, Ingram cautioned that such a response would be "a grave mistake, even though it might be applauded in some circles in the state."[40] Sitterson's nineteen-page reply, delivered more than a month later, declared that "the University intends to be responsive to the educational needs of all the people including all races, colors, and creeds." However, "the University cannot, in policy or in practice, provide unique treatment for any single race, color, or creed. To do so would be a step backward, and the University should set its sights upon a better future." Sitterson also took issue with one assumption that seemed implicit in the twenty-three demands — that the decision-making process on a university campus allowed for the immediate implementation of the BSM's agenda. At UNC, "as is the case in all large, complex institutions of higher education," responsibilities were distributed throughout the campus. The wheels of change turned slowly, Sitterson suggested.[41]

Sitterson generally expressed support for efforts to incorporate African Americans into the UNC community, although he consistently emphasized the initiatives already under way. For example, Sitterson detailed the university's efforts to recruit "those North Carolinians of all races who are presently admissible under the University's admissions standards. As a result of these efforts there was a substantial increase in the number of Negroes in the 1968 freshman class over preceding classes." He noted that the university placed great emphasis on indicators other than standardized tests but defended the use of such scores "as predictors of academic performance in college for both whites and blacks." Sitterson noted that courses in various aspects of black America were already proliferating, providing students with opportunities to specialize in African and Afro-American studies, and he contended that the university was already involved in black community problems. He flatly rejected the calls for personnel changes and for the payment of the money. Finally, Sitterson insisted that the university was working to improve the treatment of nonacademic employees. All in all, Sitterson's response was moderate in tone but gave little ground to the students.[42]

Sitterson's response, which had the approval of UNC president William C. Friday, met with disapproval not only from BSM leaders but also from white activists on the UNC campus. On 7 February, some 450 white students and faculty members marched through the campus and town and briefly occupied the ground floor of the South Building. UNC's chapter of the Southern Student Organizing Committee (SSOC), which had been in existence since the fall of 1968, was looking for an issue to mobilize and radicalize students, and the plight of black students seemed to provide an opening. The university's black students also found support from fifty-three faculty members, who signed a letter to the university community supporting the BSM's efforts and criticizing Sitterson for failing "to acknowledge the continuing racial inequality in the state and nation" and for exaggerating "the extent to which the University has already dealt with the issues raised by the BSM." The letter called for more equitable treatment of nonacademic employees and for an Afro-American curriculum.[43]

Although these developments contributed to the heightened level of activism, events outside the campus also had an impact. On 5 February, students at North Carolina Agricultural and Technical College in Greensboro occupied the administration building. The 8 February Orangeburg Massacre further heightened tensions. And then on 13 February came the Allen Building takeover at Duke, which apparently pushed members of Carolina's BSM toward a more militant posture. "At Duke they backed the man up against the wall," said Mickey Lewis, a freshman member of the BSM. "He had to come through or lose his position. I think that is what we are going to have to do here. Sitterson's a cool dude and we're going to have to rap him hard to get anything from him."[44]

While the BSM had capable leaders and the Chapel Hill movement followed its own trajectory, the events at Duke provided an impetus. The two movements also had a human connection in the form of Fuller, an organizer for the Foundation for Community Development (FCD). Fuller had been on the Duke campus throughout the negotiations following the Allen Building takeover, advising the students and at times playing a public role. But Fuller had also been a controversial figure on the Chapel Hill campus for some time. From the fall of 1967 through February 1968, he served as a part-time social work instructor, although he reportedly quit because of the competing stresses of his full-time job with the FCD.[45]

The events at Duke prompted the involvement of North Carolina governor Robert W. Scott. On 20 February, Scott issued a memorandum to the presidents of state-supported colleges and universities that declared that any students or faculty who threatened public order or harassed organized meetings would be arrested. More seriously, Scott threatened state intervention if college or university officials could not control campus conditions and contended that police officers did not need permission from campus officials to enter campuses to enforce the law. If presidents and chancellors did not call in the police in the event of an occupation of a state-owned building, Scott would send in the state highway patrol, units of the National Guard, or both if he believed that doing so was necessary. The memorandum coincided with a BSM deadline: if UNC did not give proper consideration to the group's demands by 21 February, its tactics would "change from reform to revolution." That day, about thirty-five BSM members marched to Lenoir Hall, the university cafeteria, chanting, "We're gonna burn this place down." Two days later, sixteen or seventeen food service employees walked off the job, with some one hundred workers joining the strike on 24 February. BSM members moved into nearby Manning Hall and, with workers and other students, established a strike center and makeshift dining hall, while the *Daily Tar Heel* called on students to boycott food services until workers' grievances were addressed.[46]

The student paper, edited by Wayne Hurder, a senior whose politics had moved to the left following his participation in Speaker Ban demonstrations during his freshman year, supported the strike. The student legislature also passed a resolution supporting the cafeteria workers and calling on all members of the university committee to eat lunch and dinner in Manning Hall.[47] The campus SSOC chapter looked for ways to participate in the events, conducting "stall-ins" at Lenoir Hall, disrupting service by deliberately moving slowly through cafeteria lines. A 4 March stall-in led to a disturbance that prompted about a dozen helmeted, club-carrying policemen to close the building. Pushing and shoving matches broke out between stall-in participants and regular customers. SSOC member Joel Polin received a six-inch gash on his head when a student hit him with a sugar shaker. At one point, BSM leader Dobbins called all blacks into a huddle at the north end of the hall; after ten minutes of conferring, he stood on a table and announced to the crowd, "If you white people and SSOC people want out, you better come over here now because we got no way to know you." At that point, about thirty-five blacks and an equal number of white supporters marched through the hall, overturning tables and chairs.[48]

Lenoir Hall remained closed until 6 March, when, under orders from Governor Scott, the building opened under the protection of forty state patrolmen equipped for riot duty. By sending in troops, Scott had acted against the wishes of Sitterson and Friday, and the presence of troops prompted picketing by members of the university community and townspeople. With troops on campus and with one violent skirmish already behind them, BSM and SSOC leaders began to emphasize their nonviolent goals. They received the support of the *Daily Tar Heel*'s Hurder, who editorialized, "Anyone who has stayed around

Manning Hall for the last two days and attended some of the meetings would quickly realize that the workers and their supporters are not interested in confrontation and the creation of anarchy."[49] Nevertheless, Scott continued with his public law-and-order stand. On 13 March, under orders from Scott, state troopers moved on Manning Hall, secured it, and locked it up. Fuller had received warning that the troopers would clear the building, and he encouraged the demonstrators to evacuate before the officers arrived to show that the movement was peaceful and not seeking a confrontation. Earlier that day, Chapel Hill police chief William Blake, also under the direction of Scott, walked into Manning Hall and presented arrest warrants for seven black students and one white student involved in the disruption in Lenoir. Shortly before the building was cleared, three of the students turned themselves over to police. Six of the students eventually were tried and convicted in district court, fined $150, and placed on two years' probation. The university did not institute separate disciplinary actions.[50]

Scott's intervention galvanized the campus against him, and one observer estimated that as many as 75 to 80 percent of students supported the workers' grievances. But most students also opposed the BSM and SSOC, despite their careful efforts to present their actions as moderate and nonviolent, and refused to participate in the boycott. Nevertheless, university officials ultimately agreed to a series of concessions, including retroactive pay raises, payment of overtime, and reclassification of some workers to a higher wage level. The Daily Tar Heel later editorialized that university officials had not taken the striking workers seriously until the 4 March episode.[51]

Regardless of the BSM's tactical approach, the food workers' strike had dramatized the issues of racial and labor exploitation for UNC students. In the process, the strike also somewhat tarnished the university's liberal reputation. Friday had sought to protect the university's freedom by striking a balance between accommodation and repression — to prevent both "student unrest" and conservative politicians from disrupting the university's operations and integrity. But this defensive position allowed the food workers and student activists to take the moral high ground, even when their rhetoric and actions bordered on the violent. The strike also diverted attention from the BSM's education-related goals, although these issues did not go away. In fact, university officials eventually acceded to several of the BSM's most important objectives, including a black studies curriculum with a major in African and Afro-American studies and increased emphasis on recruiting black students. However, tensions surfaced again in the fall of 1969, when Carolina cafeteria workers struck after Saga Corporation, a California-based catering contractor that took over the dining halls in 1969, cut back the workforce and increased hours and overtime without pay. The strike again prompted support from black and white campus activists, but with Scott no longer directly involving himself, the events never reached the previous level of intensity.[52]

The larger issue of racial equality soon receded somewhat on the Chapel Hill campus, as it did at Duke. In its place, the war in Vietnam increasingly dominated headlines of the student newspapers. Nevertheless, during the 1970s, both institutions continued to struggle with the meaning of integration for curricula, admissions, and student life as well as with larger institutional issues. The University of North Carolina fought a protracted battle with federal civil rights officials over its desegregation plan. As in the 1960s, Friday again sought first to protect the university's independence — this time from federal officials who wanted to merge UNC's programs with those of predominantly black schools. But this time, students were much less involved.[53]

Black Power, White Response

The black student movements at Duke and UNC represented the most dramatic showdowns over racial issues at the South's predominantly white institutions in the late 1960s. The schools were two of the region's elite universities — a private research university with a liberal president making a push to enter the ranks of the nation's elite universities and a public institution with a reputation as a bastion of southern liberalism. The trajectory of black protest at these schools represented the limits of possibility for change at predominantly white southern schools. Duke and UNC gave as much ground to black demands as did any institution in the South. The concessions included curricular modifications, special efforts to increase black presence on the campuses, and recognition — at least at some level — of the extent to which racial discrimination and inequality were entrenched at the university. Nevertheless, the most radical elements of the demands — calls for an end to grading for black students as well as control for black students of certain curricular and hiring decisions — went unrealized. At both institutions, these sorts of demands met with resistance from defenders of traditional academic practices and standards. One Duke faculty member, John Buettner-Janusch, expressed the concerns of traditionalists in a letter to professor Alan Kerckhoff, who chaired a faculty committee on student concerns. To Buettner-Janusch, the call for educational modifications to make Duke's curriculum more relevant to the concerns of African Americans bore a resemblance to all calls for relevance, which he viewed as part of a larger trend in which various segments of society made anti-intellectual demands on the university. "We have put up with it although I have always protested," Buettner-Janusch commented. He regarded "the subversion of the curriculum for the mentally disadvantaged" who played college athletics as simply the first of many departures from academia's true path: "We have prostituted ourselves for the good of industry, government, research establishments, medicine, and for other social demands upon us." Drawing on the trenchant criticisms of University of Chicago president Robert M. Hutchins, Buettner-Janusch concluded that the "academic banner" had become "a cornucopia on a field of guided missiles."[54]

Similar criticisms surfaced at Emory University. Like Duke — and, for that matter, the South's other privately controlled research universities, including Tulane, Vanderbilt, and Rice — Emory had desegregated quietly in the aftermath of the more public and volatile desegregation crises at state-supported public institutions. Black students at Emory had encountered many of the same difficulties in carving out a cultural space in an often unfriendly environment. And like their cohort on other predominantly white campuses, they had formed an organization, the Black Student Association (BSA), as a sort of mutual support network. By 1969, frustration with the slow pace of change was beginning to show; in the aftermath of the Allen Building takeover at Duke, Emory's student newspaper, the *Wheel*, took its first close look at campus race relations. At first glance, members of the BSA at Emory appeared to be more moderate than their colleagues in North Carolina. In early March 1969, BSA chair J. Henry Ambrose commented that the Duke students' demand for a black studies program was not unreasonable, "but to say 'Give it to me tomorrow' might be unreasonable." Nevertheless, Ambrose noted that Emory's black students were becoming impatient with the slow pace of integration on the campus: "After you have been here for awhile and you can't integrate things, you begin to get frustrated and you may change your tactics in order to get things done."[55]

Members of the BSA presented a list of eight "proposals" to the Emory administration on 12 March. By May, believing that the university was not acting quickly enough on the demands, the group stepped up the pressure with a series of demonstrations at the university's Cox Hall dining facility. The BSA questioned the meaning of integration and asked the university to "evaluate the objectives of the 1963 decision to bring black students to Emory." Was that decision "an attempt to assimilate a small minority into a white-oriented culture, thereby detaching them from a black-oriented culture?" The students proposed that Emory admit more black students, with financial aid and on the basis of academic promise, not standardized test scores or high school background. The BSA also called on Emory to fund a tutorial program and an orientation program to be run by the BSA. The black students also called on Emory to provide a "Black House," "a place where black students can come together as black people" and preserve their culture and benefit from mutual understanding. Other proposals called for a full-time black administrator to deal with the concerns of black students; a black psychiatrist to assist in emotional, academic, and social adjustments; an Afro-American studies program geared toward "providing city, private and federal governments with trained personnel in urban problems";

joint professorships with the Atlanta University Center; and an Afro-American Reading Room in the library.[56]

The desire to increase black enrollment was an especially thorny issue. Black students wanted Emory to concentrate more resources on recruitment and open more avenues by relaxing entrance requirements and providing tutorial programs to help black students succeed. University officials responded that they were actively recruiting African American students but that they faced stiff competition from other universities for a small pool of qualified applicants. Moreover, administrators contended that the university lacked the funds for scholarships and remedial programs geared toward black students, especially in inflationary economic times. Emory president Sanford Atwood argued that public institutions were better positioned to enroll large numbers of black students, whereas "Emory is the kind of institution which offers maximum opportunities" for a select number of academically qualified students.[57]

If the president's stance was ambiguous, members of the BSA found solid support in the outgoing and incoming student government presidents, who publicly expressed their belief that "white racism" was endemic at Emory. "We have continued to co-operate with Emory's institutional bias toward white skin," declared Stephen Abbott, the outgoing student government president, who at the time was fighting draft-evasion charges. "Either, like the Administration, we have shut our eyes and refused to see let alone fight racism or, what is equally bad, we have sought to paternalistically 'help' and 'support' Blacks assuming they were somehow inferior and thus needed our Great White Father control to guide them along."[58] With the support of Abbott and his successor, Charles Haynes, the university soon agreed to a resolution in which Atwood signed a statement acknowledging that "racism exists at Emory University" and pledged to cooperate with students, faculty, and administration to "openly commit themselves to its eradication." In exchange, members of the BSA modified their stance — "asking rather than demanding," according to Ed Ducree, a black faculty member and director of the Upward Bound program. The resolution was announced at a 28 May university-wide convocation. University officials and student activists subsequently began a lengthy process in which, as Atwood later phrased it, members of the university community "worked together" on twelve issues.[59]

This pledge of cooperation engendered some opposition. The chemistry department became the source of the most strident objection to relaxed admission requirements and special assistance for black students as well as to the university's official pledge to end racism. To department chair Leon Mandell, the BSA's agenda had "little to do with our drive towards achieving excellence in education." Moreover, the BSA's proposals were based on the false premise "that Emory University is guilty of racism and must atone for injustices that the blacks have suffered and are suffering." Guilt, Mandell argued, was an individual rather than corporate concept. If individual acts of racism had occurred, they should be charged and dealt with: "The general indictment of racism is meaningless and usually reflects some paranoia on the part of the indicter." Mandell then criticized each of the BSA's proposals, generally suggesting that they fell outside the purview of the university's mission: the university had no responsibility to raise the economic level of its janitors, to furnish group therapy for its students, or to "provide 'special' administrators for 'special groups.' . . . These requests attack much that is fundamental to an educational system that has provided more opportunity for more people than any other such program the world has devised."[60]

In contrast, white liberals within the Student Government Association embraced the charge that they helped perpetuate racism at Emory. Following a trend within the Black Power movement, black students had targeted white liberals for criticism. On 25 May, several black students interrupted the Sunday religious service in the campus's Durham Chapel. Four or five black students stopped the sermon and delivered a series of prepared speeches with several broad themes: Emory was a racist institution; the Christian community at Emory — that is, the white liberals — represented one of the most glaring examples of racism; and whites' role was no longer involvement in the ghettos or working with blacks but rather destroying racism in white communities.[61]

Seeking to respond positively to these charges, Emory's Student Government Association devised a program of noncredit classes on racism. The program, which included speakers and films, recognized that racism was "self-perpetuating phenomenon existing at every level of society" and sought to "deal with the causes and not the effects of racism." Class leaders would include Abbott, now a third-year graduate student in English; Haynes, a junior religion major; the Reverend Emmett Herndon, the Presbyterian campus minister; Philip Morgan, a political science instructor and specialist in African politics; Eugene Winograd, an assistant professor of psychology; and others. A suggested reading list offered a range of perspectives on racism, from *The Autobiography of Malcolm X* and Jonathan Kozol's *Death at an Early Age* to historical studies such as Winthrop Jordan's *White over Black*, C. Vann Woodward's *The Strange Career of Jim Crow*, and Leon Litwack's *North of Slavery*.[62]

One significant implication of white liberals' acceptance of their complicity in the perpetuation of racism was a reorientation of a tutorial program for black children conducted by the Community Services Committee. The program had provided participating white students with a firsthand introduction to the problems of the black ghetto. Indeed, in the spring of 1969, eighteen of the program's twenty-two participants sought continued involvement, and fourteen said they had benefited more from the program than had the children they had tutored.

Nevertheless, Community Service Committee leaders asked pointed questions about the program's worth. Starting with the premise that "the black man is saying that the white man has no place in the black man's ghetto," leader Helen Stanton argued that the tutorial programs were at best "band-aid" solutions to difficult problems. "At worst," she said, "they help to create more tension and misunderstanding between blacks and whites than existed beforehand." While community service programs had great value for white participants, they often served only to salve white consciences, she suggested. As a result, during the 1969–70 academic year, the Community Service Committee became the Committee for Community Action. Stanton, the chair of the reformulated program, declared that the new group would focus on action rather than service, although the exact meaning of this reorientation was unclear. Indeed, Stanton suggested that activities during the fall of 1969 would concentrate on exploring exactly how whites should respond to the changing terrain. Her comments revealed not optimism but a sort of grim realism that bordered on pessimism. "Community Action may still have a realistic place," she suggested. "Yet perhaps students, who are more concerned with getting their degree than anything else, have no right to meddle in the affairs of something they cannot possibly understand."[63]

Programs such as Emory's Community Service Committee were common on predominantly white southern campuses during the 1960s, both a natural outgrowth of student desires for greater relevance in their education and an avenue for uninvolved students to become activists. Indeed, leaders in both the SSOC and the Southern Project of the U.S. National Student Association (NSA) viewed community service programs as valuable tools to get students involved in social issues. Leaders of the Community Action Council of Tulane University Students (CACTUS) described their program as "a thorn in the side of indifference." The program had originated in 1964 with Project Opportunity, a tutorial program sponsored by the Southern Association of Colleges and Schools. For two years, it attracted only minimal student interest. But in 1966, Donald Mintz, a second-year law student, took control and created CACTUS as a new umbrella group for community service, and some 150 students soon were involved in four projects. But at Tulane, as at Emory, the changing racial terrain posed problems. In 1968, William Hill, a black undergraduate, found a way to keep white students involved without falling into the paternalism trap: "There is no longer a need for confused, frustrated, neurotic, guilty people," he declared. But by early 1970, the same kind of confusion that had emerged within Emory's community service program was appearing in CACTUS's ranks. In one issue of the CACTUS Newsletter, participant Gary Bair attempted a reconsideration of the organization in light of the rise of Black Power: "Where does this leave the students at Tulane? I really don't know. I have been seriously questioning each of CACTUS' programs in an attempt to measure its effectiveness." In the wake of April 1970 demonstrations by the Student Liberation Front, Bair tentatively concluded that white students should concentrate on winning power on campus before venturing into poor black neighborhoods. In the same issue, sociology professor George Ritzer offered a more blunt assessment: "I would conclude that whites should leave the black community alone. If whites want to do something, there is plenty to be done within the white community." Such conclusions might have spelled the end of CACTUS, but the program survived and continues to offer Tulane students an opportunity to involve themselves in New Orleans's problems.[64]

Black Power in the Deep South

At the University of Alabama, the rise of Black Power seemed to cause less uncertainty, in part, perhaps, because the black student movement there was somewhat less militant than those at the region's more elite institutions. Community service programs at Alabama originated in 1965 when the Student Government Association joined forces with the National Association for the Advancement of Colored People to sponsor the Tuscaloosa Opportunity Project, the local affiliate of Operation Head Start. Shortly thereafter, with the help of the NSA's Tutorial Assistance Center, 'Bama students created the Tutorial Assistance Project, which during the next three years attracted hundreds of students to volunteer to tutor potential high school dropouts in poor Tuscaloosa neighborhoods. In 1968, the Student Government Association created the Campus-Community Organization Program, again with help from the NSA. In this program, student volunteers spent time organizing recreational programs in depressed areas near Tuscaloosa.[65]

Like black student organizations at other Deep South public universities, Alabama's Afro-American Association (AAA) never employed radical tactics such as building takeovers to push its agenda. While the AAA at various times issued lists of demands, the organization only occasionally employed direct-action tactics, much less violence. The first set of demands came in April 1968, when the AAA called for full-time black faculty members; a course in Afro-American history; a black policeman as part of the campus security force; housing without discrimination, guaranteed by the university; and equal representation in the student government through appointments to vacancies and committees.[66] An August follow-up memo to the university community restated most of the earlier grievances and added others, including a guide to pronunciation ("the word N-E-G-R-O is pronounced knee-grow or Black"). The AAA also took on a sacred cow, calling on the university actively to seek out black athletes and offer them scholarships.[67]

The association recorded an impressive list of achievements during the 1968–69 academic year. Some of these gains were overtly political, while others were more concerned with providing on-campus social outlets for black students. The AAA began creating a black sorority; selected black students for standing university committees; created an intramural athletic team; pushed for and aided a faculty recruitment program; brought the first suit under the 1968 Fair Housing Act to open off-campus housing to black students; pushed for and achieved new courses pertaining to black Americans; won the first appointment of black students to major student government committees and the first black policeman on the campus police force; created a student recruitment program; participated in a voter registration drive for a congressional candidate; sponsored a float and a black queen in the homecoming parade; sponsored black candidates for the student government elections, including one who became the first black student elected to the student legislature; and "played a significant role in the recruitment of Alabama's first scholarship black athlete."[68]

By November 1969, continued pressure from the AAA, including a sit-in at the Union Building, prompted President F. David Mathews to create an Afro-American Grievance Committee made up of faculty and students. The committee dealt with seven demands: the creation of a black studies department, an orientation program for black students, and an Afro-American center; better benefits and working conditions for black campus employees; the hiring of more black professors; the immediate desegregation of fraternities and sororities; and the end of the athletic department's discriminatory practices. When the committee issued its final report in August 1970, the AAA had not achieved all of its demands. In particular, the committee rejected a black studies program, arguing that the "establishment of a black studies department is a step toward separatism or 'neo-segregation'" and that similar departments at other institutions had achieved only marginal success. However, the committee recommended the establishment of a minor in black studies within the American studies program. Similarly, the grievance committee recognized the social needs that produced the demand for an Afro-American center but balked establishing a facility that "would be totally inconsistent with the University's efforts to create an absolutely non-discriminatory environment dedicated to fostering educational opportunities for all its constituencies." Instead, committee members proposed allocating office space for the AAA and creating a lounge that any student group could reserve. The committee supported a black orientation program and the hiring of more black professors, although it pointed out the difficulties posed by a shortage of African Americans with doctoral degrees. The committee endorsed the concept of desegregating fraternities and sororities but failed to recommend any means of doing so. On the questions of conditions for black workers and discrimination within the athletic department, the committee essentially denied that problems existed. The AAA issued a nineteen-page response that by turns chided the committee for its lack of understanding on some issues, praised it for its understanding on others, and declared the intention to continue working on the grievances. But the group did not mount a direct-action campaign on the lines of the AAS at Duke or even the BSA at Emory.[69]

The experiences of Alabama's AAA resembled those of the black student unions at the Universities of Georgia and Mississippi. In all three cases, though the groups used rhetoric that was sometimes heated, they employed nonviolent measures. At Ole Miss, African American students had only limited free space in which to address controversial issues. As late as 1965, integration remained a controversial enough idea that segregationist protests took place. When an integrated group from Tougaloo College came to Oxford for the annual Southern Literary Festival, nearly five hundred Ole Miss students gathered outside the dorm where the black men were staying and chanted, "8-6-4-2 — send them back to Tougaloo" and "We don't want nigger lovers at Ole Miss." Nevertheless the tone of discourse in the state and on the campus gradually moderated. The Ole Miss law school, under the leadership of Joshua M. Morse III, became a center of liberal activism, as a handful of Yale-educated professors recruited black students, encouraged students to mobilize against the war in Vietnam and a restrictive policy on outside speakers, and spearheaded a controversial legal-services program for poor residents of northern Mississippi. In the wake of Martin Luther King Jr.'s assassination, a group of "Several Black Students" charged the university with harboring an atmosphere of "Bigotry, Bias and Racial Prejudice" and submitted a list of demands that mirrored those of other black student organizations. In early 1969, the group received a university charter as the Black Student Union, although officials insisted that membership could not be restricted only to African Americans. The high point of black student activism came in February 1970, when nearly one hundred black students interrupted a concert at Fulton Chapel by a traveling musical group, Up with People, that had an interracial cast and encouraged cross-cultural interaction. The highway patrol arrested a total of ninety-three blacks, including nine nonstudents.[70]

Debate ensued regarding whether the arrested students should be prosecuted, and the judicial council ultimately voted to suspend eight of the protesters, who sued the university. A federal court judge permitted all eight of the suspended students to remain in school until they faced new, individual hearings before the board of trustees, which again suspended the students. However, some faculty members took an interest in the black students' demands, and the Faculty Senate appointed several committees to investigate. The most important result was the implementation of a black studies program in the fall of 1970.[71]

On 26 February 1969, black students at the University of Georgia delivered a list of twenty-two demands to President Fred C. Davison. The demands of the Black Student Union (BSU) contained all of the elements of the Black Power agenda on white southern campuses — a department of Afro-American studies, increases in the numbers of black faculty members and students, an adviser for African American students to be selected by the students themselves, abolition of the grading system for black students in favor of a pass-fail system, the establishment of an Afro-American dormitory, and a wage increase for black employees. But also present were demands that illustrated some of the differences between race relations in Deep South public universities with white constituencies still smarting from integration and private universities located in more cosmopolitan or liberal locales. An overt, visceral racism still existed on the campus and in the state in the form of racist politician Roy Harris, who served on the university's board of regents. In addition to his resignation, the BSU demanded "the establishment of an Ad Hoc Committee to investigate 'red neck' instructors" and the banning of the Kappa Alpha fraternity from campus. In April, when a reporter from the *Red and Black* interviewed BSU president Robert Benham, he predicted that violence would visit the campus. But he predicted not black revolutionary violence but violence initiated by conservative whites seeking to clamp down on black-led demonstrations.[72]

By then, Davison had issued a less-than-forthcoming response to the BSU's demands. Like UNC's Sitterson, Davison emphasized the ways in which the university already met the demands — in existing courses on Afro-American history and culture, for example, or in machinery designed to meet the academic and social needs of all students. But Davison steadfastly refused to accede to any demands for separate facilities, personnel, or functions for black students, contending that such programs would be unsound and possibly illegal.[73]

Members of the University of Georgia community subsequently struggled to negotiate a resolution to the demands of the black students. The lack of progress prompted more militant rhetoric at a May BSU rally that featured warnings of a "fire next time" and declarations that "if the administration . . . doesn't come 'round, we're going to tear it down." At the same time, however, work proceeded on a black studies program. In April, Dean H. Boyd McWhorter of the College of Arts and Sciences appointed a faculty committee, headed by assistant dean and history professor Charles E. Wynes, to study the possibility of more black studies courses. According to McWhorter, the initiative had been in the discussion stage before the BSU issued its demands. The committee included no black students, but a subcommittee consulted with two black students, including Benham, in a meeting that Wynes described as "quite constructive." By late May, the committee had announced that it was almost ready to announce a new coordinator for the Afro-American studies program.[74]

Nevertheless, the pace of change remained too slow for black students, and in May 1971, the BSU issued a new list of thirteen demands, again centering on the university's small number of black students and teachers. The university had already hired a black admissions counselor, Benjamin J. Colbert, who had helped increase the number of black freshmen from four in the fall of 1969 to eighty-three a year later. But the BSU called on the university to bring the percentage of black students at the university up to 30 percent, in line with the state's African American population. Colbert believed that 10 percent was a more realistic goal, at least as long as UGA continued to provide an environment that was unfriendly to black students. "These students prefer to be in an all-black situation because of the problems involved in trying to cope with the almost all-white situation here," he told the *Red and Black*. BSU members also expressed dissatisfaction with the fledgling Afro-American studies program, which seemed to have greater success in attracting white students than black students. The BSU called for a black director of the program, a goal that two central figures in the program, white professors Charles Crowe and David E. Foley, supported. "There's nothing genetic about this thing," said Crowe, "but most white instructors don't have the point of view necessary."[75]

While some differences surfaced between black student movements in public universities in the Deep South and private universities in the peripheral South, the movements were generally more alike than different. Drawing on the currents of Black Power, student rhetoric reflected the militance and separatism that were hallmarks of the late-1960s black freedom struggle. Nevertheless, black student actions on predominantly white campuses in the South were generally nonviolent and pursued goals that were ultimately pluralistic. Even when they called for separate dormitories and different admissions standards and grading policies, they sought incorporation into the university community. "We only asked for those rights and privileges the other students already have," noted Harold Curry, the first president of the University of Alabama's AAA, after the organization issued its initial set of demands.[76] At Tulane, senior Nelson Brown suggested in 1968 that whites never had understood the meaning of integration: "White Americans, when they think of integration, think of the Negro being processed and changed from his original self, so he comes out stamped and approved and can integrate into society as acceptable." According to Brown, Tulane's black student organization represented "an effort to gain and retain this black consciousness as needed, the purpose of which is: one day when America progresses far enough, the white man and the black man will be able to confront each other as they are, will accept each other as they are."[77]

CHAPTER EIGHT

The War in the South

STUDENT ACTIVISM reached its second zenith in the South in the two years that preceded May 1970. On most of the region's major public and private university campuses, activists forced at least one dramatic confrontation between early 1968 and the end of the 1969–70 academic year. These confrontations involved large numbers of students — often hundreds and sometimes even thousands. The issues that resonated during these demonstrations varied. The autonomy of students as masters of their own private lives and active participants in their own educational lives provided mobilizing issues on a number of campuses. And racial issues loomed especially large in a region in which desegregation proceeded haltingly down an uncertain path. These issues all had roots in the desegregation-related crises of the early 1960s.

American involvement in Vietnam, which stretched back to the 1950s but nevertheless did not emerge as a large-scale issue until after 1965, provided the final ingredient for late-1960s activism. But Vietnam was more than simply one of a list of issues that concerned students. Instead, it joined race as one of the two dominant issues on southern campuses. In an increasingly polarized climate, support for or opposition to the war in Vietnam often served as a litmus test of political orientation, much in the same way that support for integration had indicated a willingness to dissent on a number of issues.

Vietnam never completely replaced race as the most important issue on southern campuses, and many students became adept at weaving the two issues into one analysis. For black students, racial issues still dominated, though the concerns associated with Black Power modified black students' dissent. Black students who addressed Vietnam often incorporated the issue into a larger concern with racism — "No Vietnamese Ever Called Me a Nigger."

To be sure, racial politics and the war were not mutually exclusive. Black and white activists pointed out connections between racial discrimination at home and American policy abroad from the earliest days following escalation.

In the midst of the Selma clashes in March 1965, John Lewis asked why the United States could send troops to Vietnam and not to the South to protect civil rights workers. At a May 1965 teach-in at Berkeley, Student Nonviolent Coordinating Committee (SNCC) activist Bob Moses suggested that black people were members of the Third World, a mirror that facilitated a clearer understanding of American policies in other parts of the world. In the following years, opposition to the war was evident in student newspapers on black campuses, and African American students participated in some demonstrations against the war. Members of a generation for whom American policy in Vietnam represented a core issue, black southern students added their voices to protests against the war.[1]

However, as historian Simon Hall suggests, black people had particular reasons for opposing the war. They questioned the necessity of supporting and fighting abroad when they were treated as second-class citizens at home. And they criticized the draft, which was at times applied unfairly to activists and which was carried out with little African American participation on selective service boards. Finally, the growing tendency to see African Americans as linked with people of color in other parts of the world fed black opposition to the war. When Moses looked at a photo of a Vietnamese boy being captured by a U.S. Marine, he saw "a little colored boy, standing against a wire fence, with a big, huge white marine with a gun at his back. But what I knew was that the people in this country saw a communist rebel." Black and white Americans "travel in different realities."[2]

Those different realities seemed to forestall significant levels of cooperation between black and white students in the southern antiwar movement, although a few exceptions existed. In 1967, SNCC made antidraft activity part of its southern campus program. "The campus traveler can initiate mobilization around the anti-draft program which can become a central issue," a February 1967 SNCC report suggested. Nevertheless, this issue was buried on a list with various other items that received more prominent play, including university reform, the distribution of independent publications, and the application of pressure on student governments.[3] On historically black and predominantly white campuses, the application of Black Power to the campus loomed larger for African American students than did the war. And while many black students expressed opposition to the war, the public face of the student antiwar movement in the South was white.

Racial issues continued to resonate for white students as well; for those who hailed from the South, coming to terms with the racist aspects of their upbringing often constituted an important part of their political awakening. Nevertheless, by 1969, Vietnam provided the foundation for much of the South's white student activism. The war's emergence as a resonant issue signaled two important developments on the path of southern student activism.

First, the conflict in Vietnam played an important role in pushing southern student activists toward a more radical orientation, much as the war did for students in other parts of the country. This radical orientation often incorporated a dark view of the university as a member of a military-industrial-academic complex that was prosecuting an immoral war. When radical students targeted the specific examples of this complicity — the presence of the Reserve Officers' Training Corps (ROTC), recruiters from the armed services or napalm-maker Dow Chemical Corporation, or military research on campus — they did so not so much to reform the university as to contribute to broader, more fundamental social change. In the South, however, such activists were in the minority of the student body at large and of antiwar activists in particular. More common and often more influential were liberal activists who opposed involvement in the war but accepted established American institutions, including the university.

In the division between radical and liberal activists, the student antiwar movement in the South resembled the national antiwar movement, which also split along liberal/radical lines. This similarity was part of a broader pattern that fits into the second major effect of antiwar activism in the South: the Vietnam issue's tendency to eliminate some of the "southern distinctiveness" from southern student activism. This foreign-policy issue spoke to American rather than southern sins. To the extent that Vietnam joined racism as a defining issue for white southern student activists, it contributed to the incorporation of southern students into national political and cultural patterns. In this respect, the advent of activism in general and antiwar activism in particular formed part of a larger trend in which southern higher education entered the national mainstream. All along, the drive within southern colleges and universities for excellence based on national standards had produced tensions. Some administrators who longed for the prestige associated with academic excellence sometimes chafed at the corresponding threats to orthodoxy and order. And at a time when the most dramatic examples of student activism seemed to emanate from America's most elite campuses, southern students and faculty members sometimes saw activism as a sign of a campus's entry onto the national scene. In the aftermath of April 1968 sit-ins related to women's curfews at the University of Georgia, history professor Charles Crowe, a key member of the university's activist community, suggested that the demonstrations would help improve the institution's national reputation. "The rest of the nation will know that we have students interested in expressing their views," Crowe argued. "It will help destroy the image of apathy that this University has contracted."[4] Similarly, when Jerry Rubin delivered an unauthorized speech at the University of Alabama in May 1970, some students rejoiced at the implications.[5]

The South's colleges and universities tended to be less involved in the anti-war movement than were educational institutions in other parts of the nation. At the height of American student activism, the Cambodia/Kent State/Jackson State protests of May 1970, the number of southern institutions that experienced demonstrations, though significant, still lagged behind the rest of the country. A survey conducted in the aftermath of the student strike found "significant impact" on campus operations at 76 percent of the institutions in the Northeast, 68 percent of those in the Pacific states, 51 percent in the Midwest, 52 percent in the mountain states, and only 41 percent in the Southeast. The South's participation rate of 41 percent was far lower than the national rate of 57 percent.[6]

Southern students not only protested the war less frequently than did their colleagues in other parts of the country but also were more moderate in their tactical approach to activism. Nationally, the war was perhaps the main ingredient in the rapidly rising militance of the New Left. Members of the Weatherman faction of Students for a Democratic Society (SDS), who eventually went underground to become self-styled guerrilla warriors, represented the extreme version of this militant tendency. But the violence within some factions of the New Left's national leadership held little fascination for most southern student activists, and antiwar protest in southern institutions was on the whole nonviolent. By 1969 and early 1970, antiwar activism in the South exhibited a tendency toward more confrontational tactics, but these incidents usually were more disruptive than violent; violence often occurred only when law enforcement officials overreacted while attempting to shut down demonstrations. In a few instances, unexplained fires broke out on campuses while students were demonstrating. For example, in May 1970, World War II–era barracks buildings burned at Tulane University and the University of Alabama. In both cases, the buildings were already scheduled for demolition, and in both cases, rumors circulated in the aftermath that agents provocateurs were responsible, rumors that were confirmed in the Alabama incident by an investigation conducted by local American Civil Liberties Union attorneys and journalists.[7] Nevertheless, the strongest strain of antiwar activism on southern campuses was liberal, not radical. It aimed for an end to American involvement in the war without the destruction of the basic American social or economic structure and thus testified to the degree to which the movement base had broadened to include traditional student leaders as well as campus rebels. However, this phenomenon also testified to southern student activism's tendency to flow into established channels.

The Path of the Southern Antiwar Movement

The South had no autonomous peace movement before 1965. When it developed, the southerners who took the lead came out of the civil rights movement.

In many cases, the connections between the desegregation-related activism of the early 1960s and the anti–Vietnam War movement of the late 1960s was direct. The Southern Student Organizing Committee (SSOC) became a primary vehicle for antiwar activism in significant portions of the region, especially the Carolinas, Virginia, and Georgia. On individual campuses, faculty members and students who had participated in sit-ins and picketing against segregation often moved easily into opposition to the war.

The antiwar movement was slow to develop in much of the South, no doubt in part because of strong promilitary sentiment in the region. The first wave of teach-ins barely touched the South. When debate and discussion concerning Vietnam finally emerged on southern campuses, the prowar faction was particularly vocal. Nevertheless, the debate and discussion of 1965–67 provided the necessary prelude for bolder, more organized expressions of opposition to the war in 1967 and 1968. The first locales to experience these early examples of activism were usually the areas in which dissenters had relative freedom to voice their views without placing their lives or careers in danger. As in the early 1960s, these southern free spaces tended to be in the urban South and outside Mississippi, Alabama, Georgia (except Atlanta), South Carolina, and Louisiana (except New Orleans).

By 1969, the widespread dissatisfaction with the war, which had grown in the wake of the January–February 1968 Tet Offensive, was in full bloom on southern campuses. But the "movement" — the organized expression of that discontent — often sputtered, the result of divisions among those students actively opposed to the war and the occasional emergence of other issues that pushed Vietnam from center stage. Indeed, because of activists' multi-issue orientation, separating the antiwar issue from the larger student movement can be difficult. Antiwar activism took aim not only at American foreign policy in a broad sense but at specific policies and practices on southern campuses — including the existence of both compulsory and voluntary ROTC, the involvement of southern universities in military research, and campus visits by military recruiters. While southern students added their voices to a national outcry that played some role in the eventual end of the war,[8] the southern student antiwar movement ultimately tallied its most measurable victories and defeats on those particular issues.

America's ties to the conflict in Southeast Asia dated to the immediate period after World War II, when Vietnamese nationalists, led by Ho Chi Minh, a French-educated communist, began a push to end the French colonial regime that had been in place since the late 1800s. Fearing the spread of communism in the region, the United States became more involved after the defeat of the French at Dienbienphu in 1953, eventually bestowing American backing on the South Vietnamese regime of the U.S.-educated Ngo Dinh Diem. American support deepened during John F. Kennedy's administration, and despite his campaign promises that he sought "no wider war," Lyndon B. Johnson's interpretation of Vietnam as a 1960s version of Czechoslovakia in the 1930s and Ho Chi Minh as a modern Adolf Hitler pushed the United States toward an unprecedented commitment in 1965. While hiding behind lies and half-truths about the absence of a "far-reaching strategy," Johnson committed the first combat troops in March.[9]

These developments prompted a renewal of the U.S. peace movement. Opponents of American involvement in Vietnam were a diverse lot. Pacifists who opposed all war joined activists who objected specifically to the commitment in Vietnam. The ranks included liberals who accepted the basic outlines of American life and radicals who sought broader and deeper social change. The divisions were often significant, and no one group assumed primary leadership. In fact, the antiwar movement developed a dual identity. It was a broad coalition, encompassing "church people, organized women, traditional peace workers, intellectuals, students, and assorted leftists." But even as this broad coalition gained impressive cultural power, it remained politically weak, in part because of its inherent divisions.[10]

In the wake of American escalation, college campuses in many parts of the United States temporarily became the primary staging grounds for antiwar activism. Following the first teach-in against the war in March 1965 at the University of Michigan, a wave of similar events swept campuses on the two coasts and in the Midwest. The teach-ins represented an implicit critique of the state of higher education, as students targeted a curriculum that was irrelevant to current world problems. In the South, where battles over speaker bans revealed a continuing conflict over whether controversial issues could be debated on campus, teach-ins occurred less frequently than in other regions of the country.[11]

Nevertheless, the college-based teach-ins and antiwar demonstrations set the tone for the emergence of discussion and debate on southern campuses. On the editorial pages of campus newspapers, students began debating not only whether escalation was proper but also whether demonstrations and teach-ins were a proper response to the escalation. Individual campus political milieus structured the form and content of the antiwar movements that developed on those campuses in the late 1960s. Examples in two sections of the South illustrated the possibilities, as well as the limitations. In Atlanta and Athens, supporters of the war at Emory University and the University of Georgia, who were reacting to the opposition of students on their own campuses as well as in other parts of the country, seized the early momentum by organizing a massive prowar rally in Atlanta. This strong stance signaled and solidified early support for the war on these campuses and helped limit the development of a student antiwar movement. In Durham and Chapel Hill, North Carolina, however, the prowar element was less vocal. Moreover, traditional student leaders at both Duke and the University of North Carolina expressed serious doubts about the war effort in 1966, while pockets of increasingly radical students made Vietnam a central part of their agenda.

Prowar Students and the Beginnings of the Antiwar Movement: Georgia

"Conversation: Viet Nam," the South's first Vietnam teach-in, occurred at Emory University in late October 1965 and attracted some twelve hundred people. The product of students who were veterans of civil rights activities and a controversial Emory theologian, the teach-in spawned not only a significant local antiwar movement but also a statewide, student-driven prowar rally, "Affirmation: Viet Nam," that dwarfed its predecessor and helped defenders of U.S. foreign policy seize the early momentum in Atlanta and Athens.

Among the Emory students who had been active in Atlanta's civil rights movement were Jody Palmour, a religion major from Gainesville, and Gene Guerrero, an Atlantan who had served as SSOC's first chair in 1964. In the fall of 1965, Emory theologian Thomas J. J. Altizer, who had participated in the University of Michigan teach-in the previous March, approached a handful of activists that included Palmour and Guerrero and encouraged them to organize a similar event.[12] The students put together a committee and, influenced by Southern Christian Leadership Conference dialogue programs that featured interracial conversations about civil rights, decided to give equal time to the prowar point of view. The 29 October program packed the house and featured keynote addresses by *Atlanta Constitution* editor Eugene Patterson, who spoke in favor of the Johnson administration's policy, and socialist Norman Thomas, who spoke against it. Other participants included Nanci Gitlin of SDS, activist scholar Staughton Lynd, Georgia representative James Mackay, and Young Republican Arthur Collingsworth.[13]

Shortly thereafter, several Emory students spearheaded a drive that seemed designed to counter the campus-based opposition to the war. Dubbed "Affirmation: Viet Nam" (AVN), clearly a spin on the earlier teach-in, the effort was putatively intended to gauge Georgia college students' feelings on the Vietnam issue. Organizers on campuses throughout Georgia set about publicizing a "poll" that asked respondents whether they supported American policy in Southeast Asia but was designed to show support for the war: "Although the affirmative reply is desired, negatives will be accepted."[14] The climax came at a February 1966 rally at brand-new Atlanta–Fulton County Stadium. A driving rain kept attendance at less than half organizers' goal of fifty-five thousand, but those who turned out heard Secretary of State Dean Rusk, Georgia governor

Carl Sanders, Senators Richard B. Russell and Herman Talmadge, and Atlanta mayor Ivan Allen. During his keynote address, Rusk noted the presence of anti-war protesters outside the stadium carrying signs that read "Peace in Viet Nam." The Georgia native told the crowd that he had been delivering precisely that message "to every capital of the world."[15]

The centerpiece of the rally was the presentation of the "poll," which not surprisingly found that 96.6 percent of the respondents, who included students at forty-seven of the state's fifty colleges and universities, supported the nation's commitment in Vietnam. In the following months, the AVN defined the war debate at Emory. In early 1967, AVN organizers received the George Washington Honor Medal from the Freedoms Foundation, and Emory president Sanford Atwood joined the students in traveling to Valley Forge, Pennsylvania, to accept the award, telling reporters, "We've hit the big leagues now." The AVN had racked up a two-thousand-dollar debt, which the university helped to pay off, prompting concern among Emory students who criticized the university's explicit support.[16]

By 1967, Emory students' opposition to the war was becoming more vocal, even if supporters probably still held the majority. An Atlanta SSOC chapter comprising students from Emory University, Georgia State University, Agnes Scott College, and Atlanta University formed in 1967.[17] The Atlanta chapter followed the larger organization's lead, adopting a multi-issue orientation. Atlanta SSOC's initial mobilizing issue, however, came from the gubernatorial campaign of former segregationist restaurateur Lester Maddox. When the victorious Maddox was inaugurated in January 1967, SSOC conducted a coffin-carrying demonstration that symbolized the death of the state's political freedom. The organization followed with demonstrations at the State Capitol supporting increased funding for higher education. University reform remained an important issue for the organization, but members turned to Vietnam in the spring of 1967. On 11 April, the Atlanta SSOC chapter conducted a teach-in on the Emory campus as part of the nationwide Spring Mobilization against Vietnam. About seventy-five people heard speeches by Emory political science professor Lyle Downing, Spelman historian Vincent Harding, former SNCC research director Jack Minnis, and Nick Golman of the Morehouse history department.[18]

The Atlanta student antiwar movement also included a healthy dose of draft resistance.[19] On 16 October 1967, Palmour and another Emory student, James Everett, publicly turned in their draft cards, exposing themselves to possible sentences of fifteen years in prison and/or fifteen thousand dollars in fines. Neither man had been in danger of being drafted.[20] Shortly thereafter, Emory graduate student Stephen Abbott, who would serve as the university's 1968–69 student government president, refused induction in Atlanta after his Lincoln, Nebraska, draft board rejected his application for conscientious-objector status.

Abbott, a Christian pacifist who had spent two years studying in a Benedictine seminary in Nebraska, eventually was found guilty of draft evasion and sentenced to three years in prison.[21] And in December, Guerrero refused induction after losing a two-year battle for conscientious-objector status. Guerrero was indicted for draft evasion in early March 1968.[22]

These personal acts of resistance accompanied an increase in antiwar activism. In October 1967, several students voiced their opposition to the war at a proto-countercultural "happening" that organizers dubbed "Sgt. Pepper's Peace Parade and Carnival." One of these students was Ned Williams, an African American freshman from Savannah, who delivered a short speech opposing American involvement in the war and then began a one-man demonstration against the war, sitting in the library beneath a display of Affirmation: Viet Nam's Freedoms Foundation award. He stayed there until shortly after eleven o'clock that night. Williams also began a fast. The next month, about twenty students, led by Abbott and another graduate student, Tom Coffin, picketed a Dow Chemical Company recruiter at Emory. The demonstrations against Dow continued after students returned from Christmas break. On 8 January 1968, a group of students staged a lunchtime skit that featured the unveiling of the "Third World man," a wrought-iron statue covered with melted plastic that represented a person charred by napalm.[23]

On the eve of the Tet Offensive, a student-government-sponsored referendum on Vietnam revealed a campus divided on the issue. The referendum asked respondents to answer yes or no to five possible options for American involvement in Vietnam. Most of the approximately 1,300 respondents opposed increasing the U.S. commitment in the region, but a majority also opposed both continuing with the present policy and deescalating with a goal of eventual withdrawal. Only about one-third of respondents believed that the United States should stop bombing North Vietnam, and just 15 percent thought that the United States should immediately and unilaterally withdraw from Vietnam. Though it was not a scientific survey, the referendum, which attracted more voters than any previous such measure at Emory, suggested that most students were both dissatisfied with the Johnson administration's policy and unwilling to endorse the peace movement's goals.[24]

Roughly an hour away, at the University of Georgia in Athens, activists had even more difficulty building broad-based opposition to American involvement in Vietnam. As they did at Emory, supporters of American foreign policy in Athens were numerous enough and vocal enough to create difficulty for antiwar students. In October 1965, the UGA campus newspaper, the *Red and Black*, conducted a poll on a two-pronged question: "What do you think of the recent demonstrations protesting U.S. involvement in Viet Nam and Sen.

Herman Talmadge's suggestion to draft the demonstrators?" The reporter noted that most students in the unscientific poll "opposed the demonstrations because they felt they were unpatriotic and bad for morale." Most respondents "agreed that the demonstrations were Communist inspired." Although the reporter did not provide an indication of how many people responded positively or negatively to the second part of the question, the few responses she quoted indicated at least some support for Talmadge's suggestion. Rick Wingo, a senior political science major, noted that "student demonstrators are college students who have student exemption from the draft," yet they were cutting classes to demonstrate. He supported the idea of reclassifying the demonstrators to be eligible for the draft.[25]

The following month, two University of Georgia students organized a "bleed-in," which the campus newspaper described as "a demonstration in which the participants donate blood . . . for American soldiers in Viet Nam." The two students named the drive the "Isaacs Movement," after a Texas native who had been killed in action in Vietnam the previous year. According to one of the students, the Isaacs Movement sought "to erase the stigma attached to college students and to show the soldiers in Viet Nam that the people of the U.S. are behind them."[26]

The show of support continued with preparations for Affirmation: Viet Nam. University president O. C. Aderhold lent official credibility to the cause by being the first on campus to sign the opinion poll. His statement left no doubt where he stood on the issue. People outside the United States, he said, too often envied America's luxuries: "They do not understand that these achievements are the result of a way of life that produces intelligent, responsible, and dedicated men." Aderhold suggested that the Affirmation drive would be a constructive contribution to national politics and to a nation that was becoming increasingly disturbed by student revolt.[27]

Despite this support, the petition drew the ire of a few students who opposed the stridency of the Affirmation: Viet Nam supporters. Shortly before the rally in Atlanta, two students picketed the main library, where AVN organizers were soliciting signatures, and eventually attracted a crowd of 150 onlookers. The women, both sophomores from Atlanta, seemed primarily to oppose the "poll's" vague wording and those who signed it without understanding it rather than to oppose U.S. Vietnam policy itself. "We only want students to think before they sign the Affirmation poll," said Barbara Blanton.[28] Similarly, finance professor Richard Timberlake Jr. criticized the AVN drive in a February 1966 letter to the editor of The Red and Black. If the Affirmation campaign was merely an effort to lend moral support to the soldiers in Vietnam, Timberlake suggested, then it was banal; "if it is an attempt to swing uninformed people onto a band wagon, it is mischievous and biased." Timberlake then asked whether

Affirmation organizers had even considered arguments against American involvement in Vietnam: "Have they even listened to their political science teachers on the subject?"[29]

In fact, debate and discussion concerning Vietnam had been proliferating in *The Red and Black*'s pages. Some writers talked of ending compulsory ROTC at the university, a proposal that the paper's editors opposed on the grounds that "if one great leader is produced, or if one person receives a better understanding of this country and its doctrine, the program is a success." But as Timberlake's letter suggested, not all members of the university community unquestioningly supported the nation's Vietnam policy. One student, Don Rhodes, argued against continuing the commitment: "We basically have a choice between moving forward or compromising. If this compromise is called backing down by our allies, why not back down if it will save the lives of thousands of other young Americans?"[30] Another student found the debate refreshing: "For once in their lives, many students finally had a cause to support, whether it was the 'Isaacs Movement,' anti-compulsory ROTC or anti–Viet Nam war," noted managing editor Mickey Mills. "There have never been more petitions circulated or more letters written to The Red and Black than there have been in the fall quarter of 1965." In contrast, "the average University student" had previously been "thought to be, and in most cases was, an apathy-minded, dull-minded, hell-raiser whose only problem each day was deciding whether or not to go to class."[31]

In the wake of the Affirmation rally, the debate over Vietnam, the draft, and compulsory ROTC seemed to die down somewhat. When it resurfaced, it did so as a result of the formation of a campus chapter of SDS in the spring of 1967. Searching for a mobilizing issue with broad appeal, members of the chapter circulated a newsletter that intentionally flouted a university regulation that all student publications be approved by the Office of Student Activities. But members of the chapter also organized an antiwar demonstration when Vice President Hubert H. Humphrey visited Athens that spring. During the summer, the chapter circulated a petition asking for immediate negotiations to stop bombing North Vietnam. While the student rights issues resonated with students who wanted to shed the restrictive regulations that governed their nonacademic lives, SDS's antiwar actions seemed to limit the possibility for broad-based organizing. Mills perceived SDS's antiwar actions as poorly timed and suggested that the chapter might have attracted more followers if it had stuck with the student rights issues: "If a new organization, which has in mind the idea of being a responsible, forceful voice in a university community, needs to gain the confidence of students, it can't do it by entering the limelight with demonstrations against the Vice-President of the United States." Mills added that the decision to mount the Humphrey protest was especially bad at an institution where "a great majority of the students favor — sometimes with overzealous patriotism — the war in Viet Nam."[32]

Members of the SDS chapter did not heed Mills's advice. They not only continued their vocal opposition to the war but increasingly turned their attention to a visible symbol of the university's ties with the military — the existence of compulsory ROTC. On many campuses, ROTC provided an accessible issue around which to organize opposition to university-military ties. During the 1960s, federal spending policy had the intended effect of including institutions that were outside the small circle of the nation's most prestigious research universities. Initiatives such as the National Defense Education Act of 1964 and Project THEMIS, a military-research program conducted between 1967 and the early 1970s, enabled a growing number of southern universities to take advantage of the opportunities for institutional advancement that federal Cold War spending provided. For example, thirteen of the forty-one Project THEMIS grants awarded in 1967 went to universities in nine southern states. And in most cases, the grants went to the institutions where activism was least likely to occur. Many of the recipients prominently featured such activist-unfriendly programs as engineering and agriculture — Auburn, Georgia Tech, North Carolina State, and Texas A&M.[33]

But uncovering the ways in which southern universities participated in the war effort through their research capabilities required investigation, and southern student activists often did not dig deeply enough. ROTC, in contrast, was both more accessible and more tangible to students. In fact, some southern campuses still required male students to take ROTC courses. The Morrill Land Grant Act of 1862 had made money available to all state universities and colleges that offered but did not necessarily compel participation in a Reserve Officers' Training Program. By the late 1950s, state legislatures or administrators had mandated that state universities and independent or private institutions require male students to take two years of basic ROTC training. In time, ROTC programs shifted their emphasis from the training of reserve officers to the selection and preparation of professional career officers. Thus, ROTC provided a pool of college-educated men from which a few highly motivated officers could emerge. Congressional legislation passed in the mid-1960s facilitated this change; the ROTC Vitalization Act revamped and added flexibility to the traditional program by increasing scholarship offerings and instituting a two-year officer training program. The act also instituted a junior ROTC program for high school. However, criticism of ROTC had already begun to circulate on some campuses. In the late 1950s, the U.S. National Student Association (NSA) argued that compulsory ROTC was problematic for several reasons. It infringed on students' academic freedom; its academic value was at best questionable; and it wasted students' time. The NSA argued for a voluntary system, which would be more cost-effective and produce better graduates. The intensifica-tion of American involvement in Vietnam raised the stakes of the ROTC debate. Students enrolled in ROTC received an advantage in continued draft deferment. Moreover, the escalation in Vietnam increasingly made ROTC a target for anti-war activists, who saw it as a visual manifestation of a military machine waging war on innocent people. Antiwar activists sought to pare back ROTC's campus presence by making the program voluntary rather than compulsory, by making its course offerings noncredit, or by removing it from the campus entirely.[34]

Leading the charge against compulsory ROTC at Georgia was Paul W. McBride, a doctoral student in history whose background gave him a unique perspective from which to address both the ROTC issue in particular and the Vietnam issue in general. A married father of two, McBride was a U.S. Army veteran who had served a two-year stint in Vietnam. He had joined the army in 1965, with visions of making the military a career, but the reality of military life had not equaled his visions. "The Army took little time to turn my enthusiasm first to disillusion and finally to disgust," McBride noted in a lengthy letter to *The Red and Black* that detailed his complaints. The crux of McBride's critique was that the military fostered obedience at the expense of intellectual curiosity. This trait was objectionable within the regular army but had implications that he found particularly disturbing in the university setting when students were forced to participate: "The manual 145-45 used now at the University of Georgia still refers to the danger of the 'Sino-Soviet conspiracy.' It is pardonable to be wrong, but when error is forced upon the civilian college system, and when the military instructors are forbidden to vary from doctrine, then the situa-tion is intolerable in an educational context."[35] McBride subsequently laid out a more detailed critique of the university's ROTC curriculum and faculty, arguing that instructors lacked the necessary academic credentials to be teaching in college and supporting his argument in part by listing the names and highest degrees of each department member. None of the five faculty members of the army ROTC program held a postgraduate degree of any kind. Four of the seven instructors in the air force ROTC program had master's degrees, but they were in business administration. None held any degree remotely related to interna-tional relations or political philosophy, the general thrust of the curriculum. Military Science I, for example, included a "a study of international and global affairs (which includes a comparative analysis of Democracy and Communism particularly emphasizing the U.S.S.R. and Chinese Communist threat to world stability)." Said McBride, "It is deplorable that these men teach history, politi-cal philosophy and international relations. What is worse, under a compulsory ROTC program, the student cannot avoid the incompetence."[36]

Whatever the merits of his argument, McBride's military background gave his political views as well as his membership in SDS more legitimacy in the eyes of University of Georgia students, a connection he highlighted: "In the last two years my attitude has become increasingly anti-military, not because I am faced with the problem of avoiding the draft, but because I have served with the Army." McBride argued that membership in SDS was not unpatriotic but that the organization opposed an education that included a "forced diet of military propaganda." Moreover, SDS believed that "the only relationship between the University and its adult student body should be an academic and intellectual one."[37]

SDS ultimately championed a bill before the student senate in favor of abolishing compulsory ROTC. In early April 1968, the measure passed in a 46–4 vote, and the university made participation in the ROTC program voluntary prior to the 1969–70 academic year. Participation immediately dropped by more than 50 percent, from 746 enrolled freshmen in the fall of 1968 to 339 a year later.[38]

But by that time, the issue of "coed equality" had taken center stage. Indeed, the ROTC story was a minor one in comparison with the April 1968 sit-in at the Administration Building, a protest that drew hundreds of students to the first on-campus mass demonstration since the riots against Charlayne Hunter's and Hamilton Holmes's matriculation in January 1961. This time, students demonstrated in opposition to the university's restrictive rules for women students. The issue had long been brewing on campus, and it demonstrated a greater potential than ROTC or Vietnam to mobilize more than a handful of liberal to radical students, although SDS members were deeply involved. As a consequence of his participation, the university suspended SDS leader David Simpson, who went on to become an SSOC organizer in Georgia.[39] Vietnam did not again serve as a legitimate mobilizing issue at the University of Georgia until the fall of 1969.

Compared to events in other parts of the South and the country, the Administration Building sit-in was tame. In the wake of Martin Luther King Jr.'s 4 April assassination, campuses and cities had exploded with violence. Two days after King's murder, representatives from UGA, Emory, Georgia State, Georgia Tech, and the Atlanta Alliance for Peace had gathered at Emory's air force ROTC building to coordinate antiwar demonstrations. They spent the morning debating how to deal with the defection of so many "potential recruits" to the Kennedy-McCarthy camp, which organizers believed would fail radicals in 1968 as Johnson had done in 1964. Some participants argued that antiwar radicals should work for Kennedy and McCarthy "without blunting their criticisms." But most of the discussion that day centered on the appropriate white radical response to black revolution. The night of King's death, one thousand Atlanta University Center students had held an all-night meeting and had then marched through the city's Hunter Street area; violence occasionally broke out. Thomas Gardner, an SSOC organizer who was in town for the 6 April conference, encouraged attendees to organize a teach-in on Black Power that might mobilize people against racism as Vietnam teach-ins had done against the war. Others called for more violent responses. "All this is liberal bullshit," one person reportedly said, suggesting that radicals should be willing to start a fire at Rich's department store as a way to forward the revolution. "A few comments later," reported Howard Romaine in the *Great Speckled Bird*, "the gathering disintegrated into workshops, which disintegrated into tired people having found no solutions, only bigger and bigger problems."[40]

The division and uncertainty that plagued the conference seemed to affect the upcoming antiwar demonstrations. Activists had gathered to coordinate activities in conjunction with SDS's International Days of Protest and SSOC's Southern Days of Secession, scheduled for 20–30 April. None of the college campuses in Atlanta and Athens planned to participate in the student strike that would occur in other parts of the country. On 27 April, more than 250 people gathered at the Federal Building on the corner of Peachtree and Eighth Streets to protest the war, the draft, and racism. A march and a rousing guerrilla-theater performance in Piedmont Park followed, and "a heavy influx of hippies and collegians boosted the normal peace ranks." At Emory, the academic year ended with antiwar candidate Eugene McCarthy winning a mock election and Abbott winning the race for student government president. Activism — and frustration — grew during the 1968–69 academic year, but racial politics loomed larger than the war. Black students took the stage as lead actors, and white students struggled to respond.[41]

Liberals, Radicals, and the Antiwar Movement: North Carolina

Throughout the 1960s, activists at the University of North Carolina in Chapel Hill and Duke University in Durham fed off of each other. As the war in Vietnam entered the consciousness of Chapel Hill/Durham activists, it became difficult at times to separate the UNC antiwar movement from its counterpart at Duke. A similar dynamic had been at work between University of Georgia students in Athens and activists in Atlanta, but three factors differentiated the Chapel Hill–Durham axis from its Georgia counterpart. One factor, difficult to measure, was the proximity of Chapel Hill and Durham. While some sixty miles separated Athens and Atlanta, the Duke and UNC campuses were only a little more than ten miles apart. This proximity fueled both cooperation and competition between activists on the two campuses. Second, the histories of both North Carolina institutions as well as the political environment in Chapel Hill and Durham provided a better foundation for activism than did Athens and Atlanta. UNC's storied liberalism, though perhaps overstated, offered a relatively tolerant atmosphere for activism. Duke lacked the same liberal reputation, but its aspirations to enter American higher education's elite ranks brought increasing numbers of students and faculty from outside the region. Finally, North Carolina's political atmosphere was more volatile than that of Georgia, and the Tarheel State had become one of the South's most vibrant centers for black as well as antiwar activism.

Unlike most other campuses in the South, UNC had a peace movement of sorts that predated the escalation of the Vietnam War. Students chartered a chapter of the Student Peace Union (SPU) in 1961. The group's early activities, however, centered not on disarmament or other issues that were international in scope but rather on segregation. The liberal student group went to some pains to connect the SPU's larger goals with the civil rights movement, suggesting in a 1963 resolution, for example, that the "problems of world peace and the problems of civil rights and human freedom are not separate." Instead, these problems constituted parts of "our concern for the human community as a whole, a part of an effort toward reconciliation and understanding between men of different backgrounds and views." The SPU thus refused to patronize thirteen Chapel Hill establishments that maintained discriminatory practices and said that if negotiations to resolve the matter failed, "we shall take whatever action we deem necessary and within our power, including picketing."[42]

The SPU provided models for UNC students who wanted to connect national, international, and local issues and for students who were inclined to act publicly on moral and political issues. Nevertheless, the SPU did not usher in an early and vibrant antiwar movement. A UNC chapter of SDS, formed in the spring of 1965, set its sights first on the Speaker Ban and ultimately played a crucial role in generating the student movement against it. But SDS subsequently had trouble mobilizing students on other issues, including Vietnam. In December 1966, Gary Waller laid out the war-related issues that concerned the chapter's members. The use of grades, which draft boards used as a way to determine likely candidates, "raises serious questions concerning the nature and purpose of the university," he wrote to the *Daily Tar Heel*. Moreover, the use of university facilities for war research was another important issue, but "unfortunately there has been no serious public discussion of the justification for such policies." He chastised other campus organizations for their failure to follow SDS's lead and begin debating the implications of the escalating war. An editor's note took issue with Waller's suggestion that no other organizations had addressed the war. A number of organizations, including the Westminster Fellowship and the Di-Phi Senate, had held debates, although "the attendance for these events did by no means indicate that the campus was overly interested in the issues." The editors noted, however, that student body president Robert Powell had proposed a teach-in and a student referendum on the draft.[43]

Shortly thereafter, Powell raised eyebrows by signing a letter to President

Johnson expressing doubt about U.S. involvement in Vietnam. Student leaders from one hundred colleges and universities — representing, according to the *New York Times*, "a far more moderate university group than members of the student New Left" — signed the letter, which demanded candor and honesty concerning "a perplexing military and moral dilemma." The letter offered a list of issues that were "now agitating the academic community," including whether the United States had vital interests in Southeast Asia and whether the war that the United States was conducting could produce a stable and prosperous Vietnam. The letter had originated in the NSA's 1966 annual conference, which Powell attended. During a discussion concerning whether liberals or radicals were more effective in protesting the conduct of the war, Allard Lowenstein, former NSA president and a UNC graduate, suggested writing a letter.[44]

Powell's decision to sign the letter was somewhat controversial. Though he contended that he spoke only for himself, some observers believed that he was using his standing to issue a position on the war on behalf of all UNC students. When Powell and the president of the Harvard University student body led a delegation of signers to discuss their concerns with Secretary of State Dean Rusk, Powell's critics became even more concerned. Powell stated publicly that the students who had signed the letter were "terrified" by college youth's growing mood of "increased resistance" to American involvement in Vietnam. Powell thus seemed to believe, somewhat naively, that the letter might convince the Johnson administration to work more diligently for a negotiated settlement. If such a settlement did not occur soon, he believed that "widening non-cooperation" would result.[45]

Later that month, as many as fifty-five protesters, organized by UNC's SDS chapter, picketed Vice President Humphrey's appearance in Chapel Hill. They carried signs that read: "Hubert, you lie," "Hubie is a murderer of Vietnamese children," "Drop Rusk and [Secretary of Defense Robert] McNamara, not na-palm," and "Shame on you, Hubert." Despite the protests, Humphrey defended the administration's policy in Vietnam before a panel of questioners that in-cluded Powell. Powell's participation while SDS members remained outside the meeting hall seemed to signify the differences in political and tactical orienta-tion between the liberal Powell and the more radical SDS. Nevertheless, neither pointed questions inside the building nor a demonstration outside prompted Humphrey to give ground. Continued bombing, he argued, was making North Vietnamese infiltration into South Vietnam costly; if the United States stopped, the infiltration would increase. Humphrey suggested that the administration was ready to negotiate but only if it could get assurance that "it will not be just talk."[46]

Activism around the war gained momentum. Other organizations joined SDS in pushing the issue. Some students and townspeople conducted a weekly silent peace vigil outside the Chapel Hill post office. The Friends Meeting of Chapel Hill coordinated the vigils, but one organizer said that anyone was welcome. According to the *Daily Tar Heel*, "There was no particular category of people involved" in the first demonstration, held in early January 1967. "There were professors, undergraduates, graduate students, businessmen, and several very elderly people." Also present were three graduate students from Duke, who vowed to return every week unless a similar vigil was started in Durham.[47]

The Vietnam issue, like activism in general, developed slowly but steadily on the Duke campus. Writing in the fall of 1966, student Andy Moursuno noted that only four years earlier, "Duke was considered a school almost exclusively for 'southern gentlemen' by its admirers and detractors alike." The beginning of a change in the campus political atmosphere occurred in the fall of 1963, with the admission of the first black undergraduates. During that academic year, more than 100 students joined the campus chapter of the Congress of Racial Equality; at the same time, the Young Republicans "suffered from no lack of activity themselves during the Goldwater campaign." In the spring of 1965, students and faculty members organized a teach-in that, to Moursuno, suggested the potential power that students possessed. "After all, didn't the State Department send a speaker down right away to rebut what was said at the teach-in?" But by September 1966, Moursuno's optimism had subsided. Officials in Washington had not taken seriously the ideas expressed at the teach-in, and the war continued. "The only way ever to affect basic change at a University is to do it the way they did it at Berkeley," Moursuno concluded, "and the chances of this happening at Duke are about as great as those of Stokely Carmichael volunteering for the U.S. Army."[48]

Indeed, by the spring of 1967, some Duke students and faculty still seemed more inclined to muse about the lack of activism on their campus than to attempt to generate it. A March *Sports Illustrated* article labeled Duke students "The Timid Generation" and contrasted the common view of American youth in revolt with the students who inhabited the school's placid campus. "The kids seem to constrict themselves, shut things out and go about their business with a quiet anxiety," said Jack Preiss, a Duke sociology professor. "You have to push them, cajole, almost coerce them into saying what they think."[49]

Nevertheless, enough had happened for the student newspaper, the *Chronicle*, to declare 1966–67 the academic "year of the activist." Three forces had created the changes. First, a group of about four hundred activist students generated growth in the number of petitions and pickets. Second, increasingly vocal black students began setting an activist pace that white students would follow. Finally, a number of rousing speakers prodded students toward bolder action. Visitors to the Duke campus included Stanford student body president and draft resistance leader David Harris, Stokely Carmichael, U.S. senator and war opponent Wayne Morse, and Yale chaplain William Sloane Coffin.[50] At the same time, traditional student leaders took stands against the war. In a November 1966 editorial, *Chronicle* editor David Birkhead called for the United States to negotiate with the Viet Cong. And in January 1967, both women's Student Government Association president Mary Earle and men's Student Government Association president Joe Schwab joined UNC's Powell in signing the open letter to President Johnson expressing doubts about the war.[51]

The small number of potential activists benefited from a number of factors. First, proximity to the activists in Chapel Hill helped lessen the isolation that Duke dissenters might otherwise have felt. Intercollegiate demonstrations that included not only Duke and UNC but also North Carolina State in Raleigh and North Carolina Central in Durham were common. Second, Durham's vibrant community of black activists contributed to a heightened level of activism in general that provided an indirect lift to students inclined to mobilize on the war issue. And third, local SSOC organizers kept the Vietnam issue on the table.

SSOC's involvement was particularly important after 1967. That summer, SSOC spearheaded Vietnam Summer activities in the region. Created by Gar Alperovitz, a former State Department and congressional aide, Vietnam Summer was a national community-organizing project aimed at reaching people who were concerned about the war but not yet active in opposing it. Endorsed by such nationally known figures as Martin Luther King Jr. and Benjamin Spock, the project attracted more than twenty-six thousand volunteers throughout the country. In the South, the organizing took a variety of forms, from passing out leaflets and door-to-door canvassing to vigils and draft counseling. At the center was a series of training institutes in Florida, North Carolina, and Virginia that attracted some two thousand participants. These institutes helped generate local action, as participants went back to their communities with visions of organizing statewide rallies, speakers' bureaus, newspapers, draft resistance networks, and vigils.[52] Post–Vietnam Summer reality often failed to meet such visions, however. At Duke, two students who participated in the summer activities organized the Durham Peace Committee, an antiwar group that focused on off-campus activities but also hoped to attract students. But a *Duke Chronicle* reporter noted in September that "relatively few students are actively involved on campus at the present time."[53]

The same month, as black activists were marching in Durham for jobs and housing, students and faculty from Duke and UNC organized a teach-in that featured a debate among a State Department official, two professors, and a soldier who recently had returned from Vietnam and opposed the war. In October, a fledgling group, the North Carolina Student Committee against the War, organized a conference on the war and the draft at the Duke Methodist Center.

The group's temporary chair, Randy Shannon, a Duke junior, was one of the organizers of the Durham Peace Committee. Shannon also found support from Frederick Krantz, an associate professor of Asian history, and Peter Klopfer, an associate professor of zoology and a participant in early 1960s desegregation demonstrations, as well as from full-time organizers outside the campus, including antiwar activist Lee D. Webb and SSOC veteran Sue Thrasher. About twenty-five campuses, including North Carolina State, UNC, and Duke, were represented at the meeting. Klopfer led a session on draft counseling, during which he explained the nuances of conscientious-objector status.[54]

A few weeks later, Duke's student government conducted a referendum on the war: 218 of the roughly 700 students who participated (less than 10 percent of the 8,000 students on campus) favored complete withdrawal, and 560 disapproved of the conduct of the war. The referendum also found support for the Johnson's administration's policies — 125 said they supported the president's handling of the issue, and 174 said they favored increased bombing. The *Chronicle* somewhat exaggeratedly described the referendum as an indication of "widespread dissent on the Duke campus with the present conduct of the Vietnam War." With no clear-cut consensus on the war, Duke resembled national trends. While more people were voicing opposition to the war and while activists were beginning to create some momentum against it, significant disagreements existed within the ranks of the peace movement over tactics and strategy as well as basic philosophical assumptions. These disagreements came to a head during the planning for demonstrations in Washington, D.C. Activists within the National Mobilization Committee, known as the Mobe, which spearheaded the project, had agreed to hold a multitactical protest on 21 October that would combine legal demonstration with nonviolent confrontation. But many of those involved opposed the outrageous plans of countercultural activist Abbie Hoffman, who announced that protesters would collectively levitate the Pentagon and cause it to turn orange and vibrate until all evil emissions were gone. One student Mobe leader, former Tuskegee student and NSA Southern Project staffer Gwen Patton, complained dryly, "Black people are not going to go anywhere to *levitate* the Pentagon, okay. We don't find that cute."[55] On the day of the demonstration, more than 100,000 people, predominantly young but including people of all ages and from all walks of life, gathered at the Lincoln Memorial, where they listened to speeches and then began a march toward the Arlington Memorial Bridge. The subsequent events, chronicled by Norman Mailer in *Armies of the Night*, featured violent, almost surreal clashes between demonstrators and troops at the Pentagon. By the end of the siege, police had arrested 683 people, and an untold number had been injured.[56]

The *Duke Chronicle* had warned against precisely this sort of violence in the previous day's paper. Revealing the divisions on the Duke campus, the *Chronicle* editors noted that they opposed the war — not necessarily a common position among the southern student press — but added that they also opposed the Mobe's call for "immediate unilateral withdrawal," which they likened to such dubious phrases as "self-determination for Black America" and "from dissent to resistance." The editorial concluded with a call for a "dignified and responsible" demonstration.[57]

Nearly one hundred Duke students traveled from Durham to Washington, where they experienced a far cry from such a "dignified and responsible" show of opposition. "The whole thing was unreal," wrote Alan Shusterman, the *Chronicle's* assistant managing editor, who attended the mobilization primarily as a demonstrator. Sitting in front of the Pentagon, Shusterman and six other current and former Duke students became the antiwar movement in microcosm, debating how far to take their protest. "Choices presented themselves: to leave or stay first of all, then to move, to scale the walls or to try to see what we could accomplish," Shusterman recalled. "Could we afford to be arrested?" The Duke group remained seated as soldiers slowly moved toward the demonstrators and demanded that they move back. If a demonstrator refused, "he was grabbed, clubbed repeatedly and viciously with rifle butts, and thrown behind the military lines to be arrested," Shusterman wrote. He continued, "It's a type of calm terror that captures you when this happens repeatedly, six feet away, and you know that your turn could come. I had difficulty reconciling the fact that I love my country with the fact that these were Americans committing this needless violence." The members of Shusterman's group eventually left, apparently before being beaten, but the experience had made an impression: "Call us 'lost' or 'traitors,' if you will, but something's wrong here, and we've seen it first hand."[58]

North Carolina antiwar activists hoped to capitalize on this kind of disillusionment, and the various factions of the peace movement began to replicate themselves. In November, Michael Smedburg, a twenty-year-old veteran of the Berkeley Free Speech Movement, moved to North Carolina as a full-time organizer. Smedburg was an early member of the Resistance, a group that started in the spring of 1967 in California as the brainchild of former Stanford student body president David Harris, who had participated in Duke's symposium on university reform the previous fall, and several other opponents of the war. Its name recalled the European resistance to Nazi occupation during World War II, and its organizers built on the idea of a national draft card turn-in that fall. After arriving in North Carolina, Smedburg joined UNC junior Robert Eaton and graduate student George Vlasits in creating a chapter that they hoped would grow "by personal confrontation." They circulated a statement of support for noncooperation with the draft that thirty UNC professors signed. But Resistance leaders had more trouble convincing students to be so bold, and "found an unwillingness on the part of students to take the same steps taken by activists at Berkeley in opposing or non-cooperating."[59]

Antiwar organizers faced another obstacle in a new "pickets and protest" policy that greeted Duke students returning from Christmas vacation in January 1968. The new policy recognized "the right of legitimate forms of picketing and protest" but prohibited "illegitimate" demonstrating, a heading that included any action that disrupted the "orderly operation of the institution" or that "might in any way jeopardize public order or safety." Students who participated in illegal protests were "liable to separation from the University." The Duke administration's concerns grew from one demonstration and one threatened demonstration in late 1967. On 13 November, black students held a "study-in" to protest the absence of a ban on student organizations' use of segregated off-campus facilities. During the seven-hour demonstration, the students at times blocked the entrance to the president's office and other offices in the Allen Building. Antiwar students also threatened to picket a visit by U.S. Navy recruiters, leading Duke officials to ask the recruiters to postpone their visit. The new policy was released shortly before army and navy recruiters were again scheduled to come to campus.[60]

The new policy, which the school's president, Douglas M. Knight, argued would prevent action that was "destructive to the pursuit of learning and of a free society," raised the ire of activist students. It received its first test in early February, when recruiters from Dow Chemical Corporation visited Duke. On 5 February, more than seventy-five students and others demonstrated against the recruiters, who had set up shop in the Engineering Building. University officials quickly ruled that picketers could not enter the building, and most demonstrators chose to comply. University officials later allowed a "representative group" of ten people to enter the building, providing the opportunity for one of the demonstrators, Buddy Tieger, a Duke law student, to challenge the Dow recruiter to participate in a debate at a Liberal Action Committee meeting. The recruiter refused, though he offered to discuss the issues "over a beer."[61]

The demonstrations escalated the next day, as protesters blocked the door to a booth where the Dow recruiter was interviewing, violating the new policy on picketing. Given a warning to move in five minutes, the protesters waited until mere seconds remained before moving. On the following day, demonstrators changed their tactics, launching a study-in on the lawn facing the entrance to the Allen Building. Discussion among the demonstrators keyed on the university's moral responsibility vis-à-vis the war. Birkhead argued that the university had already taken positions on segregated facilities and Durham housing, thereby ruling out the possibility that the institution was "amoral." With these precedents in place, the university should be free to "take positions that are in harmony with its purposes as a university." Vietnam, Birkhead argued, should top the list. But Birkhead wanted more than a broad denunciation of the war. The real issue, he said, was "the right of students to protest the investment policy of the university, which helps support a war which is considered by many to be immoral and contrary to the expressed ideals of the university."[62]

Birkhead thus invoked what New Left activists often referred to as "complicity" — the university's participation in a military-industrial-academic complex that was prosecuting the war. This approach reflected the New Left's increasing tendency to reject American higher education as an important tool in reforming an exploitative society. The 1962 Port Huron Statement had singled out the university as a base from which to launch a new political movement. By 1966, however, SDS's move to the left incorporated a more radical and darker view of the university. Carl Davidson generated and reflected SDS's souring vision of higher education in "Toward a Student Syndicalist Movement; or, University Reform Revisited." [63]

Conservative students at Duke, alarmed at the election of reformist student government officers during the 1966–67 academic year, attempted to connect Davidson's working paper with a public address in which women's student government president Mary Earle called for various student power goals. At a student forum in March 1967, students James A. Martin Jr. and Eaton Merritt passed out 350 copies of Davidson's paper. Martin delivered a speech in which he suggested that the reformist student politicians were perhaps unwittingly pursuing policies that would lead to the university's destruction. Martin and Merritt forwarded to Knight copies of "Toward a Student Syndicalist Movement," Earle's address, and a letter to the editor written by Martin. An accompanying cover letter suggested that Knight was familiar with the conservative students' actions and thanked him for his help.[64]

In attempting to connect SDS's radical interpretation of student activism with liberal student government leaders, the conservative students and possibly Knight had fallen victim to overdrawn logic. Nevertheless, the general thrust of Davidson's argument — that the university was intimately tied into a large, oppressive system and that student activists should locate and expose those connections — increasingly permeated the actions of activists at Duke and UNC. Following the Dow demonstrations, four Duke students drove all night to New York City to present a statement to the investment committee of the university's board of trustees asking Duke to sell its stock in Dow. The committee refused to meet with the students, who then picketed along Sixth Avenue.[65]

A member of the Student Committee against the War, which was essentially indistinguishable from SSOC's operations in Chapel Hill and Durham, won a meeting with Thomas Perkins, the chair of the investment committee. During the interview, an unnamed student, probably Tieger, asked Perkins whether the university's possession of Dow stock "is consistent with the stated goals of Duke University, to advance Christianity and Christian values and to pro-vide a Christian education for its students." Perkins responded that "the only guideline of our investment policy is the return" but added that "the Investment Committee has made a moral stand in support of Dow's production of napalm, because we own the stock." Turning the tables on the student, Perkins suggested that Dow would have been immoral if its country had asked it to make napalm and it had refused. The discussion then turned to whether citizens had a moral or legal responsibility for acts done at the government's request. When the stu-dent asked about the German soldiers convicted at the Nuremburg trials for obeying orders, Perkins replied, "I think the Nuremburg trials were wrong. No individual has a right to act against authority." He subsequently modified that statement when the student asked Perkins whether he would have led Jews to the ovens at Auschwitz if ordered to do so: "There is a question as to how far down the line duty goes."[66]

Writing in the aftermath of the Dow protests at Duke, UNC's Vlasits in-terpreted the events as "a new stage in the development of a radical student movement in N.C." The demonstrations had not stopped Dow from recruit-ing or forced Duke to sell its stock in the company; however, they had raised the issue of complicity as well as the "side issue" of Duke's repressive policy on demonstrations.[67] Vlasits's commentary also suggested the increasing inter-connectedness of the student movements against the war at Duke and UNC. A "worklist mailing" detailing antiwar activities in Durham and Chapel Hill showed a variety of ongoing and to some extent coordinated activities taking place at both institutions, including draft counseling, draft resistance, "guerilla theater" groups, dorm talks, and films. Activists also circulated antiwar peti-tions at Duke and UNC and organized "concerned faculty" groups on both cam-puses. The faculty group at UNC was working on position papers on specific topics, such as Attorney General Ramsey Clark and Vice President Humphrey, as well as conducting "general research on university complicity." One faculty member was looking for students and faculty who were interested in working on the issue of ROTC's academic status.[68]

The list also noted planning for SSOC's Southern Days of Secession, sched-uled for the last ten days of April. At Chapel Hill, the plans called for a guer-rilla theater production of a war-crimes tribunal, trying the university for com-plicity as well as a student and faculty moratorium on classes. Duke students also planned a war-crimes tribunal, trying their university for its ownership of stock in Dow and other defense-related industries. Students from both univer-sities planned an antiwar march in Durham. Students at the all-women Queens College in Charlotte, North Carolina, planned an "unapproved" teach-in on the war and a draft-counseling booth for the students' "dates during their big May Day weekend," the first significant show of activism at Queens. Other North

Carolina campuses with students who planned to participate in the Days of Secession events included Davidson College, Atlantic Christian College, North Carolina Wesleyan College, Belmont Abbey College, and Appalachian State.[69]

In Durham and Chapel Hill, however, the emergence of black student activism took some of the momentum from these activities. This dynamic was especially apparent at Duke, where the assassination of Martin Luther King Jr. prompted the multiday silent vigil centering on the issues of racism within the university and the institution's treatment of its predominantly black support staff. In terms of student involvement, the silent vigil was easily the activist event of the decade, attracting the participation of thousands of Duke students. Students such as Birkhead who had been active in the antiwar movement helped lead the vigil. On the night of 5 April, when some two hundred students entered President Knight's home, Knight used his earlier call for negotiations in Vietnam to support a contention that he had "felt that frustration . . . as much as you feel it."[70] Although ssoc celebrated the emergence of widespread activism on the Duke campus during the silent vigil, the issues that emerged during this chain of events temporarily relegated Vietnam to secondary importance, thus taking some of the wind out of the sails of the Days of Secession.

SSOC, SDS, and the War

As the "secession" moniker suggested, ssoc was attempting to fashion a distinctly southern — specifically, a *white* southern — approach to antiwar organizing. Although ssoc had originated in early 1964 from pockets of white opposition to segregation, issues of international politics had concerned many of its earliest members. As Thomas Gardner, an ssoc member from Virginia, recalled, these activists had debated such issues as nuclear disarmament, Cuba, and especially the escalating war in Vietnam. Like their compatriots on the campuses in North Carolina and Georgia, activists associated with ssoc throughout the South moved from debates and discussion of Vietnam to more overt declarations of opposition to American involvement. By 1967, according to Gardner, more than forty southern cities had experienced some kind of peace vigil or demonstration, often as the result of an alliance between church-related peace proponents in a community and students and faculty on a campus. William Jeffries, the southeast regional peace secretary for the American Friends Service Committee, had worked especially closely with ssoc in some of these demonstrations.[71]

The year 1967 represented a turning point for ssoc's antiwar efforts. Early in the year, the organization and the Southern Conference Educational Fund cosponsored a peace tour through college campuses in Florida. Delegation members Gardner, David Nolan, and Nancy Hodes gave public presentations, held workshops, showed films, set up literature tables, and met with local activists, generating some positive response, although their attempts to speak at Miami-Dade Junior College failed. They were eventually arrested, and the house in which they had been staying while in Miami exploded a week after they departed. Nevertheless, the Florida peace tour was promising enough to prompt a decision to mount peace tours in North Carolina, South Carolina, Arkansas, and Tennessee. The response was not always positive. At Appalachian State Teachers College in Boone, North Carolina, several hundred students joined forces to evict the "outside agitators" from the campus, a move that drew praise from the North Carolina legislature. Although ssoc organizers made many important contacts, especially in North Carolina, "few groups sustained themselves past September, and only in a few cases did a lasting community coalition against the war grow out of Vietnam Summer South."[72]

These efforts, like the peace movement as a whole, seemed to accomplish little in the face of continued escalation in Vietnam. ssoc members became increasingly frustrated with the lack of tangible results. This frustration, combined with growing contact with radicals outside the South whose analysis increasingly labeled capitalism and American imperialism the sources of worldwide exploitation, resulted in souring the view within ssoc of the U.S. role in the world. A handful of ssoc members joined international tours to socialist countries and participated in contacts with Third World revolutionaries. In 1967, two ssoc members visited Cuba, while another participated in a trek to Czechoslovakia that featured a weeklong meeting with representatives from both the National Liberation Front (the Vietnamese organization fighting for the overthrow of the South Vietnamese government) and the Democratic Republic of Vietnam. "By 1969," Gardner recalled, "there was a growing, though incomplete, sense of solidarity with third-world revolutionary movements and an increased understanding of the nature of U.S. imperialism."[73]

As ssoc became radicalized in the mid-1960s, members willingly accepted their new mandate to organize the white community but disagreed about which white community to organize. Some favored a concentration on labor organizing, while others wanted to continue to organize students. In practice, the organization pursued both strategies with mixed success. ssoc attempted to organize North Carolina textile workers at the same time that some ssoc members turned their attention to developing a radical analysis that portrayed the university as a social-control mechanism for the establishment.[74]

ssoc members developed a sort of southern nationalist interpretation of social change, an extension of the southern emphasis that had been present since the group's inception. Many ssoc members resented what they saw as the "Yankee paternalism" radicals from outside the region exhibited. The emphasis on southern distinctiveness also had a practical aspect: ssoc members believed that by encouraging pride in a southern heritage but pointing it in a radical direction, they could reach white southerners who might otherwise be put off by the New Left. But celebrating the South without giving in to racism proved difficult. Intermittently throughout its existence, ssoc used as its symbol black and white hands clasped in front of a Confederate battle flag. The message was that interracialism should be part of the New South, but some people had trouble setting aside the racist connotations of the Confederate flag. In addition, some sds members questioned whether a separate southern New Left organization was necessary. These issues came to a head in May 1967, when ssoc held a conference at Buckeye Cove, North Carolina, on "The Role of the Southern Radical in the American Left." sds representative Mike James proposed a merger of sds and ssoc, but ssoc members voted down the proposal. Florida ssoc members then decided to go off their own, severing their ties with ssoc. Individuals within in sds, mainly members of the Progressive Labor Party, subsequently worked within sds to undermine ssoc and to build sds in the South. Progressive Labor strongholds developed at Florida State University and in New Orleans, eventually playing an important role in ssoc's downfall.[75]

ssoc's southern nationalism faded during 1968, but not solely because of leftist intrigue. The continued importance of the Vietnam War, an international problem that seemed to have little relevance to southern distinctiveness, complicated efforts to maintain an analysis that emphasized southern particularity. The Days of Secession represented one of the last gasps of this phase. ssoc leaders built this campaign on what they saw as a too-often-ignored history of white southern dissent. While the standard interpretation of southern history might have been a story of white southerners fighting for slavery and against integration, ssoc built a historical narrative on examples of white southern dissent during the Civil War and the late-nineteenth-century Populist movement. The ssoc worldview merged the New Left opposition to capitalist imperialism with a view, not new to ssoc, that the South was a colony of the industrial North. These views were neatly encapsulated in ssoc's flyer advertising the Days of Secession. Headlined "WE SECEDE," the flyer began by disassociating *secede* from its common connotations relating to southern states that severed their ties with the United States in 1861 over the issue of slavery. "Secession also has a radical tradition in the South," the flyer noted; during the War between the States, some two hundred southern counties had in effect seceded from the secessionists. The people of Winston County, Alabama, for example, refused to fight for the Confederacy, and "their young men" consequently spent almost the entire Civil War in prison.[76] The flyer noted that during the 1960s, young southerners (the word *white* appeared nowhere in the flyer but was implicit) had rejected racism and placed their faith in the federal government "as the guarantor of the rights of all." This faith was misplaced, ssoc argued. American business, government, and military had shown their oppressive nature; a "Free South in a Free and Peaceful World" would come only when young southerners placed their hope for change in each other. Then came the rallying cry:

> As young Southerners we hereby SECEDE from:
> THE WAR AGAINST THE VIETNAMESE
> RACISM AND EXPLOITATION OF THE POOR
> THE SELECTIVE SERVICE SYSTEM.[77]

In this sense, *secede* had no formal political connotation but rather served as a stand-in for *dissent*. SSOC leaders apparently chose *secede* for the images that it conjured. The wording of the flyer implied that SSOC leaders believed that that young white southerners opposed both the war and racism but also had a strong sense of regional identity — some sort of identification with southern "heritage." SSOC leaders clearly were hoping to find language that would appeal to these southerners.

The Days of Secession corresponded with SDS's International Days of Protest and the Student Mobilization Committee's international student strike on 26 April 1968. But some in the national movement both inside and outside the South saw SSOC's southern nationalism as becoming increasingly untenable. The international implications of the concept of imperialism, for which American involvement in Vietnam provided an object lesson, clashed with the idea that the American South was distinctive enough to require a separate analysis. By early 1969, the Progressive Labor element was leading a movement for SDS to disassociate itself from SSOC and implement separate organizing efforts in the region. This drive would lead directly to SSOC's June 1969 vote to dissolve the organization. Meanwhile, Progressive Labor played a similarly divisive role within SDS that would lead to the group's fatal break-up later the same year.[78]

SDS and the South

Although the number of SDS chapters in the South increased most rapidly after 1968, the various debates that took place within SDS's national ranks during the late 1960s — old guard versus Prairie Power, Revolutionary Youth Movement versus Progressive Labor Party — meant little to most southern student activists. The cadre of New Left activists on individual campuses might have debated these distinctions, but student newspapers, which were more representative of the sentiments of average students, rarely mentioned these issues. Nevertheless, SDS and its regional counterpart, SSOC, played an important role in the development of antiwar protest in the South. The dissolution of SDS and SSOC resulted from a number of internal and external factors. Internally, both groups struggled to construct an effective ideology, and these struggles caused bitter factional disputes, which at times were encouraged by external repression from government intelligence operations. Both organizations dissolved precisely when many southern schools were experiencing their first serious tastes of activism. Activists on these campuses might have benefited from experienced counsel but instead were left on their own.

SDS's perceived radicalism made it a tough sell on southern campuses still struggling with basic academic-freedom issues. Students who attempted to form SDS chapters often had difficulty winning formal recognition from their universities. Although chapters formed at the University of Texas in 1964 and at the University of North Carolina in 1965, few others existed prior to 1967. As in the country as a whole, however, that number subsequently mushroomed as SDS came to signify the student movement in general and the antiwar movement in particular. But as SDS turned from protest to resistance to revolution, it began to lose touch with its campus base. By the spring of 1969, media coverage ensured that SDS would be an important symbol, though the meaning of that symbolism varied according to the interpreter. Conservative critics often charged that the organization was part of a communist conspiracy, while journalists (and some subsequent historians) often saw SDS as "the movement" incarnate.[79]

SDS's influence in the South varied. On some campuses — for example, at the Universities of North Carolina, Texas, Georgia, and Kentucky and at Tulane and Vanderbilt — chapters played key roles in generating and sustaining student activism.[80] On other campuses, SDS had less direct influence. At the University of Alabama, for example, SDS was merely one of several activist organizations at work in the late 1960s. Founded in early 1968, the chapter's driving force was Paul Scribner, a transfer student from the University of Arizona. A former supporter of Eugene McCarthy, Scribner had joined SDS after attending the 1968 Democratic National Convention and becoming disillusioned with the establishment. By December 1968, Scribner claimed that Alabama's SDS chapter had thirty-six members.[81] The chapter was not the most effective activist organization on the Alabama campus, a distinction that likely went to the Democratic Students Organization (DSO), formed in late 1967. The DSO was a liberal rather than radical group, although the university's conservatism often made the organization's actions seem radical. DSO's members came from the ranks of the university's traditional leadership, a development that might have been surprising on other campuses but was not necessarily so at 'Bama. Student government loomed large at the university, and ambitious students often used campus politics and particularly the law school as a training ground for a political career. By the late 1960s, the law school had a couple of liberal professors who were open about their political inclinations and who influenced a core of campus activists. The DSO's founding members included a former student government president and a former student government representative; the president of the university's Young Democrats chapter; and the chair of the Tutorial Assistance Program, which offered students the opportunity to work with disadvantaged children in Tuscaloosa. The DSO would be a force for "progressive action," which its founders defined to include support for McCarthy's presidential campaign, backing for the university's fledgling Experimental College, and opposition to the war in Vietnam. In March 1968, the DSO began holding weekly peace vigils on the steps of the University Union. The first vigil, a fifteen-minute affair, attracted 95 protesters and 150 spectators. The SDS chapter attracted a small core of members as well as the suspicion of conservatives who knew of the national organization's reputation but accomplished little in the way of substantive change.[82]

If the influence of individual SDS chapters varied, then the group at least played an important symbolic role. Students might not have monitored the specific ideological battles within the national SDS but were aware of the rising militance within the organization and within the movement at large. Historian Douglas Rossinow believes that the war in Vietnam was the primary ingredient in pushing the New Left toward a conflation of militance and radicalism: "Anger at the war became the fuel on which the left ran, and when the fuel ran out, the movement sputtered."[83]

This rising tide of anger, vividly demonstrated in high-profile confrontations such as the April 1968 showdown at Columbia University and the August 1968 clashes at the Democratic National Convention in Chicago, helped increase the number of participants in a southern, campus-based antiwar movement that had previously been fairly small. Existing campus movements, built on a triad of student-oriented concerns, racial issues, and the war, provided the foundation for heightened activity and rising levels of participation fueled by anger at the war. Two national antiwar events, the moratoria of October and November 1969 and the Cambodia/Kent State explosion, brought antiwar activism to its peak. The campus response usually was conditioned by administration officials' boundaries concerning what kinds of actions were permissible. These boundaries often became the dominant issue on particular campuses. But the issues that the southern student movement had already placed on the table — free speech, student power, racism, and increasingly women's rights in addition to war-related issues such as ROTC and military research — provided the raw materials for showdowns.

Antiwar Activism, 1969

Nationally, the spring of 1969 saw a concerted push to excise ROTC programs from college campuses. This effort soon reached the South, where many schools had already experienced antiwar activism directed at ROTC. At the close of the food workers' strike at the University of North Carolina, campus activists turned their attention to ROTC: "The rest of this semester — if you believe the so-called radical elements on campus — is going to be 'Get Rid of ROTC Time,'" noted the editors of the *Daily Tar Heel*. The effort to limit ROTC's influence had already borne fruit at Yale, Princeton, Dartmouth, and Stanford, which had discontinued academic credit for their ROTC programs. In mid-April, the editors of the University of Michigan's student newspaper sought to convince other college dailies to publish and endorse an anti-ROTC editorial arguing that ROTC programs were "antithetical to the ultimate purposes of higher education" and "contrary to basic pedagogical principles." But the editorial also tied a general indictment of ROTC as an educational program to specific foreign-policy transgressions in Vietnam. In response to critics who argued that the university should adopt a neutral position and accept ROTC, the editorial suggested that at a time "when the military is an integral element in an expansionist foreign policy . . . the ROTC program is as partisan in its own way" as SDS. The *Duke Chronicle* also ran the editorial.[84]

At Tulane University, the intensification of the national anti-ROTC campaign corresponded with heightened antiwar activism on campus. Concern over ROTC's educational value had already prompted the Curriculum Committee of the College of Arts and Sciences to initiate a review of officer-training programs. In mid-April, the committee urged the retention of ROTC programs but also proposed modifications that supporters of ROTC opposed. The committee suggested that the military services should make greater use of regular university faculty for instruction in several courses of study, including modern languages and sciences. Moreover, active military officers should not teach courses with "substantive political or policy content." Finally, "all drill, indoctrination and training in military skills" should be noncredit activities, confined to the summer, or totally extracurricular. The release of the committee's report coincided with the publication in the campus newspaper, the *Hullabaloo*, of the nationally distributed anti-ROTC editorial.[85]

A few days later, antiwar activists on campus began a series of demonstrations aimed at ROTC drills. At the same time, campus debate over the value of ROTC flourished; a 25 April rally in which students spoke for and against granting credit for ROTC courses attracted some five hundred students. Following the rally, members of Tulane's SDS chapter escalated their demonstrations. At the same time, university officials more clearly defined the limits for demonstrations. On 29 April, as members of the air force ROTC prepared to drill on the University Center quadrangle, campus police chief Robert Scruton announced through a bullhorn that the field, within specified parameters, was a "classroom." Any interference within those parameters by demonstrators would constitute disruption of a university-sanctioned educational program. About fifty demonstrators disregarded the warning and sat on the field.

Scruton ordered their arrest, and campus police dragged thirteen students and mathematics professor Edward Dubinsky, the SDS chapter's adviser, off the field. All were subsequently released but remained subject to university disciplinary procedures. Dubinsky's case soon became a central campus issue. A University Senate committee determined that Dubinsky's actions, while constituting a "serious violation of university policy," did not merit his dismissal; however, Tulane president Herbert Longenecker overruled the committee's decision and recommended to the Tulane Board of Administrators that the math professor's appointment be terminated. The board obliged, and Dubinsky responded by filing a complaint with the American Association of University Professors. The situation dragged on for two years, but the university ultimately avoided censure.[86]

The spring 1969 demonstrations at Tulane represented a high point of sorts in the campus antiwar movement, although the war, combined with other issues, continued to generate controversy. Tulane students were conspicuous participants in New Orleans peace marches in October and November 1969. Some of these students were involved in a reemergence of campus politics in early April 1970, when the two student presidential candidates held a debate. The debate extended into the night, and the two sides eventually formed a loose coalition, the Tulane Liberation Front (TLF), which subsequently took over the University Center and called for a strike of all classes until the university met TLF demands, which combined university reform with a better environment for African Americans, limitations on ROTC, and Dubinsky's reinstatement. The university-reform-related demands included faculty self-rule, student evaluation of the faculty, elimination of arbitrary social rules, and implementation of a student bill of rights, to be written by students and faculty together and to be legally binding on the administration. After six days, the occupation ended when the University Senate endorsed amnesty for participating students and prompt action on a student bill of rights.[87]

At one point in the TLF occupation, student leaders declared that they were changing their movement's focus from a political to a cultural "revolution." Given the showdown's modest outcome, *revolution* was too strong a word. The unorganized nature of the occupation and the hodgepodge quality of the demands, which amounted to a catalog of campus issues that had arisen during the previous two years, revealed the strengths and weaknesses of the campus movement in the South. The TLF takeover, which was followed the next month by large-scale demonstrations in the wake of the Kent State shootings, achieved the largest levels of student participation in campus demonstrations that Tulane had experienced. Never before had so many students been so actively and overtly engaged in social and political issues. Nevertheless, the Tulane "movement" was diffuse and unfocused. It struck at everything at once, attracting participants who formerly had been on the sidelines, but seemed to generate few concrete accomplishments.

This dynamic was replicated to varying degrees on other campuses throughout the South. At Loyola University, the Jesuit-affiliated institution that bordered Tulane's campus, the post-Kent demonstrations eventually led to a takeover of the university's student union, the Danna Center. The similarities between the occupation of Tulane's University Center and the Loyola takeover were not coincidental. Activists on the two campuses fed off each other. On 7 May, about seven hundred students from Tulane, Loyola, and Louisiana State University in New Orleans marched from Tulane to Jackson Square, where protesters and police narrowly avoided a confrontation. When Tulane students won an option not to attend classes for the remainder of the semester, Loyola students wanted the same privilege. The school's official policy stipulated that individual teachers and students should make their own arrangements, and student opposition merged with larger issues, leading to the Danna Center takeover. On 13 May, about three hundred students met, with a majority voting to end the occupation; about fifteen students and faculty members refused to leave, however. At two o'clock on the morning of 14 May, about twenty-five policemen entered the center and arrested the remaining protesters.[88]

At both Tulane and Loyola, Vietnam underlay the demonstrations in a profound sense, but the actual issues for which activists fought concerned campus matters. This tendency struck one administrative official at the University of Alabama, where the Kent State shootings generated a circus of activity. "I thought it was very amusing — and pointed this out to students that came in with a rally over Vietnam — and what their demands consisted of was to eliminate visitation restrictions to dormitories, something related to the food in the cafeteria, a series of parietal rules, and these kinds of things, totally unrelated to the war," recalled Joab Thomas, a biology professor and interim student affairs administrator. "There were some who wanted to eliminate final exams that year . . . the kind of thing that had no relationship to the war and [was] in some ways trivial."[89]

From 6 May until the end of the semester, the Tuscaloosa campus saw meetings, demonstrations, and counterdemonstrations. The first night's activities began with a candlelight vigil joined by some one thousand Alabama students. Many then moved on to the university president's mansion, but President F. David Mathews was not home. The demonstrators then continued to the Student Union, where they stayed through the night. That same night, an intramural sports building slated for demolition burned to the ground. Protests continued, prompting Mathews to invite the state police to campus to maintain order. On 13 May, city and state police stepped in to avert a potential clash between pro- and antiadministration students, indiscriminately arresting a total of nearly sixty participants and bystanders. At times, according to critics, the officers used unnecessary force.[90]

The administration had attempted to keep events under control by instituting a nighttime curfew and prohibiting demonstrations during the day. Students responded by rallying against the restrictions. For several days, the activities had little order. Some campus observers complained that activism was a fad for many participants.[91] Many students became involved even though they had not played a part in any previous movement activities, whatever their sympathies may have been. Moreover, activism at Alabama had been fragmented and unorganized, making organizing difficult after Kent State. Jack Shelton, a Methodist campus minister who had identified with many of the movement's causes, nevertheless saw "few very thoughtful persons" and "a lot of people who were incompetent" among the campus radicals. Shelton believed that being a good radical meant knowing "how to organize, how to run a mimeograph machine, how to have a schedule, how to stick with it, how to function within a strict structure. . . . I thought the radicals here were grossly disorganized; they were full of rhetoric but they didn't work very hard and they didn't work very effectively and they couldn't keep things on track."[92]

Nevertheless, a coalition of faculty and students met frequently during the May disturbances to hammer out a list of demands that would create some order out of the chaos, basing the list on recent events. The group's primary issues included restrictions on women, the concerns of black students, and free speech. In a profound sense, the Vietnam War was the leverage point for all of the students' concerns. Peace vigils had been taking place from time to time on Fridays since 1967, and some protests against ROTC had occurred on campus during the 1969–70 academic year. Moreover, in October 1969, the national Vietnam Moratorium received support not only from activist organizations but also from the Student Government Association, which was now under the liberal leadership of Warren Herlong. Nevertheless, none of the coalition's demands pertained either to the war or to ROTC or complicity.[93] The demands included the repeal of special rules for women; the elimination of mandatory food contracts; administrators' acceptance of the new student government constitution; student control of student funds; an end to speaker bans; student representation in campus governance; the satisfaction of the demands previously issued by black student groups; the payment of the guaranteed federal minimum wage for university-associated employees; the right to collectively bargain for university employees; a prohibition against outside police forces on campus; monthly student meetings with President Mathews; and amnesty from any disciplinary action for participants in coalition activities.[94]

As was true on most campuses throughout the country, activists at Alabama were unable to maintain the intensity of the post-Kent demonstrations. While coalition participants were formulating and pushing their agenda, conservative students were also visible on campus. Administration officials feared a violent clash between opposing sides. In fact, to Mathews, who had been an undergraduate at the university in the late 1950s, the entire scene recalled the riots that surrounded Autherine Lucy's attempt to integrate the university in 1956, and he called in the state police to prevent such rioting.[95] Activists roundly criticized the decision. "I think it was really a tremendous overreaction on his part," said Jack Drake, a graduate of 'Bama's law school who was a Tuscaloosa activist. "I thought he handled that situation very, very poorly."[96]

Mathews's invitation to the state police reflected a major subplot of the demonstrations. Dissatisfaction with the war had risen, but so had public revulsion at radicals' violent rhetoric and actions. Richard Nixon, elected to the presidency in November 1968, had embraced a "silent majority" and promised "law and order." Alabama governor George C. Wallace's strong showing in the presidential campaign had to a great extent developed as a result of these sentiments, which were as strong in the South as in any part of the country. Thus, university officials were caught between competing pressures from students and from the public to clamp down on the demonstrations. At the University of Kentucky, post-Kent demonstrations prompted Governor Louie B. Nunn to call in National Guardsmen and police. At Nunn's instigation, university officials also imposed a curfew on students.[97] In Maryland, Governor Marvin Mandel ordered three hundred National Guard troops to the University of Maryland's College Park campus after violence flared between state police and students. In West Virginia, Governor Arch Moore called in state police to shut down demonstrations despite a history of little student activism.[98] At the University of South Carolina in Columbia, demonstrators took over the student center. The next week, while university trustees considered the cases of thirty-one students who had participated in the takeover, about two hundred students broke into the treasurer's office, tearing up records, overturning desks, and throwing paper and computers out the windows. Fighting then broke out between the protesters and highway patrolmen. That night, more than six hundred police officers swept through the campus with tear gas. Students and supporters were subsequently banned from gathering on the campus.[99]

Even campuses with only weak student movements exploded briefly in early 1970. At the University of Georgia, administrative sanctions against one of the most important student activists and a filtered-down version of the split between sds and ssoc weakened the already small movement. David Simpson, who had founded the school's sds chapter, was suspended from the university after the May 1968 protests. Simpson converted most of chapter's members to ssoc before leaving to work for the group as an organizer in the state. Simpson seemed to realize the practical difficulties of organizing in the South. "There are a lot of SDS people who come down here to 'freak everybody out' or 'get the pigs,'" Simpson said. "What they don't understand is that they've got to win over those rednecks they're trying to freak out. So what I say to Northerners who come down here is to put your heart in the revolution in Dixie or get out."[100] Despite his pragmatism, however, UGA's student movement became splintered and unfocused. On the one hand, more people than ever participated in antiwar demonstrations during the 1969–70 academic year; on the other, participants fell under a framework of several organizations that ran the ideological gamut from conservative to radical, and many students probably did not identify with any of the organizations. When antiwar students and faculty organized a mid-October rally to coincide with the National Moratorium, the Young Democrats assumed the most conspicuous role among university organizations.[101] But a small SDS chapter re-formed in early 1970 under the leadership of two sophomores, while the Student Mobilization Committee played a central role in antiwar activism. In April, a rally against the war attended by some two hundred people led an estimated thirty to forty people to "invade" the military building. The protesters interrupted classes in progress before Lieutenant Colonel James O. Youngblood, an assistant professor of military science, offered to speak with a representative. But one of the protesters responded that "the group was composed of individuals and had no authoritative systemic structure which provided for one person to speak for them." People milled around for about twenty minutes before leaving the building.[102]

The Kent State shootings attracted larger numbers of students to the streets of Athens. On the night of 6 May, some three thousand demonstrators gathered outside the Academic Building, where many jeered while President Fred C. Davison attempted to persuade them not to strike. University officials had declared class attendance optional in the wake of the deaths. The massive outpouring of anger continued for several days but seemed to have no acknowledged leaders and no agenda. Instead, a more general sentiment that sought a sign of support from university officials prevailed. "Other universities are out of classes — we should go to the Academic Building and demand that they shut down in sympathy for the people who got killed," one student declared. "If we give a damn that's what we ought to do."[103] After two days of demonstrations, Davison announced that the board of regents had authorized him to suspend classes on Friday, 8 May, and Saturday, 9 May. The university also obtained a restraining order barring students from entering any campus building on 8 May "for any purpose other than the conduct of the educational and business affairs normally . . . carried out in such buildings." The demonstrations then fizzled out.[104]

Despite the concrete achievements of the antiwar movement at the University of Georgia, such as the institution of a voluntary ROTC program before the beginning of the 1969–70 academic year, the lack of focus and of any sort of support from Davison limited the possibilities for further victories. Antiwar activists at Emory University were somewhat more successful. In the wake of a post-Kent student strike, faculty of Emory College voted to discontinue air force ROTC; after some wrangling, the program was formally deactivated in 1974. Demonstrators at Emory also received backing from university president Sanford Atwood, who on 5 May declared his support for striking students in a telegram to Nixon. According to Atwood, the students acted "not against the University, but against the policies of our government regarding the Vietnam War," and he thus urged the president "to consider the prompt withdrawal of all United States troops from Vietnam and Cambodia."[105] The events at Emory represented a trend at institutions with more liberal presidents, many of which had better academic reputations and more geographically diverse student bodies.[106]

To some extent, the University of North Carolina followed this trend. Its traditional student liberalism began to show cracks in April 1969, when conservative opponents of the NSA finally won a referendum forcing the university to disassociate itself from the organization.[107] UNC's activism had always had definite limits. After the spring 1969 food workers' strike, the university's board of trustees had instituted a new set of procedures to deal with student unrest, threatening to suspend, expel, or dismiss any student or faculty member involved in obstructing "the normal operations or functions of any of the component institutions of the University."[108]

UNC nevertheless experienced significant levels of activism in the fall of 1969. In January 1970, opponents of ROTC won a mixed victory when a faculty committee recommended continuing ROTC but making it part of a new Curriculum on War and Defense that would "be concerned with war not as a vocational specialty, governed by technical principles and experience, but as a paramount human problem, a phenomenon that is social, political, psychological, and ethical." The committee also proposed limiting the number of hours of credit students could receive for ROTC as well as the amount of time the program could devote to drills. Opponents complained that the committee had not gone far enough to scale back ROTC, but the report significantly circumscribed the existing programs.[109] The following April, activists organized a two-day antiwar "festival" that attracted thousands of participants. The next month, the Cambodian incursion initiated another flurry of activity, which intensified after Kent State. Marches involving thousands of students and countless petitions accompanied a call for a student strike. Taking the lead in the activities was student government president Thomas Bello, a junior from Raleigh and a Morehead scholar who had won the presidency as an independent — that is, outside the established student party structure. After Kent State, Bello attempted to combine support for the strike with calls for nonviolence. An arsonist set fire to UNC's air force ROTC building, but despite this action and demonstrations on and off campus, classes continued without a violent showdown between demonstrators and troops. Striking students ultimately won the opportunity to receive grades for the work they had completed prior to the walkout.[110]

Students, the War, and Political Mobilization: Culmination and Conclusions

May 1970 represented the culmination of antiwar activism in the South, but it was an artificial end. Opposition to the war had been building, but most campus-based antiwar movements remained small. Kent State mobilized students who had not become directly involved in the antiwar movement. As the ranks of demonstrators swelled, they often brought in other concerns that had been present on southern college campuses. Nevertheless, the end of the academic year quickly followed. When students returned to campus in the fall, the antiwar movement resumed at a pace that more closely resembled the pre-Kent months than the tumultuous days of early May. At Tulane University, for example, a feature in the 1971 yearbook presented several students' and faculty members' answers to the question of why there were "quite literally only one-tenth the number of campus disturbances this year as compared to last."[111]

The war in Vietnam had provided the impetus for all kinds of activism, and when this impetus faded away, the general levels of activism declined. As a result, the student movement's broader campus-related aims remained largely unrealized. In the early 1970s, some activists still envisioned students as key players in a progressive alliance of black and working-class white voters that would take power away from huge financial interests. These visions proved unrealistic, for the South remained a stronghold of the "silent majority." A late May 1970 appearance by President Nixon at the University of Tennessee illustrated the limits of student political mobilization. Nixon's appearance, the first since the Kent State shootings, took place in the football stadium on a southern college campus during a religious revival led by the Reverend Billy Graham. Some 250 activists, including Tennessee students, chanted and jeered at the president during the program, but, in the words of one participant, they were "250 Lions to 90,000 Christians."[112]

CHAPTER NINE

Southern Campuses
at Decade's End

IN FEBRUARY 1968, Joseph P. Long was a disappointed freshman. Long had come to Vanderbilt from Springfield, Tennessee, some twenty miles north of Nashville, to study mechanical engineering in hopes of one day becoming an astronaut. A decade before, the "avowed Southern conservative" probably would have felt quite comfortable on the Nashville campus. But Long found Vanderbilt too liberal and too politically apathetic. While watching news coverage of Vietnam in his dorm, Long heard fellow students laugh or "seem oblivious" to events. These were dark days for American involvement in Southeast Asia. The Tet Offensive, which began on 31 January, shook the confidence of many Americans that victory was near and in fact seemed to suggest the Viet Cong's willingness to fight indefinitely. But while Tet prompted many Americans to reconsider their support for the war, Long was not among them. His commitment made the comments of his dorm mates all the more difficult to bear. Long described the incident to the *Nashville Banner* and expressed his concerns not only about the antiwar sentiments but also about urban problems, racial rioters, and hippies. "America is imperiled as never before," he declared.[1]

For Long, as for many college students in the late 1960s, the war in Vietnam was a personal issue. "A few guys from my county have been killed in the war," he told the Vanderbilt *Hustler* a few days after the *Banner* printed his letter. "It bothers me to see people ungrateful for this sacrifice. I just don't like to see people being happy about it." Long was determined, however, to channel his discontent in productive directions. He spoke as if he were mounting an evangelical crusade that sought to reconvert Vanderbilt to conservatism but confessed that he sometimes felt like "the only conservative on the entire campus. . . . I take liberalism here as a sort of challenge. I'm going to change every one of these liberals to conservatives if it kills me. And it probably will kill me."[2]

But Long's characterization of Vanderbilt as a liberal institution was hardly the consensus opinion on campus. Judy LeKashman had left Vanderbilt in 1967 after attempting to prod the school toward change, especially in regard to women's issues. LeKashman had written a series of controversial articles in the *Hustler* and an article on birth control in the campus humor magazine, the *Dirty We'jun*, and she had publicly criticized what she called "archaic" school rules, including the social regulations that hemmed in women on campus. At Brandeis, LeKashman found a more open, progressive, and intellectually adventurous campus, but she still was not happy. "It was the intellectual extreme [opposite] of Vanderbilt," LeKashman told the *Hustler*. "Whereas here the only student questions concern future test dates, the questions there were excessive. Brandeis students assume they are smarter than the professors. Instead of listening, then arguing — they just argue." She left Brandeis and returned to Vanderbilt in early 1968, but she was not sure she would stay. She seemed troubled by the continued power of what she called "immature" fraternities: "They're too conservative and too much of a closed society to influence social progress and liberality on campus."[3]

Long and LeKashman's experiences combine to offer a composite portrait of southern college campuses in the midst of a significant transformation. The transformation was far-reaching, incorporating the daily lives of students, the cultural contours of the campuses they inhabited, the form and content of their academic programs, and the political environment in which students wrestled with the issues of the period. The transformation was not by any means complete. Even at the height of the movement, students could continue to replicate many of the collegiate patterns established before 1960. Nevertheless, southern campuses were different places in 1970 than they had been in 1960. Student activism did not single-handedly cause the changes that occurred. The forces shaping youth culture, higher education, and southern and American politics were varied and complex. Nevertheless, the political mobilization of southern college students had played an important role in reshaping the campuses on which this mobilization occurred. Describing and measuring changes in the contours of campus life and culture by the early 1970s, therefore, indicates the impact of the southern student movement.

At the most basic level, southern student activism, which always had a strong civil libertarian component, opened up campuses so that rebels could voice their opinions in ways that had not previously been possible. Activism dissolved the larger patterns of orthodoxy and self-censorship that blighted intellectual life. Colleges and universities may not have become places in which the dominant culture featured students brimming with intellectual curiosity and willing to challenge even the most sacred ideas, but at least people who exhibited such tendencies had more room in which to operate. But the changes went beyond the point of simply creating space for exploring previously controversial ideas.

Activism helped to expand the cultural spectrum on southern college campuses. Students are a transient population, but the cultural space they inhabit is not transient. Student life comprises campus subcultures handed down from generation to generation, and those subcultures play a central role in establishing the possibilities and limits for all aspects of student life, including patterns for political engagement.[4] In 1960, the student cultural spectrum on southern college campuses was truncated. The fraternity/sorority subculture exercised a disproportionate amount of power, controlling the machinery of student politics and generally avoiding engagement with substantive political issues. The extent to which this dynamic held varied throughout the region according to political geography and institutional type, and the subculture dominated at some schools outside the South. But in the region, the collegiate subculture was exaggerated by other forces, including conservative evangelical religion, traditional ideas about gender roles, and, most important, the maintenance of a color line that paralyzed higher education. In short, southern colleges looked like the South. They reflected their communities and instilled the values of a rural region defined by its communitarian social relations.

Larger social and economic forces were already chipping away at southern folkways in 1960, and college campuses might have continued to evolve along with the rest of the region. But the color line presented a fundamental obstacle. Southern higher education could not enter the national mainstream with segregation intact. Liberal gradualists would have continued a slow march toward managed desegregation, but the civil rights movement made liberal gradualism untenable, and the sit-in movement dealt it a fatal blow.

The sit-in movement provided a new avenue for political mobilization that required a physical commitment. It forced students to take sides, to declare their allegiances. On southern college campuses, the sit-in movement ultimately shook up established cultural patterns. But it was not simply the introduction of nonviolent direct action that created the disruption, though such tactics were disruptive enough. It was the use of nonviolence to challenge segregation, the institution that played the largest role in setting the South apart from the rest of the nation. Southern student activists eventually addressed a wide range of issues, but segregation was the first item on the agenda. Activists on both sides of the color line challenged beliefs and practices that were central to daily life in the Jim Crow era.

But what should desegregation look like? How far should it proceed? These questions produced no consensus, either in the South or elsewhere in the United States. Southern student activists continued to explore the meaning of desegregation in the South's formerly segregated institutions, simultaneously addressing the full range of issues that the 1960s generation faced and doing so in ways that blurred the lines between on-campus and off-campus. In the process, activists fleshed out new models of campus rebellion and carved out space for political engagement that had not previously existed. The cultural challenge was far-reaching. By the late 1960s, for example, activists also challenged assumptions about women's roles on campus and thereby helped equalize the opportunities afforded to male and female southern college students.

The Counterculture and the Campus

These cultural changes were intertwined with the rebellion against mainstream American conventions known as the counterculture. As employed in the popular media, the term encompassed a wide range of behavior, including the rejection of traditional boundaries for sexuality and the use of drugs for the expansion of consciousness as well as unconventional modes of attire, hairstyles, and music, practices that combined to seem to represent a rejection of dominant American values. But defining the counterculture can be tricky, in part because the movement had few structural or organizational markers. Within the narrative of the rise and fall of the New Left, the counterculture has been a controversial concept. Old guard activists and historians such as Todd Gitlin and James Miller have portrayed the counterculture as one of several elements — including a propensity toward violence and a romantic view of Third World nationalist movements — that contributed to the New Left's downfall.[5] Other scholars, more sympathetic to the radical activists, have disagreed with the declension narrative of the old guard and have found much of value in the movement's rejection of bourgeois social relations.[6]

What impact did the counterculture have on the southern student movement? First, the counterculture must be separated from other cultural trends. For example, the counterculture resonated with the "sexual revolution" (the increasing sexualization of American culture that in some respects dated back to the 1920s), but the sexual revolution was a separate entity. The counterculture also resonated with youth culture, but it too followed its own trajectory. "While America was full of young people sporting long hair and beads," suggests one historian, "the committed revolutionaries (of a cultural stripe) were few in number and marginal at best." Or, in Gitlin's words, "There were many more weekend dope-smokers than hard-core 'heads'; many more readers of the *Oracle* than writers for it; many more co-habitors than orgiasts; many more turners-on than droppers-out."[7]

If judged by the presence of hippie attire or casual drug use, southern campuses of the late 1960s and early 1970s may be said to have assumed many countercultural trappings. But while much of the southern student movement was indigenous, the counterculture was not a particularly southern development; New York and San Francisco had the greatest claims to genuine rebellion against prevailing cultural norms. When the counterculture reached the South, cities were first to feel the effects. By the late 1960s, the South contained some pockets of cultural rebellion. In Atlanta and New Orleans in particular, alternative newspapers documented the presence not only of the counterculture but also of all manner of leftist politics. College campuses also harbored cultural rebels. Despite a reputation for unfriendliness to dissent, even Jackson, Mississippi, had an alternative newspaper, the *Kudzu*. Moreover, the popularity of rock music and the commercialization of youth culture caused even the most conservative of campuses to feel some effects.[8]

Within Students for a Democratic Society (SDS), the counterculture made its first appearance in the mid-1960s in the form of new radicals from midwestern and southwestern campuses. Sporting handlebar moustaches and long hair, they tended toward anarchy rather than centralized discipline. Significantly, the avatars of Prairie Power came from more conservative locales. For example, activists from the University of Texas won a reputation within SDS as anarchists who were enthusiastic about psychedelic drugs. While Austin was tolerant relative to much of the Deep South, it was considerably more conservative than the East and West Coast campuses that produced much of the SDS old guard.[9]

As a heuristic device, the separation of the counterculture and the New Left illuminates the divergence between activists who sought structural social change through political mobilization and those who emphasized personal liberation as a preface to broader social change. But historians' tendency to create sharp divisions between the counterculture and the New Left is less useful when examining the southern student movement. As a historian of Austin's New Left has argued, conservative locales tended to create circumstances in which political and cultural rebels saw more similarities than differences.[10] To be sure, differences of opinion at times emerged along the counterculture/New Left axis. In Gainesville, Florida, for example, a division between hippies and politically active students began to develop after 1965. Morning glory seeds, which could be used as a psychedelic drug, grew in popularity, along with changes in attire. Marshall Jones, a University of Florida professor and activist, later recalled his alarm at the developments: "How the hell were we supposed to do anything with a bunch of people who were dropping seeds, winding themselves into incredible sexual tangles, and talking out of their heads about a new dimension in human experience?" As Jones saw it, the hippies and the activists drew from the same critique of American society, but their conclusions diverged. Hippies believed that the best way to forward a process of radical change was to behave as if it had already run its course. A frontal assault on mainstream America was futile and would involve concessions and compromises that would ultimately corrupt the challenge. Activists responded that while it was all well and good to behave as if the revolution had already occurred, it had not. The hippie community, moreover, lacked a viable economic base and made no allowances for people over thirty or with children. Finally, hippies' naïveté exposed them to "commercialism on one side and hard narcotics on the other." Despite their differences, Gainesville's two factions eventually worked out an alliance of sorts. When the hippies got into trouble with the university administration or police, the activists defended them. Moreover, as Jones recalled, the activists eventually came to appreciate the value of nonconformists in the community. The hippies, in turn, showed up at demonstrations and "were always ready to include us in the proceedings of a quieter mode of life."[11]

A similar convergence of counterculture and New Left politics occurred in Austin, Texas, where the white counterculture had been distinct from the political Left in the early 1960s. While the predecessors of the New Left organized around civil rights activism in the late 1950s and early 1960s, cultural rebels rarely participated in these demonstrations and instead concentrated on the local folk music scene. Nevertheless, these two constituencies maintained ideological ties. While the political rebels focused on antiracist activism, they also used marijuana and peyote and experimented with sexual liberalization. The ties strengthened in the wake of the rise of Black Power, which generated a transition in the New Left in Austin. Black Power called into question the value of an interracial civil rights movement; as a result, New Left activists in Austin increasingly concluded that their task was to create a cultural revolution within white America. These leftists had always believed that a revolution in values must form a meaningful part of a broader political revolution, but the revolution in values increasingly occupied the central role in the New Left analysis. "In Texas," Douglas Rossinow argues, "making a new counterculture gradually became the new left's main strategy for creating fundamental social change."[12]

On the University of Texas campus, the most public manifestations of the Austin SDS chapter's countercultural turn were the *Rag* and a festival, Gentle Thursday, organized in the fall of 1966. The festival, held on the UT campus's West Mall, was intended to contrast with an annual invitation-only costume party run by campus fraternities. Organizers declared that Gentle Thursday was a "celebration of our belief that there is nothing wrong with fun." Attendees drew peace symbols in chalk on the sidewalks and drew graffiti on a fighter plane mounted in front of the Reserve Officers' Training Corps building. Gentle Thursday went over well with students, and activists on other campuses throughout the country, including some southern schools, soon produced their own versions of this countercultural happening.[13]

At the University of Alabama, a version of Gentle Thursday developed in connection with the Experimental College, which was not a radical political organization but nevertheless served as an incubator for political and cultural as well as educational ferment. Small numbers of cultural rebels had been present on the campus in the late 1950s and early 1960s in the form of "bohemians" who gathered in the University Union for discussions over coffee. But fraternities and sororities, which monopolized the machinery of student government, dominated campus politics. In fact, the Machine, a secret confederation of fraternities, reportedly met every year to select its candidates for campuswide offices, which often served as springboards for state political careers. By 1967, however, moderate to liberal leaders had won positions of student government power and supported the Experimental College, a student-run institution that resembled the free universities created elsewhere around the same time.[14]

While Alabama's Experimental College offered its share of nontraditional courses, a series of festivals that it sponsored in the Woods Hall Quadrangle in 1969 received the most attention and caused the most controversy. The Woods Quads were not quite the scenes of hedonism that some members of the public perceived them to be, but the presence of loud music and hippies alarmed some Tuscaloosa residents, who complained to the university administration. In October 1969, in the midst of one of the Quads, officials cut off electricity to the festival's amplifiers and electric guitars. Within five minutes, organizers commandeered a generator, and the music continued. Policemen then consulted university officials before attempting to confiscate the generator, but students gathered around to protect it, and the officials backed down. The next day, about fifty students held a sit-in in front of President F. David Mathews's office following rumors that he was going to ban the concerts. Mathews criticized what he called the students' intimidation tactics but eventually ruled that the Quads could continue as long as participants complied with a handful of regulations. The meetings between the students and the president were contentious. In the polarized world of 1969, the dispute seemed to symbolize more than the actual issues at stake, especially to the students. "The Administration doesn't realize that the Quad is a people's thing," said Bill Moody, the student who directed the Experimental College. "They don't want to deal with the people, they want to deal with us three or four [at a time]. For the first time in the history of the University, we are on the offensive. We're not going to be oppressed because a lot of townspeople don't like hippies getting together after dark."[15]

Moody's comments illustrated the widening gap between conservative "townspeople" and students and campus rebels for whom opposition to the war in Vietnam and constricting cultural limitations were often closely connected. Those divisions rose to the surface on several occasions. In October 1968, Tuscaloosa policemen raided a student-run establishment, the Haight Hut, that sold beads, posters, Indian water pipes, incense, and the like. Police suspected that the student proprietors were dealing drugs and on 4 October arrested six people in the Haight Hut on vagrancy charges. Those arrested included Bud Silvis, a university student and chemistry lab instructor, who was later indicted by a grand jury but shot and killed himself before the trial began. One person wrote anonymously to the *Crimson White* that the episode exemplified the Tuscaloosa police's efforts to crack down on students who were not "their kind" — that is, students who had "different ideas from the Tuscaloosa police, who wear 'funny clothes' or long hair, or . . . 'act like they're not in their right minds.'" The problem, according to the writer, was deeper than the use of drugs. It was "a question of being able to live one's life and think one's thoughts, and have one's views as he wishes."[16]

The Woods Quad and Haight Hut incidents represented Tuscaloosa's version of a counterculture, with the political content limited to calls for the right to open-air festivals and head shops. But other 'Bama students attempted to combine some of the trappings of the counterculture with a political agenda. Ernest Hallford, a graduate student in English from McKenzie, Alabama, responded to the Woods Quad clash by forming the Committee for the Liberation of All People (CLAP). In November 1969, he and thirty other demonstrators interrupted a U.S. Army Reserve Officers' Training Corps drill session to protest the fact that military courses carried academic credit. Hallford described the demonstration as a "yippie tactic." And indeed, his attire seemed to constitute a self-conscious protest. "It's a real happening in McKenzie when I go home," he told a *Crimson White* reporter, noting that he had been a clean-cut, small-town student for the first two years of his collegiate career before becoming a "freak."[17]

The deliberately outlandish attire and tactics of activists such as Hallford at times impeded serious efforts at mass mobilization among Alabama students, few of whom were prepared to repudiate the visible symbols of middle-class orthodoxy. In this respect, a temporary mobilization of 'Bama students during the demonstrations that occurred in the wake of Cambodia and Kent State was somewhat misleading. One student activist, Mike O'Bannon, later suggested that although a small number of people "were very into the whole political thing, into changing themselves, into a whole different view of what the world could be like," for most people, political activism "was as much a fad as streaking or goldfish swallowing was in the '50s."[18] However, the post-Kent demonstrations did suggest the significant division between conservatives and students who at some level opposed American foreign policy or identified with one or more strands of dissent. In fact, fear of a violent clash between these opposing sides prompted Mathews to call for reinforcements from state police. While Mathews's decision drew the ire of campus activists, letters from conservative students suggested a different perspective. "Today, my sorority sisters and I were talking and we all say *hurray* for America, Nixon and our University!" wrote one student shortly after the Kent State shootings. "I support the Nat'l Guardsmen, after all what could they do — get stoned to death?"[19] These demonstrations suggested that the split between the counterculture and the New Left was not the primary story at Tuscaloosa or in much of the rest of the South. The more fundamental split was between conservatives and dissenters of any persuasion. Vietnam and Kent State threw these differences into high relief.

Consciously countercultural forms of activism sometimes represented a tacit acknowledgment that an outright political victory was impossible, as in the April 1970 Tulane Liberation Front takeover of the university's student center. Leaders of the demonstration ultimately abandoned their most ambitious idea, a boycott of classes intended to shut the university down, because they lacked the necessary student support. Instead, they called for an ill-defined "cultural revolution" to be headquartered at the University Center.[20]

In a region with a history of resistance to dissent and a tradition of progressive politics rooted in liberal gradualism, the split between the counterculture and the New Left took a backseat to the larger cultural and political divide. Politically, a cleavage existed between the student Left and the student Right. But this characterization suggests a formality or rigidity that did not exist on campuses where many students, even at the height of the movement, remained apolitical or only casually involved in politics. A more accurate characterization would be that the division between the collegiate subculture, dominated by fraternities and sororities, and campus rebels, which included elements of both the New Left and the counterculture, had become more pronounced. The collegiate subculture remained much in evidence, and fraternities generally could be counted on to oppose progressive change. At the same time, however, the Greek societies' stranglehold over campus social life was loosening on many campuses, opening up opportunities for outsiders who were neither campus rebels nor members of fraternities and sororities. The extent and experience of this cultural blurring varied from campus to campus.

Women and Activism

For most of the 1960s, leadership roles in campus movements fell almost exclusively to men. The ranks of college rebels had always included women, but many women — especially white women — who participated in the decade's social movements found themselves relegated to secondary or support roles. The centrality of civil rights to other forms of campus protest made it all but inevitable that people would eventually see an analogy between women's marginalization and the oppression of black people, and the civil rights movement and the New Left thus give birth to the women's liberation movement.[21] This new form of explicitly feminist activism sought first and foremost to free women from confining assumptions and regulations and to create a more congenial atmosphere for them to explore the meaning of their lives as women, and groups devoted to this goal sprung up on and around many southern college campuses.

Concern about the place of women on the campus frequently took the form of protest concerning rules that colleges and universities had always applied more stringently to women than to men. Old assumptions about the role of women at the university and in society provided the foundation for gender-specific codes of conduct. Throughout the 1960s, universities operated under the assumptions of in loco parentis, but at most institutions, the regulations that grew from this philosophy restricted women more than men. During the second half of the 1960s, these regulations increasingly came under attack from activists looking for an issue to mobilize students and from more moderate — sometimes even conservative — students who wanted more freedom but did not incorporate this desire into a larger political agenda.

The unfair application of nonacademic regulations to women frequently appeared on lists of issues in late-1960s student protests. In some cases, it served as the primary organizing issue for student demonstrations, most notably in April 1968 at the University of Georgia, when hundreds of students took over an administration building to protest inequality in campus regulations for women. A pamphlet that circulated around the time of the two-day sit-in lampooned the authority of Louise McBee, the university's dean of women, who oversaw the enforcement of the regulations laid out in the *Georgia Belle* handbook and thus earned the moniker "Queen Bee." *Dear Queen Bee*, "an advice column for puzzled coeds," offered a series of satirical questions and responses, including one in which "Over 21" asked, "I am a married woman attending the University of Georgia. Last night my husband said he wanted me to have a child. What is your advice?" Queen Bee responded, "According to THE GEORGIA BELLE, married women may have children only if parental permission is obtained and a university approved chaperone is present at conception."[22]

In the aftermath of the April 1968 demonstrations, university officials substantially revised curfews on campus, although they contended that such a revision had already been in the works. The demonstrations did not, however, indicate the formation of a full-fledged feminist movement on the University of Georgia campus. The activists who took the lead in the movement couched demands for equal treatment of women in the language of student power and the New Left's larger democratic vision. But subsequent efforts to generate momentum around women's liberation seemed to fall flat. In 1971, an avowedly leftist organization, Women's Oppression Must End Now (WOMEN) formed, but it appealed to only a small number of students. WOMEN revealed its political colors in the spring of 1971 by sponsoring a speech by Linda Jenness, the 1970 Socialist Workers' Party candidate for governor of Georgia.[23]

The Georgia demonstrations nevertheless made an impression on students and administrative officials at the University of Alabama. One student there, Sondra Nesmith, noted the protests in an August 1968 column opposing the university's housing policy in particular and its paternalistic attitude toward students in general. According to Nesmith, students were organizing to oppose such regulations everywhere except at the University of Alabama: "Let's lay it on the line — at this institution STUDENTS ARE NIGGERS, and the dean of women treats the coeds on this campus as something much less."[24] If feminism was only implicit in Nesmith's larger student rights argument, it nevertheless stood in stark contrast to the opposing viewpoint on the same page. Beth Caldwell, president of the association of sororities, defended the regulations as necessary for the protection of women students: "Young women do have a moral and social standard to uphold. I don't feel that they are supposed to have the same rights as young men do concerning hours, off-campus living, etc."[25]

By 1968, however, defenders of curfews for women were increasingly in the minority among 'Bama students. Fearful that activists might exploit the issue, the administration moved to revise the regulations. Starting in the fall of 1968, women seniors who were over twenty-one and had parental consent could live off campus. The following spring, the university began allowing visitation privileges in men's residence halls. By September 1969, women students who were twenty-one or who were seniors and had parental consent were exempt from curfews. In December, the university extended the curfew from eleven o'clock to midnight. And in early 1970, women students with sixty credit hours and parental consent no longer had a curfew.[26]

The gradual phasing out of separate nonacademic regulations for women did not necessarily indicate the emergence of feminism on the Alabama campus. In fact, as late as 1970, feminism remained muted. Nevertheless, a women's liberation group was formed during the 1969–70 academic year, and it organized a series of candlelight vigils as part of the May 1970 demonstrations. The visibility of these women activists helped ensure that the women's curfew would be at the top of the list of concerns voiced during those demonstrations. Other developments pointed to a sea change in attitudes toward women's roles on campus. For example, the president of the Association of Women Students for 1970–71, Cathy Wright, a junior political science major, proclaimed that the women's student government organization would no longer be "cute and gimmicky. We're getting rid of all the crème puff." Rather than tracking down female students who had not signed into their dorms at night, the group would work to get women involved in university activities, including some that had been previously restricted to men. Wright also adopted a style that the feature editor of the Crimson White described as "almost a walking replica of what Cosmopolitan and Mademoiselle would call the 'new woman.'" Flouting atavistic expectations for women's attire, Wright declared, "I rarely take off my blue jeans — even on a Friday night." She attributed her willingness to reject traditional conceptions of the coed to an upbringing that, because of her father's military career, included frequent relocations. The mobility "kept me from getting really entrenched in one set of cultural biases."[27] Wright's feminism represented a significant departure from traditional conceptions of the Bama Belle.

If women's liberation was only inchoate at such Deep South schools as the Universities of Georgia and Alabama, then it was more fully developed in other locales. At Duke University, women looking for organizational opportunities to explore liberation had at least four options. On the left, a women's liberation group, Female Liberation No. 11, formed in the fall of 1969. The fifteen or so founders were oriented toward socialism and believed that the "oppression of women is institutional, not individual, and will not end until there is a change in the economic base of society." One founder, Mary Thad Ridge, was also presiding chair of Praxis, which emerged in October 1969 as part of an effort to "de-studentize" the Student Liberation Front and move into the community. Similarly, members of Female Liberation No. 11 expressed a desire to organize around issues that would unite women on campus with women, especially those from the working class, in Durham. In March 1970, the group organized a two-day symposium, "Women: The Longest Revolution," as an alternative to a more moderate symposium taking place at the same time, "Directions for Educated Women." The main speaker at the Female Liberation conference was *Feminine Mystique* author Betty Friedan, who argued that a redefinition of women's roles would only come with a restructuring of society. The moderate symposium, which took place in conjunction with the thirtieth anniversary of the Women's College, was geared more toward professional opportunities for college-educated women and featured an address by historian Carl Degler, who argued that women should have "more options" so that they could live "more complete lives." During the same academic year, the campus YWCA organized a women's liberation group that sponsored a series of consciousness-raising sessions. Whereas Female Liberation pursued an overtly political agenda that included goals such as child-care centers for working mothers, the YWCA group eschewed a broader political agenda in favor of a concentration on "personal politics." Finally, the SDS Committee on Female Liberation sponsored a March 1970 rally in support of working women that featured speeches by a union leader and a leftist journalist. Fifty students then marched to Chancellor Barnes Woodhall's office and posted on his door a statement supporting women workers.[28]

Duke's multiple pathways to women's liberation mirrored trends within the larger women's movement. While some women activists argued that the oppression of women grew from capitalism and would be eliminated when capitalism was replaced with socialism, others placed men at the center of oppression.

Gainesville, Florida, produced two of the earliest and most vocal exponents of what would soon be called radical feminism. In June 1968, Beverly Jones and Judith Brown, both veterans of the Congress of Racial Equality and the Gainesville SDS, published "Toward a Female Liberation Movement." The position paper, which soon became known as the Florida Paper, conceptualized women's struggle for equality as a battle against all men and rejected the idea that women's struggle should take second place behind the struggle to eliminate capitalism. Later that summer, Brown and Carol Giardina cofounded the South's first women's liberation group, Gainesville Women's Liberation.[29]

As usual, the fine points of debate within movement circles — in this case, whether oppression of women would end with the end of capitalism or whether women should work separately to end their oppression — filtered down to southern campuses in a belated and incomplete form. Nevertheless, in early 1969, when an activist for the Southern Students Organizing Committee (SSOC) set out to list the examples of college women organizing for themselves, she found a number of women's liberation groups as well as a significant level of pressure for modifications in dorm regulations and other unfairly applied social rules. At the University of Arkansas, women activists passed out leaflets calling for mass meetings about campus rules. At New College in St. Petersburg, Florida, a faculty wives women's liberation group had been formed. Women's liberation groups also had formed in and around campuses in Durham and Greensboro, North Carolina; the University of South Carolina in Columbia; Nashville; and Richmond. In Atlanta, a group of women had been meeting regularly and worked with SSOC to organize a regional women's conference.[30]

This February 1969 conference focused on women's problems on campus. One series of presentations offered "action models" for galvanizing campus support for a women's movement. One speaker discussed the "coed equality movement" at the University of Georgia. Brown discussed developments in Gainesville. A third speaker covered "counter-orientation" activities at the University of North Carolina at Greensboro, now a coeducational institution after years as the Women's College of the University of North Carolina. Other workshops dealt with "Grad Schools and Women," "Dorm and Person-to-Person Organizing," and "Guerrilla Theater." However, the conference also offered programs meant to attract women from outside college campuses. One session focused on "Southern Women's Struggle for Her Own and Others' Freedom," featuring historical sketches on the Grimké sisters, Georgia populist Rebecca Felton, and Unionist women from West Virginia during the Civil War. Anne Braden of the Southern Conference Educational Fund offered a presentation on women in the modern movement. Other workshops dealt with women as consumers, a class analysis of women in the South, and "the Southern Sex Myth."[31]

A sample "campus survey" indicated the student women's issues on which organizers hoped to capitalize as well as the broader issues that helped give rise to a somewhat separate regional variant of women's liberation. Respondents were asked to document discrimination in a number of areas, from social rules to curricular matters. "Are there courses required or 'recommended' for women which mold women into socially acceptable roles (such as home ec or marriage and family)?" "Are there courses that women are not permitted or are discouraged from taking?" "Do counselors encourage women out of certain majors?" "Can you get birth control info, devices, etc. from school nurse or doctor?" "How do women's dorms compare with men's?" The survey's final section, "Movement Stuff," demonstrated that conference organizers were attuned to the discrimination women faced within the movement itself: "What is the general role of women in your group?" "Do women do all the typing? Mimeographing? Other shit-work? Are women actively recruited?" "Do women in your group talk together about women's problems? How do they feel about women's liberation? What is the reaction of men in your group?"[32]

One male ssoc organizer, Thomas Gardner, recalled that men within the organization were somewhat slow to embrace women's issues: "There was not a single male on the ssoc staff level who did not express some reluctance about devoting ssoc resources to women's liberation organizing." Women in ssoc diverged from the radical feminism of the Gainesville women and encouraged the engagement of women's issues within the context of a movement that sought "total change." Led by Lyn Wells, a longtime ssoc organizer, these women "were uncomfortable with the middle-class, academic nature of much of the women's liberation movement" and "could not accept as realistic the call for a totally feminist revolution." They recognized, however, that consciousness-raising groups could serve as useful tools to organize women within a revolutionary movement. "Although the problem has *personalized symptoms*," Wells wrote in December 1968, "it is an *institutionalized menace*, and must be approached as that."[33]

The women in ssoc had little chance to pursue their version of liberation under the group's umbrella, since it dissolved shortly after Wells wrote that pamphlet. At southern colleges and universities, however, as in the nation at large, the women's movement generated significant changes. During the 1970s and 1980s, progressive transformation — and some continuity and backlash — occurred in the arena of women's rights and gender relations. By 1992, women made up 56 percent of the southern college student population, up from 38 percent in 1960. Women also increasingly entered formerly male disciplines, while formerly female disciplines were redefined.[34] At the University of Georgia, for example, the name of the School of Home Economics was changed to the College of Family and Consumer Sciences in the late 1980s. Campuses with coordinate colleges for women experienced a long process of dissolving the lines that divided the men's and women's units. The University of Richmond's Westhampton College for women and Richmond College for men formally continued to exist, but their roles were limited largely to nonacademic functions, and all classes were coeducational. A similar process played out at Tulane University, where Newcomb College for women remained a separate but somewhat limited entity until the aftermath of 2005's Hurricane Katrina, when the college was dissolved as part of a university-wide reorganization.[35]

At the most fundamental level, day-to-day gender relations underwent dramatic changes on southern college campuses during the 1970s and 1980s. Many campuses saw the merger of men's and women's student government associations, an indication of the dissolution of the "separate spheres" for men and women that had existed throughout much of the twentieth century. After a period of decline in the 1970s, fraternities and sororities, still in some ways guardians of traditional gender roles, experienced a revival in the 1980s.[36] Yet while sorority members continued to play roles assigned decades earlier (as participants in the Kappa Alpha fraternity's Old South ball, women wore frilly dresses while men dressed as Confederate soldiers), sororities increasingly emphasized community service. By the 1990s, despite continuing concerns that men were likely to hold campus leadership positions and to dominate classroom discussion, a liberal brand of feminism that emphasized the expansion of professional opportunities for middle-class women could be seen as ascendant on southern college campuses.

Race was a complicating factor in the emerging women's movement, creating a division that proved difficult to transcend. Black women did not tap into the same sense of second-class status felt by white women in the civil rights movement such as Casey Hayden and Mary King. But African American women sometimes described feeling excluded from a liberal feminism that seemed to emphasize the experiences of middle-class white women. Yet the institutional settings for black and white women on southern college campuses created a common experience. Black colleges started the decade with a similar understanding about what education for women was supposed to mean and if anything tended to be even more restrictive than white colleges. In a 1968 column headlined "We've Come a Long Way, Baby," Fisk student Beatryce Nivens celebrated not only the loosening of restrictions in general at Fisk but also the relaxation of regulations that disproportionately affected female students: "How many girls can remember the strict curfews that were enforced in the '65–'66 school year? Remember the late minutes and social probation? What about the hard-core 'no riding in vehicles' rule? In those days everything one did had to be checked, re-checked and double checked by the Dorm mother and the Dean of Women. Fortunately, we Fiskites have come a long way!"[37] As at the predominantly white Universities of Georgia and Alabama, any sort of explicitly feminist consciousness appears to have been inchoate. At Fisk, as at other historically black institutions, the drive for Black Power and a black university dominated student mobilization. A fuller questioning of gender roles on historically black as well as predominantly white campuses awaited the 1970s.

Race and the Culture of the Southern Campus

Race stood at the center of southern student activism throughout the 1960s. Southern student activists played a central role in dismantling legalized segregation. By embracing nonviolent direct action, infusing it with a generational identity, and taking advantage of the organizational opportunities presented by their proximity to each other on college campuses, African American students reinvigorated the civil rights movement. The sit-in movement was a rare event—pitch-perfect for its time, attuned to the idealism of a Cold War America not yet weighed down by a realization of limits that would come later in the decade. Viewed from the perspective of the early twenty-first century, the sit-in movement seems almost naive in its embrace of American ideals.

Yet an analysis of the sit-in movement from the perspective of southern college campuses underscores the radicalism of both the technique of nonviolent direct action and the movement it helped to generate. Those unsettled by the activism of black students included not only segregationist whites but also moderate whites and conservative African Americans. For conservative blacks, especially those at the helm of vulnerable colleges and universities, the movement threatened to undermine the fragile power they had so carefully cultivated and maintained. Presidents such as Southern University's Felton Grandison Clark, acting at the behest of segregationist politicians and white-controlled state boards, clamped down, especially in public institutions of the Deep South, where the sit-in movement struggled to achieve victories and where academic freedom suffered the most. But opposition on black campuses was not simply about preserving fiefdoms or about buckling under pressure from white politicians. Some black faculty members and administrators believed that nonviolent direct action distracted students from what should have been their primary agenda—getting an education. These elders saw activism and education as incompatible.

Despite such resistance, however, the sit-in movement won widespread participation on many historically black college campuses, especially in the Upper South and in larger cities in the Deep South. Participation often crossed campus subcultural dividing lines, encompassing not only students who might fit comfortably in the category of campus rebels but also outsiders and mainstream campus leaders. For some schools, the movement took on the appearance of a semi-sanctioned activity, earning glowing reports in alumni publications and support in the black community. Indeed, such support was a crucial determinant of the ultimate success or failure to end segregated public facilities. This dynamic was not permanent; by 1962, the mass phase of the sit-in movement was over. Pockets of activity continued to operate in and around black campuses, and black students continued to participate in challenges to segregation and disfranchisement. But much of the movement's early leadership had left the campus, either graduating or moving into the ranks of full-time activists in organizations such as the Student Nonviolent Coordinating Committee and the Congress of Racial Equality. And while those two organizations never completely lost sight of college students and campuses, their focus shifted to voter registration and community organizing, especially in the rural Deep South. Moreover, the philosophy and practice of nonviolent direct action was losing its hold on the imaginations of activists. Finally, especially after the rejection of the full Mississippi Freedom Democratic Party delegation at the Democratic National Convention in August 1964, white liberals' motives and dependability increasingly came into question.

This transition toward what would eventually be called Black Power occurred just as a small but significant number of southern white students were becoming active. The delay resulted from predominantly white campuses' reaction to nonviolent direct action. White liberal gradualists who sought an orderly and measured process toward a desegregated South found the sit-in movement difficult to process. They often viewed the movement against the backdrop of desegregation crises — Autherine Lucy's thwarted effort to desegregate the University of Alabama, the integration of Central High School in Little Rock. Those episodes seemed to convey the message that order was central to racial progress. Indeed, at the University of Alabama, taking a stand in favor abiding by the law was a relatively safe but coded way to support integration. But the sit-in movement forced southern liberal gradualists to reconsider the meaning of order, and in the earliest days of the movement, participation by white southern students was rare. Participants often came from or found support from campus religious organizations. Secular campus organizations, such as the University of North Carolina's chapter of the Student Peace Union, which mounted a nonviolent campaign against segregated restaurants in the early 1960s, were relatively rare. In any event, the white students who were willing to put their bodies on the line for integration tended to be campus rebels or outsiders. And if they were not on the outside when they started, their activism quickly put them there.

By 1963 and 1964, pockets of white student activism, primarily targeting segregation, were developing, not coincidentally, in the same places that had served as the most effective incubators of the sit-in movement in the spring of 1960. This development that gave rise to the Southern Student Organizing Committee (ssoc). ssoc represented a milestone in that its formation indicated that the number of white students willing to challenge racial discrimination had reached a critical mass.

Thus, race structured the student movement that unfolded from the sit-in movement. Ironically, though activists set out to dismantle segregation, the development of the southern student movement underlined the continuing existence of the color line. This is not to say that activism in the South was completely segregated. The idea of interracialism held a great deal of power, as the integrated programs organized by the U.S. National Student Association's Southern Project demonstrated. Nevertheless, activism among black and white students largely developed along separate but parallel lines. The two groups followed similar processes centered on the incorporation of nonviolent direct action, but the timing differed.

The parallel lines continued during the second half of the 1960s, even as levels of white student activism began to approach those of black students and as Black Power became a rallying cry for African American students. Though the issues that students addressed were often similar — lessened restrictions on nonacademic life, more student participation in the campus decision-making process, more relevant courses — Black Power cast a very different tone on those issues. Both black and white students felt a sense of generational liberation, but in the context of Black Power, rebellion against repressive campus regulations became associated with racial liberation. At the same time, black student activism on predominantly white campuses focused on changing recently desegregated institutions to allow black students to succeed while still embracing their racial identities. White activists' agendas often incorporated black students' goals, effectively creating a pluralist interpretation of Black Power. White students would organize the white community while fighting for the liberation of African Americans. But the interracialism that so animated early white converts to activism was partially set aside.

Many black students recognized that any kind of integration that accepted formerly all-white campuses as they were at the time of the first matriculation of African American students was integration from inequality. These institutions were created as *white* institutions, and even after African American students began to gather in dozens rather than twos and threes, little cultural space was available in which black students could develop on their own terms. Demonstrations inspired by Black Power pointed out the whiteness of newly desegregated campuses. At the most basic level, these demonstrations raised awareness, but they also prompted administrators and faculty members to reconsider course offerings and social space. The results included academic and nonacademic changes. In the popular imagination, Black Power has often borne connotations of violence and separatism; on predominantly white campuses, however, violence was minimal. And while black students on predominantly white campuses tapped into currents that called for African Americans to control their own institutions and lives, what emerged was pluralistic, not separatist. The new vision featured a restructured campus in which African Americans could participate without surrendering their racial identities.

By the mid-1970s, African American students appeared to be entering the mainstream of campus life on predominantly white campuses, though the evidence of racial progress at times rested side by side with evidence of limitations. At the University of Alabama, African American Cleophus Thomas was elected student body president in 1976. But more than thirty years later, no other black student had won the office. In 1983, the University of Mississippi discontinued the practice of distributing Confederate battle flags at football games after John Hawkins, a cheerleader and president of the Black Student Union, refused to wave the flag. The group also demanded an increase in the number of black faculty and administrators, a black studies program, and the hiring of a black affirmative action officer, but the symbols received the largest amount of attention, both on and off campus. As late as 1998, associations with the university's racist past continued to hamper President Robert Khayat's effort to raise the university's national academic profile.[38]

On many campuses, some institutions within the university community — notably the Greek societies — continued to resist change. Most southern fraternities and sororities remained completely segregated in the late 1990s, and they still exerted a significant amount of power. Moreover, black students had become ambivalent at best about the need to challenge such institutions.[39] On a broader scale, integration seemed to have stalled, thanks to a combination of "political fatigue, court rulings, and admissions and financial-aid policies." A 1998 study by the Southern Education Foundation found that in the nineteen states that formerly operated dual systems of higher education, historically black colleges remained overwhelmingly black, while whites dominated flagship state institutions in numbers disproportionate to their share of the population.[40]

Moreover, historically black colleges often struggled financially, and student activism declined on these campuses as elsewhere. By the mid-1980s, observers worried that black institutions, plagued with financial problems and competing with better-funded predominantly white institutions, would not survive. Fisk University, for years a giant in African American education, provided the prism through which many viewed the problems. Student enrollments at the Nashville university sagged, and President Walter Leonard frequently found himself asking benefactors for donations to pay employees. At the same time, Leonard's management style, which political scientist Manning Marable likened to the traditional autocratic black college president, angered faculty members and some students. According to Marable, a central problem at Fisk, as at all black colleges, was "the historic failure of these institutions to articulate a clear pedagogy and practice of liberation." In other words, the Black Power movement had failed to achieve its central educational goal. In fact, Marable noted that although a few "Black Power era" scholars had won presidential appointments at black colleges, "the vast majority of black administrators are dominated by the corporate world, and have little if any sympathy for black studies and the radical pedagogical departures which gave birth to a new generation of black scholarship in the 1960s and early 1970s."[41]

The problems at public black colleges continued into the 1990s. Short on resources, these institutions had always had to do more with less. But desegregation provided alternatives for black students with better academic preparation and capabilities. Critics charged that financial mismanagement often lay at the core of the problems; defenders of the institutions complained that public financing of public black institutions remained low. "Almost every state with a public black college has a public black college in trouble," a reporter for the *Chronicle of Higher Education* noted in 1996.[42]

However, some private black institutions experienced something of a resurgence during the late 1980s and 1990s. One factor appeared to be cost: tuition at private black schools ran about half the tuition at their predominantly white counterparts. But at least as important was a growing sense among black students that historically black colleges provided a more nurturing atmosphere.[43] In 1999, when *Black Enterprise* magazine published a list of the best fifty colleges for African Americans, half, including the top nine, were historically black institutions. The magazine published the list "to help African American parents and students make the most enlightened choices about where to attend college and identify where students are most likely to be successful." The rankings were computed by weighing, among other factors, academic reputation among black educators and success in graduating black students.[44]

The resurgence of private black colleges came as racial tensions resurfaced on predominantly white campuses. The reconsideration of black schools thus may have constituted part of a larger tendency to look back nostalgically at black institutions of the segregation era.[45] To some extent, the resurgence of black institutions, accompanied by a sense of black consciousness and pride, also testified to the successes of Black Power in the cultural if not political sphere. But the goal of black liberation had become intermingled with the goals of individual achievement and especially career advancement.

Politics, Culture, and the Americanization of the Campus

The 1960s southern student movement thus had mixed outcomes. Activist students helped nudge southern schools toward acceptance at some level of what historian Roger Geiger terms the "ideology of egalitarianism and social justice" that increasingly dominated American higher education.[46] Given the state of southern higher education at the end of the 1950s, this was no small feat. But the institutions that emerged were not so much instruments of liberation as mirrors of American pluralism.

More precisely, southern universities nurtured the kinds of individualism that defined American culture at the close of the twentieth century. Meritocratic individualism — the idea that people should be able to rise or fall according to their abilities — had provided ammunition for the assault on southern segregation. Subsequent movements encouraged an expressive individualism that sought personal liberation from constraints and societal limits.[47] As the 1960s concluded, both forms of individualism continued to exist and even thrive on southern campuses at the same time that the organized mobilization of students declined. Concurrent legal trends — specifically, the end of in loco parentis as a viable legal idea — buttressed a tendency toward a new version of student life in which students were free agents outside the classroom. But activists who envisioned students using this freedom to explore intellectual or political interests were disappointed. When combined with the economic downturn of the late 1960s and 1970s, these forces took the culture of the campus in a direction that activists never intended. A weak job market for college graduates combined with expanding access to a college education meant that students who wanted to find good jobs or attend graduate or professional schools needed high grades. Such an environment left little room for activism. Indeed, these forces created a dominant campus culture of grim professionalism. The outsiders, who viewed college primarily as an avenue of upward mobility, now dominated. In the words of historian Helen Lefkowitz Horowitz, the nerds took revenge.[48]

By the 1980s, critics on the left commonly complained that the vast majority of students were either politically conservative or focused on obtaining a college degree that would serve as a union card for the white-collar workforce. Campus culture seemed to mirror political culture, emphasizing individual material accumulation over concerns about collective social health. Moreover, in an ironic twist, the South now seemed to set the nation's political tone. The ascendant Republican Party, building on Richard Nixon's "southern strategy," tailored a message to appeal to white southerners disaffected by social movements. In a move laden with symbolism, Ronald Reagan kicked off his 1980 presidential campaign in Neshoba County, Mississippi, where three civil rights workers had been murdered sixteen years earlier. In a country shifting politically to the right, the South now seemed to fit within national norms. Or perhaps the nation had become southern.[49]

When commentators pondered the decline in activism among college students, they rarely differentiated between southern campuses and those outside the region. The salient difference was not so much between southern and northern students as between students of the 1960s and students of the 1980s. To be sure, southern students, like southern Americans, still grappled with the meaning of southern identity. And when they clashed over symbols — the display of Confederate flags at campus functions, for example, or the playing of "Dixie" at football games — the region's history of segregation and racial discrimination was never far from the surface.[50] Even when such polarizing symbols did not lie at the center of debate, the continuing vestiges of the South's history of racial discrimination seemed imposing. Writing for a 1989 *New York Times* opinion section devoted to race relations on campus, an undergraduate student at the University of Georgia noted that despite the obvious signs of progress nearly thirty years after Charlayne Hunter and Hamilton Holmes had broken segregation at that institution, tensions continued to exist "at the personal level, where we live and work together every day." Transcending the past, the writer suggested, indeed represented a formidable task. "The most difficult part of integration — creating, day to day, an environment of understanding — is just beginning," he concluded. However, the *New York Times* also included columns by students at the University of Michigan and Stanford University who detailed similar challenges.[51]

As some observers perceived a revival in student activism in the last half of the 1990s, southern schools played a part. In the progressive magazine *Mother Jones*'s 1998 annual survey of the nation's "top ten activist schools," for example, five — Duke University, Spelman College, the University of Texas, James Madison University, and the University of North Carolina — were located in the South. The rankings were more anecdotal than scientific. Nevertheless, just as southern higher education had to a large extent entered the national mainstream in terms of institutional quality, the region's students no longer seemed uniformly less — or, for that matter, more — politicized than students in other parts of the country.[52]

The normalization of both southern political culture and campus political culture revealed the successes and limitations of 1960s student activism. Southern student activists' most substantial achievements had been their successes in challenging segregation and in opening up the region's campuses to dissent. But southern higher education still faced problems. The difference was, however, that they were now largely the same problems that faced the entire nation.

NOTES

INTRODUCTION

1. O'Bannon, interview; "The Aggressive Moderates," *Time*, 2 June 1970, 81.

2. "The Aggressive Moderates."

3. An important exception is Michel, *Struggle for a Better South*, which examines white student activism in the South through the prism of an organization. Important studies of the civil rights organizations that reveal the involvement of students include Carson, *In Struggle*; Meier and Rudwick, *CORE*. Arsenault, *Freedom Riders*, is an outstanding examination of the primarily CORE-led Freedom Rides of 1961. And Hogan, *Many Minds, One Heart*, offers a fresh examination of SNCC. Key state-level studies include Dittmer, *Local People*, on Mississippi; Fairclough, *Race and Democracy*, on Louisiana; Tuck, *Beyond Atlanta*, on Georgia. Important local studies are Norrell, *Reaping the Whirlwind*, on Tuskegee, Alabama; Chafe, *Civilities and Civil Rights*, on Greensboro, North Carolina; Eskew, *But for Birmingham*, on the Birmingham, Alabama, movement.

4. Breines, "Whose New Left?" See also Rossinow, *Politics of Authenticity*, 8–9.

Important studies of New Left leadership at the national level include Sale, *SDS*; Unger, *Movement*; relevant chapters of Matusow, *Unraveling of America*; Miller, *Democracy Is in the Streets*; Gitlin, *Sixties*; Breines, *Community and Organization*; Isserman and Kazin, "Failure and Success"; Isserman and Kazin, *America Divided*; Barber, *Hard Rain Fell*.

Local studies include Rorabaugh, *Berkeley at War*; Heineman, *Campus Wars*, which analyzes the antiwar movement at four midwestern state universities; Rossinow, *Politics of Authenticity*; Billingsley, *Communists on Campus*, which devotes significant attention to the campus left at the University of North Carolina; Monhollon, *This Is America?*; Wynkoop, *Dissent in the Heartland*.

To suggest, however, that national studies comprised the entirety of the body of scholarship on the New Left until recently would be misleading. In fact, the earliest studies of 1960s student activism were often studies of a handful of prestigious institutions, with Berkeley and Columbia dominating. Scholars who spent time at the University of California at Berkeley during the 1960s represented an important subset of the first wave of activism studies. For a list of Berkeley-connected studies, see Julian Foster, "Student Protest: What Is Known, What Is Said," in *Protest!*, ed. Foster and Long, 28–29.

5. The starting point for analyzing the South since World War II is Bartley, *New South*. On broader economic trends, see Cobb, *Selling of the South*; Schulman, *From Cotton Belt to Sunbelt*. A vast literature exists on the question of regional identity in the modern South. For one relatively recent assessment of southern identity, see Cobb, "Epitaph."

6. An exception can be seen in Williamson, *Black Power on Campus* and *Radicalizing the Ebony Tower*.

7. Van Deburg makes this argument in *New Day in Babylon*, but the nature of his topic prevents him from exploring the idea.

8. On Austin, see Rossinow, *Politics of Authenticity*; on Chapel Hill, see Billingsley, *Communists on Campus*. Historians of the New Right have launched their own challenge to the conventional understandings of the 1960s. Klatch, *Generation Divided*, argues that the emergence of the New Right, in the form of Young Americans for Freedom, constitutes an "untold story"—and an important one, as a number of the group's leaders went on to play key roles in the conservative backlash of the 1970s and 1980s. On Young Americans for Freedom, see also Andrew, *Other Side of the Sixties*. I have chosen not to widen this study to include an analysis of conservative organizations on southern campuses and instead have focused on left-liberal or progressive activists and groups. Historians await a good study of conservative student mobilization on southern college campuses in the 1960s. However, the nature of southern campus political culture meant that progressive students found themselves challenged by and engaged in an ongoing debate with conservative students. Thus, conservative voices can be heard in this study.

9. *Southern Patriot*, January 1966, 1.

10. *Wheel*, 21 September 1967, 5.

11. See, for example, Isserman and Kazin, *America Divided*, where the only extended discussion of any southern university concerns the Wallace incident (90–91).

12. Schrag, "New Beat," 42.

13. Durwood Long and Julian Foster, "Levels of Protest," in *Protest!*, ed. Foster and Long, 81–88. In 1967, all but 8 of the nation's 112 predominantly black institutions were in fifteen southern and border states extending from Texas and Oklahoma to Maryland (Robert F. Campbell, "Negro Colleges Have a Job," 2).

14. For accounts of late-1960s protest movements on black campuses, see Bass and Nelson, *Orangeburg Massacre*; Spofford, *Lynch Street*. See also Williamson, *Radicalizing the Ebony Tower*.

15. Cash, *Mind of the South*, 90–91.

16. Dyer, "Higher Education," has suggested that "southern colleges and universities appear to have confronted fewer crises over the freedom to teach and inquire than did those in other parts of the nation" in the twentieth century (134). Nevertheless, Dyer provides a brief but telling list of conflicts over academic freedom and efforts to limit dissenters on college and university campuses.

17. On the growing ties between the federal government and southern higher education and southern institutions' early moves from the periphery to the center of national life, see Mohr, "World War II and the Transformation."

CHAPTER ONE. *Southern Campuses in 1960*

1. Lott, *Herding Cats*, 24–25, 41–42. Lott describes his undergraduate days in chapter 2, "The Legacy of Ole Miss."

2. Lewis with D'Orso, *Walking with the Wind*, 69–70.

3. Ibid., 71.

4. Kerr, *Uses of the University*, 66.

5. Mohr, "World War II and the Transformation," 33–55.

6. Ibid., 48–49.

7. Roger Geiger, editor's introduction, *History of Higher Education Annual* 19 (1999): 13.

8. *New York Times*, 23 December 1947, 17.

9. Kousser, "Progressivism"; James D. Anderson, *Education of Blacks*, esp. chapter 7, "Training the Apostles of Liberal Culture: Black Higher Education, 1900–1935"; Wolters, *New Negro on Campus*, 3–15; Geiger, editor's introduction, 13–15; Logan, *Negro in American Life and Thought*.

10. Wolters, *New Negro on Campus*, 3–15.

11. Ibid., 65–69.

12. Other protests occurred at Howard University in Washington, D.C., Hampton Institute in Virginia, Florida A&M, Morehouse College in Georgia, Storer College in West Virginia, Livingstone College in North Carolina, Lincoln Institute in Kentucky, Knoxville College in Tennessee, Johnson C. Smith University in North Carolina, St. Augustine Junior College in North Carolina, Alcorn A&M in Mississippi, North Carolina A&T; and Shaw University in North Carolina (Wolters, *New Negro on Campus*, 276–77).

13. Ibid., 278.

14. Moody, *Coming of Age in Mississippi*, 218–19, 241–42, 245–47.

15. Bartley, *New South*, chapter 8, "God and Society in the Modernizing South."

16. "The Younger Generation," *Time*, 5 November 1951, 46, 52.

17. Horowitz, *Campus Life*. Similarly, sociologists Clark and Trow posited the existence of four student subcultures: "academic," "collegiate," "vocational," and "non-conformist" ("Determinants of College Student Subcultures").

18. *Hustler*, 18 February 1955, 4.

19. Ibid., 25 February 1955, 4.

20. Ibid.; Patricia Foster, *All the Lost Girls*, 218–19; Conkin, *Gone with the Ivy*, 529.

21. Horowitz, *Campus Life*, 220–21.

22. Ibid., 11–13, 119, 144 (quotation).

23. Trillin, *Education in Georgia*, 73–74.

24. Willie Morris, *North toward Home*, 168, 170–71.

25. *Fisk News*, Winter 1960, 7.

26. James D. Anderson, *Education of Blacks*, 276; Frazier, *Black Bourgeoisie*, 24, 78–85.

27. Meier, *White Scholar*, 88–98.

28. Ellison, *The Invisible Man*, 115–50.

29. *Forum*, 29 January 1957, 2.

30. Egerton, *Speak Now against the Day*, 285–86.

31. Norrell, *Reaping the Whirlwind*.

32. Mohr, "World War II and the Transformation," 43–45 (see n.35 for enrollment ranges); McCandless, *Past in the Present*, 127.

33. Carol Roberts, "UGA Lib Began with '68 march," *Red and Black*, 3 December 1971, 1, 6.

34. Carmer, *Stars Fell on Alabama*, 14–15; Cash, *Mind of the South*, 332–33.

35. During the 1968–69 academic year, the *Crimson White* replaced the "Bama Belle" with "The Beautiful People," which featured photos of men as well as women.

36. Boroff, *Campus U.S.A.*, 123–24; McCandless, *Past in the Present*, 219.

37. *Richmond Collegian*, 26 April 1957, 1.

38. Zinn, *Southern Mystique*, 115, 118.

39. Walker, *Meridian*, 95.

40. Solomon, *In the Company of Educated Women*, 186–98.

41. Dorothy Dawson Burlage, "Truths of the Heart," in Curry et al., *Deep in Our Hearts*, 97.

42. Ibid., 87–130, esp. 94–99.

43. Joan C. Browning, "Shiloh Witness," in ibid., 39–83, esp. 56–63.

44. Bartley, *New South*, 270–73, 290–94; Rossinow, *Politics of Authenticity*, 53–54.

45. *Richmond Collegian*, 4 February 1955, 1 (first quotation); 11 February 1955, 1 (second quotation).

46. *Hustler*, 21 January 1955, 1, 6.

47. Daniel, *Lost Revolutions*, 267–70.

48. Will D. Campbell, *Brother to a Dragonfly*, 112–30.

49. *Hustler*, 24 February 1956, 1.

50. Dyer, *University of Georgia*, 225–40.

51. Another episode that pitted state officials against dissenting students at the University of Georgia occurred in 1953, when editors at the *Red and Black* criticized the efforts to prevent an African American, Horace Ward, from entering the law school. The editorials attracted the attention of Roy V. Harris, a segregationist member of the board of regents, and eventually prompted the Georgia legislature to debate a resolution to force the editors to resign. Seeking to quell the disturbance, university officials instituted new controls on the content of the student newspaper, and four editors resigned in protest. By that time, the controversy had won national attention. See Pratt, *We Shall Not Be Moved*, 30–41.

52. Horowitz, *Campus Life*, 168–72.

53. Schrecker, *Age of McCarthyism*, 82–84. Schrecker, *No Ivory Tower*, provides a detailed account of the impact of anticommunism on American colleges and universities.

54. Heale, *McCarthy's Americans*, 217. See also Woods, *Black Struggle, Red Scare*.

55. Billingsley, *Communists on Campus*.

56. J. Angus Johnston, "Student Activism in the United States before 1960: An Overview," in *Student Protest*, ed. DeGroot, 12–26; for the founding of the NSA, see 22–23. See also Constance Curry, "Wild Geese to the Past," in Curry et al., *Deep in Our Hearts*, 3–35 (for Curry's extensive involvement in the 1950s and 1960s, see 7–25); Rossinow, *Politics of Authenticity*, 43. Johnston, "United States National Student Association," chronicles the history of the organization from its founding to 1978.

57. Harry H. Lunn Jr. to Constance Curry, 8 March 1955, U.S. Student Association Records, Box 68, Wisconsin Historical Society.

58. Ibid.

59. Ibid.

60. Eli Evans, *Provincials*, 177.

61. Ibid., 178–79.

62. Ibid., 180–84.

63. On UNC's liberalism in the 1950s and 1960s, see Billingsley, *Communists on Campus*. Billingsley's study, like Chafe, *Civilities and Civil Rights*, emphasizes the limitations of North Carolina liberalism in responding to the politics of the 1960s. In his contribution to a collection of essays on the Berkeley Free Speech Movement, Henry Mayer, who was an undergraduate student at UNC before attending graduate school at Berkeley, suggests that UNC had a history of greater freedom but lost ground during the 1960s as a result of the "Speaker Ban" controversy. Conversely, Berkeley could not claim a history of support for free speech but gained ground in the aftermath of the Free Speech Movement ("A View from the South," in *The Free Speech Movement: Reflections on Berkeley in the 1960s*, ed. Cohen and Zelnik, 167).

64. Eli Evans, *Provincials*, 177–78.

65. Wiggins, *Desegregation Era*, 6.

66. Ibid., 6; Bartley, *New South*, 155–56.

67. Weisbrot, *Freedom Bound*, 11–13 (quotation on 13).

68. Newberry, "Without Urgency or Ardor," 500–501; Sosna, *In Search of the Silent South*, 205–6; Bartley, *New South*, 28–30.

69. "Justice for All"; Michael G. Wade, "Four Who Would: *Constantine v. Southwestern Louisiana Institute* (1954) and the Desegregation of Louisiana's State Colleges," in *Higher Education and the Civil Rights Movement*, ed. Wallenstein, 60–91.

70. Kean, "'At a Most Uncomfortable Speed'"; Mohr and Gordon, *Tulane*, 131–54. On desegregation at Vanderbilt, see Conkin, *Gone with the Ivy*, chapter 19.

71. E. Culpepper Clark, *Schoolhouse Door*, 1–113. See also Synnott, "Federalism Vindicated," 298.

72. For a survey of the process of desegregation throughout the South, see Wallenstein, "Black Southerners and Non-Black Universities" (revised as "Black Southerners and Nonblack Universities: The Process of Desegregating Southern Higher Education, 1935–1965," in *Higher Education and the Civil Rights Movement*, ed. Wallenstein, 17–59).

73. Clark, *Schoolhouse Door*, 84; for student participation in and reaction to the riots, see 62–68, 71–84, esp. 83–84.

74. Ibid., 83.

CHAPTER TWO. *Nonviolent Direct Action and the Rise of a Southern Student Movement*

1. Nash, interview.

2. Long, interview.

3. Nash, interview.

4. Meier and Rudwick, *CORE*, 3–97; Arsenault, *Freedom Riders*, 11–92; Laue, "Direct Action and Desegregation," 63–71; Oppenheimer, "Sit-In Movement," 26–36.

5. Franklin McCain, interview by Jim Schlosser, December 1997, excerpt,

"Greensboro Sit-Ins: Launch of a Civil Rights Movement," http://www.sitins.com/ (accessed 12 August 2005).

6. *New York Times*, 26 March 1960, 10.

7. Fellowship of Reconciliation, *Martin Luther King and the Montgomery Story*, http://www.ep.tc/mlk/ (accessed 2 July 2007).

8. *New York Times*, 15 February 1960, 1. For a brief description of the Greensboro sit-ins, see Sitkoff, *Struggle for Black Equality*, 61–64. For more detailed discussions, see Chafe, *Civilities and Civil Rights*; Wolff, *Lunch at the 5&10*.

9. *New York Times*, 3 February 1960, 22.

10. Ibid., 9 February 1960, 16.

11. Ibid., 15 February 1960, 1.

12. Southern Regional Council, "The Student Protest Movement: A Recapitulation," September 1961, Zellner Papers, Box 1, Wisconsin Historical Society. For a chronological list of the first wave of sit-ins and related demonstrations, see Laue, "Direct Action and Desegregation," 329–34; see also 76–77.

13. Martin Luther King Jr., "The Time for Freedom Has Come," *New York Times Magazine*, 10 September 1961, 25.

14. Southern Regional Council, "Student Protest Movement."

15. *New York Times*, 26 March 1960, 10.

16. Matthews and Prothro, *Negroes and the New Southern Politics*, 416–24. Zinn, *SNCC*, 26; Sellers, with Terrell, *River of No Return*, 19. Matthews and Prothro draw their conclusions from interviews conducted in early 1962 with 264 students at thirty institutions throughout the region; see 496–97 for an explanation of the data collection procedures.

17. For discussions of the factors in the spread of sit-in activities in 1960, see Oppenheimer, "Sit-In Movement," 19–36; Laue, "Direct Action and Desegregation," 75–83; Carson, *In Struggle*, 11–18; Charles U. Smith, *Student Unrest*, xi–xx.

18. Bond, interview.

19. Aldon D. Morris, *Origins of the Civil Rights Movement*, 188–228.

20. "Minutes of the Meeting of the SNCC Executive Committee, December 27–31, 1963," Highlander Folk School Manuscript Collection, microfilm, Reel 38, Amistad Research Center, Tulane University, New Orleans.

21. Orbell, "Protest Participation." Orbell based the majority of his conclusions on data gathered by Matthews and Prothro for *Negroes and the New Southern Politics*.

22. Williamson, *Radicalizing the Ebony Tower*, 3–4.

23. Oppenheimer, "Sit-In Movement," 98.

24. *Crimson White*, 18 June 1964, 11, 25 March 1965; *New York Times*, 10, 13 June 1964; on Rogers, Hester B. Rogers, "The Reverend T. Y. Rogers, Jr.: His Life and Work," unpublished manuscript in the possession of E. Culpepper Clark; Wendt, "God, Gandhi, and Guns."

25. Lewis with D'Orso, *Walking with the Wind*, chapter 5.

26. Halberstam, *Children*, 11–17.

27. Ibid., 2–24, 40–50, 60–63; Lewis with D'Orso, *Walking with the Wind*, 91–92.

28. Halberstam, *Children*, 176.

29. Ibid., 64–65.

30. Ibid., 105; Lewis with D'Orso, *Walking with the Wind*, 80 (quotation).

31. On the philosophy of nonviolent action and Gandhi's contribution to its development, see Sharp, *Politics of Nonviolent Action*, 7–16, 82–87.

32. Lewis with D'Orso, *Walking with the Wind*, 86, 93, 87.

33. Ibid., 91, 107.

34. *Nashville Tennessean*, 14 February 1960, 10-A, 19 February 1960, 4, 21 February 1960, 2-A.

35. *New York Times*, 24 February 1960, 28.

36. *Nashville Tennessean*, 28 February 1960, 1, 6.

37. Ibid., 6 (quotation); Lewis with D'Orso, *Walking with the Wind*, 93.

38. *Nashville Tennessean*, 29 February 1960, 1, 2.

39. Lewis with D'Orso, *Walking with the Wind*, 109; *Fisk University Forum*, 24 March 1960, 2 (quotation); *Fisk News*, Spring 1960, 16–18.

40. Lewis with D'Orso, *Walking with the Wind*, 185.

41. Hogan, *Many Minds, One Heart*, 53.

42. Carson, *In Struggle*, 23.

43. "Statement of Purpose," SNCC Papers (microfilm), Reel 1, reprinted in Carson, *SNCC*, 23–24.

44. Tuck, *Beyond Atlanta*, 54–66, 120–21.

45. On the Atlanta student movement, see Garrow, *Atlanta, Georgia*; Zinn, *Southern Mystique*; Zinn, *SNCC*; Fleming, *Soon We Will Not Cry*; Tuck, *Beyond Atlanta*, 107–27.

46. On Atlanta University, see Bacote, *Story of Atlanta University*; on Spelman, see Read, *Story of Spelman College*, and Manley, *Legacy Continues*; on Morehouse, see Edward Allen Jones, *Candle in the Dark*, Rovaris, *Mays and Morehouse*, and Mays, *Born to Rebel*; on Clark, see Brawley, *Clark College Legacy*; on Morris Brown, see Sewell and Troop, *Morris Brown College*.

47. *Atlanta Journal-Constitution*, 13 March 1960, 11B.

48. Mays, interview.

49. Bond, interview; King, interview.

50. Zinn, *Southern Mystique*, 118.

51. Fleming, *Soon We Will Not Cry*, 48, 50.

52. Bond, interview.

53. Zinn, *Southern Mystique*, 115–17; Howard Zinn, "A Quiet Case of Social Change," typescript, Zinn Papers, Box 3, Wisconsin Historical Society.

54. Zinn, *SNCC*, 232; Fort, "Atlanta Sit-In Movement," 164.

55. Brawley, interview.

56. Mays, interview.

57. Hornsby, interview.

58. Herschelle Sullivan to Howard Zinn, 13 April 1961, Zinn Papers, Box 3, Folder 7.

59. Bond, interview.

60. Notes on workshop sessions can be found in SNCC Papers (microfilm), Reel 1.

61. Carson, *In Struggle*, 31.

62. Ibid., 31–55.

63. Meier and Rudwick, *CORE*, 101–21.

64. On the idea of free space, see Sara M. Evans and Boyte, *Free Spaces*.

65. Willa B. Player, interview by the Greensboro Public Library, 3 December 1979, "Greensboro Sit-Ins: Launch of a Civil Rights Movement," http://www.sitins.com/multimedia.shtml (accessed 19 September 2008).

66. Chafe, *Civilities and Civil Rights*, 98–116, 83–84, 133.

67. Wolff, *Lunch at the 5&10*, 166.

68. Chafe, *Civilities and Civil Rights*, 110–13, 122–25.

69. Ibid., 127.

70. Ibid., 126–28.

71. Fairclough, *Race and Democracy*, 284.

72. Kim Lacy Rogers, *Righteous Lives*, 23–24.

73. Harry Lunn Jr. to Constance Curry, 8 March 1955, U.S. Student Association Records, Box 68, Wisconsin Historical Society.

74. R. Bentley Anderson, *Black, White, and Catholic*.

75. Fairclough, *Race and Democracy*, 219, 271.

76. Ibid., 271–84; Kim Lacy Rogers, *Righteous Lives*, 67–70; Lombard, interview.

77. Jerah Johnson, *UNO Prisms*, 111; Cassimere, interview by author.

78. Cassimere, interview by author; Jerah Johnson, *UNO Prisms*, 112–13.

79. Fairclough, *Race and Democracy*, 276–80, 295–96; Haley, interview.

80. Haley, interview.

81. Meier and Rudwick, *CORE*, 116, 169.

82. Hine, "Civil Rights and Campus Wrongs," 310–20.

83. Ibid.

84. Ibid., 320–25; Oppenheimer, "Sit-In Movement," 168–73.

85. U.S. National Student Association, "A Survey of the Southern Student Sit-In Movement and National Student Activity," 10–12, in U.S. Student Association Records, Box 105. See also Bromley and McCabe, "Impact of the 'Sit-In' Movement"; Branch, *Parting the Waters*, 280–84.

86. *St. John Dixon et al. v. Alabama State Board of Education et al.*, U.S. Court of Appeals, Fifth District, 294 F.2d 150; 1961 U.S. App.

87. Oppenheimer, "Sit-In Movement," 165.

88. Ibid., 157–62; Rabby, *Pain and the Promise*, chapter 5.

89. Fairclough, *Race and Democracy*, 265–71; Lomax, *Negro Revolt*, 209 (quotation).

90. Adolph L. Reed to Felton G. Clark, 24 January 1962, CORE Papers (microfilm), Reel 40. See also Adolph Reed, "Crisis on the Negro Campus," *The Nation*, 10 February 1962, 111–13, which contains the same passage.

91. Bromley and McCabe, "Impact of the 'Sit-In' Movement," 66–67; Fairclough, *Race and Democracy*, 265, 267–69.

92. Adolph L. Reed to Felton G. Clark, 24 January 1962, CORE Papers (microfilm), Reel 40.

93. Reed, "Crisis on the Negro Campus," 112.

94. D'Army Bailey to Julian Bond, 4 August 1962, SNCC Papers (microfilm), Reel 5; Fairclough, *Race and Democracy*, 289–91; David Dennis to Fredricka Teer, 24 February 1962, CORE Papers (microfilm), Reel 22.

95. Zellner with Curry, *Wrong Side of Murder Creek*, chapter 12; Fairclough, *Race and Democracy*, 291.

96. *Southern Patriot*, September 1962, 4.

97. Moody, *Coming of Age in Mississippi*, 239, 246.

98. Clarice T. Campbell and Rogers, *Mississippi*, 198–201.

99. *Southern Patriot*, November 1961, 1–2; Clarice T. Campbell and Rogers, *Mississippi*, 201–3.

100. Clarice T. Campbell and Rogers, *Mississippi*, 212–17. On Beittel's resignation, see Williamson, "'This Has Been Quite a Year.'"

101. Moody, *Coming of Age in Mississippi*, 273, 277.

102. Maxine D. Jones and Richardson, *Talladega College*, 175.

103. Ibid., 176–78.

104. Ibid., 179–80; *Student Voice*, April 1962.

105. Maxine D. Jones and Richardson, *Talladega College*, 180–81.

106. Ibid., 181–82.

107. Ibid., 185–87.

108. News Release, 4 October 1962, SNCC Papers (microfilm), Reel 18 (quotation); Zellner with Curry, *Wrong Side of Murder Creek*, 216.

109. Martin Luther King Jr., "Time for Freedom Has Come," 25.

110. Halberstam, *Children*, 268–69.

111. Minutes of Staff Meeting, 6 March 1962, SNCC Papers (microfilm), Reel 3.

112. "Proposed Educational Program for Full-Time Civil Rights Workers in the South," n.d., SNCC Papers (microfilm), Reel 11.

113. Zinn, *SNCC*, 236.

CHAPTER THREE. *White Students, the Campus, and Desegregation*

1. Raines, *My Soul Is Rested*, 107.

2. Woodward, "Unreported Crisis," 89.

3. Ibid.

4. Ibid., 82–83.

5. Silver, *Mississippi*, 107–9. See also Sansing, *Making Haste Slowly*; Cohodas, *Band Played Dixie*.

6. *Hustler*, 12 January 1962, 4.

7. The regulation stated, "It shall be the duty of every student to discourage disorderly assemblage in large groups on or off the campus. . . . Students found at the scene of a riot or in an unruly mob shall be subject to immediate expulsion from the University whether or not they are active participants" (Ibid., 4 March 1960, 1, 2).

8. Ibid., 4.

9. Ibid., 11 March 1960, 1, 4.

10. Ibid., 29 April 1960, 4.

11. Ibid., 23 September 1960, 1, 6.

12. Ibid., 14 October 1960, 4.

13. Ibid., 17 February 1961, 1; 24 February 1961, 1; 3 March 1961, 1, 3.

14. Ibid., 9 February 1962, 1, 10; 16 February 1962, 1.

15. Ibid., 20 April 1962, 4.

16. Ibid., 11 May 1962, 4.

17. Ibid., 30 November 1962, 1; 4 January 1963, 1, 2; 14 December 1962, 1; 17 May 1963, 2; 11 January 1963, 4, 10.

18. Ibid., 17 May 1963, 3; 18 October 1963, 1. I have not been able to determine what, if anything, the apparent acronym PROD stood for.

19. Ibid., 1 November 1963, 1; 8 November 1963, 4.

20. Lukas, *Don't Shoot*, 153.

21. Ibid., 138–53; Michel, *Struggle for a Better South*, 25–31. The Knoxville student movement was connected to the Nashville movement through Barry, who had left Fisk for graduate study at the University of Tennessee. Students for Equal Treatment conducted sit-ins in Knoxville restaurants and picketed an award ceremony at which *Look* magazine named Knoxville an all-American city. Forty-nine activists were arrested during this demonstration, including a white student, Phillip Bacon, who began fasting in jail. Bacon's actions galvanized many other white students: according to Barry, "What is so unique about Knoxville and U-T is the number of white students who have joined in the fight for equal rights for all. Two-thirds of [Students for Equal Treatment] is made up of white students, and Bacon has become the symbol of the protest movement here" (*Southern Patriot*, May 1963, 4).

22. *Hustler*, 1 May 1964, 1, 4.

23. Cusick, interview.

24. *Daily Tar Heel*, 7 January 1961, 1; 16 February 1961, 2.

25. Ibid., 22 March 1961, 2.

26. Alex McIntire to Russell Banks, Tucker Clark, John Gunn, Art and Barbara Lester, Ciaran Mercier-Johansen, and Saundy G. Mercier, August 1985 (first quotation), October 1985 newsletter, edited by Alex McIntire (second quotation), both in Alex McIntire, ed., "From the Tables Down at Harry's: Chapel Hill's Other Alumni of the Sixties: A Triumphant Return," an undated collection of memoranda and articles related to a 1986 reunion, North Carolina Collection, University of North Carolina, Chapel Hill.

27. *Daily Tar Heel*, 11 October 1961, 1; 13 February 1962, 2.

28. "Prospectus for Spring Conference," 8 December 1961, series 1, no. 3, SDS Papers (microfilm); Minutes, SDS National Executive Committee Meeting, Chapel Hill, 6–7 May 1962, series 1, no. 5, SDS Papers (microfilm).

29. *Daily Tar Heel*, 7 January 1961, 2.

30. Ehle, *Free Men*, 4, 17–32; quotation on 29. See also Billingsley, *Communists on Campus*, 29–31.

31. Billingsley, *Communists on Campus*, 29–31; Ehle, *Free Men*, 103 (quotation).

32. Ehle, *Free Men*, 323.

33. Ibid., 326, 331–35.

34. Sam Shirah, "A Proposal for Expanded Work among Southern White Students," Shirah Papers, Box 1, Wisconsin Historical Society.

35. Rabby, *Pain and the Promise*, 2.

36. Ibid., 61–63.

37. Ibid., 92, 133–34.

38. Ibid., 92–95.

39. Ibid., 132–34, 124–25.

40. Ibid., 155–57; Patricia Stephens Due, "Report to National Action Council," 7 November 1963, Shirah Papers, Box 1; Parr, "The Forgotten Radicals," 72–77.

41. Mike Geison to Patricia Stephens Due, 24 May 1964, CORE Papers (microfilm), reel 22.

42. Marshall B. Jones, "Berkeley of the South."

43. Rabby, *Pain and the Promise*, 157–58; Giardina, "Judith Brown," 256–73; Michel, *Struggle for a Better South*, 94–98.

44. Chappell, *Inside Agitators*, 4–7. On Haygood, see also Mann, *Atticus Greene Haygood*.

45. Jane Stembridge, "Meeting of Emory Students to Discuss Their Role in the Racial Situation in the South Today," Southern Student Human Relations Project Papers, Box 27, Martin Luther King Jr. Center for Nonviolent Social Change.

46. *Wheel*, 10 November 1960, 1.

47. "A Biographical Sketch of Richard Stevens," Stevens Papers, Box 16, Emory University.

48. Robert L. Tenney, "Prospectus for Atlanta for the White Southern Student Project," Shirah Papers, Box 1.

49. Rossinow, *Politics of Authenticity*, 23–57.

50. Rossinow, "'Break-Through to New Life,'" 326–29; Rossinow, "Breakthrough," 22–29, 150–53.

51. Rossinow, *Politics of Authenticity*, 9.

52. Fairclough, *Race and Democracy*, 274–75. On the New Orleans student movement, see Fairclough, *Race and Democracy*, 272–79, 295–96; Kim Lacy Rogers, *Righteous Lives*, 69–123; Murray, "Struggle for Civil Rights"; Mohr and Gordon, *Tulane*, 351–63.

53. Mohr and Gordon, *Tulane*, 353–57.

54. *Hullabaloo*, 12 October 1962, 1; 16 November 1962, 1; Mohr and Gordon, *Tulane*, 216–27.

55. Fairclough, *Race and Democracy*, 295–96.

56. Mohr and Gordon, *Tulane*, 290–91.

57. Ibid., 294–95; *Hullabaloo*, 17 December 1964, 1.

58. *Maroon*, 6 April 1962, 1.

59. Thomas H. Clancy, S.J., unpublished memoir, 147, Loyola University Archives, New Orleans.

60. Curry, interview.

61. *Maroon*, 6 October 1961, 1; 11 May 1962, 4.

62. Ibid., 19 February 1965, 1.

63. *Crimson White*, 11 October 1962, 1; "Talk on Captives Hits Snag in Cuba; Release Delayed," *New York Times*, 11 October 1962, 1; Thomas J. Hamilton, "Khrushchev Offers a Deal on Cuba and Berlin Crises," *New York Times*, 15 October 1962, 1; Tad Szulc, "Radio Free Dixie in Havana Praises Negro 'Revolt' in South," *New York Times*, 8 October 1962, 1. On Radio Free Dixie, see Tyson, *Radio Free Dixie*.

64. Wallenstein, "Black Southerners and Non-Black Universities," 142.

65. Pratt, *We Shall Not Be Moved*, 109, 100. On desegregation at the University of Georgia, see Pratt, *We Shall Not Be Moved*; Dyer, *University of Georgia*, chapter 14; Trillin, *Education in Georgia*; Cohen, "'Two, Four, Six, Eight.'"

66. Pratt, *We Shall Not Be Moved*, 92–106, quotation on 105.

67. Ibid., 106–7.

68. *Red and Black*, 11 January 1961, 1.

69. Pratt, *We Shall Not Be Moved*, 114.

70. Michel, *Struggle for a Better South*, 95.

71. Trillin, *Education in Georgia*, 125–26.

72. Pat Knight, Report on University of Georgia, 24 April 1964, Southern Student Human Relations Project Papers, Box 29.

73. Lott, *Herding Cats*, 29.

74. Thomas Buckley, "Mississippi U. Students Found Isolated in Culture and Outlook," *New York Times*, 21 October 1962, 65.

75. Lott, *Herding Cats*, 31–33; Bob Zellner, "Report on Oxford," Braden Papers, Box 64, Folder 11, Wisconsin Historical Society.

76. Cohodas, *Band Played Dixie*, 84–86. The most thorough treatment of the desegregation of the University of Mississippi is Barrett, *Integration at Ole Miss*.

77. Cohodas, *Band Played Dixie*, 93–97.

78. Meredith, *Three Years in Mississippi*, 245 (quotation), 286. On the Rebel Underground's treatment of white students who ate with Meredith, see also Barrett, *Integration at Ole Miss*, 202–3.

79. Zellner, "Report on Oxford."

80. Buckley, "Mississippi U. Students"; Zellner, "Report on Oxford."

81. E. Culpepper Clark, *Schoolhouse Door*, xii–xiii. Wallace, not a part of the fraternity system that dominated campus politics, failed in his efforts to win student political offices.

82. Ibid., *Schoolhouse Door*, 143.

83. John Robert Zellner, Report on White Southern Student Project (School Year of 1961–62), Braden Papers, Box 64.

84. E. Culpepper Clark, *Schoolhouse Door*, 160–62. Though Meyer received the death threats, staffer Robert E. Roberts had penned the editorial that was the focus of segregationist ire (Robert E. Roberts to Constance Curry, n.d., U.S. National Student Association Southern Project Papers, Martin Luther King Jr. Center for Nonviolent Social Change). For more on Roberts and the editorial, see chapter 4.

85. *Crimson White*, 15 November 1962, 4.

86. E. Culpepper Clark, *Schoolhouse Door*, e.g., 239–40.

87. David Mathews, "Reflections on Student Activism," July 2001, in author's possession.

88. *Crimson White*, 15 November 1962, 4; 9 June 1963, 4.

89. Ibid., 27 June 1963, 4.

90. E. Culpepper Clark, *Schoolhouse Door*, 170, 240–46.

91. On Gainey and Clemson, see "The Quotes of the Year: An Interpretive Report from the S.C. Student Council on Human Relations," Shirah Papers, Box 1. On Auburn, see Olliff, "'Just Another Day on the Plains'"; J. R. Bullington, Letter to the Editor, *Auburn Plainsman*, 2 April 1999. Kean, "'At a Most Uncomfortable Speed,'" effectively points out the mythology of desegregation that has developed at four private southern research institutions.

92. Cohen, "'Two, Four, Six, Eight.'"

93. Muir and McGlamery, "Trends in Integration Attitudes," 965.

94. Student questionnaires in Lowenstein Collection, Box 2, Folder 13, University of North Carolina.

95. *New York Times*, 12 December 1964, 22.

96. Ibid., 9 December 1964, 32.

97. Ibid., 8 March 1965, 1; 16 March 1965, 1.

98. Ibid., 15 March 1965, 1.

CHAPTER FOUR. *Building a Southern Movement*

1. Anne Braden to Mary, 8 October 1963, Shirah Papers, Box 1, Wisconsin Historical Society.

2. See "Field Report," n.d., Shirah Papers, Box 1.

3. *Southern Patriot*, January 1964, 1.

4. On Lowenstein's involvement in NSA, see Chafe, *Never Stop Running*, 82–108.

5. Altbach, *Student Politics in America*, 122–32; Chafe, *Never Stop Running*, 93–95.

6. Altbach, *Student Politics in America*, 122–32. On the South and the NSA, see Johnston, "Openings to Equality"; Johnston, "Habit of Talking."

7. Altbach, *Student Politics in America*, 128.

8. Johnston, "Habit of Talking," 5–6. Johnston covers the founding of the NSA Southern Project in "The United States National Student Association," 253–59.

9. Curry, interview; Curry, *Silver Rights*, 21–22.

10. Johnston, "Habit of Talking," 11; Zellner, interview; Curry interview.

11. Application of Clifford Hewitt, Southern Student Human Relations Project Papers, Box 13, Martin Luther King Jr. Center for Nonviolent Social Change.

12. Box 13, Miles Lovelace File, Southern Student Human Relations Project Papers.

13. "A Bell Tolls," *Crimson White*, n.d., in ibid.; see also E. Culpepper Clark, *Schoolhouse Door*, 160–62.

14. Robert E. Roberts to Constance Curry, n.d., Box 13, Robert E. Roberts File, Southern Student Human Relations Project Papers. Curry distributed the editorial,

which she said made her cry, to a number of publications. It eventually appeared in the Southern Regional Council's quarterly publication, *New South*.

15. On scef, see Klibaner, *Conscience of a Troubled South*; Reed, *Simple Decency and Common Sense*.

16. Mary King, *Freedom Song*, 37.

17. Ibid., 61–62.

18. Bartley, *New South*, 29–31.

19. Anne and Carl Braden noted the implications of involvement in the state human relations council in Alabama in "Is There a Significant Place for the White Southerner in the Integration Struggle," a discussion paper prepared for the 1962 sds conference in Chapel Hill (sds Papers (microfilm), Series 1, No. 4).

20. Johnston, "Habit of Talking," 22; Zellner, interview.

21. Edgar A. Love, "Claiming the Right to Choose: A Profile," Braden Papers, Box 64, Wisconsin Historical Society. Zellner addresses his experiences at Huntingdon in Zellner with Curry, *Wrong Side of Murder Creek*, 48–88.

22. For example, in October 1962, Zellner worked to get white students to a Pete Seeger concert at the Miles College auditorium. About twenty students from Birmingham-Southern College attended (John Robert Zellner, "Prospectus for Month of November — White Students Project," 30 October 1962, Box 1, Zellner Papers, Wisconsin Historical Society).

23. John Robert Zellner, Report on White Southern Student Project (School Year of 1961–62), Braden Papers, Box 64.

24. Zellner, interview. In later years, some founding members of ssoc expressed resentment over Zellner's identification with sncc, which they said kept him from contributing more to ssoc's efforts at organizing white southern students. The ssoc's Gene Guerrero declared that Zellner had not been the best man for the job because he "spent most of his time involved in regular demonstrations, sit-ins and stuff, and did not reach out to many white people." sncc staffer Stanley Wise described Zellner as having "assimilated a sncc personality," which made him seem "sort of weird to white students" (Simon, "Southern Student Organizing Committee," 4–5).

25. *Southern Patriot*, June 1963, 1; Sam Shirah, "A Proposal for Expanded Work among Southern White Students," n.d., Shirah Papers, Box 1.

26. Wise was referring to a boycott of the city bus system, which encountered difficulties in late 1964 but ultimately succeeded by 1965. See Wendt, "God, Gandhi, and Guns," 50–51.

27. Stanley L. Wise notebook, September 1964–June 196[5], sncc Papers (microfilm), Series 4, No. 412.

28. Hayden looms especially large in Miller, *Democracy Is in the Streets*; on Hayden's experiences in McComb, see 58–60.

29. Ibid., 48–60, quotation on 59.

30. Sale, *SDS*, 36.

31. Minutes, sds National Executive Committee Meeting, Chapel Hill, 6–7 May 1962, sds Papers (microfilm), Series 5, No. 1. For more on the Chapel Hill conference, see chapter 3.

32. Robb Burlage to SDS National Executive Committee, 25 December 1962, SDS Papers, Series 2a, No. 1.

33. "State of SDS Chapter Organization — 12/63" SDS Papers, Series 2a, No. 3.

34. SDS's national office frequently had trouble tallying the exact number of chapters, so it is somewhat difficult to say with precision how many chapters existed at any time in the South. A February 1967 list shows 143 total chapters, 10 of them in the South — in Birmingham, Alabama; at the Universities of Florida, Louisville, Kentucky, North Carolina, Texas, and Virginia; at Duke University; at Clemson University, and in Lexington, Virginia (*New Left Notes*, 3 February 1967).

By the spring of 1969, SDS leaders could only guess at the number of chapters, let alone the number of members. The best tally of chapters during the period probably comes from the U.S. Senate Committee on Government Operations, which found 304 chapters, including 48 in the South. Of these, 34 were identifiable as campus chapters. They included (alphabetically by state), Alabama: University of Alabama, Auburn; Florida: University of Florida, Florida State, Florida Presbyterian, New College, University of Miami; Georgia: Emory, University of Georgia, Georgia State; Kentucky: University of Kentucky; Louisiana: Louisiana State University, Loyola, Northwestern Louisiana State, Tulane; Mississippi: Mississippi State; North Carolina: Duke, University of North Carolina; South Carolina: University of South Carolina; Tennessee: LeMoyne-Owen, Memphis State; Texas: East Texas State, Houston, North Texas State, Rice, Southern Methodist, Stephen F. Austin State, University of Texas, Texas A&M, Texas Tech, Trinity, West Texas State; Virginia: Old Dominion, University of Virginia, Virginia Commonwealth (Sale, *SDS*, 529–31).

35. Lukas, *Don't Shoot*, 153.

36. Michel, *Struggle for a Better South*, 37; for the founding of SSOC, see chapter 2.

37. Ibid., 36.

38. On the SSOC founding document, see ibid., 39–45; the biographical sketch of Burlage is drawn from 40. On the regionalists, see Singal, *War Within*, esp. chapters 5, 10. On the agrarians, see Conkin, *Southern Agrarians*.

39. In 1962, Burlage wrote an SDS position paper, "The South as an Underdeveloped Country," in which he argued that the South's racial mores were intimately connected with its economic woes and that any real solution would have to deal with both problems (SDS Papers [microfilm], Series 4b, No. 46).

40. "We'll Take Our Stand," Highlander Folk School Manuscript Collection (microfilm), Reel 37.

41. As Michel notes in *Struggle for a Better South*, many of the questions introduced at SSOC's founding meeting continued to trouble the organization throughout its existence (37).

42. Anne and Carl Braden, "Is There a Significant Place for the White Southerner?"

43. Ed Hamlett, "What Is the Role of the Southern White?" *Southern Patriot*, April 1964, 1.

44. Leslie Dunbar to Philip Sherburne, 24 November 1965, Papers of the U.S.

National Student Association, Box 2, Martin Luther King Jr. Center for Nonviolent Social Change.

45. Philip Sherburne to Leslie W. Dunbar, 1 December 1965, in ibid.

46. Johnston, "Habit of Talking."

47. Leslie Dunbar to Philip Sherburne, 24 November 1965, Papers of the U.S. National Student Association, Box 2.

CHAPTER FIVE. *From the Community to the Campus, from University Reform to Student Power*

1. *Daily Tar Heel*, 4 May 1965, 4.

2. Hayes Mizell, "Vision from Olympus: The NSA Southern Project Looks at SSOC," 20 December 1964, U.S. Student Association Records, Box 109, Wisconsin Historical Society.

3. *Report of the President's Commission on Campus Unrest*, 22–41.

4. Breines, *Community and Organization*, 12.

5. Savio, Walker, and Dunayevskaya, *Free Speech Movement and the Negro Revolution*, 17. The most comprehensive treatment of the FSM is Goines, *Free Speech Movement*. A number of insightful essays appear in Cohen and Zelnik, *Free Speech Movement*. Rorabaugh places the movement in the context of the social movements of the 1960s as they developed in the city of Berkeley (*Berkeley at War*, 8–47). See also Draper, *Berkeley*.

6. The Summer Project's roots lay in the strategic stalemate that confronted SNCC's Mississippi operation in the fall of 1963. Despite exhibiting great courage, the organization's workers had achieved few concrete victories. The preceding July, liberal activist Allard Lowenstein investigated Mississippi's racial situation and suggested a protest vote to demonstrate blacks' desire to participate in the electoral process. The SNCC staff endorsed the plan, and some one thousand blacks cast votes in the state primary. Encouraged, SNCC planned a "Freedom Vote" for the November general election. To provide the labor for this effort, Lowenstein helped recruit white students from the North. Nearly eighty thousand blacks then cast votes (McAdam, *Freedom Summer*, 35–39, 41–44).

7. Ibid., 117.

8. Ibid., 161–69; quotation on 169.

9. Ibid., 43.

10. *Red and Black*, 25 October 1965, 4.

11. *Wheel*, 22 April 1965, 7.

12. *Daily Tar Heel*, 11 December 1964, 4.

13. *Wheel*, 30 April 1965, 2.

14. *Red and Black*, 4 October 1965, 4.

15. *Hustler*, 22 October 1965, 4.

16. On the Speaker Ban episode, see Billingsley, *Communists on Campus*; Link, *William Friday*, 109–41.

17. Henry Mayer, a 1963 UNC graduate who had begun graduate studies at Berkeley

when the FSM began, provides an instructive comparison of the two universities in "A View from the South: The Idea of a State University," in *Free Speech Movement*, ed. Cohen and Zelnik, 157–69. Mayer suggests that prior to their respective free-speech clashes, the University of North Carolina had the stronger tradition of academic freedom. But the FSM heralded a period of greater freedom at Berkeley, while the Speaker Ban controversy initiated a period of retrenchment at UNC: "My alma mater was losing its soul just as my new campus discovered it needed one" (167).

18. *Daily Tar Heel*, 16 February 1965, 1; 20 February 1965, 1; Billingsley, "Speaker Ban," 421–22.

19. *Daily Tar Heel*, 4 May 1965, 1, 2.

20. Ibid., 13 September 1966, section 2, p. 11. On the student government budget, see the inaugural address of David L. Grigg, 31 March 1960, Student Organizations and Activities: Student Government Records, Series 1: Executive Records, Subseries 1: Presidents' Records, University of North Carolina Archives.

21. Billingsley, *Communists on Campus*, 125–49, 170–82.

22. Mohr and Gordon, *Tulane*, 479–80.

23. James S. Turner, "Ohio State: Free Speech and Student Power," in *Protest!*, ed. Julian Foster and Long, 345–61.

24. Link, *William Friday*, 133; "Statement to Board of Trustees by Paul Dickson," Student Organizations and Activities: Student Government Records, Series 1: Executive Records, Subseries 1: Presidents' Records.

25. Link, *William Friday*, 135; Billingsley, *Communists on Campus*, 190.

26. *Daily Tar Heel*, 6 November 1966, 1.

27. *Crimson White*, 15 March 1966, 1.

28. "Southern Student Organizing Committee Campus Contact Report, 4 February 1965," in SDS Papers (microfilm), Series 2a, No. 66.

29. *Crimson White*, 23 February 1965, 1.

30. University Human Rights Forum Statement of Position, U.S. National Student Association Papers, Box 26, Martin Luther King Jr. Center for Nonviolent Social Change.

31. *Crimson White*, 18 March 1965, 3.

32. Ibid., 4.

33. Ibid., 12 April 1966, 1; 25 April 1966, 1; 28 April 1966, 1; 16 June 1966, 1; 23 June 1966, 2.

34. Ibid., 6 April 1967, 1; 10 April 1967, 1; 19 February 1968, 1.

35. Ibid., 10 October 1968, 1; 15 October 1968, 1.

36. Ibid., 5 March 1970, 1; 9 March 1970, 1.

37. Sansing, *Making Haste Slowly*, 203–5.

38. Ibid, 205–6.

39. *Hustler*, 26 April 1968, 9.

40. On progressive education, a good starting point is Cremin, *Transformation of the School*. On progressive education in the South, see Link, *Hard Country and Lonely Place*; Leloudis, *Schooling the New South*.

41. Altbach, *Student Politics in America*, 125.

42. "Joint Statement on the Rights and Freedoms of Students," 13–14 November 1966, found in Student Government Association of Emory University Papers, Box 1, Emory University.

43. *New York Times*, 21 August 1967, 1, 17. Drake recalled the congress as an important event in the formulation of his opinions on student-related issues. Drake later worked to get a student named to the search committee for a new University of Alabama president in 1969 (Drake, interview).

44. Edward Schwartz, "Student Power," in *Student Power*, rev. ed., ed. Schwartz, 4–6.

45. "The Port Huron Statement," reprinted in Miller, *Democracy Is in the Streets*, 329–74; quotations on 333–35, 373–74.

46. The elections of Davidson and Calvert signaled the rise within the SDS leadership of Prairie Power, a development that reflected a change not only in the geographical distribution of power but also in philosophical orientation. Prairie Power implied a distrust of almost any kind of organization and in practice veered toward anarchy (Sale, *SDS*, 279–85). On Davidson, see Heineman, *Campus Wars*, 95–97.

47. Carl Davidson, "Toward a Student Syndicalist Movement; or, University Reform Revisited," August 1966, Office of the President, Douglas M. Knight Subject Files, "Student Rights and Activism, 1966–68" Folder, Duke University.

48. Carl Davidson, "Student Power: Radical View," in *Student Power*, ed. Schwartz, 7–10.

49. For example, the presidents of both Tulane and Duke Universities saved copies of Davidson's working paper. Tulane president Herbert E. Longenecker distributed the paper to all of the university's academic deans (Mohr and Gordon, *Tulane*, 324). Duke president Douglas M. Knight corresponded with conservative students who distributed copies of Davidson's paper in an effort to demonstrate the revolutionary and therefore dangerous implications of the university's reformist student government (James A. Martin Jr. and Eaton Merritt to Douglas M. Knight, 10 March 1967, Office of the President, Douglas M. Knight Subject Files, "Student Rights and Activism, 1966–68" Folder, Duke University). For more on Martin and Merritt's effort, see chapter 8.

50. Sale, *SDS*, 264; Dittmer, *Local People*, 257–61.

51. Sale, *SDS*, 264–69.

52. *Daily Tar Heel*, 7 December 1966, 1.

53. *Duke Chronicle*, 5 November, 1; 8 November, 1, 4, 5; 11 November 1966, 1.

54. *Daily Tar Heel*, 19 February 1967, 4.

55. David Kiel and Terry Fowler, "A Report on the Experimental College of the Student Government of the University of North Carolina," August 1967, Southern Student Human Relations Project Papers, Box 30, Martin Luther King Jr. Center for Nonviolent Social Change.

56. *Daily Tar Heel*, 5 January 1967, 1.

57. "A History of Freedom Party," Southern Student Human Relations Project Papers, Box 27; Marshall B. Jones, "Berkeley of the South," 42 (quotation).

58. Marshall B. Jones, "Berkeley of the South," 44.

59. Ibid., 44–53.

60. Free University of Florida fund-raising pamphlet, n.d., Southern Student Human Relations Project Papers, Box 27.

61. Ibid.

62. Marshall B. Jones, "Berkeley of the South," 58–59.

63. Michel, "We'll Take Our Stand," 186–89.

64. Young, "*The Kudzu*," 22–136.

65. Director's Report, NSA Southern Project, 1967–68, Southern Student Human Relations Project Papers, Box 2.

66. SSOC's periodical, *New South Student*, devoted at least two issues in the late 1960s to analyses of higher education. Both demonstrated the connections between corporate capitalism and the university. In March 1968, a "special university issue" included an article by Bill Towe, "Who Runs the School?" Towe argued that the university was a microcosm of American society and that revealing the universities' power structures would uncover the mechanisms by which the university—and society—oppressed people. Research along these lines, Towe suggested, "can show how the great liberal universities that talk about truth and beauty are the same ones that buy land and kick poor ghetto Negroes out and pay their non-academic employees next to nothing" (*New South Student*, March 1968, 10). The January 1969 edition included radical analyses of the University of Arkansas and Duke University as well as an essay by SSOC activist and former University of Virginia student David Nolan decrying "white control of black education."

67. Curry, interview.

68. For a later analysis of this dilemma, see Ed Hamlett, "Whither SSOC?" *New South Student*, February 1967, 22.

69. Director's Report, NSA Southern Project, 1967–68 (first quotation); Howard Romaine to Leslie Dunbar, executive director of the Field Foundation, 31 October 1968 (second quotation), 6 October 1969, both in Southern Student Human Relations Project Papers, Box 39. Unfortunately for Romaine, he did not have the opportunity to find out whether the NSA Southern Project could capitalize on these circumstances. After failing to receive continued funding from the Field Foundation, the Southern Project shut down in the summer of 1968.

CHAPTER SIX. *Student Power and Black Power at the South's Negro Colleges*

1. Robert Goodman, "White Teach-Black School," *Great Speckled Bird*, 9 December 1968, 5.

2. Ture and Hamilton, *Black Power*, 32, 44.

3. Bayard Rustin, "Black Power and Coalition Politics," *Commentary*, September 1966, 35–40.

4. Van Deburg, *New Day in Babylon*, 8–10. Van Deburg's book is the best scholarly assessment of the Black Power movement. For Van Deburg's definition of Black Power, see chapter 1, "What Is 'Black Power'?" 11–28.

5. Ibid., 65–82.

6. *Courtbouillon* (Dillard University), April 1968, 1; *Le Diable Bleu* (Dillard University), 1969, 4; *New Orleans Times-Picayune*, 24 October 1968, 1.

7. Third World Commission of the U.S. National Student Association, "Black Students in Higher Education: A Proposal for the Creation of a National Association of Black Students," [1969], U.S. Student Association Records, Box 108, Wisconsin Historical Society.

8. Ibid.

9. Warnat, "Role of White Faculty."

10. On Bishop and South Carolina State, see Rosenthal, "Southern Black Student Activism," 125; Clancy, "Fight for Equality on Two Negro Campuses," 37–39. On Talladega, see Maxine D. Jones and Richardson, *Talladega College*, 219.

11. C. Vann Woodward, "Unreported Crisis."

12. Lynd and Yancey, "Southern Negro Students," 40, 41.

13. Ibid., 39–40.

14. For example, Tougaloo College in Mississippi and Brown University developed an exchange program for students. More common, however, was the development of relationships between black and white institutions in the same city — for example, between Emory University and the institutions of the Atlanta University Center. See "Notes on Some Cooperative Programs with Atlanta University," n.d., Judson C. Ward Papers, Box 16, Emory University. Tulane and Dillard universities also created cooperative programs in the late 1960s (Mohr and Gordon, *Tulane*, 491).

15. Chisum, "At Miles College," 17. Monro was not the only northern white college administrative official to quit his job and go South. Vincent C. De Baun, president of Lasell Junior College in Boston, resigned his position in 1968 after attending a memorial service for Martin Luther King Jr. and became professor of the humanities at Talladega College (Maxine D. Jones and Richardson, *Talladega College*, 207).

16. Robert F. Campbell, "Negro Colleges Have a Job," 4–5, 9.

17. Van Deburg, *New Day in Babylon*, 31–32.

18. Ibid., 9–10.

19. *Southern Patriot*, June 1963, 1; Samuel Shirah, "A Proposal for Expanded Work among Southern White Students," n.d., Box 1, Shirah Papers, Wisconsin Historical Society.

20. Michel, *Struggle for a Better South*, 82–83.

21. Norrell, *Reaping the Whirlwind*, 175; Forman, *Sammy Younge, Jr.*, 91.

22. Forman, *Sammy Younge, Jr.*, 110.

23. Norrell, *Reaping the Whirlwind*, 170–72.

24. Ibid., 178.

25. Ellison, *Invisible Man*, 36; Norrell, *Reaping the Whirlwind*, 182.

26. Patton's late 1966–early 1967 tenure with the Southern Project exposed racial tensions within the National Student Association. In a letter to Edward Schwartz, the association's vice president for national affairs, UNC student and association coordinator Teddy O'Toole complained that Patton was using the Southern Project to fund "a personal crusade . . . to convince southern Negroes that militant separatism is the only an-

swer to their dilemma" (O'Toole to Schwartz, 7 February 1967, U.S. Student Association Records, Box 125, Wisconsin Historical Society).

27. *New York Times*, 5 March 1966, 10; 5 April 1966, 1.

28. Ibid., 6 April 1966, 1; 7 April 1966, 26.

29. ssoc's efforts took the form of a fact sheet distributed to college students throughout the region calls for a "Southern Education General Protest." The ssoc missive argued that the Alcorn situation was "a caricature of southern education in general" and suggested that southern students "relate what they are trying to do to our own deplorable conditions" ("Southern Education General Protest," [April 1966], Papers of the Southern Student Organizing Committee and Thomas N. Gardner, Box 1, University of Virginia).

30. Simon, "Southern Student Organizing Committee," 38.

31. Herman Carter, "Protest at S.U.," n.d., 1–3, Southern Student Human Relations Project Papers, Box 29, Martin Luther King Jr. Center for Nonviolent Social Change.

32. Ibid., 8.

33. Ibid.

34. *New York Times*, 9 April 1967, 1; 10 April 1967, 1; 11 April 1967, 16 (quotation).

35. Ibid., 9 November 1967, 41.

36. Ibid., 30 September 1967, 20.

37. *Southern Patriot*, January 1968, 1.

38. A group of female student activists, the Informerettes, eventually joined their male compatriots, though the division of labor reflected some gender inequalities. The Informerettes, according to a protest pamphlet issued during the abbreviated student movement, "did the necessary paper work, etc." (*MDS Newsletter*, December 1967, 8, sds Papers [microfilm], Series 3, No. 36).

39. *MDS Newsletter*, December 1967, 2–11, sds Papers (microfilm), Series 3, No. 36; Fairclough, *Race and Democracy*, 410–11.

40. *MDS Newsletter*, December 1967, 8, sds Papers (microfilm), Series 3, No. 36.

41. Ibid., 4.

42. Ibid.

43. Darwin T. Turner, "Black University," *Negro Digest*, March 1968, 19.

44. For one perspective on the early 1960s student movement at Howard, see Sellers with Terrell, *River of No Return*, 57–80, in which Sellers characterizes his fellow students as materialistic and conformist.

45. On Howard's institutional history, see Logan, *Howard University*; on activism at Howard in the 1960s, see Lawrence B. de Graaf, "Howard: The Evolution of a Black Student Revolt," in *Protest!*, ed. Julian Foster and Long, 319–44.

46. de Graaf, "Howard," 323–25.

47. Hare, "Final Reflections on a 'Negro' College," 43.

48. Ibid., 44–45; de Graaf, "Howard," 346.

49. de Graaf, "Howard," 329–32.

50. Ibid., 333–38.

51. Ibid., 338.

52. Van Deburg, *New Day in Babylon*, 77–82. For several visions of a black university, see *Negro Digest*, March 1968, an issue devoted to the concept.

53. Hine, "Civil Rights and Campus Wrongs," 326–30.

54. Ibid., 130; Sellers with Terrell, *River of No Return*, 206–7; Bass and Nelson, *Orangeburg Massacre*, 18–21.

55. Bass and Nelson, *Orangeburg Massacre*, 15–78, provide the most detailed description of these events. See also Watters and Rougeau, *Events at Orangeburg*, 1–16 (quotation on 5).

56. Bass and Nelson, *Orangeburg Massacre*, 37–47.

57. Ibid., 49–77.

58. Nelson's commentary, "Orangeburg to Kent State," which originally appeared in the *Los Angeles Times* in May 1970, is reprinted as an appendix to Bass and Nelson, *Orangeburg Massacre*, 235–38.

59. Bass and Nelson, *Orangeburg Massacre*; Watters and Rougeau, *Events at Orangeburg*. On the whole, however, the events in Orangeburg received little national news coverage. *Time* magazine did not even mention the episode in 1968 (Bass and Nelson, *Orangeburg Massacre*, viii).

60. Bass and Nelson, *Orangeburg Massacre*, 89.

61. *New York Times*, 11 February 1968, 36.

62. Watters and Rougeau, *Events at Orangeburg*, 27–29.

63. Ibid., 41.

64. Bass and Nelson, *Orangeburg Massacre*, 87–88.

65. Chafe, *Civilities and Civil Rights*, 176.

66. *Southern Patriot*, April 1968, 2.

67. Forman, *Sammy Younge, Jr.*, 263–67.

68. Ibid., 267–71 (quotation on 270).

69. Ibid., 271.

70. Ibid., 271–75 (quotation on 274).

71. Ibid., 276.

72. *Student Protests 1969 Summary*, 3, 14–15, in Longenecker Papers, Box 67a, Tulane University.

73. Stanley H. Smith, "Administrators Should Heed Student Views."

74. *Southern Patriot*, May 1969, 1.

75. Hunter, "Black Colleges and the Black Mood," 30; Robert L. Terrell, "Black Awareness versus Negro Traditions," 35.

76. Hunter, "Black Colleges and the Black Mood," 30; Robert Goodman, "Atlanta 'Instant Negro' U," *Great Speckled Bird*, 25 November 1968, 7; Terrell, "Black Awareness versus Negro Traditions," 29.

77. "Black Power."

78. Cook, "Tragic Myth of Black Power," 60.

79. Albert E. Manley, "The Negro Rebellion: Past, Present, and Future," *Spelman Messenger*, November 1966, 22.

80. Terrell, "Black Awareness versus Negro Traditions," 31.

81. Ibid., 29–30; "Spelman College Speaks Out," *Spelman Messenger*, February 1969, 23.

82. "The Harkness Hall Incident (April 1969): A Chronology of Events at Morehouse College," Vertical Files — College and University Files, Atlanta University Center.

83. Ibid.

84. Ibid.

85. Ibid.; *Atlanta Voice*, 27 April 1969, 1.

86. "The Harkness Hall Incident (April 1969): A Chronology of Events at Morehouse College," Appendix II and III, Vertical Files — College and University Files.

87. "Afro-American and Third World Courses," Appendix A, "The Martin Luther King, Jr. Memorial Center: A Draft Proposal for the Second Element: The Institute for Advanced Afro-American Studies," October 1968, in Horace Mann Bond Papers (microfilm), Reel 24, Part 2, Howard-Tilton Library, Tulane University, New Orleans.

88. Manley, *Legacy Continues*, 51–52.

89. "Afro-American and Third World Courses," Appendix A, "The Martin Luther King, Jr. Memorial Center: A Draft Proposal for the Second Element: The Institute for Advanced Afro-American Studies," October 1968, 1, in Horace Mann Bond Papers (microfilm), Reel 24, Part 2, Howard-Tilton Library, Tulane University, New Orleans; Van Deburg, *New Day in Babylon*, 81–82.

90. "Malcolm X U. Dedicated," *Black Ink*, November 1969, 1; Chafe, *Civilities and Civil Rights*, 175, 220. See also Fergus, *Liberalism, Black Power, and the Making of American Politics*, 38–53.

91. On the Jackson State shootings, see Spofford, *Lynch Street*.

92. Jerah Johnson, *UNO Prisms*, 10–12, 37–40.

93. In 1969, SUNO had one white in a student body of eighteen hundred (Fairclough, *Race and Democracy*, 432).

94. Southern University at New Orleans Office of Institutional Research, *Traject-o-scope '74*, September 1974, Southern University at New Orleans Library.

95. *Southern University Digest*, 17 May 1968, 1; Fairclough, *Race and Democracy*, 432.

96. Lynn French, "Progress at SUNO High School," *Plain Truth of New Orleans*, 21 October 1969, Political Ephemera Collection, Tulane University.

97. "Separate but Equal?" *Ungarbled Word*, 6–12 February 1969. Political Ephemera Collection, Tulane University.

98. Hugh T. Murray Jr., "Black Eruption: Southern Style," 11–12, Murray Papers, Tulane University; Harlette Smith, "SUNO Revolts," *Southern University Digest*, 24 April 1969, 5, 7.

99. On the flag-raising controversy and SUNO in the late 1960s, see Fairclough, *Race and Democracy*, 429–33.

100. Ferdinand, interview.

101. *New Orleans Times-Picayune*, 4 April 1969, section 1, p. 8.

102. Murray, "Black Eruption," 19–22.

103. Ferdinand, interview; *New Orleans Times-Picayune*, 10 April 1969, 1.

104. *New Orleans Times-Picayune*, 10 April 1969, 1.

105. Ferdinand, interview. Ferdinand's background reveals the potential for activism that existed at SUNO. A native of New Orleans's Lower Ninth Ward, an area inhabited by poor and working-class people, Ferdinand attended St. Augustine High School, a Catholic institution that prided itself on sending black students to good colleges. As a high school student, Ferdinand was a member of the NAACP Youth Council and participated in the picketing on Canal Street from 1961 to 1963. He graduated from St. Augustine in 1964 and that fall was one of eight entering black freshmen at Carleton College in Minnesota. Ferdinand was not comfortable with the Carleton social setting and left in March 1965 to join the army, where he was tracked into repairing nuclear missiles. He served for a year in Korea and then for a period in El Paso, Texas. By the time Ferdinand left the army in 1968 and returned to New Orleans to enter SUNO, he had a wide range of experiences. And he was not the only one with this type of background. Of the seven students who lowered the American flag and replaced it with the flag of black liberation on 2 April, Ferdinand later recalled, three were military veterans. Moreover, Ferdinand's activism apparently ran in the family. His brother, Kenneth, led a series of demonstrations at nearby Xavier University shortly after the SUNO uprising. And another brother, Keith, was among the gun-toting black students at Cornell who gained renown with their demonstrations in 1969.

106. Murray, "Black Eruption," 11–12; Harlette Smith, "SUNO Revolts," *Southern University Digest*, 24 April 1969, 5, 7.

107. Ferdinand, interview.

108. *Louisiana Weekly*, 13 September 1969, 1; 13 December 1969, section 2, p. 3.

109. Cassimere, "Crisis of Public Higher Education"; "To Be or Not to Be? That Is Big Southern Question," *New Orleans Times-Picayune*, 7 April 1973, 18.

110. Thomas, "Student Movement at Southern University"; "Southern Crisis Traced to Quiet Student Protest," *New Orleans Times-Picayune*, 19 November 1972, 42; "Southern University: One Year After," *Black Collegian* 4 (November–December 1973): 40.

CHAPTER SEVEN. *Black Power on White Campuses*

1. Trillin, *Education in Georgia*, 2.

2. Edwin Lombard, interview.

3. *Crimson White*, 17 June 1965, 1.

4. The *Crimson White* published a three-part series on black students at the university on 22, 24, and 29 February 1968; quotation is from the 24 February article.

5. Crump, interview.

6. Ibid.

7. Ibid.

8. *Hullabaloo*, 10 May 1968, 11, 12.

9. *Daily Tar Heel*, 16 November 1961, 1.

10. Ibid., 30 September 1966, 1.

11. Dobbins, interview.

12. *Daily Tar Heel*, 17 November 1967, 1.

13. Dobbins, interview; *Daily Tar Heel*, 16 February 1968, 1; 17 February 1968, 1; 17 September 1968, 1.

14. Trillin, *Education in Georgia*, 76.

15. Black Student Union flyer, [1969], Vertical Files, "Georgia, University, BSU," University of Georgia.

16. See *New York Times*, 21 April 1969, 1.

17. Chafe, *Civilities and Civil Rights*, 220.

18. On desegregation at Duke, see Kotelanski, "Prolonged and Patient Efforts."

19. Yannella, "Race Relations," 5, 8–9.

20. In his memoir of the 1960s, Knight later portrayed himself as caught in the cross fire between the forces of social change and the forces of white, conservative reaction. "My mother remarked later that when she saw the first news story describing me as 'Yankee-born and Yale-educated,' she braced herself for trouble," he noted (*Street of Dreams*, 137).

21. Charles E. M. Dunlop to Douglas M. Knight, 10 April 1967, Office of the President, Douglas M. Knight Subject Files, "Civil Rights, 1963–67" Folder, Duke University.

22. Knight to Dunlop, 13 April 1967 [draft], 29 April 1967, both in ibid. According to a note attached to the letters, Dunlop was the son of an Evanston, Illinois, minister. He entered Duke in the fall of 1965 and held an eighteen-hundred-dollar graduate assistantship for the 1966–67 academic year.

23. *Duke Chronicle*, 8 August 1968; Kornberg and Smith, "'It Ain't Over Yet,'" 104. On the silent vigil, see also Segal, "New Genesis."

24. Kornberg and Smith, "'It Ain't Over Yet,'" 112; Hobson, *But Now I See.*

25. The treatment of nonacademic employees had long been an issue on the Duke campus. Led by activist Harry Boyte, the Duke CORE chapter placed the wages of Duke's nonacademic employees at the top of its list of concerns in a May 1964 pamphlet on discrimination at the university. See "Suggestions from Duke CORE in Regard to Discrimination and Unfair Employment Practices at Duke University," [May 1964], Office of the President, Douglas M. Knight Subject Files, "Civil Rights, 1963–67" Folder. In February 1965, the predominantly black nonacademic employees organized themselves into an independent union, the Duke Employees Benevolent Society, and in September 1965 the society affiliated with the American Federation of State, County, and Municipal Employees, AFL-CIO, as Local 77. According to two labor organizers involved in the Local 77 cause, the plight of the nonacademic employees provided for students an example of "the hypocracy [*sic*] of the beautiful paternal factory that teaches enlightenment but practices humiliation." See Peter Brandon and Nancy Park, "A Brief History of Duke Employees Local 77, AFSCME, AFL-CIO," April 1966, in folder titled Boyte Family Papers, Harry C. Boyte Series, Box 16, "SSOC, 1963–64" Folder, Duke University.

26. Frank L. Ashmore, "A Crisis in Conscience," Sanford L. Atwood Papers, Box 63, Emory University.

27. Kornberg and Smith, "'It Ain't Over Yet,'" 112.

28. Knight to Members of the Board of Trustees, 3 February 1969, Office of the President, Douglas M. Knight Subject Files, "Afro-American Situation, February 1969 — Miscellaneous Material, 1968–69" Folder.

29. Duke University Office of Information, "Duke Taking Steps to Improve Conditions for Minority Group Students on Campus," 4 February 1969, Knight Papers, "Afro-American Situation, February 1969 — Miscellaneous Material, 1968–69" Folder.

30. Kornberg and Smith, "'It Ain't Over Yet,'" 107.

31. The name provides an indication of the connections between events at Duke and the eventual formation of Malcolm X Liberation University, discussed in chapter 6, which opened the following March. See Fergus, *Liberalism, Black Power, and the Making of American Politics*, 33–39.

32. Kornberg and Smith, "'It Ain't Over Yet,'", 120. Other demands were reinstatement of black students who had withdrawn because of academic difficulties; an increase in the black student population to equal 29 percent by 1973; a black adviser selected by black students; more black representation in the university power structure; financial reassurance for black students; a black student union; self-determination of working conditions by nonacademic employees; and total amnesty for students involved in the sit-in.

33. *New York Times*, 14 February 1969, 1; Knight, *Street of Dreams*, 135–36; *Duke Chronicle*, 8 March 1969, 5; Kornberg and Smith, "'It Ain't Over Yet,'" 108.

34. *New York Times*, 17 February 1969, 1; Meeting Minutes, 15 October 1968, Statement by Dr. Douglas Knight for wDBS Radio (quotation), 16 February 1969, Report of Faculty Committee on Student Concerns, 17 February 1969, all in Knight Papers, "Afro-American Situation, February 1969 — Miscellaneous Material, 1968–69" Folder; "Duke to Permit Peaceful Protests, but Sets Penalties for Violators," draft of news release, Knight Papers, "Pickets and Protest Policy, 1967–68" Folder.

35. *Duke Chronicle*, 31 March 1969, 1. In a memoir of his experiences during the 1960s, Knight later referred to his "forced resignation by various trustees," although he declined to discuss the specifics of Duke politics (*Street of Dreams*, 139).

36. *Duke Chronicle*, 11 March 1969, 1; 18 March 1969, 1; Elizabeth Tornquist, "Duke U.," *Great Speckled Bird*, 24 March 1969, 6. The abortive exodus apparently was connected with the opening of the Malcolm X Liberation University. But the students insisted that their decision to stay at Duke did not represent an abandonment of the Malcolm X idea, which they said would "meet our immediate needs." For a transcript of the AAS statement, see *Duke Chronicle*, 18 March 1969, 1.

37. Elizabeth Tornquist, "Duke: The Southern Struggle," *Great Speckled Bird*, 24 February 1969, 4, 18.

38. Transcript of Address by Stokely Carmichael, 21 November 1968, Chancellor's Papers: J. C. Sitterson Series, University of North Carolina.

39. "Reply by Chancellor J. Carlyle Sitterson of the University of North Carolina at Chapel Hill to a Set of Demands Presented to Him by the Black Student Movement, December 11, 1968," 24 January 1969, Friday Collection, Subgroup 1, Series 7, Subseries 1, Campus Disruption (Student Unrest): Black Student Movement: Statements, 1968–69, University of North Carolina.

40. James C. Ingram to Sitterson, 16 December 1968, in "Black Student Movement," Chancellor's Papers: Sitterson Series.

41. Ibid., 3–4.

42. Ibid., 5–7, 9–10 (quotation on 6).

43. *Daily Tar Heel*, 8 February 1969, 1; 11 February 1969, 3.

44. Link, *William Friday*, 143; *Greensboro Daily News* clipping, 18 February 1969, "Black Student Movement — Clippings," Chancellor's Papers: Sitterson Series.

45. *Duke Chronicle*, 7 March 1969, 2; *Daily Tar Heel*, 22 September 1967, 1; 17 February 1968, 1.

46. Link, *William Friday*, 145–46; *Daily Tar Heel*, 25 February 1969, 1, 2.

47. *Daily Tar Heel*, 2 April 1969, 2; 28 February 1969, 1.

48. Ibid., 5 March 1969, 1.

49. Ibid., 9 March 1969, 2.

50. Ibid., 14 March 1969, 1; Link, *William Friday*, 151, 156.

51. *Daily Tar Heel*, 21 March 1969, 7; 22 March 1969, 2.

52. Link, *William Friday*, 156–57.

53. Ibid., 249–366.

54. John Buettner-Janusch to Alan Kerckhoff, 3 March 1969, Office of the President, Douglas M. Knight Subject Files, "Afro-American Situation, February 1969 — Letters Concerning" Folder.

55. *Wheel*, 6 March 1969, 9.

56. Ibid., 27 May 1969, 1.

57. Ibid., 12.

58. Ibid., 2.

59. The issues included the BSA's original demands as well as the concerns of workers, black membership on college committees, budgetary relations with the Student Government Association, and "inter-relations with all Emory students" (Sanford S. Atwood to university faculty and staff members, 15 September 1969, draft, Box 1, Student Government Association of Emory University Papers, Emory University).

60. Leon Mandell to Sanford S. Atwood, 23 July 1969, Judson C. Ward Papers, Box 16, Emory University.

61. Emory University Office of Development and Planning, "A Summary of Events of May 25–28, 1969, on the Emory University Campus Concerning Student Demonstrations and Subsequent Actions by University Faculty and Administration," 6 June 1969, Atwood Papers, Box 64.

62. "Preview: Student Government Education Program on White Racism," Student Government Association of Emory University Papers, Box 1.

63. Helen Stanton, Memo Regarding Committee for Community Action, n.d., Student Government Association of Emory University Papers, Box 1.

64. Egerton, "CACTUS Is the Word"; Mohr and Gordon, *Tulane*, 492–93; *CACTUS Newsletter*, April 1970, Political Ephemera Collection, Tulane University.

65. *Corolla* (University of Alabama), 1968, 75, W. A. Hoole Special Collections Library, University of Alabama.

66. Afro-American Association and Other Concerned Students to Frank Rose, n.d., Mathews Papers, Box 21, University of Alabama; *Crimson White*, 2 May 1968, 1.

67. Afro-American Association to University Community, 1 August 1968, Mathews Papers, Box 21.

68. "Programs and Accomplishments of the 1968–69 Administration of the Afro-American Association," n.d., Mathews Papers, Box 22. In a move that underlined the importance of football at the university, the AAA eventually sued the University of Alabama and Paul (Bear) Bryant to force the active recruitment of African Americans for intercollegiate athletics. A legend has developed that Bryant decided to recruit black athletes after the University of Southern California's Sam Cunningham ran roughshod over the Crimson Tide defense. Whether or not this story is true, the often-overlooked suit by the AAA suggests at least some agency on the part of black students at Alabama. See papers related to *Afro-American Association of the University of Alabama v. Paul "Bear" Bryant et al.*, Mathews Papers, Box 21.

69. "Report to the President of the Afro-American Grievance Committee," 19 August 1970, "Comments on the Report to the President of the Afro-American Grievance Committee," both in Mathews Papers, Box 21.

70. James, "Demand for Racial Equality," 108.

71. Ibid., 119.

72. *Red and Black*, 27 March 1969, 1; 8 April 1969, 5.

73. Ibid., 27 March 1969, 1, 4.

74. Ibid., 6 May 1969, 5; 15 April 1969, 1; 22 May 1969, 1.

75. Ibid., 13 May 1971, 1.

76. *Crimson White*, 2 May 1968, 1.

77. *Hullabaloo*, 10 May 1968, 11.

CHAPTER EIGHT. *The War in the South*

1. Bob Moses remarks at Vietnam Day Rally, 21–23 May 1965, http://www.lib.berkeley.edu/MRC/pacificaviet/#ucbteachin (accessed 9 January 2009).

2. Simon Hall, *Peace and Freedom*, 9–11; Moses, remarks at Vietnam Day.

3. "SNCC Campus Program," report for Staff Meeting, 7 May 1967, SNCC Papers (microfilm), Reel 3.

4. *Red and Black*, 28 May 1968, 1.

5. O'Bannon, interview.

6. Peterson and Bilorusky, *May 1970*, 15, 59–60.

7. Wolfe, *University of Alabama*, 225; Drake, interview.

8. Most accounts of the antiwar movement assume its effectiveness in shortening the war. The most fully developed statement of this position is Wells, *War Within*. Garfinkle takes the opposite position in *Telltale Hearts*. And although it is not a central point in his argument, Heineman, *Campus Wars*, 1–2, also suggests that the antiwar movement did not end the war. On the antiwar movement in general, see also DeBenedetti with Chatfield, *American Ordeal*; Mitchell K. Hall, *Because of Their Faith*; Small and Hoover, *Give Peace a Chance*.

9. For an overview of American involvement in Vietnam, see Herring, *America's Longest War*.

10. DeBenedetti with Chatfield, *American Ordeal*, 4.

11. On the teach-ins, see Menashe and Radosh, *Teach-Ins.*

12. Altizer soon raised eyebrows with his highly publicized "God is dead" theory, which received prominent play in *Time* magazine, among other publications (*Wheel*, 18 November 1965, 7).

13. Michel, *Struggle for a Better South*, 104; *Wheel*, 4 November 1965, 2.

14. *Red and Black*, 11 January 1966, 1.

15. *Wheel*, 15 February 1966, 1.

16. *Wheel*, 2 March 1967, 4.

17. The formation of the Atlanta chapter followed a decision by ssoc to convert from a leadership organization that sought to encourage existing manifestations of the student movement — regardless of the organizational vehicle — to a membership organization that more closely resembled and in fact duplicated sds (Michel, *Struggle for a Better South*, 126–29; Simon, "Southern Student Organizing Committee," 57).

18. *Wheel*, 19 January 1967, 1; 9 February 1967, 1; 20 April 1967, 2; 11 May 1967, 3.

19. In March 1966, the Selective Service announced that college men would be deferred only if they were full-time students who ranked in the upper half of their class. The government expected colleges to supply draft authorities with lists of class ranking for all students. Students could also choose to take a government-sponsored College Qualification Test. Undergraduates were required to score at least 70, while graduate students had to score 80 or higher. In August 1966, the Johnson administration announced the highest monthly draft call since the Korean War — 46,200 men. Draft boards were ordered to conscript men in categories that had previously been considered deferred, such as childless married men under age twenty-six. During the summer of 1967, the Selective Service revoked draft deferments for all of the country's 650,000 graduate students except for those in medical and dental school. Following the Tet Offensive, Johnson announced the cancellation of a number of occupational deferments. The National Security Council later issued a directive, superseding Selective Service regulations, that continued deferments for graduate students in engineering, mathematics, and the natural sciences (Rudy, *Campus and a Nation in Crisis*, 171–72). The starting point for understanding the draft is Baskir and Strauss, *Chance and Circumstance.*

20. *Wheel*, 2 November 1967, 3.

21. Ibid., 9 January 1969, 1; 16 January 1969, 1; 17 April 1969, 1; *Great Speckled Bird*, 15–28 March 1968, 2.

22. *Southern Patriot*, March 1968, 4.

23. *Wheel*, 19 October 1967, 1, 2; 9 November 1967, 1; 11 January 1968, 3.

24. Ibid., 11 January 1968, 1.

25. *Red and Black*, 26 October 1965, 2.

26. Ibid., 4 November 1965, 1.

27. Ibid., 11 January 1966, 1.

28. Ibid., 8 February 1966, 1.

29. Ibid., 17 February 1966, 4.

30. Ibid., 16 November 1965, 4.

31. Ibid., 2 December 1965, 4.

32. Ibid., 6 April 1967, 1; 12 July 1967, 9; 27 July 1967, 4.

33. Heineman, *Campus Wars*, 18; on federal military spending during the Cold War, see 13–20.

34. *Daily Tar Heel*, 28 October 1959, 2; Peterson and Bilorusky, *May 1970*, 23; *Duke Chronicle*, 24 April 1969, 4.

35. *Red and Black*, 24 October 1967, 5.

36. Ibid., 16 January 1968, 4.

37. Ibid., 24 October 1967, 4–5.

38. Ibid., 11 April 1968, 1; 7 October 1969, 5.

39. *Athens Daily News*, 31 May 1968, 1.

40. *Great Speckled Bird*, 12–25 April 1968, 12.

41. *Wheel*, 16 May 1968, 1; 30 May 1968, 1.

42. "A Resolution of the UNC Chapter of the Student Peace Union," 17 March 1963, in Student Organizations and Activities: Student Government Records, Series 1: Executive Records, Subseries 1: Presidents' Records, University of North Carolina. For more on the SPU's sit-in activities, see chapter 3.

43. *Daily Tar Heel*, 2 December 1966, 2.

44. Ibid., 4 January 1967, 1; 5 January 1967, 1.

45. Ibid., 1 February 1967, 1.

46. Ibid., 1 March 1967, 1.

47. Ibid, 5 January 1967, 1.

48. *Duke Chronicle*, 29 September 1966, 2.

49. William Johnson, "Timid Generation," 75.

50. *Duke Chronicle*, 17 May 1967.

51. Ibid., 30 November 1966, 1; 5 January 1967, 1.

52. Wells, *War Within*, 138–39, 168–70; *Southern Patriot*, August 1967, 8.

53. *Duke Chronicle*, 27 September 1967, 1.

54. Ibid., 9 October 1967, 1.

55. Wells, *War Within*, 174–81, quotation on 180.

56. Ibid., 195–203; Mailer, *Armies of the Night*.

57. *Duke Chronicle*, 20 October 1967, 2.

58. Ibid., 23 October 1967, 1.

59. Wells, *War Within*, 125; *Duke Chronicle*, 13 November 1967, 1.

60. *Duke Chronicle*, 8 January 1968, 1; "Duke to Permit Peaceful Protests, but Sets Penalties for Violators," draft of news release, Office of the President, Douglas M. Knight Subject Files, "Pickets and Protest Policy, 1967–68" Folder, Duke University.

61. *Duke Chronicle*, 5 February 1968, 1.

62. Ibid., 9 February 1968, 1.

63. Carl Davidson, "Toward a Student Syndicalist Movement or University Reform Revisited," August 1966, Office of the President, Douglas M. Knight Subject Files, "Student Rights and Activism, 1966–68" Folder. For more on Davidson's working paper, see chapter 5.

64. James A. Martin Jr. and Eaton Merritt to Douglas M. Knight, 10 March 1967, in ibid.

65. Student Committee against the War, Worklist No. 5, SDS Papers (microfilm), Series 3, No. 55; *Duke Chronicle*, 16 February 1968, 1.

66. "Chairman of Duke Investments Explains Why Duke Supports Dow," 29 February 1968, SDS Papers (microfilm), Series 3, No. 55. Although the student interviewer is not named, he acknowledges at one point during the interview that he is a law student, and Tieger had coordinated the effort to meet with Perkins. A participant in desegregation sit-ins in the early 1960s, Tieger also gained notoriety in December 1967 when he and Vlasits publicly notified the commanding officer at the Raleigh induction center that they would refuse induction. On Tieger and the effort to meet with Perkins, see *Duke Chronicle*, 16 February 1968, 1. On Tieger's draft resistance, see *Southern Patriot*, March 1968, 4.

67. Student Committee Against the War, Worklist #5.

68. "Durham–Chapel Hill: Worklist Mailing #1, [spring 1968], SDS Papers (microfilm), Series 3, No. 55.

69. *New Left Notes*, 25 March 1968, 7.

70. Knight had signed a "Negotiate Now" statement in the *New York Times* (David M. Henderson, ed., "A Journal of the Duke Vigil," Appendix 1, Duke University Archives; quotation from Item 3, "Dr. Knight speaking with group in his living room," 5 April 1968).

71. Thomas N. Gardner, "The Southern Student Organizing Committee," 14 October 1969, 27–28, Papers of the Southern Student Organizing Committee and Thomas N. Gardner, Box 6, University of Virginia. On SSOC and Vietnam, see Michel, *Struggle for a Better South*, 108–14, 143–52; on SSOC's efforts to weave a peculiarly southern argument against American involvement in Vietnam, see 193–94.

72. Gardner, "Southern Student Organizing Committee," 29.

73. Ibid., 30.

74. The March 1968 issue of the *New South Student*, SSOC's monthly magazine, was devoted to an analysis of the university. The featured article was Bill Towe, "Who Runs the Schools?" On SSOC and Labor, see Michel, *Struggle for a Better South*, 153–60.

75. See Michel, *Struggle for a Better South*, chapter 8, "Falling Apart: The Dissolution of SSOC." See also Simon, "Southern Student Organizing Committee," 70–71.

76. Other versions of SSOC's call for secession were more specific in their denouncement of the North's exploitation of the South. In *New Left Notes*, for example, SSOC called for secession "in the tradition of other Southerners and Southern movements that have resisted Yankee imperialism whether directed against South Vietnam or our own South" (*New Left Notes*, 25 March 1968, 7).

77. "Call to Southern Days of Secession," in Southern Student Organizing Committee Papers, Box 4, University of Virginia.

78. On the Progressive Labor–Weatherman split in SDS, see Sale, *SDS*, chapter 24. On the demise of SSOC, see Michel, *Struggle for a Better South*, chapter 8.

79. Sale, *SDS*, 518–25.

80. On SDS at the University of Texas, see Rossinow, *Politics of Authenticity*, chapter 5. On Tulane, see Mohr and Gordon, *Tulane*, chapters 6, 7, esp. 568–74. On Kentucky, see Mitchell K. Hall, "'Crack in Time.'"

81. *Crimson White*, 17 December 1968, 2.

82. Ibid., 14 December 1967, 1; 18 March 1968, 1.

83. Rossinow, *Politics of Authenticity*, 246.

84. *Daily Tar Heel*, 18 April 1969, 2; *Duke Chronicle*, 16 April 1969, 2.

85. Mohr and Gordon, *Tulane*, 591–92.

86. Ibid., 593–606. For a summary of the Dubinsky episode, see *Hullabaloo*, 5 February 1971, 10–16.

87. *Hullabaloo*, 10 April 1970; *New Orleans States-Item*, 10 April 1970, 1; 15 April 1970, 1.

88. *New Orleans States-Item*, 5 May 1970, 1; 8 May 1970, 1; 14 May 1970, 1, 6; *Maroon*, 12 May 1970, 1.

89. Thomas, interview.

90. *Crimson White*, 14 May 1970, 1; Wolfe, *University of Alabama*, 225.

91. O'Bannon, interview.

92. Shelton, interview.

93. In fact, in an effort to prepare for possible protest activities concerning war-related research at the university, Arts and Sciences dean Douglas E. Jones issued a May 1969 memorandum in which he wrote that one chemistry professor had "an army research grant which might be used as an excuse to create some sort of disturbance around that building." He also noted that "someone over this past weekend rigged 'booby traps' of acid on several lab doors in [the chemistry] building. They were discovered in time to avoid injury" (Douglas E. Jones to David Mathews, Raymond McLain, Willard Gray, Larry McGehee, and John Blackburn, 16 May 1969, Box 20, Mathews Papers, Box 21, University of Alabama).

94. "Demands of Student-Faculty Coalition," n.d., Mathews Papers, Box 20.

95. Mathews, "Reflections on Student Activism," 13–14. Mathews also contended that the city police, invited by the campus police chief without Mathews's knowledge, were more violent than the state police, who were "seasoned professionals." The director of the state force was Floyd Mann, who had gained respect for protecting Freedom Riders against violent segregationists.

96. Drake, interview. Drake provided legal representation to some of the students who were arrested during the demonstrations.

97. Mitchell K. Hall, "'Crack in Time,'" 39. University of Kentucky president Otis A. Singletary was on record as opposing "slogan shouters." Singletary succeeded John Oswald, who had resigned in the spring of 1968 after a prolonged battle with Nunn and conservative elements in the state legislature.

98. Drobney, "Generation in Revolt."

99. *Daily Tar Heel*, 12 May 1970, 1; 13 May 1970, 1.

100. *Atlanta Constitution*, 16 April 1969, in Vertical Files, "Georgia — University — Students for a Democratic Society," Hargrett Rare Book and Manuscript Library, University of Georgia. After ssoc's demise, Simpson went on to affiliate with the Revolutionary Youth Movement within sds (*Red and Black*, 21 April 1970, 2).

101. *Red and Black*, 16 October 1969, 1.

102. Ibid., 16 April 1970, 1.

103. Ibid., 7 May 1970, 1, 2.

104. Ibid., 12 May 1970, 1.

105. *Wheel*, 26 May 1970, 1; Bassett, "Some of the Anguish," 14.

106. At Duke University, for example, new president Terry Sanford, a former governor of North Carolina, lent his name and support to an antiwar festival held in Chapel Hill in April 1970 (*Duke Chronicle*, 11 April 1970, 1). At the University of Virginia, President Edgar F. Shannon Jr. sent a May 1970 statement to Virginia's senators opposing the bombing of Cambodia (Dabney, *Mr. Jefferson's University*, 521–22). At Vanderbilt, President G. Alexander Heard, did not overtly back student demonstrations but "came close to an endorsement of their opposition to President Nixon." Heard subsequently served as a special adviser to Nixon on campus unrest but issued reports that "were often sharply critical, offending the conservative press and disappointing Nixon staffers" (Conkin, *Gone with the Ivy*, 628, 630).

107. *Daily Tar Heel*, 23 April 1969, 1.

108. Ibid., 16 September 1969, 1.

109. Ibid., 15 January 1970, 1.

110. For Bello's background, see *Daily Tar Heel*, 3 March 1970, 1. On the Cambodia/ Kent State demonstrations, see *Daily Tar Heel*, May 1970.

111. *Tulane Jambalaya*, 1971, Book 4, 9.

112. Thompson, "'Taste of Student Power,'" 90.

CHAPTER NINE. *Southern Campuses at Decade's End*

1. *Hustler*, 20 February 1968, 7.

2. Ibid.

3. Ibid., 8 March 1968, 7.

4. On American student subcultures, see Horowitz, *Campus Life*.

5. Miller, *Democracy Is in the Streets*; Gitlin, *Sixties*. Although both authors place the counterculture firmly within the "declension narrative" of the New Left, Rossinow notes that they have complex views of the counterculture. Gitlin, for example, acknowledges the "direct line from the expressive politics of the New Left to the counterculture's let-it-all-hang-out way of life" and the salutary effects of thousands of "counterinstitutions" that hippies helped build ("New Left in the Counterculture," 80–81).

6. Examples of this approach include Breines, "Whose New Left?"; Sara M. Evans, *Personal Politics*; Echols, *Daring to Be Bad*. I have drawn on Rossinow's typology for this condensation of views on the counterculture. Rossinow adds a third view — that of conservatives and neoconservatives, who have tended to view the New Left and the counterculture as two wings of one (unfortunate) movement. See Rossinow, "New Left in the Counterculture," 80–85.

7. Bailey, "Sexual Revolution(s)," 257, 255; Gitlin, *The Sixties*, 214.

8. Atlanta's underground newspaper was the *Great Speckled Bird*, which emerged from the Southern Project of the U.S. National Student Association in 1967. See "Director's Report, NSA Southern Project, 1967–68," in Southern Student Human Relations Project Papers, Martin Luther King Jr. Center for Nonviolent Social Change. In New Orleans,

the *Nola Express* emanated from a small community of leftists who operated under the banner of Movement for a Democratic Society. Other alternative newspapers in the South included the *Rag* in Austin, Texas; and the *Radish* in Durham, North Carolina. The *Kudzu* was produced by two men associated at one time with Millsaps College — one a graduate and the other a former instructor. See Young, "*The Kudzu*."

9. Rossinow, "New Left in the Counterculture," 86–87.

10. Ibid., 87.

11. Marshall B. Jones, "Berkeley of the South", 55–57.

12. Rossinow, "New Left in the Counterculture," 90–95, quotation on 95.

13. Ibid., 96–97.

14. According to an investigative report by a reporter for the *Crimson White*, the student newspaper, the Machine, which adopted the Greek letters Theta Nu Epsilon, had been on the campus at least since the 1930s and possibly since the 1910s. It included representatives from eleven of the campus's most politically powerful fraternities. By 1968, political differences were developing within the Machine, and if the *Crimson White* investigative report was accurate, some of the most important campus activists in the late 1960s and early 1970s emanated from the Machine itself. These students included Newman Strawbridge, the 1968–69 student government secretary-treasurer, and Ralph Knowles. As student body president during the 1966–67 academic year, Knowles reportedly upset some members of the Machine by appointing non-Greeks to some posts. See *Crimson White*, 23 March 1968, 1.

15. Ibid., 27 October 1969, 1; 30 October 1969, 1.

16. Ibid., 8 October 1968, 1; 29 October 1968, 4; 18 February 1969, 1.

17. Ibid., 20 November 1969, 1; 18 December 1969, 6.

18. O'Bannon, interview.

19. Barbara Williams to F. David Mathews, 6 May 1970, Mathews Papers, Box 21, "Student Demonstrations 1970, General Correspondence May 1–13, 1970" Folder, University of Alabama.

20. *Hullabaloo*, 14 April 1970, 17 April 1970.

21. Horowitz, *Campus Life*, 242; Sara M. Evans, *Personal Politics*.

22. "UGA Lib Began with '68 March," *Red and Black*, 3 December 1971, 1; *Dear Queen Bee*, [April 1968], Vertical File, "Georgia — University — Student Demonstrations," University of Georgia.

23. *Red and Black*, 3 December 1971, 1.

24. The overstated comparison of the exploitation of students and African Americans was common at the time. The originator apparently was Jerry Farber, who published an essay, "The Student as Nigger," in 1967 (Farber, *Student as Nigger*).

25. *Crimson White*, 12 August 1968, 3.

26. Report on Women's Rules, n.d., "An Evaluation of the Request for Self-Regulated Hours," 8 August 1969, both in Mathews Papers, Box 20.

27. *Crimson White*, 19 February 1970, 1.

28. *Duke Chronicle*, 30 September 1969, 3; 7 October 1969, 1; 3 March 1970, 1; 7 March 1970, 7; 10 March 1970, 1; 20 May 1970, 11-A.

29. Echols, *Daring to Be Bad*, 62–63.

30. *Great Speckled Bird*, 24 February 1969, 2.

31. Southern Student Organizing Committee, "Women, Students, and the Movement," conference itinerary, 7–9 February 1969, Anne and Carl Braden Papers, Box 81, Wisconsin Historical Society.

32. Ibid.

33. Thomas N. Gardner, "The Southern Student Organizing Committee," 14 October 1969, 27–28, 31–32, Papers of the Southern Student Organizing Committee and Thomas N. Gardner, Box 6, University of Virginia.

34. McCandless, *Past in the Present*, 260.

35. Mohr, "Coming Together (and Falling Apart)."

36. McCandless, *Past in the Present*, 254, 276.

37. *Fisk Forum*, 25 October 1968, 1.

38. *New York Times*, 30 November 1991, 29; 3 May 1983, A16; 1 November 1998, ED20.

39. Gose, "U. of Alabama Studies."

40. *New York Times*, 28 August 1998, 1.

41. Marable, "Quiet Death of Black Colleges," 35, 36.

42. Healy, "Public, Historically Black Colleges."

43. Tift, "Black by Popular Demand," 59.

44. LaVeist and Whigham-Desir, "Top 50 Black Colleges," 73.

45. Mohr, "Schooling, Modernization, and Race," 448.

46. Geiger, *Research and Relevant Knowledge*, 258.

47. See Bellah et al., *Habits of the Heart*, 27, which argues that American individualism is comprised of two variants, "utilitarian" and "expressive."

48. Horowitz's chapter on student cultures after the 1960s is "The Nerds Take Revenge" (*Campus Life*, 245–62).

49. Egerton, *Americanization of Dixie*; Applebome, *Dixie Rising*; Cobb, "Epitaph for the North."

50. On these battles at the University of Mississippi, see Cohodas, *Band Played Dixie*, 193–204, 251–54.

51. Jeff Turner, "Race Relations on Campus: University of Georgia," *New York Times*, 5 April 1989, 27.

52. *Mother Jones*, September–October 1998, 21. The following year, the University of Texas was the only southern school to make the list (*Mother Jones*, September–October 1999, 20).

BIBLIOGRAPHY

MANUSCRIPT COLLECTIONS

Atlanta University Center, Atlanta

Robert W. Woodruff Library

Thomas D. Jarratt Papers
Vertical Files — College and University Files

Duke University, Durham, North Carolina

Duke University Archives, Perkins Library

Allen Building Takeover Collection
Office of the President, Douglas M. Knight Subject Files

Special Collections Library

Boyte Family Papers

Emory University, Atlanta

Special Collections, Robert W. Woodruff Library

Sanford Atwood Papers
Richard L. Stevens Civil Rights and Peace Movement Papers
Student Government Association of Emory University Papers
Judson C. Ward Papers

Martin Luther King Jr. Center for Nonviolent Social Change, Atlanta

Archives and Library

Papers of the U.S. National Student Association, 1955–69

Tulane University, New Orleans

Amistad Research Center

Daniel Webster Wynn Papers

Special Collections

   Hugh T. Murray Jr. Papers
   Political Ephemera Collection

Tulane University Archives

   Herbert E. Longenecker Papers

University of Alabama, Tuscaloosa

W. A. Hoole Special Collections Library

   F. David Mathews Papers

University of Georgia, Athens

Georgia Room, University of Georgia Library

   Vertical Files

University of North Carolina, Chapel Hill

Southern Historical Collection, Wilson Library

   William C. Friday Collection
   Allard K. Lowenstein Collection

University of North Carolina Archives

   Chancellor's Papers: J. C. Sitterson Series
   William C. Friday Papers
   Student Organizations and Activities: Student Government Records Series

University of Virginia, Charlottesville

Alderman Library

   Papers of the Southern Student Organizing Committee and Thomas N. Gardner
   Social Movements Special Collection
   Southern Student Organizing Committee Papers

Virginia Union University, Richmond

Virginia Union University Archives

   Vertical Files

Wisconsin Historical Society, Madison

Archives

   Anne and Carl Braden Papers

Samuel C. Shirah Jr. Papers
U.S. Student Association Records
John Robert and Dorothy Zellner Papers

MICROFILM COLLECTIONS

Congress of Racial Equality Papers, 1941–1967. Sanford, N.C.: Microfilming
  Corporation of America, 1980.
Students for a Democratic Society Papers, 1958–1970. Glen Rock, N.J.: Microfilming
  Corporation of America, 1977.
Student Nonviolent Coordinating Committee Papers, 1959–1972. Sanford, N.C.:
  Microfilming Corporation of America, 1982.

INTERVIEWS CONDUCTED BY AUTHOR

Raphael Cassimere, 11 September 1997
Constance Curry, 3 August 1998
Jack Drake, 7 April 1998
Michael Kane, 25 April 1995
Edwin Lombard, 18 November 1997
Joab Thomas, 16 May 1998
John Robert Zellner, 25 April 1995, 26 January 1999

INTERVIEWS

Georgia Government Documentation Project, Georgia State University, Atlanta
(all interviews conducted by Vincent Fort)

Julian Bond, 10 April 1979
James Brawley, 24 April 1979
Alton Hornsby, 3 May 1979
Lonnie King, 20 April 1979
Carolyn Long, 13 July 1979
Benjamin E. Mays, 29 November 1978
Lois Moreland, 1 December 1978
Margaret Rowley, 22 November 1978
Wendell Whalum, 21 November 1978
Mary Ann Smith Wilson, 13 April 1978

Kim Lacy Rogers and Glenda Stevens Oral History Collection, Amistad Research
Center, Tulane University, New Orleans (all interviews conducted by Kim Lacy Rogers)

Raphael Cassimere, 9 November 1978
Vallery Ferdinand III (Kalamu ya Salaam), 17 June 1988, 18 May 1979
Oretha Castle Haley, 27 November 1978
Rudolph Lombard, 7 June 1988

Southern Oral History Program, Southern Historical Collection, Wilson Library, University of North Carolina, Chapel Hill

> Pat Cusick, 19 June 1989
> Preston Dobbins, 4 December 1974
> Sharon Rose Powell, 20 June 1989

Louisiana State University Oral History Collection, Baton Rouge

> Maxine Crump, 8 July 1992
> Arden French, 24 March 1977

Transcripts of Interviews in the Possession of E. Culpepper Clark, University of Alabama, Tuscaloosa

> Mike O'Bannon, [1977]
> Jack Shelton, 11 April 1977

Henry Hampton Collection, Film and Media Archive, Washington University Libraries, St. Louis (http://digital.wustl.edu/e/eop/browse.html)

> Diane Nash, interview by Blackside, 12 November 1985, for *Eyes on the Prize: America's Civil Rights Years (1954–1965)* (accessed 14 October 2008)

NEWSPAPERS

> *Black Ink*, University of North Carolina, Chapel Hill 1969–72
> *Courtbouillon*, Dillard University, 1965–72
> *Crimson White*, University of Alabama, Tuscaloosa, 1960–70
> *Daily Tar Heel*, University of North Carolina, Chapel Hill, 1959–70
> *Driftwood*, Louisiana State University in New Orleans, 1960–70
> *Duke Chronicle*, Duke University, Durham, North Carolina, 1960–70
> *Fisk News*, Fisk University, Nashville, Tennessee, 1960–70
> *Fisk University Forum*, Fisk University, Nashville, Tennessee, 1957–70
> *Hullabaloo*, Tulane University, New Orleans, 1960–70
> *Hustler*, Vanderbilt University, Nashville, Tennessee, 1955–70
> *Louisiana Weekly*, New Orleans, 1968–70
> *Maroon*, Loyola University, New Orleans, 1960–70
> *MDS Newsletter*, New Orleans, 1967–69
> *New Left Notes*, 1962–68 (in Students for a Democratic Society Papers [microfilm])
> *New South Student*, 1965–69 (Southern Regional Council News Clipping Collection, Archives Division, Auburn Avenue Research Library on African-American Culture and History, Atlanta–Fulton County Public Library System)
> *The Panther*, Virginia Union University, Richmond, 1960–70
> *Red and Black*, University of Georgia, Athens, 1960–70
> *Richmond Collegian*, University of Richmond, Virginia, 1957–70
> *Southern University Digest*, Southern University, Baton Rouge, Louisiana, 1960–70

Southern Patriot, 1958–70 (bound volume in Howard-Tilton Memorial Library, Tulane University)

Spelman Messenger, Spelman College, Atlanta, 1960–70

Student Voice, University of Richmond, Virginia, 1960–65 (bound volume in University of Richmond Library, Virginia)

Wheel, Emory University, Atlanta, 1960–70

SECONDARY SOURCES

Altbach, Philip G. "Student Activism." In *International Higher Education, an Encyclopedia*, ed. Philip G. Altbach, 247–60. New York: Garland, 1991.

——. *Student Politics in America: A Historical Analysis*. New York: McGraw-Hill, 1974.

Anderson, James D. *The Education of Blacks in the South, 1860–1935*. Chapel Hill: University of North Carolina Press, 1988.

Anderson, R. Bentley. *Black, White, and Catholic: New Orleans Interracialism, 1947–1956*. Nashville: Vanderbilt University Press, 2005.

Anderson, Terry H. *The Movement and the Sixties*. New York: Oxford University Press, 1995.

Andrew, John A., III. *The Other Side of the Sixties: Young Americans for Freedom and the Rise of Conservative Politics*. New Brunswick: Rutgers University Press, 1997.

Applebome, Peter. *Dixie Rising: How the South Is Shaping American Values, Politics, and Culture*. New York: Times Books, 1996.

Arsenault, Raymond. *Freedom Riders: 1961 and the Struggle for Racial Justice*. New York: Oxford University Press, 2006.

Astin, Alexander W., Helen S. Astin, Alan E. Bayer, and Ann S. Bisconti. *The Power of Protest*. San Francisco: Jossey-Bass, 1975.

Bacote, Clarence A. *The Story of Atlanta University: A Century of Service, 1865–1965*. Atlanta: Atlanta University, 1969.

Bailey, Beth. "Sexual Revolution(s)." In *The Sixties: From Memory to History*, ed. David Farber, 149–74, 235–62. Chapel Hill: University of North Carolina Press, 1994.

Barber, David. *A Hard Rain Fell: SDS and Why It Failed*. Jackson: University Press of Mississippi, 2008.

Barrett, Russell H. *Integration at Ole Miss*. Chicago: Quadrangle, 1963.

Bartley, Numan V. *The New South, 1945–1980*. Baton Rouge: Louisiana State University Press, 1994.

Baskir, Lawrence M., and William A. Strauss. *Chance and Circumstance: The Draft, the War, and the Vietnam Generation*. New York: Knopf, 1978.

Bass, Jack, and Jack Nelson. *The Orangeburg Massacre*. 2nd ed. Macon, Ga.: Mercer University Press, 1984.

Bassett, Beth Dawkins. "Some of the Anguish: The Turbulent Sixties." *Emory Magazine*, June 1982, 6–15.

Bellah, Robert P., Richard Madsen, William M. Sullivan, Ann Swidler, and Steven M. Tipton. *Habits of the Heart: Individualism and Commitment in American Life*. Berkeley: University of California Press, 1985.

Billingsley, William J. *Communists on Campus: Race, Politics, and the Public University in Sixties North Carolina*. Athens: University of Georgia Press, 1999.

——. "Speaker Ban: The Anti-Communist Crusade in North Carolina, 1963–1970." Ph.D. diss., University of California, Irvine, 1994.

"Black Power: The Widening Dialogue." *New South*, Summer 1966, 65–80.

Blassingame, John W., ed. *New Perspectives on Black Studies*. Urbana: University of Illinois Press, 1971.

Boroff, David. *Campus U.S.A.: Portraits of American Colleges in Action*. New York: Harper, 1960.

Branch, Taylor. *Parting the Waters: America in the King Years, 1954–1963*. New York: Simon and Schuster, 1988.

——. *Pillar of Fire: America in the King Years, 1963–1965*. New York: Simon and Schuster, 1988.

Brawley, James P. *The Clark College Legacy: An Interpretive History of Relevant Education, 1869–1975*. Atlanta: Clark College, 1977.

Breines, Wini. *Community and Organization in the New Left, 1962–1968: The Great Refusal*. New Brunswick: Rutgers University Press, 1989.

——. "Whose New Left?" *Journal of American History* 75 (September 1988): 528–45.

Bromley, Dorothy Dunbar, and Susan McCabe. "Impact of the 'Sit-In' Movement on Academic Freedom." *Negro Education Review* 12 (April 1961): 63–71.

Brubacher, John S., and Willis Rudy. *Higher Education in Transition: An American History: 1636–1956*. New York: Harper, 1958.

Cade, Cathy. *A Lesbian Photo Album: The Lives of Seven Lesbian Feminists*. Oakland, Calif.: Waterwoman, 1987.

Campbell, Clarice T., and Oscar Allan Rogers Jr. *Mississippi: The View from Tougaloo*. Jackson: University Press of Mississippi, 1979.

Campbell, Robert F. "Negro Colleges Have a Job." *Southern Education Report*, November 1967, 2–9.

Campbell, Will D. *Brother to a Dragonfly*. New York: Seabury, 1977.

——. *The Stem of Jesse: The Costs of Community at a 1960s Southern School*. Macon, Ga.: Mercer University Press, 1994.

Carmer, Carl. *Stars Fell on Alabama*. Rahway, N.J.: Quinn and Boden, 1934.

Carmichael, Stokely, and Charles V. Hamilton. *Black Power: The Politics of Liberation in America*. New York: Vintage, 1967.

Carson, Clayborne. *In Struggle: SNCC and the Black Awakening of the 1960s*. Cambridge: Harvard University Press, 1981.

Cash, W. J. *The Mind of the South*. 1941; New York: Vintage, 1991.

Cassimere, Raphael. "Crisis of Public Higher Education in Louisiana." *Integrated Education*, October 1975, 8–13.

Chafe, William H. *Civilities and Civil Rights: Greensboro, North Carolina, and the Black Struggle for Freedom*. New York: Oxford University Press, 1980.

———. *Never Stop Running: Allard Lowenstein and the Struggle to Save American Liberalism*. New York: Basic Books, 1993.

Chappell, David L. *Inside Agitators: White Southerners in the Civil Rights Movement*. Baltimore: Johns Hopkins University Press, 1994.

Chisum, James. "At Miles College, a Mere Lack of Knowledge Is No Bar." *Southern Education Report*, May 1967, 14–19.

Chomsky, Noam, Ira Katznelson, R. C. Lewontin, Laura Nader, Richard Ohmann, David Montgomery, Immanuel Wallerstein, Ray Siever, and Howard Zinn. *The Cold War and the University: Toward an Intellectual History of the Postwar Years*. New York: New Press, 1997.

Clancy, Paul. "The Fight for Equality on Two Negro Campuses." *Reporter*, 13 July 1967, 37–39.

Clark, Burton, and Martin Trow. "Determinants of College Student Subcultures." In *College Peer Groups: Problems and Prospects for Research*, edited by Theodore M. Newcomb and Everett K. Wilson, 17–70. Chicago: Aldine, 1966.

Clark, E. Culpepper. *The Schoolhouse Door: Segregation's Last Stand at the University of Alabama*. New York: Oxford University Press, 1993.

Cobb, James C. "An Epitaph for the North: Reflections on the Politics of Regional and National Identity at the Millennium." *Journal of Southern History* 66 (February 2000): 3–24.

———. *The Selling of the South: The Southern Crusade for Industrial Development, 1936–1990*. 2nd ed. Urbana: University of Illinois Press, 1993.

Cohen, Robert. "'Two, Four, Six, Eight, We Don't Want to Integrate': White Student Attitudes toward the university of Georgia's Desegregation." *Georgia Historical Quarterly* 80 (Fall 1996): 616–45.

———. *When the Old Left Was Young: Student Radicals and America's First Mass Student Movement, 1929–1941*. New York: Oxford University Press, 1993.

Cohen, Robert, and Reginald E. Zelnik, eds. *The Free Speech Movement: Reflections on Berkeley in the 1960s*. Berkeley: University of California Press, 2002.

Cohodas, Nadine. *The Band Played Dixie: Race and the Liberal Conscience at Ole Miss*. New York: Free Press, 1997.

Conkin, Paul K. *The Southern Agrarians*. Knoxville: University of Tennessee Press, 1988.

Conkin, Paul K., assisted by Henry Lee Swint and Patricia S. Miletich. *Gone with the Ivy: A Biography of Vanderbilt University*. Knoxville: University of Tennessee Press, 1985.

Cook, Samuel Du Bois. "The Tragic Myth of Black Power." *New South*, Summer 1966, 58–64.

Cremin, Lawrence A. *The Transformation of the School: Progressivism in American Education, 1876–1957*. New York: Knopf, 1961.

Curry, Constance. *Silver Rights*. Chapel Hill, N.C.: Algonquin, 1995.

Curry, Constance, Joan C. Browning, Dorothy Dawson Burlage, Penny Patch, Theresa Del Pozzo, Sue Thrasher, Elaine Delott Baker, Emmie Schrader Adams, and Casey Hayden. *Deep in Our Hearts: Nine White Women in the Freedom Movement*. Athens: University of Georgia Press, 2000.

Dabney, Virginius. *Mr. Jefferson's University: A History*. Charlottesville: University Press of Virginia, 1981.

Daniel, Pete. *Lost Revolutions: The South in the 1950s*. Chapel Hill: University of North Carolina Press, 2000.

DeBenedetti, Charles, with Charles Chatfield. *An American Ordeal: The Antiwar Movement of the Vietnam Era*. Syracuse, N.Y.: Syracuse University Press, 1990.

DeGroot, Gerard J., ed. *Student Protest: The Sixties and After*. London: Longman, 1998.

Dickey, Ouida, and Doyle Mathis. *Berry College: A History*. Athens: University of Georgia Press, 2005.

Dittmer, John. *Local People: The Struggle for Civil Rights in Mississippi*. Urbana: University of Illinois Press, 1994.

Doddy, Hurley. "The Sit-In Demonstrations and the Dilemma of the Negro College Presidents." *Journal of Negro Education* 30 (Winter 1961): 1–3.

Draper, Hal. *Berkeley: The New Student Revolt*. New York: Grove, 1965.

Drobney, Jeffrey A. "A Generation in Revolt: Student Dissent and Political Repression at West Virginia University." *West Virginia History* 54 (1995): 105–22.

Durden, Robert F. *The Launching of Duke University, 1924–1949*. Durham: Duke University Press, 1993.

Dyer, Thomas G. "Higher Education in the South since the Civil War: Historiographical Issues and Trends." In *The Web of Southern Social Relations: Women, Family, and Education*, ed. Walter Fraser Jr., R. Frank Saunders Jr., and Jon L. Wakelyn, 127–45. Athens: University of Georgia Press, 1985.

———. *The University of Georgia: A Bicentennial History, 1785–1985*. Athens: University of Georgia Press, 1985.

Echols, Alice. *Daring to Be Bad: Radical Feminism in America, 1967–1975*. Minneapolis: University of Minnesota Press, 1989.

Egerton, John. *The Americanization of Dixie: The Southernization of America*. New York: Harper's Magazine Press, 1974.

———. "CACTUS Is the Word." *Southern Education Report*, September 1968, 27–29.

———. *Speak Now against the Day: The Generation before the Civil Rights Movement*. Chapel Hill: University of North Carolina Press, 1994.

Ehle, John. *The Free Men*. New York: Harper and Row, 1965.

Ellison, Ralph. *The Invisible Man*. 1947; New York: Vintage, 1989.

English, Thomas H. *Emory University, 1915–1965: A Semicentennial History*. Atlanta: Emory University Press, 1966.

Eskew, Glenn T. *But for Birmingham: The Local and National Movements in the Civil Rights Struggle*. Chapel Hill: University of North Carolina Press, 1997.

Evans, Eli. *The Provincials: A Personal History of Jews in the South*. 1973; New York: Atheneum, 1976.

Evans, Sara M. *Personal Politics: The Roots of Women's Liberation in the Civil Rights Movement and the New Left*. New York: Knopf, 1979.

Evans, Sara M., and Harry C. Boyte. *Free Spaces: The Sources of Democratic Change in America*. New York: Harper and Row, 1986.

Eynon, Bret. "Cast upon the Shore: Oral History and the New Scholarship on the Movements of the 1960s." *Journal of American History* 83 (September 1996): 560–70.

Fairclough, Adam. *Race and Democracy: The Civil Rights Struggle in Louisiana, 1915–1972*. Athens: University of Georgia Press, 1995.

Farber, Jerry. *The Student as Nigger: Stories and Essays*. New York: Pocket, 1970.

Farrell, James J. *The Spirit of the Sixties: The Making of Postwar Radicalism*. New York: Routledge, 1997.

Fergus, Devin. *Liberalism, Black Power, and the Making of American Politics, 1965–1980*. Athens: University of Georgia Press, 2009.

Fleming, Cynthia Griggs. "Black Women Activists and the Student Nonviolent Coordinating Committee: The Case of Ruby Doris Smith Robinson." *Journal of Women's History* 4 (Winter 1993): 64–82.

———. *Soon We Will Not Cry: The Liberation of Ruby Doris Smith Robinson*. Lanham, Md.: Rowman and Littlefield, 1998.

Forman, James. *The Making of Black Revolutionaries*. New York: Macmillan, 1972.

———. *Sammy Younge, Jr.: The First Black College Student to Die in the Black Liberation Movement*. New York: Grove, 1968.

Fort, Vincent D. "The Atlanta Sit-In Movement, 1960–1961, an Oral Study." In *Atlanta, Georgia, 1960–1961: Sit-Ins and Student Activism*, ed. David J. Garrow, 113–80. Brooklyn, N.Y.: Carlson, 1989.

Foster, Julian, and Durwood Long, eds. *Protest! Student Activism in America*. New York: Morrow, 1970.

Foster, Patricia. *All the Lost Girls: Confessions of a Southern Daughter*. Tuscaloosa: University of Alabama Press, 2000.

Frazier, E. Franklin. *Black Bourgeoisie*. Glencoe, Ill.: Free Press, 1957.

Garfinkle, Adam. *Telltale Hearts: The Origins and Impact of the Vietnam Antiwar Movement*. New York: St. Martin's, 1995.

Garrow, David J., ed. *Atlanta, Georgia, 1960–1961: Sit-Ins and Student Activism*. Brooklyn, N.Y.: Carlson, 1989.

———. *Bearing the Cross: Martin Luther King, Jr., and the Southern Christian Leadership Conference*. New York: Morrow, 1986.

Geiger, Roger L. *Research and Relevant Knowledge: American Research Universities since World War II*. New York: Oxford University Press, 1993.

Giardina, Carol. "Judith Brown: Freedom Fighter." In *The Human Tradition in the*

Civil Rights Movement, ed. Susan M. Glisson, 255–74. Lanham, Md.: Rowman and Littlefield, 2006.

Gitlin, Todd. *The Sixties: Years of Hope, Days of Rage*. New York: Bantam, 1987.

———. *The Whole World Is Watching: Mass Media in the Making and Unmaking of the New Left*. Berkeley: University of California Press, 1980.

Goines, David Lance. *The Free Speech Movement: Coming of Age in the 1960s*. Berkeley, Calif.: Ten Speed, 1993.

Goldfield, David. *Black, White, and Southern: Race Relations and Southern Culture, 1940 to the Present*. Baton Rouge: Louisiana State University Press, 1990.

Gose, Ben. "U. of Alabama Studies Why Its Fraternities and Sororities Remain Segregated by Race." *Chronicle of Higher Education*, 5 December 1997, A54–55.

Greene, Christina. "'We'll Take Our Stand': Race, Class, and Gender in the Southern Student Organizing Committee, 1964–1969." In *Hidden Histories of Women in the New South*, ed. Virginia Bernhard, Betty Brandon, Elizabeth Fox-Genovese, Theda Perdue, and Elizabeth Hayes Turner, 173–203. Columbia: University of Missouri Press, 1994.

Halberstam, David. *The Children*. New York: Random House, 1998.

Hall, Mitchell K. *Because of Their Faith: CALCAV and Religious Opposition to the Vietnam War*. New York: Columbia University Press, 1990.

———. "'A Crack in Time': The Response of Students at the University of Kentucky to the Tragedy at Kent State, May 1970." *Register of the Kentucky Historical Society* 83 (Winter 1985): 36–63.

Hall, Simon. *Peace and Freedom: The Civil Rights and Antiwar Movements in the 1960s*. Philadelphia: University of Pennsylvania Press, 2006.

Hare, Nathan. "Final Reflections on a 'Negro' College." *Negro Digest* 17 (March 1968): 40–46, 70–76.

Heale, M. J. *McCarthy's Americans: Red Scare Politics in State and Nation, 1935–1965*. Athens: University of Georgia Press, 1998.

Healy, Patrick. "Public, Historically Black Colleges Face Myriad of Problems." *Chronicle of Higher Education*, 17 May 1996, A-6.

Heineman, Kenneth J. *Campus Wars: The Peace Movement at American State Universities in the Vietnam Era*. New York: New York University Press, 1993.

Herring, George C. *America's Longest War: The United States and Vietnam, 1950–1975*. New York: McGraw-Hill, 1996.

Hine, William C. "Civil Rights and Campus Wrongs: South Carolina State College Student Protest, 1955–1968." *South Carolina Historical Magazine* 97 (October 1996): 310–31.

Hobson, Fred C. *But Now I See: The White Southern Racial Conversion Narrative*. Baton Rouge: Louisiana State University Press, 1999.

Hogan, Wesley, C. *Many Minds, One Heart: SNCC's Dream for a New America*. Chapel Hill: University of North Carolina Press, 2007.

Holt, Len. *The Summer That Didn't End*. New York: Morrow, 1965.

Horowitz, Helen Lefkowitz. *Campus Life: Undergraduate Cultures from the End of the Eighteenth Century to the Present*. Chicago: University of Chicago Press, 1987.

Hunter, Charlayne. "Black Colleges and the Black Mood." *Southern Education Report*, May 1969, 28–31.

Hunter-Gault, Charlayne. *In My Place*. New York: Farrar, Straus, Giroux, 1992.

Isserman, Maurice. *If I Had a Hammer . . .: The Death of the Old Left and the Birth of the New Left*. New York: Basic Books, 1987.

———. "The Not-So-Dark and Bloody Ground: New Works on the 1960s." *American Historical Review* 94 (October 1989): 990–1010.

Isserman, Maurice, and Michael Kazin. *America Divided: The Civil War of the 1960s*. New York: Oxford University Press, 2000.

———. "The Failure and Success of the New Radicalism." In *The Rise and Fall of the New Deal Order, 1930–1980*, edited by Steve Fraser and Gary Gerstle, 212–42. Princeton: Princeton University Press, 1989.

Jacoby, Russell. "Pollyanna Goes to College." *Dissent*, Winter 1997, 115–19.

Jaffe, A. J., Walter Adams, and Sandra G. Meyers. *Negro Higher Education in the 1960s*. New York: Praeger, 1968.

James, Anthony W. "A Demand for Racial Equality: The 1970 Black Student Protest at the University of Mississippi." *Journal of Mississippi History* 62 (Summer 1995): 97–120.

Johnson, Jerah. *UNO Prisms, 1958–1983*. New Orleans: University of New Orleans, 1983.

Johnson, William. "The Timid Generation." *Sports Illustrated*, 11 March 1967, 68–78.

Johnston, J. Angus. "The Habit of Talking: The USNSA Southern Seminars, 1958–65." Unpublished paper, in author's possession.

———. "Openings to Equality: The South and the U.S. National Student Association in the Sixties." Paper presented at the 1997 annual meeting of the History of Education Society, Philadelphia, in author's possession.

———. "The United States National Student Association: Democracy, Activism, and the Idea of the Student, 1947–1978." Ph.D. diss., City University of New York, 2009.

Jones, Edward Allen. *A Candle in the Dark: A History of Morehouse College*. Valley Forge, Pa.: Judson, 1967.

Jones, Marshall B. "Berkeley of the South: A History of the Student Movement at the University of Florida, 1963–1968." Unpublished paper, Special Collections, George A. Smathers Libraries, University of Florida, Gainesville.

Jones, Maxine D., and Joe M. Richardson. *Talladega College: The First Century*. Tuscaloosa: University of Alabama Press, 1990.

Joye, Harlon. "Dixie's New Left." *Transaction* 7 (September 1970): 50–56, 62.

"Justice for All." *La Louisiane*, Spring 1997, 24–27.

Kean, Melissa Fitzsimons. "'At a Most Uncomfortable Speed': The Desegregation of the South's Private Universities, 1945–1964." Ph.D. diss., Rice University, 2000.

Kerr, Clark. *The Uses of the University*. Cambridge: Harvard University Press, 1963.

King, Mary. *Freedom Song: A Personal Story of the 1960s Civil Rights Movement*. New York: Morrow, 1987.

Klatch, Rebecca. *A Generation* Divided: The New Left, the New Right, and the 1960s. Berkeley: University of California Press, 1999.

Klibaner, Irwin. Conscience of a Troubled South: The Southern Conference Educational Fund, 1946–1966. Brooklyn, N.Y.: Carlson, 1989.

Knight, Douglas M. Street of Dreams: The Nature and Legacy of the 1960s. Durham: Duke University Press, 1989.

Kornberg, Allan, and Joel Smith. "'It Ain't Over Yet': Activism in a Southern University." In Black Power and Student Rebellion, ed. James McEvoy, 100–121. Belmont, Calif.: Wadsworth, 1969.

Kotelanski, Jorge. "Prolonged and Patient Efforts: The Desegregation of Duke University, 1948–1963." Honors thesis, Duke University, 1990.

Kousser, J. Morgan. "Progressivism — For Middle Class Whites Only: North Carolina Education, 1880–1910." Journal of Southern History 46 (May 1980): 160–94.

Kuhlman, Martin. "Direct Action at the University of Texas during the Civil Rights Movement, 1960–1965." Southwestern Historical Quarterly 98 (April 1995): 551–66.

Laue, James H. "Direct Action and Desegregation, 1960–1962: Toward a Theory of the Rationalization of Protest." Ph.D. diss., Harvard University, 1965.

LaVeist, Thomas, and Marjorie Whigham-Desir. "Top 50 Black Colleges for African Americans." Black Enterprise, January 1999, 71–80.

Leloudis, James L. Schooling the New South: Pedagogy, Self, and Society in North Carolina, 1880–1920. Chapel Hill: University of North Carolina Press, 1996.

Lewis, John, with Michael D'Orso. Walking with the Wind: A Memoir of the Movement. New York: Simon and Schuster, 1998.

Link, William A. A Hard Country and Lonely Place: Schooling, Society, and Reform in Rural Virginia, 1870–1920. Chapel Hill: University of North Carolina Press, 1986.

———. William Friday: Power, Purpose, and American Higher Education. Chapel Hill: University of North Carolina Press, 1995.

Logan, Rayford. Howard University: The First One Hundred Years, 1867–1967. New York: New York University Press, 1969.

———. The Negro in American Life and Thought: The Nadir, 1877–1901. New York: Dial, 1954.

Lomax, Louis E. The Negro Revolt. New York: Harper, 1962.

Lord, Walter. The Past That Would Not Die. New York: Harper and Row, 1965.

Lott, Trent. Herding Cats: A Life in Politics. New York: Morrow, 2005.

Lukas, J. Anthony. Don't Shoot — We Are Your Children! New York: Random House, 1968.

Lynd, Staughton, and Robert Yancey. "Southern Negro Students: The College and the Movement." Dissent, Winter 1964, 39–45.

Mailer, Norman. The Armies of the Night. New York: New American Library, 1968.

Manley, Albert E. A Legacy Continues: The Manley Years at Spelman College, 1953–1976. Lanham, Md.: University Press of America, 1995.

Mann, Harold W. Atticus Greene Haygood. Athens: University of Georgia Press, 1965.

Marable, Manning. "The Quiet Death of Black Colleges." Southern Exposure, March–April 1984, 31–39.

Mathews, F. David. "Reflections on Student Activism." March 1999. Unpublished paper, in author's possession.

Matthews, Donald R., and James W. Prothro. Negroes and the New Southern Politics. New York: Harcourt, Brace, and World, 1966.

Matusow, Allan J. The Unraveling of America: A History of Liberalism in the 1960s. New York: Harper and Row, 1984.

Mays, Benjamin E. Born to Rebel: An Autobiography. 1971; Athens: University of Georgia Press, 1987.

McAdam, Doug. Freedom Summer. New York: Oxford University Press, 1988.

McCandless, Amy Thompson. The Past in the Present: Women's Higher Education in the Twentieth-Century American South. Tuscaloosa: University of Alabama Press, 1999.

McCormick, Richard P. The Black Student Protest Movement at Rutgers. New Brunswick: Rutgers University Press, 1990.

McEvoy, James, ed. Black Power and Student Rebellion. Belmont, Calif.: Wadsworth, 1969.

McGrath, Earl J. The Predominantly Negro Colleges and Universities in Transition. New York: Bureau of Publications, Teachers College, Columbia University, 1965.

Meier, August. A White Scholar and the Black Community, 1945–1965. Amherst: University of Massachusetts Press, 1992.

Meier, August, and Elliott Rudwick. CORE: A Study in the Civil Rights Movement, 1942–1968. Urbana: University of Illinois Press, 1975.

Menashe, Louis, and Ronald Radosh, eds. Teach-Ins, U.S.A.: Reports, Opinions, Documents. New York: Praeger, 1967.

Meredith, James. Three Years in Mississippi. Bloomington: Indiana University Press, 1966.

Michel, Gregg L. "A Greater Division of Labor." Paper presented at the 1998 annual meeting of the American Historical Association, Seattle, in author's possession.

——. Struggle for a Better South: The Southern Student Organizing Committee, 1964–1969. New York: Palgrave Macmillan, 2004.

——. "We'll Take Our Stand: The Southern Student Organizing Committee and the Radicalization of Southern White Students, 1964–1969." Ph.D. diss., University of Virginia, 1999.

Miller, Jim. Democracy Is in the Streets: From Port Huron to the Siege of Chicago. Cambridge: Harvard University Press, 1994.

Mohr, Clarence L. "Coming Together (and Falling Apart): Tulane University and H. Sophie Newcomb Memorial College in the Postwar Decades." Louisiana History 49 (Winter 2008): 53–92.

———. "Schooling, Modernization, and Race: The Continuing Dilemma of the American South." American Journal of Education 106 (May 1998): 439–50.

———. "World War II and the Transformation of Southern Higher Education." In Remaking Dixie: The Impact of World War II on the American South, ed. Neil R. McMillen, 33–55. Jackson: University Press of Mississippi, 1997.

Mohr, Clarence L., and Joseph E. Gordon. Tulane: The Emergence of a Modern University. Baton Rouge: Louisiana State University Press, 2001.

Monhollon, Rusty L. This Is America? The Sixties in Lawrence, Kansas. New York: Palgrave, 2002.

Montgomery, James Riley, Stanley J. Folmsbee, and Lee Seifert Green. To Foster Knowledge: A History of the University of Tennessee, 1794–1970. Knoxville: University of Tennessee Press, 1984.

Moody, Anne. Coming of Age in Mississippi. 1968; New York: Dell, 1976.

Morgan, Chester M. Dearly Bought, Deeply Treasured: The University of Southern Mississippi, 1912–1987. Jackson: University Press of Mississippi, 1987.

Morris, Aldon D. The Origins of the Civil Rights Movement: Black Communities Organizing for Change. New York: Free Press, 1984.

Morris, Willie. North toward Home. Oxford, Miss.: Yoknapatawpha, 1967.

Muir, Donald E., and C. Donald McGlamery. "Trends in Integration Attitudes on a Deep-South Campus during the First Two Decades of Desegregation." Social Forces 62 (June 1984): 963–72.

Murray, Hugh T., Jr. "The Struggle for Civil Rights in New Orleans in 1960: Reflections and Recollections." Journal of Ethnic Studies 6 (Spring 1978): 25–42.

Neufeldt, Harvey, and Clinton Allison. "Education and the Rise of the New South: An Historiographical Essay." In Education and the Rise of the New South, ed. Ronald K. Goodenow and Arthur O. White, 250–93. Boston: Hall, 1981.

Newberry, Anthony Lake. "Without Urgency or Ardor: The South's Middle-of-the-Road Liberals and Civil Rights, 1945–1960." Ph.D. diss., Ohio University, 1982.

Norrell, Robert J. Reaping the Whirlwind: The Civil Rights Movement in Tuskegee. New York: Knopf, 1985.

Olliff, Martin T. "'Just Another Day on the Plains': The Desegregation of Auburn University." Alabama Review 54 (April 2001): 104–44.

Oppenheimer, Martin. "The Sit-In Movement of 1960." Ph.D. diss., University of Pennsylvania, 1963.

Orbell, John M. "Protest Participation among Southern Negro College Students." American Political Science Review 61 (June 1967): 446–56.

Palcic, James L. "The History of the Black Student Union at Florida State University, 1968–1978." Ph.D. diss., Florida State University, 1979.

Parr, Stephen Eugene. "The Forgotten Radicals: The New Left in the Deep South, Florida State University, 1960 to 1972." Ph.D. diss., Florida State University, 2000.

Payne, Charles. I've Got the Light of Freedom: The Organizing Tradition and the Mississippi Freedom Struggle. Berkeley: University of California Press, 1995.

Perlstein, Rick. "Who Owns the Sixties?" Lingua Franca, May–June 1996, 30–37.

Peterson, Richard E., and John A. Bilorusky. May 1970: The Campus Aftermath of Cambodia and Kent State. Berkeley: Carnegie Commission on Higher Education, 1971.

Piliawsky, Monte. Exit 13: Oppression and Racism in Academia. Boston: Beacon, 1982.

Pratt, Robert A. We Shall Not Be Moved: The Desegregation of the University of Georgia. Athens: University of Georgia Press, 2002.

Rabby, Glenda Alice. "Out of the Past: The Civil Rights Movement in Tallahassee, Florida." Ph.D. diss., Florida State University, 1984.

———. The Pain and the Promise: The Struggle for Civil Rights in Tallahassee, Florida. Athens: University of Georgia Press, 1999.

Raines, Howell. My Soul Is Rested: Movement Days in the Deep South Remembered. New York: Putnam, 1977.

Read, Florence Matilda. The Story of Spelman College. Princeton: Princeton University Press, 1961.

Reed, Linda. Simple Decency and Common Sense: The Southern Conference Movement, 1938–1963. Bloomington: Indiana University Press, 1991.

The Report of the President's Commission on Campus Unrest. Washington, D.C.: U.S. Government Printing Office, 1970.

Richardson, Joe M. A History of Fisk University, 1865–1946. University: University of Alabama Press, 1980.

Rogers, Kim Lacy. Righteous Lives: Narratives of the New Orleans Civil Rights Movement. New York: New York University Press, 1993.

Roland, Charles P. The Improbable Era: The South since World War II. Lexington: University Press of Kentucky, 1975.

Rorabaugh, W. J. Berkeley at War: The 1960s. New York: Oxford University Press, 1989.

Rosenthal, Joel. "Southern Black Student Activism: Assimilation vs. Nationalism." Journal of Negro Education 44 (Spring 1975): 113–29.

Rossinow, Douglas. "'The Break-Through to New Life': Christianity and the Emergence of the New Left in Austin, Texas, 1956–1964." American Quarterly 46 (September 1994): 309–40.

———. "Breakthrough: White Youth Radicalism in Austin, Texas, 1956–1973." Ph.D. diss., Johns Hopkins University, 1994.

———. "The New Left in the Counterculture: Hypotheses and Evidence." Radical History Review 67 (Winter 1997): 79–120.

———. The Politics of Authenticity: Liberalism, Christianity, and the New Left in America. New York: Columbia University Press, 1998.

Rovaris, Dereck J., Sr. Mays and Morehouse: How Benjamin E. Mays Developed Morehouse College, 1940–1967. Silver Spring, Md.: Beckham House, 1990.

Rudy, Willis. The Campus and a Nation in Crisis: From the American Revolution to Vietnam. Madison, N.J.: Fairleigh Dickinson University Press, 1996.

Sale, Kirkpatrick. SDS. New York: Vintage, 1973.

Sansing, David G. Making Haste Slowly: The Troubled History of Higher Education in Mississippi. Jackson: University Press of Mississippi, 1990.

Savio, Mario, Eugene Walker, and Raya Dunayevskaya. The Free Speech Movement and the Negro Revolution. Detroit: News and Letters, 1965.

Scales, Junius. Cause at Heart: A Former Communist Remembers. Athens: University of Georgia Press, 1987.

Schrag, Peter. "New Beat in the Heart of Dixie." Saturday Review, 20 March 1971, 42–45, 56–59.

Schrecker, Ellen W. The Age of McCarthyism: A Brief History with Documents. Boston: Bedford/St. Martin's, 1994.

———. No Ivory Tower: McCarthyism and the Universities. New York: Oxford University Press, 1986.

Schulman, Bruce. From Cotton Belt to Sunbelt: Federal Policy, Economic Development, and the Transformation of the South, 1938–1980. 1991; Durham: Duke University Press, 1994.

Schwartz, Edward, ed. Student Power — A Collection of Readings. Washington, D.C.: U.S. National Student Association, 1968.

———. Student Power — A Collection of Readings. Rev. ed. Washington, D.C.: U.S. National Student Association, 1969.

Segal, Theodore David. "A New Genesis: The Silent Vigil at Duke University, April 5th–12th, 1968." Senior honors thesis, Duke University, 1977.

Sellers, Cleveland, with Robert Terrell. The River of No Return: The Autobiography of a Black Militant and the Life and Death of SNCC. New York: Morrow, 1973.

Sewell, George A., and Cornelius V. Troup. Morris Brown College: The First Hundred Years, 1881–1981. Atlanta: Morris Brown College, 1981.

Sharp, Gene. The Politics of Nonviolent Action. Boston: Sargent, 1973.

Silver, James. Mississippi: The Closed Society. New York: Harcourt, Brace, and World, 1963.

Simon, Bryant. "Southern Student Organizing Committee: A New Rebel Yell in Dixie." Honors essay, University of North Carolina, 1983.

Sitkoff, Harvard. The Struggle for Black Equality, 1954–1980. New York: Hill and Wang, 1981.

Singal, Daniel J. The War Within: From Victorian to Modernist Thought in the

South, 1919–1945. Chapel Hill: University of North Carolina Press, 1982.

Small, Melvin, and William D. Hoover, eds. Give Peace a Chance: Exploring the Vietnam Antiwar Movement. Syracuse, N.Y.: Syracuse University Press, 1992.

Smith, Charles U., ed. Student Unrest on Historically Black Campuses. Silver Spring, Md.: Beckham House, 1994.

Smith, Stanley H. "Administrators Should Heed Student Views." Southern Education Report, June 1969, 41–45.

Snider, William D. Light on the Hill: A History of the University of North Carolina at Chapel Hill. Chapel Hill: University of North Carolina Press, 1992.

Solomon, Barbara Miller. In the Company of Educated Women: A History of Women and Higher Education in America. New Haven: Yale University Press, 1985.

Sosna, Morton. In Search of the Silent South: Southern Liberals and the Race Issue. New York: Columbia University Press, 1977.

Spofford, Tim. Lynch Street: The May 1970 Slayings at Jackson State College. Kent, Ohio: Kent State University Press, 1988.

Straus, William A. Chance and Circumstance: The Draft, the War, and the Vietnam Generation. New York: Knopf, 1978.

Student Protests 1969 Summary. Chicago: Urban Research Corporation, 1970.

Sullivan, Patricia. Days of Hope: Race and Democracy in the New Deal Era. Chapel Hill: University of North Carolina Press, 1996.

Synnott, Marcia. "Desegregation in South Carolina, 1950–1963: Sometime 'Between "Now" and "Never."'" In Looking South: Chapters in the Story of an American Region, ed. Winfred B. Moore Jr. and Joseph F. Tripp, 51–64. Westport, Conn.: Greenwood, 1989.

——— . "Federalism Vindicated: University Desegregation in South Carolina and Alabama, 1962–1963." Journal of Policy History 1 (July 1989): 292–318.

Terrell, Robert L. "Black Awareness versus Negro Traditions: Atlanta University Center." New South, Winter 1969, 29–40.

Thomas, Tim. "The Student Movement at Southern University." Freedomways, First Quarter 1973, 14–27.

Thompson, Ruth Anne. "'A Taste of Student Power': Protest at the University of Tennessee, 1964–1970." Tennessee Historical Quarterly 57 (Spring–Summer 1998): 80–97.

Tift, Susan E. "Black by Popular Demand." Time, 20 March 1989, 59.

Trillin, Calvin. An Education in Georgia: Charlayne Hunter, Hamilton Holmes, and the Integration of the University of Georgia. 1964; Athens: University of Georgia Press, 1991.

Tuck, Stephen G. N. Beyond Atlanta: The Struggle for Racial Equality in Georgia, 1940–1980. Athens: University of Georgia Press, 2003.

Ture, Kwame, and Charles V. Hamilton, Black Power: The Politics of Liberation. New York: Vintage, 1992.

Turner, Darwin T. "The Black University: A Practical Approach." Negro Digest 17 (March 1968): 14–20, 64–69.

Twelve Southerners. I'll Take My Stand: The South and the Agrarian Tradition. New York: Harper, 1930.

Tyson, Timothy B. Radio Free Dixie: Robert F. Williams and the Roots of Black Power. Chapel Hill: University of North Carolina Press, 1999.

Unger, Irwin. The Movement: A History of the American New Left, 1959–1972. Lanham, Md.: University Press of America, 1974.

Van Deburg, William L. New Day in Babylon: The Black Power Movement and American Culture, 1965–1975. Chicago: University of Chicago Press, 1992.

Vincent, Charles. A Centennial History of Southern University and A&M College, 1880–1980. Baton Rouge: Southern University, 1981.

Walker, Alice. Meridian. New York: Harcourt Brace Jovanovich, 1976.

Wallenstein, Peter. "Black Southerners and Non-Black Universities: Desegregating Higher Education, 1935–1967." History of Higher Education Annual 19 (1999): 121–48.

———, ed. Higher Education and the Civil Rights Movement: White Supremacy, Black Southerners, and College Campuses. Gainesville: University Press of Florida, 2008.

Wallerstein, Immanuel, and Paul Starr, eds. The University Crisis Reader. 2 vols. New York: Random House, 1971.

Warnat, W. I. "The Role of White Faculty on the Black College Campus." Journal of Negro Education 45 (Summer 1976): 334–38.

Watters, Pat, and Weldon Rougeau. Events at Orangeburg. Atlanta: Southern Regional Council, 1968.

Weisbrot, Robert. Freedom Bound: A History of America's Civil Rights Movement. New York: Norton, 1990.

Wells, Tom. The War Within: America's Battle over Vietnam. Berkeley: University of California Press, 1994.

Wendt, Simon. "God, Gandhi, and Guns: The African American Freedom Struggle in Tuscaloosa, Alabama, 1964–1965." Journal of African American History 89 (2004): 36–56.

Wiggins, Samuel P. The Desegregation Era in Higher Education. Berkeley, Calif.: McCutchan, 1966.

Williamson, Joy Ann. Black Power on Campus: The University of Illinois, 1965–1975. Urbana: University of Illinois Press, 2003.

———. Radicalizing the Ebony Tower: Black Colleges and the Black Freedom Struggle in Mississippi. New York: Teachers College Press, 2008.

———. "'This Has Been Quite a Year for Heads Falling': Institutional Autonomy in the Civil Rights Era." History of Education Quarterly 44 (Winter 2004): 554–76.

Wolfe, Suzanne Rau. The University of Alabama: A Pictorial History. University: University of Alabama Press, 1983.

Wolff, Miles. Lunch at the 5&10. Rev. and exp. ed. 1970; Chicago: Elephant, 1990.

Wolters, Raymond. The New Negro on Campus: Black College Rebellions of the
1920s. Princeton: Princeton University Press, 1975.

Woods, Jeff. Black Struggle, Red Scare: Segregation and Anti-Communism in the
South, 1948–1968. Baton Rouge: Louisiana State University Press, 2004.

Woodward, C. Vann. "The Unreported Crisis in the Southern College." Harper's
Magazine, October 1962, 82–89.

Wynkoop, Mary Ann. Dissent in the Heartland: The Sixties at Indiana University.
Bloomington: Indiana University Press, 2002.

Yannella, Don. "Race Relations at Duke University and the Allen Building
Takeover." Honors thesis, Duke University, 1985.

Young, Stephen Flinn. "The Kudzu: Sixties Generational Revolt — Even in
Mississippi." Southern Quarterly 34 (Spring 1996): 122–36.

Zellner, Robert, with Constance Curry. The Wrong Side of Murder Creek: A
White Southerner in the Freedom Movement. Montgomery, Ala.: NewSouth,
2008.

Zinn, Howard. SNCC: The New Abolitionists. Boston: Beacon, 1965.

———. The Southern Mystique. New York: Knopf, 1964.

INDEX

stronghold, 251; sit-in movement, 64–66; white student activism, 101–3

Nixon, Richard, 10, 171, 197, 259, 261, 270, 283, 317n106; appearance at University of Tennessee, 1970, 262

North Carolina Agricultural and Technical College, 6, 46, 167, 212

North Carolina Speaker Ban, 37, 95, 102, 136, 137, 143–47, 213, 240, 289n63

Orangeburg, South Carolina: Orangeburg Massacre, 182–88, 204, 212; sit-in movement, 67–68

Patton, Gwen, 173, 174, 244, 304–5n26

Peabody College, 51, 89

Player, Willa B., 62–63

Port Huron Statement, 35, 129, 132, 142, 153, 247

Powell, Robert, 158, 240–41, 243

public and private colleges: effects on activism, 8, 10, 33, 36, 49–50, 54, 97–98, 146, 189

Rebel Underground (University of Mississippi), 108–9

Red and Black (University of Georgia), 141, 223, 224, 234, 235, 237

religion and activism, 28, 29–32, 52, 55–56, 100–101

Religious Emphasis Week (REW), 30–32

Reserve Officers' Training Corps (ROTC), 235–38, 254–55, 258, 260–62

restrictions on women, 264, 271–75, 277

Richer, Edward, 159

Romaine, Howard, 163–64

Rubin, Jerry, 1, 227

Salaam, Kalamu Ya. See Ferdinand, Vallery, III

Salter, John, 72

Savio, Mario, 4, 115, 139, 141

Scarritt College, 51, 55, 89

Schwartz, Edward, 152–55, 163

Scott, Robert W., 212–15

Sellers, Cleveland, 48, 181, 184, 186

Shirah, Samuel C., Jr., 89, 118–19, 124, 127, 131, 172

Simpson, David, 238, 259–60

sit-in movement: debates over educational value, 58–59, 70–71; Deep South, 67–77; Greensboro, 61–63; impact, 45; Nashville, 50–55; New Orleans, 64–66; origins, 44–50; regional variations, 60–61

Sitterson, J. Carlyle: demands of black students, 210–13; Speaker Ban, 146–47

South Carolina State College, 6, 67–68, 167, 169, 182–87

Southern Conference Educational Fund (SCEF), 118, 124–26

Southern Conference for Human Welfare, 25, 39, 124

southern distinctiveness and activism, 10, 227, 250–51

southern liberalism, 39, 81, 133, 279

Southern Patriot (Southern Conference Education Fund), 4, 12, 118, 119, 124

Southern Regional Council, 25, 47, 125, 169, 186

Southern Student Organizing Committee (SSOC): Atlanta chapter, 232; dissolution, 252; funding, 134–35; interracial period, 176; organizing strategy, 137–38; origins, 131–34; perceived as radical, 148; southern identity, 250–52; UNC food workers' strike, 213; university reform, 143, 162–63; Vietnam, 243–44, 249–52; women's liberation, 275–76

Southern University, Baton Rouge, 6, 18, 64–65, 69–71, 176–77, 278

Southern University, New Orleans (SUNO), 102, 195–99

LA
229
.T84
2010

CPSIA information can be obtained at www.ICGtesting.com
Printed in the USA
LVOW122030201011

251426LV00001B/21/P